ON FORM

On Form

Poetry, Aestheticism, and the Legacy of a Word

ANGELA LEIGHTON

OXFORD
UNIVERSITY PRESS

OXFORD
UNIVERSITY PRESS

Great Clarendon Street, Oxford OX2 6DP

Oxford University Press is a department of the University of Oxford.
It furthers the University's objective of excellence in research, scholarship,
and education by publishing worldwide in

Oxford New York

Auckland Cape Town Dar es Salaam Hong Kong Karachi
Kuala Lumpur Madrid Melbourne Mexico City Nairobi
New Delhi Shanghai Taipei Toronto

With offices in

Argentina Austria Brazil Chile Czech Republic France Greece
Guatemala Hungary Italy Japan Poland Portugal Singapore
South Korea Switzerland Thailand Turkey Ukraine Vietnam

Oxford is a registered trade mark of Oxford University Press
in the UK and in certain other countries

Published in the United States
by Oxford University Press Inc., New York

British Library Cataloguing in Publication Data
Data available

Library of Congress Cataloging in Publication Data
Data available

Typeset by Laserwords Private Limited, Chennai, India
Printed in Great Britain
on acid-free paper by
Biddles Ltd., King's Lynn, Norfolk

ISBN 978-0-19-929060-4

For Harriet

Acknowledgements

This book would not have been possible without the award of a two-year Leverhulme Major Research Fellowship, which gave me that most precious of commodities: time to think and read, and then time to change my mind about the book I was writing. If this is not quite the book I at first envisaged, I can only say that it would not have come about at all without the benign and uninterfering support of the Leverhulme Committee, who awarded me a Fellowship and then accepted a change of plan. In addition, a Fellowship at Clare Hall, Cambridge, gave me a very welcome extra year for writing up, in beautiful surroundings and in congenial company.

To friends and colleagues who have, at various points over the years, read and talked to me about this book, I am deeply in debt, and to an extent only they can know. If they seem reduced to a list of names here, that is not because I forget the time, attention, and friendship they offered. I would like to thank, in particular, James Booth, Stefan Collini, Harriet Marland, Margaret Reynolds, Marion Shaw, and David Wheatley for reading work, often at an early stage, and giving me the benefit of their invariably generous and helpful advice. In addition, Gillian Beer, Rachel Bowlby, Jonathan Ellis, Heather Glen, Matthew Campbell, Peter McDonald, and Susan Wolfson have lent me their special expertise in particular areas, and have often saved me from basic errors. For advice given, suggestions made, books lent, or just helpful exchanges of views, my thanks also to Malcolm Bowie, Paul Hamilton, Sara Johnson, Tim Kendall, John Kerrigan, Patrick McGuinness, Matthew Mitton, Adrian Poole, Brian Rigby, Frances Spurling, Patsy Stoneman, David Trotter, Carolyn Williams, and Clive Wilmer. To Roy Fisher, Heather McHugh, and Anne Stevenson I am grateful for all kinds of advice on matters of fact, and for tolerance and reticence on matters of interpretation.

Over the years, I have also had reason to be grateful to a number of libraries whose librarians have pursued requests and chased up references: in particular all the staff at the Brynmor Jones Library, Hull, for their unfailing helpfulness over many years; but also John Wells at the University Library, Cambridge, Grace Timmins at the Tennyson Research Library, Lincoln, the staff at the Poetry Library, South Bank, and those at the British Library.

Some early versions of chapters have appeared in previous publications.

'Elegies of Form: Bishop, Plath, Stevenson' is reproduced by permission from the *Proceedings of the British Academy*, 121(2003), 257–75. 'Touching Forms: Tennyson and Aestheticism' is reproduced by permission of Oxford University Press, from *Essays in Criticism*, 52(2002), 56–75. Some parts of 'Aesthetic Conditions: Pater's Re-Forming Style' were published in 'Aesthetic Conditions: Returning to Pater', in *Walter Pater: Transparencies of Desire*, ed. Laurel Brake, Lesley Higgins, and Carolyn Williams (Greensboro, North Carolina: ELT Press, 2002), 12–23, as were some parts of 'Seeing Nothing: Vernon Lee's Ghostly Aesthetic' in 'Ghosts, Aestheticism and Vernon Lee', in *Victorian Literature and Culture*, 28/1(2000), 1–14. The latter two are reproduced by permission from ELT Press and Cambridge University Press respectively.

In addition, I am very grateful to Bloodaxe Books for permission to reprint the greater part of Anne Stevenson's poem, 'The Figure in the Carpet', from *Poems: 1955–2005* (Tarset: Bloodaxe Books, 2004), 290–1, all rights reserved. Thanks, too, to the Syndics of Cambridge University Library for permission to reproduce a line from the drafts of Anne Stevenson's 'Willow Song', from the Stevenson Archive, CUL, MS. Add. 9451. For permission to quote Heather McHugh's 'What Poems are For', from *Hinge & Sign: Poems, 1968–1993* (Wesleyan University Press, 1994), 179, thanks are due to Wesleyan University Press, all rights reserved. Since this is an academic book I have taken care to ensure that all other quotations from copyright material fall within the definition of fair dealing for the purposes of literary criticism.

I am particularly aware that a book of this range of reference will be guilty of all sorts of omissions. Anyone who writes criticism today knows the problems of keeping up with innumerable specialists in every field, and therefore the dangers of failing to do so. I remain indebted and grateful to innumerable writers and critics whom I have read but not quoted, on aestheticism, form, and poetry in general, as well as to individual authors who have, over the years, helped me to work out my own interpretations. These constitute the ghostly backdrop of this book, and I can only say that, without them, it would not itself have materialized.

To my editors and copy-editors at OUP, in particular Andrew McNeillie, Eva Nyika, and Jack Sinden, I am grateful for support, patience, and advice.

Contents

∾

The philosopher cannot easily comprehend that the artist passes,
almost with indifference, from form to content and from content
to form; that form comes to the artist with the meaning that he
wishes to give it ...

Paul Valéry

(This is a form of matter of matter she sang.)

Jorie Graham

1

Form's Matter: A Retrospective

What is form? Why might form matter? Why does this word continue
to worry our accounts of art? The word is utterly familiar, yet also
unspecific, abstract, aloof. In literary criticism at least, it tends to figure
without articles, not as *a* form or *the* form, or even the form *of*, but just
'form'—as if it were one of those 'essential Forms'[1] which Plato placed
beyond the world of passing appearances, 'unchangeably in the same
state for ever'.[2] Those however, Plato also admits, 'manifest themselves
in a great variety of combinations, with actions, with material things,
and with one another'.[3] Somehow this platonic problem, of form which
is both 'essential', yet becomes visible or 'manifest' in 'material things',
transfers to the word itself. It is an abstraction from matter, removed
and immaterial; but it is also subtly inflected towards matter. As a word
it holds off from objects, being nothing but form, pure and singular; at
the same time, its whole bent is towards materialization, towards being
the shape or body of something. Form, which seems self-sufficient and
self-defining, is restless, tendentious, a noun lying in wait for its object.

One reason for this complexity, even confusion of purpose, is that
form, unlike other abstract nouns in English, has a multitude of

---

[1] Plato, *The Republic,* trans. Francis Macdonald Cornford (London: Oxford University
Press, 1941), 183.
[2] Ibid. 187.   [3] Ibid. 183.

meanings. There are more than twenty dictionary definitions of the word, among them shape, design, outline, frame, ideal, figure, image, style, genre, order, etiquette, body, beauty, mould, lair, print-type, format, desk, grade, class. The fact that so many senses whisper within earshot of form make it, somehow, dense and crowded. It is thick with possible echoes and conflicting references. The fact, too, that several of these meanings emphasize writing: a piece of school furniture, a classroom name, the type of a letter in printing, an arrangement of official words on a page, only adds to its literary resourcefulness. In addition to this mischief of potential puns, the word is pliable, enjoying a wealth of grammatical connections. It answers, for instance, to at least three different opposites: form and matter, form and content, form and formlessness, each of which, as David Pole points out, alters the sense of this 'protean monosyllable'.[4] To these might be added other notional partnerships: form and informality, form and deformity, form and information, form and reform. Certainly the 'form and' construction appears in a multitude of book and essay titles: form and feeling, form and intent, form and authority, form and contentment, form and meaning, form and time, form and format, form and poetry. It is as if there were something unfinished, even unformed, about form. It hangs on its other half, needing that support or relief. At some level an old soul–body dualism underpins these constructions, reminding us that form, without its shaping partner, might be so disembodied as to mean nothing at all. But that suggestion too is complicated by the fact that form, by itself, can also mean body, shape, or matter. As Raymond Williams points out, the dictionary definitions of the word range from 'an essential shaping principle' to 'a visible or outward shape, with a strong sense of the physical body'.[5] This is a word full of contradictions, which can switch its allegiance from any one meaning or slip the hold of any one philosophical definition.

Not only does it play with multiple significations, but form also runs into innumerable associations. What is formed may be transformed, deformed, or reformed; it may contain a formative or forming purpose; it may be formal, informed, or multiform. More distantly and archaically, form carries the meaning of beauty or comeliness, a sense which

---

[4] David Pole, *Aesthetics, Form and Emotion*, ed. George Roberts (London: Duckworth, 1983), 81.

[5] Raymond Williams, *Keywords: A Vocabulary of Culture and Society* (London: Flamingo, 1983; first pub. 1976), 138.

distinctly invokes the shape of the human body. In addition to all this buzz of possibilities, form is also one of those ordinary nuts-and-bolts words, a grammatical tool, as in 'in the form of'—a transaction which allows one thing to turn into another, and thus be transformed. All this etymological and grammatical activity presses on the singular sense of form. Although it looks like a fixed shape, a permanent configuration or ideal, whether in eternity, in the mind, or on the page, in fact form is mobile, versatile. It remains open to distant senses, distortions, to the push-and-pull of opposites or cognates. While most abstract nouns lend themselves to philosophical whittling, to definitions which reduce their sense for clarity and use, form makes mischief and keeps its signification moveable.

This very multiform potential may be the reason why artists continue to need and use the word, whether or not it is in critical fashion. It suggests in itself something of the very multi-dimensionality, the unsettled busyness, of the artwork. For form can signify both the finished object, the art form in its completion, or the parts that make up its technical apparatus. It can signify a visionary apparition in the mind, or the real, physical properties of a work. In addition, it can suggest the force that drives to completion: a resource, a goad, a ghost, an intention, a struggle, a desire. Of course in literary criticism it may also open a can of quarrels from its recurrent association with critical formalisms, old and new. Nonetheless, in spite of all this, form remains a word in common critical currency. It is, it seems, one that we cannot do without. After all, what other word could describe, with so little fuss, but also with a due sense of estrangement and embodiment, the object in question: the art form in all its integral complexity? What other word could be so wittily and succinctly resonant, drawing into its small scope such a crowd of possibilities? The evidence of its long and resilient history, among both critics and artists, is that while there may be nothing in this word, that nothing matters.

* * *

The story of form is an erratic one. It does not lend itself to chronological plotting, and its more technical meanings come and go on the tides of fashion. Nevertheless, this simple four-letter word, so basic to the idioms of speech, expresses in miniature a conundrum of language itself: that it is, and is not, the object it represents. At the same time this is a word which, at certain points in history, becomes charged with an extra load of philosophical or critical meaning. In particular, from the mid-eighteenth century onwards, it becomes associated with the growth of philosophical aesthetics and the Kantian emphasis on subjective perception. While often needing and using the word to express the art form itself, on the whole Kant does not stop to consider it, but keeps it as the maidservant of more conceptual abstractions: truth, taste, or judgement, for instance. Form helps, but it is rarely the main subject of discussion. So he writes, in the *Critique of Judgement,* that 'In painting, sculpture, and in fact in all the formative arts ... the *design* is what is essential. Here it is not what gratifies in sensation but merely what pleases by its form, that is the fundamental prerequisite for taste.'[6] He thus isolates 'form' as the essential figure of 'the formative arts', and offers it as the object of a pure, as opposed to a sensual or empirical, judgement. Alongside form he ranges 'beauty (which ought properly to be a question merely of the form)', but which is often confused with the lesser qualities of '*charm* and *emotion*'.[7] Kant's insistence on separating beauty from charm, the 'intrinsic' from mere '*ornamentation*',[8] is essential to the dual system he sets up between pure and empirical thinking. That beauty and form belong somehow to a pure kind of perception, against more ornamental, or emotional ones, is a connection which will cause trouble for those two words for the rest of the century and beyond. As he sums up: 'A judgement of taste which is uninfluenced by charm or emotion ... and whose determining ground, therefore, is simply finality of form, is *a pure judgement of taste*.'[9]   So Kant lets 'form' accept the burden of that disinterested judgement which is not confused by the muddling emotionalism of charm or ornament. He thus finds in it a word through which to assert the impersonal, purist claims of his whole aesthetic theory. Even while that theory offers an inherently subjective account of taste, it also shies away from subjective needs or feelings, and the word 'form', with its sense of simple 'finality', of nothing more to be said, suits that aim. Kant's concern, however, as Theodore Uehling points out, 'is not with any property of an object, but fundamentally with the disposition of the cognitive faculties of producer and perceiver.'[10] Although he invokes the arts, and indeed poetry in particular, which he

---

[6] Immanuel Kant, *The Critique of Judgement,* trans. James Creed Meredith (Oxford: Clarendon Press, 1952), 67.

[7] Ibid. 65.   [8] Ibid. 68.   [9] Ibid. 65.

[10] Theodore E. Uehling, Jr., *The Notion of Form in Kant's Critique of Aesthetic Judgment* (The Hague, Paris: Mouton, 1971), 112.

puts in 'the first rank among all the arts',[11] his main interest is in the mind's cognition rather than in the function of art itself.

Kant's very language, however, does offer the beginnings of an artistic formalism, which, in separating form from matter, spearheads a long and sometimes exasperating history. As Paul Guyer summarizes, 'our pleasure in beauty is a response only to the perceptible *form* of an object, not to any matter or content it may have'.[12] Yet matter and content also hover at the door of form, threatening its pure 'finality'. As Kant himself concedes, 'charms may be added to beauty to lend to the mind, beyond a bare delight, an adventitious interest in the representation of the object'.[13] The question of representation bothers his accounts of beauty and form, as if, at some level, challenging the very disinterested, even charmless, thesis he sets up. This leads to a niggling contradiction, that, as Guyer continues, there are also '*impure* forms of beauty—of no lesser value than pure beauty—where what we respond to with the free play of our imagination and understanding is harmony *between* an object's perceptible form and its matter, its content, or even its purpose.'[14] So the very things that should be distinct and separate: form and matter, disinterested beauty and 'adventitious' representation, prove not altogether separable. As in Plato, essential beauty has a tendency to touch on manifest examples of itself in the world.

While Kant gives to the nineteenth century a language for aesthetic disinterestedness, for a purity of perception, however menaced by its opposites, it is Schiller who bequeaths it a powerful and influential account of form as art form. In the 'Fifteenth Letter' of *On the Aesthetic Education of Man*, he writes:

The object of the form-drive, expressed in a general concept, we call form, both in the figurative and in the literal sense of this word: a concept which includes all the formal qualities of things and all the relations of these to our thinking faculties. The object of the play-drive ... may therefore be called living form ... what in the widest sense of the term we call beauty.[15]

This brings together terms which will be worked over for the next two centuries. Instead of abstracting 'form' into a pure noun, an idea set

[11] Kant, *The Critique of Judgement*, 191.

[12] Paul Guyer, *Values of Beauty: Historical Essays in Aesthetics* (Cambridge: Cambridge University Press, 2005), 193.

[13] Kant, *Critique of Judgement*, 67.   [14] Guyer, *Values of Beauty*, 194.

[15] Friedrich Schiller, *On the Aesthetic Education of Man: In a Series of Letters*, ed. and trans. Elizabeth M. Wilkinson and L. A. Willoughby (Oxford: Clarendon Press, 1967), 101.

apart, as Kant does, Schiller fidgets with it, trying out grammatical alternatives: 'form-drive', 'formal qualities', 'living form', as if to push the noun into new shapes, new 'forms'. So the 'play-drive' of art is a 'form-drive', a wish to make forms, and that leads to a notion of 'living form'—a phrase which will be repeated by a number of later theorists. That form might be 'living' gives it huge possibilities of movement, change, reproduction, energy. Here, it is neither purely abstract, a word unconnected with feelings or objects, nor a matter of merely inert matter. Instead, it is shifting, purposeful, tied to an organicist metaphor which makes it, grammatically and literally, moveable. Schiller finds in form, not only a definition of art, but also of the creative need for art. He links the finished work to the energies and desires of its playful creator.

His later discussion of form and matter in the 'Twenty-Second Letter' is a *locus classicus* for Victorian aesthetes:

In a truly successful work of art the content should effect nothing, the form everything ... Subject-matter, then, however sublime and all-embracing it may be, always has a limiting effect upon the spirit, and it is only from form that true aesthetic freedom can be looked for. Herein, then, resides the real secret of the master in any art: that he can make his form consume his material.[16]

This much quoted, final assertion depends, according to Schiller's editors, on 'the hidden biological metaphor in the word *vertilgen*, which they translate as 'consume'. However, they admit that this differs from more familiar nineteenth-century translations: Pater, for instance, writes 'obliterate', and Wilde, 'annihilate'. These, they argue, 'indeed make it sound as though Schiller wants to empty art of subject-matter if not of content'.[17] They insist, by contrast, that for him 'the forms of art ... are never "pure",'[18] since matter, as edible substance, is only recycled, not destroyed by form. Nevertheless, pure or impure, this passage gives to later generations a potent and memorable opposition between form as 'spirit' and matter as 'material', the one 'everything', the other 'nothing'. To make form obliterate, or annihilate, the matter will be the difficult, sometimes guilty, sometimes provocative, aim of Schiller's aestheticist followers.

Thus from German philosophy the word 'form' comes into English Romanticism with an already heightened charge. It is now loaded, not

---

[16] Schiller, *On the Aesthetic Education of Man* 155–7.
[17] Ibid. p. clxxvi.   [18] Ibid. p. clxxvi–clxxvii.

only with its old platonic overtones, but with Kant's subject-centred yet abstract epistemology, as well as with a developing sense of poetic or aesthetic integrity. The mix of all these makes form a packed and complex word by the time the Romantics come to use it. Coleridge, above all, worries over its dual affiliation to shaped thing and imaginative outline. The two, he argues, must be kept apart, as the dead from the living. So he writes that 'all form as body, i.e. as shape, & not as forma efformans, is dead.'[19] The idea of '*forma efformans*' (forming form) is a curious investment of activity in the thing. Form by itself has to be modified by a verb, as if to stop it hardening into a mere object. Form is not a body but an agent. It forms. The difference between 'forming form' and 'formed form' appears throughout Coleridge's writings and underpins much of his theory of imagination. Elsewhere, in the *Notebooks* for instance, he jots down: 'Difference of Form as proceeding and Shape as superinduced—the latter either the Death or the imprisonment of the Thing; the former, its self-witnessing, and self-effected sphere of agency'.[20] 'Shape' stays still and kills its object, while 'Form' is its communicated liveness, 'self-witnessing, and self-effected'. While we may be none the wiser as to how form is a self-witnessing thing, its own testimony and justification, what can be heard is how Coleridge shies away from the nominal mode in defining form, and turns for help to verbs and present participles. Something, whatever 'Thing' it is, starts to move as form, and to move, it seems, of its own volition. What can be heard here is not exactly a philosophical definition, but a pushing at language to bring form to life. Like the imagination, form is a shaping activity rather than a visual shape, and this leads to the curious self-involvement of what it does. It acts on itself, sees itself, is its own 'agency'. It cannot therefore be described in simile or metaphor, in a likeness to some other object, but only in a kind of grammatical tautology: 'self-witnessing, and self-effected'.

This gives rise, perhaps, to an intriguing passage in which Coleridge seems to refer specifically to the making of poems. After a briefly disparaging reference to the mere 'technical forms of Poetry', he then jots down some half-related thoughts, evidently inspired by the word itself: 'Poems.—Ghost of a mountain | the forms seizing my body, as I passed, became realities—I, a Ghost, till I had reconquered my Substance |.'[21] It is unclear whether this is a definition of 'Poems'

---

[19] *Coleridge's Notebooks: A Selection*, ed. Seamus Perry (Oxford: Oxford University Press, 2002), 124.
[20] Ibid. 131.   [21] Ibid. 27.

generally, a memory of an event, or a projected summary of a particular poem. Whichever it is, 'forms' is now an uncanny word, which can make the objects out there (presumably mountains) turn from ghosts to violent possessors of the speaker's own 'body'. In this vampiric exchange, the speaker loses his bodily matter and becomes a ghost in turn. Read beside the many addresses to the awful forms or silent forms of romantic nature poetry, it highlights the way in which the word can release objects from mere objectivity. A form, unlike the fixed view or shape, is hollow, ghostly, and therefore morphologically greedy for substance, for body or matter. The relationship between form and substance is not a given, but dramatic, risky, essentially a disjunction. 'Poems', it seems, are out to find a 'Substance', which is not, necessarily, inherent in their own 'forms'. In fact, they are born of that discrepancy. Interestingly, what happens in this passage is that the poet then snatches substance back, in order, one supposes, not to die of too much insubstantiality himself.

Romantic form, then, is already a complicated idea. It ranges from objects seen, which are still and dead, to objects which act on the imagination and may even, therefore, be peculiarly energetic, vicious, disturbing. Coleridge, when he writes about forms, is writing about something which pivots between world and mind, bringing one into the other, either as an object or as an inspiration for poetry. But both the fixity of forms and their very active independence can be a problem. They either move too little, or move too much. They might, at one extreme, harden into deadeningly unpoetic objects which cannot tickle the imagination into action, or at the other, they might become so ghostly and wilful that they steal the poet's mental stability from him. Either way, for Coleridge, there are risks. It is Shelley who, with less anxiety, acclaims the idea of a self-motivating, self-justifying form. His lines, for instance, from 'The Triumph of Life'—'the phantom of that early Form | Which moved upon its motion'—drove Empson to complain that the '*Form* is its own justification; it sustains itself, like God, by the fact that it exists.'[22] Empson disliked what he saw as the religious underpinnings of the passage, but he also perhaps misses the fact that Shelley's forms are not God-sustained at all, but self-sustaining, and thus skim across an epistemological void. The combination of two near-tautologies: the phantom of a form, and moving on motion,

---

[22] William Empson, *Seven Types of Ambiguity* (Harmondsworth: Penguin, 1961; first pub. 1930), 161.

almost defies sight, gravity (and sense) altogether. The lines do not explain or name the form, and do not offer it as a metaphor of the mind; instead, they set it afloat on a stream of language which carries it on its own momentum. Shelley lets the verbs take the weight, or weightlessness, of this phantom, which seems to exist without body or matter, on the rhythmic, self-propelling impulse of words. The anti-representational bent of the word here, doubly removed from reality in being 'the phantom' of a 'Form', makes it suited to that intercalative world of Romantic visions invoked by all these poets. Form, as in Coleridge, is a ghost, an object cut off from its original body, yet acting with an eerie independence which makes it seem autonomous and self-involved. It thus serves as the necessary, if unpredictable, intermediary between the mind and the world, in case, otherwise, they should come completely apart.

Far from going out of currency after the Romantics, form becomes one of the most precious terms in the vocabulary of Victorian aestheticism. Theories of 'art for art', while invoking form as the justification for a merely formal artistry, without political or moral point, also, contradictorily, give it a new and specific sense of bodily presence. Form is, on the one hand, thinned into mere style or manner, and, on the other, fleshed out into beauty's desirable shape. This shift might be traceable to the book which was both the holy writ and unholy scandal of the aesthetes: Gautier's *Mademoiselle de Maupin* (1835). It is not so much the soft-core narrative which provides ammunition against (Romantic) nature and middle-class Christian morality, but the recurrent association of form with beauty. If form, for the Romantics, usually involves a ghostly transaction of power, and sometimes fear, between perceiver and the natural world, Gautier's bisexual, transsexual heroine quite simply makes form human, and her own. As the hero puts it: '*J'adore sur toutes choses la beauté de la forme;—la beaut' e pour moi, c'est la Divinité visible, c'est le bonheur palpable.*'[23] (I worship beauty of form above all things;—beauty, to me, is the divine made visible, it is happiness made palpable.) The word which everywhere attaches itself to form is 'beauty'. It is an old platonic association, but here it is also real, a matter of crusading physical presence. Even when the object of desire is sexually ambivalent, the language of love is the same. The hero asks: '*pour un adorateur exclusif de la forme, y a-t-il une*

---

[23] Théophile Gautier, *Mademoiselle de Maupin*, intro. Geneviève van den Bogaert (Paris : Garnier-Flammarion, 1966), 149.

incertitude plus aimable ... ?'[24] (For a worshipper exclusively of form, is there a more lovable uncertainty?) Throughout the novel the word carries the burden of the various human bodies that fill it, as well as of an alternative morality by which '*la correction de la forme est la vertu.*'[25] (The correctness of form is virtue.) The peculiar sexlessness of English Romantic poetry is swept aside in this rehabilitation of form as desirable body. As D'Albert puts it in one place: '*Le type de beauté que je rêvais depuis si longtemps, je l'ai rencontré.—J'ai trouv' e le corps de mon fantôme.*'[26] (The type of beauty of which I dreamed for so long, I have encountered.—I have found the body of my phantom.) So beauty and the body fill up the hollow Romantic 'phantom', and make it human. Gautier's stroke of genius, and mischief, in this work is to keep the body ambiguous, ambidextrous. This is a drama of 'As You Like It', with an updated Rosalind and Orlando changing sexual places while the language remains the same. As a result, the body of the phantom form, anarchic, licentious, and impersonal, returns to fill it out.

Mademoiselle de Maupin is a prolonged metaphor about desire, pleasure, and art. It is as if the body of Coleridge's 'phantom' has turned up, in the 1830s, but without any vengeful, vampiric tendencies. Form, after Gautier, will carry this distinctly non-platonic, non-Kantian charge. It is no longer an object of perception, but an object of touch. Such a sexualizing of form is aestheticism's rather obvious, but also daring, innovation. When, in 1868, Pater published his extraordinary review of 'Poems by William Morris', later to become the Conclusion to *The Renaissance*, he explicitly connects the form–beauty ideal to 'art for art' by defending 'a kind of poetry which, assuming artistic beauty of form to be an end in itself, passes by those truths and the living interests which are connected with them'.[27] Pater, more than any other, is aware of what form, as 'an end in itself', both shuts in and shuts out. It shuts in beauty and shuts out truth, thus emphatically polarizing those two sparring partners of aestheticist thought. Meanwhile form, a word he cannot leave alone, is also one he cannot promote without qualms. For on the one hand it means 'beauty of form', the physical matter of the body; but on the other it means something which might perhaps not matter at all.

---

[24] Théophile Gautier, *Mademoiselle de Maupin*, intro. Geneviève van den Bogaert (Paris : Garnier-Flammarion, 1966), 212.

[25] Ibid. 201.   [26] Ibid. 191.

[27] Walter Pater, 'Poems by William Morris', *Westminster Review*, 34(1868), 300–12, 309.

In *Marius the Epicurean* the elderly counsellors are suspicious of Flavian's Epicureanism, 'suspecting some affectation or unreality in that minute culture of *form*:—Cannot those who have a thing to say, say it directly?'[28] they grumble. The question of 'affectation', 'unreality', minuteness, of being unable to say a thing 'directly', is a criticism that presses everywhere on Pater's own exquisitely evasive, even at times affected prose.

Wilde, by contrast, enjoys the shock and provocation of the unconditional. 'It is just because he has no new message, that he can do beautiful work. He gains his inspiration from form, and from form purely, as an artist should.' So 'form' is set unequivocally against 'message'. He then adds, for the hell of it: 'Form is everything. It is the secret of life.'[29] It is when Wilde pushes his luck too far in this direction that hell indeed catches up with him. That form is 'everything', in life as in writing, is a position which will indeed be challenged by life itself, both in the ending of *Dorian Gray* and, for Wilde himself, in the real courtroom's formal charges. His most interesting comments about form, however, are not the outrageous one-liners, but his observations about criticism. In 'The Critic as Artist' form is first of all a weapon against intentionalism. Long before twentieth-century intentionalist fallacies, Wilde writes that 'criticism of the highest kind ... does not confine itself ... to discovering the real intention of the artist and accepting that as final.'[30] Instead, it 'makes the critic a creator in his turn, and whispers of a thousand different things which were not present in the mind of him who carved the statue or painted the panel or graved the gem.'[31] This seductive whispering takes as many liberties with the work as it needs, because, in the end, it has its own necessary form. The sense of form, he insists, 'is the basis of creative no less than of critical achievement.'[32] For 'the critic is he who exhibits to us a work of art in a form different from that of the work itself'.[33] Form, here, is not artistic technique or even artistic inviolableness—the defence mechanism of the aesthetic against the world; instead, it is almost the opposite. The different 'form' of criticism, its seductive, sly, even Chinese whispering, is a freedom to play. It need not guess intention or reproduce the formal properties of the work. Instead, it discovers in its own 'form' the new meanings or relations of a work. By comparison with some of the professionalized

[28] Walter Pater, *Marius the Epicurean*, 2 vols. (London: Macmillan, 1910), i, 99.

[29] Oscar Wilde, 'The Critic as Artist', in *Intentions* (London: Methuen, 1919; first pub. 1891), 153–217, 201.

[30] Ibid. 143–4.   [31] Ibid. 146.   [32] Ibid. 200.   [33] Ibid. 157.

formats of twentieth-century critics, Victorian aestheticism offers some of the most potent, rich, sexy, if also, sometimes, outrageous or silly accounts of what literary criticism might be for.

The cachet of the word, by this time, had spread well beyond literary circles. In 1867, the year before Pater's 'William Morris' review, and in the same year that Swinburne published his seminal essay on 'William Blake', Sidney Colvin wrote an article on 'English painters and painting', which declares that 'perfection of forms and colours—beauty, in a word—should be the prime object of pictorial art.'[34] That 'beauty, in a word' sounds already self-conscious, provocative. That it is just a word is also, somehow, part of the point. The phrase has a no-getting-round-this obstinacy about it. Beauty, indeed, will continue to be as ineluctable and necessary a word for Woolf, Yeats, and Stevens, who continue to turn it over and over as if to catch its shine. For all its Nineties' over-use, its sugar-coated familiarity, there is something about this word which will not give up. If, in 1867, 'in a word' apologizes, it also, quite simply, finds no alternatives.

Colvin's abstraction of 'forms and colours' from message or subject matter is a tactic which, almost fifty years later, Clive Bell and his fellow modernists repeat, as if it represented the new triumph of the modern. Bell's famous definition of 'Significant Form', as the quality inherent in all the fine arts as well as crafts, emphasizes the same elements as Colvin:

lines and colours combined in a particular way, certain forms and relations of forms, stir our aesthetic emotions. These relations and combinations of lines and colours, these aesthetically moving forms, I call 'Significant Form'.[35]

In fact, A. C. Bradley had already used the term 'significant form'[36] in his 1901 inaugural lecture on 'Poetry for Poetry's Sake', thus making the crucial connection between it and the doctrine of 'Art for Art'.[37] In Bell's passage it is interesting how this newly claimed phrase, capitalized for significance, shifts from visible 'lines and colours', those elementary, technical ingredients of the visual arts, to unfixed, 'aesthetically moving forms'. Form becomes aesthetic when it starts to move. On the one

---

[34] Quoted in Elizabeth Prettejohn, 'Introduction', *After the Pre-Raphaelites: Art and Aestheticism in Victorian England* (Manchester: Manchester University Press, 1999), 1–14, 3,

[35] Clive Bell, *Art* (London: Chatto & Windus, 1914), 8.

[36] A. C. Bradley, 'Poetry for Poetry's Sake', in *Oxford Lectures on Poetry* (London: Macmillan, 1926), 3–34, 19.

[37] Ibid. 4.

hand the passage abstracts form into 'lines and colours', into technical parts of a painting; but on the other it also insists on those 'emotions' that are stirred. As a result, 'Significant Form', that much abused term which John Carey dismisses as the mantra of high art,[38] in fact registers a deep tension. It was Louis MacNeice who, though hostile to the phrase, noted that it is 'a contradiction in terms'.[39] Often taken to mean pure form, or form abstracted altogether from meaning, 'Significant Form' in fact registers the contrary pressure of significance, and therefore the stress of incompatibles being brought together.

Mostly, of course, Bell is simply arguing that 'lines and colours' are more significant than the thing which they represent. But the fact that 'significance', in the sense of both 'importance' and 'import',[40] is essential to form does somewhat qualify the formalist sound of the phrase. 'Bell's aesthetics,' Fishman suggests, 'appears to lie midway between an excessively purist formalism and an incipient expressionism which threatens the notion of pure form.'[41] Certainly, matters of significance in Bell are always pressing against mere lines or colours. When he writes about Cézanne's landscape paintings, for instance, the same ambiguity can be felt. 'Everything can be seen as pure form, and behind pure form lurks the mysterious significance that thrills to ecstasy.'[42] Here, the need for 'significance' compromises the purity or self-sufficiency of form. There is, it seems, something 'behind pure form', even if what it is disappears into a hazy flourish of affective rhetoric. Even in Clive Bell, it seems, the issue is one of 'form and'.

When Roger Fry offers his own, admittedly 'vague adumbration of the nature of significant form' in *Vision and Design* (1920), six years after Bell, he pushes even further towards an expressive theory. The phrase does not refer to 'agreeable arrangements of form, harmonious patterns, and the like', but to 'the effort on the part of the artist to bend to our emotional understanding by means of his passionate conviction some intractable material which is alien to our spirit.'[43] Even more of something outside seems to be pressing against form here: 'effort', emotions,

---

[38] John Carey, *What Good are the Arts?* (London: Faber, 2005), 89–90.

[39] Louis MacNeice, *Modern Poetry: A Personal Essay*, intro. Walter Allen (Oxford: Clarendon Press, 1968; first pub. 1938), 59.

[40] Solomon Fishman, *The Interpretation of Art: Essays on the Art Criticism of John Ruskin, Walter Pater, Clive Bell, Roger Fry and Herbert Read* (Berkeley & Los Angeles: University of California Press, 1963), 83.

[41] Ibid. 85. [42] Bell, *Art*, 209.

[43] Roger Fry, *Vision and Design* (London: Chatto & Windus, new and rev. edn 1923; first pub. 1920), 302.

'understanding', 'conviction', 'material'. Significant Form is worked for, not necessarily agreeably, and the effort and stuff of that work can be heard or seen in it. So Fry retains an expressive intention, a purpose or affect, in form. It is achieved by bending or hammering, or some other implied hard labour of the artist, which makes that 'intractable material' eventually tractable. Both Bell and Fry thus acknowledge the forces which contradict their own formalist agendas. The emphasis on 'lines and colours' cannot be isolated from significance, expression, artistic effort.

The word 'form', then, makes the transition from aestheticism to modernism without any sign of embarrassment or apology. Although the sexual connotations of the word disappear, the emphasis on art's non-representational bent becomes even more pronounced. Form, for the modernists, is refreshed by an association with the visual arts, particularly cubism and post-impressionism, which gives the word an extra agenda and turns it into the messenger of newness. The main impetus behind this, alongside Bell and Fry, is Ezra Pound who, in 1916 for instance, declared that 'So far as I am concerned, Jacob Epstein was the first person who came talking about "form, not the *form of anything*".'[44] This has an exhilarating assertiveness about it, even if it is wrong. Form, which is not the form of anything, goes back at least to Coleridge. But Pound, as late as 1921, could insist that 'so few people have yet dissociated form from representation' that it is still necessary to repeat the proposition that 'A work of art has in it no idea which is separable from the form.'[45] Pound's own criticism constantly returns to the banner of form, for which abstract sculpture is now the prime example. 'Brancusi', he points out, 'is meditating upon pure form free from all terrestrial gravitation; form as free in its own life as the form of the analytic geometers'.[46] That it must be abstract, even merely geometrical, is the new modernist creed. The word inflects easily to this hard, sculptured quality, to the sense of art as an almost mathematical defiance of reality, rather than a copy of it. At the same time, Pound does acknowledge his debt to Pater and Whistler,[47] recognizing that his own penchant for abstract descriptions—that 'beauty, in so far as

[44] Ezra Pound, *Gaudier-Brzeska: A Memoir* (Hessle, E. Yorkshire: The Marvell Press, 1960; first pub. 1916), 98.

[45] Ezra Pound, 'Brancusi', in *Literary Essays of Ezra Pound*, ed. T. S. Eliot (London: Faber, 1960; first pub. 1954), 441–5, 441.

[46] Ibid. 444.   [47] Pound, *Gaudier-Brzeska*, 120.

it is beauty of form, is the result of "planes in relation" '[48]—is only a development of a long aestheticist history.

One sign of this indebtedness is the repeated association of form and beauty in his work. The term 'beauty of form' trips off Pound's tongue without any apology for almost a century of use. Thus, he suggests, Brancusi's 'Ovoid' invites 'the contemplation of form or of formal-beauty',[49] the two words pairing readily as if bound by a natural tie. The old etymological association of form with comeliness, or physical beauty, lies somewhere deep in the expression. However, in Pound's hands beauty has lost its palpable allure, and couples with form only to resist any visible shaping. Thus 'formal-beauty', hyphenated into an easy hybrid, is nothing that you might see. Yet his continuing need for the word 'beauty' is protestingly asserted in 'The Serious Artist', when he claims, for instance, that: 'Beauty in art reminds one what is worth while. I am not now speaking of shams. I mean beauty, not slither, not sentimentalizing about beauty, not telling people that beauty is the proper and respectable thing. I mean beauty. You don't argue about an April wind.'[50] So he cudgels the word, as if by these verbal blows he might clear it of accreted 'shams'. In the end he is left with that familiar, self-justifying phrase, 'beauty, in a word', residual and stubborn. The difference between the Victorian aesthetes and their modernist successors is that the former suffer from a sense of guilt and intrigue in their attitudes to form and beauty; the latter do not. Pater shifts nervously round those words, feeling their human contours, their sexual potential; for Pound, the point is abstract and unarguable, an opportunity for trailblazing the values of modernity. But in both, the word provides a way of resisting art's commitments to reality, in the name of some indefinable otherness which commands endless permutations of definition.

Certainly, the word 'form' has always had a natural fit in the visual arts. Essentially, the word first comes to mind as something seen. Thus Picasso, for instance, acclaims the radically new work of Cézanne in terms which replay the old sense of opposition:

'If one occupies oneself with what is full: that is, the object as positive form, the space around it is reduced to almost nothing. If one occupies oneself primarily with the space that surrounds the object, the object is reduced to almost nothing. What interests us most—what is outside or what is inside a

---

[48] Ibid. 121.   [49] Pound, *Literary Essays*, 444.
[50] Pound, 'The Serious Artist', in *Literary Essays*, 41–57, 45.

form? When you look at Cézanne's apples, you see that he hasn't really painted apples, as such. What he did was to paint terribly well the weight of space on that circular form.'[51]

The question 'what is outside or what is inside a form?' perfectly captures the way that form is both a container and a deflector. Imagined visually, it looks two ways: to the shape it keeps in and the shape it keeps out. It is a wall or line between two objects, or between two blocks of space, and thus offers a choice: there are apples, or there is an apple-shaped 'weight of space'. Form, then, is the distribution of space caused by edging one thing against another, so that each calls attention to the other. It is not so much a dispensable holder of content, as a line, perhaps a very fine line, between two alternatives which are actually two ways of looking at a work: now-you-see (apples) and-now-you-don't. Apples, as such, are not important. They are weightlifters of the space around them, shapes upholding another shape. Nevertheless, however distantly, their shapes do recall something, with a name in the world: apples. They throw it into a kind of distant, remembered, perhaps elegiac relief. The most abstract form—even just a clean line, for instance—is still, at some level, representationally significant. It can still bring something to mind: a flagpole, say, a tree, a lighthouse. Similarly, and conversely, what seems to be an exact representation is also abstract, making a mere shape, a sound, an arrangement of rhythms on the page. To learn to cross from one dimension to the other is part of the dynamics of form itself. Particularly in literature, that most multi-dimensional of the arts, the word form might involve a choice of at least three things: the shape of the text on the page, the shape of its sounds in the air, and the matter of which it speaks. As a result it calls for what Franklin Rogers has called 'a "volumetric" reading', one which advances 'in several dimensions at once'.[52] Picasso's 'what is outside or what is inside a form?' is a reminder that the word may refer, not to a single boundary line, but to a dividing line, an outline, between different dimensions of understanding. Form, by this account, is not a fixed shape to be seen, but the shape of a choice to be made.

For the modernists, then, who take their bearings from the visual arts, form seems to become ever further removed from the nineteenth century's fascination with the tactile. The artwork is not representative

---

[51] Quoted in Franklin R. Rogers, *Painting and Poetry: Form, Metaphor, and the Language of Literature* (London and Toronto: Associated University Presses, 1985), 152–3.

[52] Ibid. 194.

of anything, but is purely itself. At the same time, however, the question of significance, of emotional affect or of interpretative choice continues to knock for attention. However much form tries to shut them out, those external needs and desires complicate its abstract purity. After all, as Picasso puts it, 'What interests us most ... ?' is a question that brings the whole problem of audience, point of view, human interest, and human needs, into the picture.

It is this complexity that is acknowledged in one of the most vibrant little books of the period: Henri Focillon's *The Life of Forms in Art* (1934). An art historian, Focillon extends his argument to include, specifically, the roles of artist and audience. Thus he begins with a familiar proposition: 'A work of art is the measure of space. It is form, and as form it must first make itself known to us.'[53] This, like Picasso's description, betrays its affiliation to the visual arts. Form is realized in space and is shaped to be seen. But this is only the starting point. Soon it is qualified by another statement: 'a work of art is motionless only in appearance. It seems to be set fast—arrested, as are the moments of time gone by. But in reality it is born of change, and it leads on to other changes.' Indeed, he continues, the appearance of stillness is deceptive: art's 'very immobility sparkles with metamorphoses'.[54] With the word 'metamorphoses' he routs the abstract fixity of modernist accounts. Form spawns life, change, movement. Far from being a finished object, integral to itself, abstract and finished, it is the start of change: 'the life of forms in the mind propagates a prodigious animism that, taking natural objects as the point of departure, makes them matters of imagination and memory, of sensibility and intellect ... Between nature and man form intervenes,' he concludes.[55] This capacious definition of form explodes the old dualisms, rejects the argument from abstraction, and offers instead a seething sense of reproductive life. Form consists of all the metamorphic interactions the artwork initiates, including ones which are 'matters of imagination and memory, of sensibility and intellect'. Far from being cut off from purpose and affect, authorial or readerly interests, form brings them all energetically into play. From the hard-edged, untouchable sculptures of modernism we have moved into a De Quincean world, where form is imagined as the uncontrollable, promiscuous 'animism' of a dream, or of nightmare.

[53] Henri Focillon, *The Life of Forms in Art*, trans. Charles Beecher Hogan and George Kubler (New York: George Wittenborn, Inc. 1948; first pub. 1934), 2.
[54] Ibid. 6.   [55] Ibid. 47.

By making transformation the essence of form, Focillon confronts again the tricky questions of subject matter and interpretation. He writes, for instance, that: 'Form is never the catch-as-catch-can garment of subject-matter. No, it is the various interpretations of subject-matter that are so unstable and insecure.'[56] Form is not a garment of thought, to hide or reveal its proper (bodily) matter, but rather a complex of already active 'interpretations'. From here it is but a short step to finding form, like God, everywhere. If this is a limitation, it is also a strength. For it allows Focillon to include something of the originally formal nature of creativity, as well as of the nature of the reader or audience. 'Now the idea of the artist is form,' he writes. 'His emotional life turns likewise to form … I do not say that form is the allegory or the symbol of feeling, but, rather, its innermost activity. Form activates feeling.'[57] That the artist feels formally to start with is a nicely inclusive formula which, at a stroke, obviates the need for translating, or annihilating, the dancing partners of form: feeling, intention, matter. All of those are already formal. As a result, form is no longer conceived as the end product, a finished museum piece, cut off, as it were, from the means of production. Instead, it is both production and reproduction, creativity and creation. Form mucks in with all the business of thinking, feeling, producing, interpreting, whether artist's or reader's, so that what it is is an object on the move, 'unstable and insecure'. The life of forms, Focillon concludes, is simply the innumerable ways in which the artwork comes to life through interpretation. It is thus always significant, but not chained to any one represented significance. Instead, it is the metamorphosing potential of art, as it becomes the point of interaction between artist and audience, maker and perceiver. Those kinaesthetic resources are form's defining feature, and they require, like Focillon's own, a tentacular, sinuous, ever-shifting critical description. Form, it seems, cannot be pinpointed by a single definition; it can only be described, progressively, on the hoof.

So by the mid-century, form has once again become an activity. If, as Focillon writes, 'form … activates feeling', then it is, to start with, an event connected with consciousness and deeply bedded in the functions of the human heart. The artist feels in forms, and thus forms feelings. The word is associated with human energies, whether creation or interpretation, and pivots the activities of hand and brain. This sense

---

[56] Henri Focillon, *The Life of Forms in Art*, trans. Charles Beecher Hogan and George Kubler (New York: George Wittenborn, Inc. 1948; first pub. 1934), 6.
[57] Ibid. 47.

of inclusive, humanized activity is developed in Susanne K. Langer's *Feeling and Form* (1953), which catches up innumerable strands of thinking from the previous hundred years. Forms, she explains, 'are either empty abstractions, or they do have a content; and artistic forms have a very special one, namely their *import*. They are logically expressive, or significant, forms.'[58] So Clive Bell's formula, tweaked by Fry's expressive '*import*' and given the extra fillip of Langer's own word 'logically', returns in full force. At the same time, as the title tells, 'Art is the creation of forms symbolic of human feeling.'[59] This certainly rejects modernism in its overt recovery of 'feeling' as part of the work of creation. 'Form and Feeling' would once have been a contradiction, but it is now a hybrid, rather like Langer's other hybrid, 'living form'[60] which, like Schiller's original, or Coleridge's 'forma efformans', or Focillon's 'life of forms', insists on life at the heart of form. Langer's amalgam of many previous accounts brings out the relational restlessness of the word, its close connections with the feelings that first impel creativity. She thus continues the project, started by Focillon, of wresting form away from the museum of untouchable (and therefore enticingly touchable) art forms, and giving it back to the human beings who make or perceive it.

This plethora of definitions from a century and more suggests the extent to which form has always been a word needed by the arts. It is volatile, evasive yet resilient, surviving the fashions which bring it to prominence and constantly recovering forgotten meanings. If, at times, it also seems trivial, self-involved, not an easy word to justify politically, it is, nonetheless, one which will not go away. It has survived its connection with aestheticism, modernism, and beyond, and continues, if sporadically, to be a word that probes the discomfiting distances of art, its aloofness, obliqueness, inwardness. Form, in its shorthand brevity and endless punning ramifications, comes close to expressing the mysterious, self-justifying nature of the literary itself.

Even in the last twenty or thirty years, when terms like text, language, the unconscious have taken centre stage in literary discussion, form appears here and there as a word still capable of resisting reduction. In Roland Barthes's essays, *The Responsibility of Forms* (1986), for instance, it denotes something which refutes the world's systems of exchange.

[58] Susanne K. Langer, *Feeling and Form: A Theory of Art Developed from Philosophy in a New Key* (London: Routledge & Kegan Paul, 1953), 52.
[59] Ibid. 40.   [60] Ibid. 65.

That forms have responsibility may imply, as Helen Vendler argues, that Barthes's 'devotion to the aesthetic was not only a natural inclination but also a fully ethical commitment.'[61] Nevertheless, at certain points in these essays art is defined as a responsibility, not to the world or society, but precisely to nothing. Lying outside the accountable, art belongs with 'all that man does "for nothing".'[62] The ambivalently highlighted phrase returns like a refrain, and gives to these essays a peculiarly aestheticist direction. Of the artist Cy Twombly, for instance, Barthes writes: 'there is always an extreme point where [the body] gives itself *for nothing*.'[63] Works of pop art, he suggests, 'incarnate the very concept of facticity—that by which, in spite of themselves, they begin to signify again: they signify that they signify nothing'.[64] That 'nothing' is both significant, and significant of nothing. The dead end of logic becomes the declared end of art. Signifying nothing, like significant form, keeps signification in view while also emptying it of matter, and of mattering too much. The old duo, of 'form and', dances on. In the essay on 'Requichot and His Body', Barthes writes that Requichot 'wanted to lose *for nothing*: he contested any exchange'.[65] That '*for nothing*' seems the opposite of responsibility. It is throwaway, careless, senseless, a piece of aestheticism recalling Pater's conclusion that 'art comes to you proposing frankly to give nothing'.[66] The possibility of something in nothing is aestheticism's continuing and tempting pipedream.

At one point, Barthes offers a definition. He writes that 'form is what is *between* the thing and its name, form is what delays the name.'[67] This is an interesting role for form. It is a go-between, an interval, an interrupter, breaking the norms of representation and obstructing the passage from thing to name. The sense of exchange, of a brisk traffic between name and thing, is broken by it, or at least delayed by it. As an extra, a surplus, a hiatus even, form is conceived by Barthes as a pause in the work of signification, which also alters the nature of signification. It is not the quick transaction that we expect, and which satisfies our expectations, but the pause which, for a moment, stops that transaction being relevant

[61] Helen Vendler, *The Music of What Happens: Poems, Poets, Critics* (Cambridge, Mass.: Harvard University Press, 1988), 74.

[62] Roland Barthes, *The Responsibility of Forms: Critical Essays on Music, Art, and Representation*, trans. Richard Howard (Oxford: Basil Blackwell, 1986; first pub. 1982), 161.

[63] Ibid. 171.   [64] Ibid. 202.   [65] Ibid. 233.

[66] Walter Pater, *The Renaissance: Studies in Art and Poetry* (London: Macmillan, 1910; first pub. 1873), 239.

[67] Barthes, *The Responsibility of Forms*, 234.

at all. The idea that form gives us pause, that it reroutes our very trains of thought, adds yet another element to this inventive and much reinvented word. Barthes suggests that form stops us in our tracks of thinking, and inserts itself in that moment of stillness. To attend to form is thus to admit some other kind of mental attention, which is not the quick route to a name or the knowledge of an object. Neither the thing nor the name, form keeps us in a place which postpones the logic of both.

Post-war commentators on form, like Barthes himself, are beset by a sense of responsibility, even guilt, as they return to a word with a perhaps frivolous history. Their advocacy of aestheticist ideas is thus uneasy, hard-won. Adorno, for instance, is both fascinated by and distrustful of an aestheticist heritage which, after the war, risks irrelevance and worse. There are moments when, in his monumental work, *Aesthetic Theory*, he suddenly seems to throw over the aesthetic altogether, as if in panic or penitence. So, towards the end of the book he writes: 'it would be preferable that some fine day art vanish altogether, than that it forget the suffering that is its expression and in which form has its substance.'[68] This, like many other comments about silence, is a baffled gesture, a piece of merely rhetorical retraction. In fact, self-evidently, suffering is no more the essential 'substance' of artistic form than are laughing, forgetting, or just the look of a vase of flowers. Having written at such passionate length about the aesthetic, this histrionic guilt on behalf of, not his own writing, but the art of others, is either ingenuous or slightly disingenuous. In several places Adorno invokes silence as a punishingly appropriate reaction to atrocity. Thus he writes, for instance: 'The prospect of the rejection of art for the sake of art is foreseeable. It is intimated by those art-works that fall silent or disappear.'[69] Each part of this proposition in fact betrays something other than what it proposes: first, that art for art's sake is still, in the 1970s, a sufficiently viable artistic creed to be worth turning away from, and secondly, that the artwork by its very nature is unlikely to want to 'fall silent or disappear'. After all, the responsibility of art is to be there, unsilent and unvanished. What it is there *for*, however, is a question that always remains to be answered.

Certainly Adorno here has touched on the raw nerve of aestheticism. The pressure from 'suffering' is not irrelevant, even if it is

---

[68] Theodor W. Adorno, *Aesthetic Theory*, ed. Gretel Adorno and Rolf Tiedemann, newly trans. Robert Hullot-Kentor (London: Athlone Press, 1997; first pub. 1970), 260.
[69] Ibid. 53.

not necessarily the 'substance' of art. The very tag 'art for art's sake' implies a shutting out, of art for someone's sake, for something's sake, for God's sake. The question of 'art *for*' leaves that something still pressing, calling from the outside. It may perhaps be true that ethical responsibility presses all the more urgently on the art which formally shuts it out than on the art which flashes its political credentials. This is something that Herbert Read suggested in 1945, a date also conducive to guilt and responsibility: 'art has never been so deliberately devoid of message as during the last fifty years,' he points out, sweeping up modernism and the Nineties together. 'At the same time, and in the true sense of the word, we can also assert that art has never been so effectively ethical.'[70] As an assertion, it betrays unease. It protests too much, depends too much on those special emphases: 'the *true* sense', '*effectively* ethical', and a 'we' which impersonates a crowd. The sense that art can be 'ethical' without a 'message' is crucial, however. Read's paradox ultimately leaves open the question of where, in art, ethical purpose or meaning are to be found.

Towards the end of her valiant defence of the aesthetic in *The Music of What Happens* (1988), Helen Vendler tackles this thorny issue when she briefly considers Czeslaw Milosz's poem 'The Poor Poet', dated '*Warsaw, 1944*'. Here, she argues, we find 'the problem of content and form in its most violent aspect, as the serenity of form (even here, in the concentric form of this lyric) tortures the anguish of content'.[71] When the content consists of massacres, annihilation, suffering, the poet distrusts his 'serenity of form'. But this does not necessarily deny the need for form; it merely deepens its complexity. Form matters in this case, not because it withdraws altogether from 'content', but because it 'tortures' it. We are back in the '*Musée des Beaux Arts*', but that may be precisely why, in the serene quiet, we might hear the 'anguish' all the more clearly. In Auden's poem, that brilliant exposé and defence of aestheticisms of all kinds, the poet forces us to consider the place, art-room or poem-room, where torture is serenely depicted. At the same time, the poem is a searing reminder that this is the room not only of art but also of life, where the daily routines continue, oblivious to horrors. Admittedly, the poem's Christian scene gives it all a saving grace. Nevertheless, this is still a reminder that, precisely in

---

[70] Quoted in Solomon Fishman, *The Interpretation of Art*, 182.
[71] Vendler, *The Music of What Happens*, 129.

the museum of the fine arts, the ethical imagination is most severely exercised. 'About suffering they were never wrong,'[72] Auden begins, giving Adorno's word pride of place in his own poem's frighteningly serene and ordered room.

* * *

Form, as a critical term, has in recent years come back into fashion. Partly as a result of various retrospectives of Victorian aestheticism and twentieth-century formalism, the word is offered, from time to time, as a timely reminder of what we might have forgotten. Denis Donoghue, for instance, breaks off a discussion of 'art for art's sake' in his book on *Walter Pater* (1995) to throw out a challenge: 'The part of Aestheticism which should now be recovered, I suggest, is its concern for the particularity of form in every work of art.'[73] Form, here, is a work's identifying mark, its structural fingerprint. That this 'particularity' has been forgotten is then repeated in his next book, *Speaking of Beauty* (2003), where, he suggests again, 'the question of form has rarely been treated as the inescapable issue. This is strange,' he adds, 'because form is the distinguishing characteristic of art; there is no reason to assume that it is unproblematically given, like the counting of syllables in an iambic pentameter.'[74] This note of caution steers the argument away from questions of verse-form or metre. Form is not a matter of correct technique; it is a force of creativity generally. 'The Force of Form', his chapter title implies, is a kind of Romantic energy, a volcanic explosion of purpose, the movement of which sweeps 'counting syllables' out of the way.

Donoghue thus returns to the Romantic basis of form. It is something in the mind, the 'force' of which is not to be resisted. This is essentially the subject of Susan Wolfson's groundbreaking book, *Formal Charges* (1997), which not only rescues critical formalism from simple-minded detractors, but also, as the title suggests, defines form as a force, an energy, a subtle *j'accuse*. The slip from noun to adjective in her title frees the word at a stroke from its contract to technical minutiae. At

---

[72] W. H. Auden, 'Musée des Beaux Arts', in *Collected Poems*, ed. Edward Mendelson (London: Faber, 1976), 146.

[73] Denis Donoghue, *Walter Pater: Lover of Strange Souls* (New York: Alfred A. Knopf, 1995), 288.

[74] Denis Donoghue, *Speaking of Beauty* (New Haven and London: Yale University Press, 2003), 121.

the same time, 'Formal Charges' invests form with the very things it has traditionally seemed to ignore: ideological and social formations. To regard form, not as a shape, an object, or technique, but as a 'charge', with all its headlong, economic, even judicial connotations, is to release it from stasis. Form does not stay still; in many senses, it 'charges'. In Romantic poetry, she concludes, 'aesthetic form has always been experimental, potentially critical, even antagonistic.'[75] This wrests back the subversive terms, experiment and critique, and gives them to form. In Wolfson's profound analysis of Romanticism, she brings form back into the social arena to show just how richly Romantic poetry exploits the interactions between aesthetics and ideology, the 'aesthetic imagination and social information'.[76]

Coincidentally, in that same year Peter McDonald published *Mistaken Identities* (1997), a book which redefines form in the context of contemporary Northern Irish poetry. Those who, for whatever political or ideological reasons, insist on worthy content 'have much to learn as a result of being outraged by "form", with all its seeming irresponsibility and impersonality',[77] he writes. By thus outraging them, form turns the ideologists and political moralists into the newly scandalized bourgeois. McDonald continues to push at the word in *Serious Poetry* (2002). By no means 'accidental or narrowly functional',[78] form, he explains, 'is the pressing reality according to which metaphors and meaning must make their way.'[79] This is not form as a hoop to be gone through, a kind of technical constriction, but form as a 'pressing reality' which itself directs 'metaphors and meanings'. Form and matter have almost changed places here, as form becomes the external idea, reality, or intention, which impels the writing. In a review of Robert Lowell, McDonald takes this further when he argues for 'a drama of form: the ways in which metre—the rhythms of lines, the comings and goings of sound, the demands and revelations of rhyme—perform their own transformations on the writing self'.[80] So the 'drama of form' is one which, ultimately, transforms and performs.

[75] Susan J. Wolfson, *Formal Charges: The Shaping of Poetry in British Romanticism* (Stanford, Ca.: Stanford University Press, 1997), 230.

[76] Ibid. 231.

[77] Peter McDonald, *Mistaken Identities: Poetry and Northern Ireland* (Oxford: Clarendon Press, 1997), 187.

[78] Peter McDonald, *Serious Poetry: Form and Authority from Yeats to Hill* (Oxford: Clarendon Press, 2002), 49.

[79] Ibid. 68.

[80] Peter McDonald, 'Beside Himself', review of Robert Lowell's *Collected Poems*, in *Poetry Review*, 93(2003–4), 62–70, 64.

Those prefixes give form hard work to do, drawing it away from mere technicalities. It becomes an action, involving an author who might be transformed and an audience for whom something is performed. A busy actor, then, form acquires an old, but rejuvenated momentum which alters the conditions by which it is created. Instead of being the object of artistic intention or readerly affect, it is their creator.

The question of form has always troubled Northern Irish poetry, and some of its best recent accounts have come from the need to justify that poetry. So Edna Longley, in *Poetry in the Wars* (1986), takes up the battle on its behalf. 'Most critics of contemporary poetry neglect form', she declares. She then offers her own definition: 'By form I mean the musical shape into which all the "sounds of sense", syntactical and rhythmical, finally settle. ... The formal completeness of a George Herbert is rare indeed', she adds. The strong 'shape' of form, although complicated by being a shape of both music and meaning, in the ear and the eye, tends towards a sense of technical completion, of perfect finish. However, there is another element at stake here. 'Form,' she suggests, 'the binding force of poetry's wholeness, is also the last ditch of its aesthetic immunity.'[81] If 'binding' and 'wholeness' sound rather neat, recalling older, well-wrought formalisms, that 'last ditch' suggests something else, something desperate and risky. What is in this 'last ditch' is 'aesthetic immunity'. The phrase lies there like a thrown gauntlet. The old, historical relationship between form and aestheticism is suddenly brought back into prominence, although in a throwaway place and phrase which might pass unnoticed. Being in the 'last ditch' sounds very like being at a last gasp. Nevertheless, 'aesthetic immunity' holds its own, possibly still immune from the, by implication, war-torn place in which it has landed. Form, then, is the final, if deeply threatened, site of a notion of the aesthetic as untouched, untroubled, perhaps immune to wars. Just how far-fetched such 'aesthetic immunity' has become in the 1980s, and how far from its more comfortable origins in art for art's sake, is signalled by that 'ditch'.

In America, as in Northern Ireland, a 'new' formalism in poetry has set poets and critics marking out the borders, lining up the armies, and hoisting form's flag. Yet once again, mere verse form is not the point. Most of the poets contributing to Annie Finch's *After New Formalism* (1999) continue to push out the boundaries of the word, so that form

---

[81] Edna Longley, 'The Singing Line: Form in Derek Mahon's Poetry', in *Poetry in the Wars* (Newcastle: Bloodaxe Books, 1996; first pub. 1986), 170.

comes to mean the very thing that makes a poem a poem. Adrienne Rich warns that form must not be allowed to slide into 'inert formula or format'.[82] It is not a group badge or an inherited trophy to prove poetic credentials. Similarly Anne Stevenson asserts that 'No poem worthy of the name can be formless, whether it is written according to metrical rules or in free verse', and concludes 'Every poem IS its form.'[83] Molly Peacock writes of 'the fallacy of the verse form as a container or the *outside* of something'. Instead, she suggests, 'Form is a body. Verse form literally embodies the emotion of the poem, in the sense that embodiment both *is* and *contains* the life it is the body of.'[84] The advantage of this well-worn organic metaphor is that it stops the dualisms of inside and outside controlling the argument. Without the necessity for a soul, this leaves form at least at home in the poem—so much at home that it might be all there is.

A recent issue of *Modern Language Quarterly* (2000) also suggests how much the word is back in currency. Most of these essays, like Wolfson's 'Reading for Form',[85] take the word as a near synonym for the nature of the literary itself. Catherine Gallagher argues 'that form contends against time',[86] but then shows how Shelley and Pater set form to time, in 'a thoroughly secular, time-embracing formalism'[87] which undermines the visual by the pulse of the narrative. Robert Kaufman goes a step further in arguing that form is in fact a new kind of knowledge. He shows how Ginsburg's 'Sunflower Sutra', with its weirdly psychedelic force field of 'mad black formal sunflowers', breaks down the dualism of form and content altogether. From this, he suggests, another term might be found. 'The form-content,' he writes, 'which does not itself guarantee any particular ethical or political subjectivity, is an in-construction capacity for *knowing*.'[88] So the poem's imaginative transformation depends, indeed, on form, but only in the sense that the word mediates the thing, formalizes it, makes it fit for a different kind of

---

[82] Adrienne Rich, 'Format and Form', in *After New Formalism: Poets on Form, Narrative, and Tradition*, ed. Annie Finch (Ashland, Or.: Story Line Press, 1999), 1–7, 1.

[83] Anne Stevenson, 'The Trouble with a Word Like Formalism', in *After New Formalism*, 217–23, 219.

[84] Molly Peacock, 'From Gilded Cage to Rib Cage', in *After New Formalism*, 70–8, 72.

[85] Wolfson, 'Reading for Form', in *Modern Language Quarterly*, 61(2000), 1–16.

[86] Catherine Gallaher, 'Formalism and Time', in *Modern Language Quarterly*, 61(2000), 229–51, 231.

[87] Ibid. 239.

[88] Robert Kaufman, 'Everybody Hates Kant: Blakean Formalism and the Symmetries of Laura Moriarty', in *Modern Language Quarterly*, 61(2000), 131–55, 141.

seeing–knowing. This is not the knowing of a matter through language, but knowing the language matter of a text. Form, then, might be a word which, as a result of all these repeated, reformulated definitions, starts to alter the very thing we mean by knowing. To be a 'capacity for', rather than an object of knowledge, shifts attention towards a kind of knowing which is an imaginative attitude rather than an accumulation of known things. Such knowledge, like form itself, gravitates towards an intransitive mode in its nature. Moreover, as a near kin to the notion of the literary itself, it does not close down into an achieved interpretation, but remains open to endless permutations of meaning.

All these accounts, then, suggest that form is still as rich and amenable a word as it always was. It means anything from the specifics of technique to the workings of creativity, from language parts to interrelations of interpretation, from artistic integrity to the nature of knowledge. It can mean the art work per se, or the whole business of how art is made and interpreted. When Derek Attridge, in *The Singularity of Literature* (2004), writes that 'the notion of singularity is entirely bound up with the notion of form,'[89] he, like Donoghue, is trying to find in the word that unique quality of art, what makes it itself. But this too is noun-bound language, and Attridge, like others before him, distrusts its fixity. Form, he continues, 'needs to be understood verbally—as "taking form," or "forming," or even "losing form" '.[90] These verbs, unlike the noun, can play for time. They draw out the event into something not quickly complete, but still, like the participle, *in medias res*. Thus we catch form in the act. It might, then, be necessary to ask: what kind of criticism could be devoted to ' "taking form," or "forming," or even "losing form" '? Perhaps to think of form as a way of knowing, not as an object of knowledge, might be the beginning of an answer. Even 'losing' it might then be appropriate.

This is the question raised by Michael Wood's *Literature and the Taste of Knowledge* (2005). Rephrasing a crucial question in Peter de Bolla's *Art Matters*,[91] Wood suggests that any reader will 'need at some stage to ask what literary forms know or know of'.[92] He, too, proposes that form is neither just a property of writing nor a characteristic of the individual artwork, but knowledge itself—a tasty, secret kind of knowledge,

---

[89] Derek Attridge, *The Singularity of Literature* (London: Routledge, 2004), 112.
[90] Ibid. 113.
[91] Peter de Bolla, *Art Matters* (Cambridge, Mass.: Harvard University Press, 2001), 31.
[92] Michael Wood, *Literature and the Taste of Knowledge* (Cambridge: Cambridge University Press, 2005), 135–6.

and one not easily grasped. 'A penny for its thoughts',[93] he quips, summarizing how we might find out what it is that literary form knows. This nice turn of phrase hints at something unexpected and chancy in literary criticism: that it might not be, necessarily, a straightforward knowing, as of knowing the meaning of something, but a kind of lucky gamble or guesswork, a down payment on nothing. If we shall need 'to ask what literary forms know or know of', this might also mean rewriting the terms of such knowledge, and being willing to listen to the strange things that are said. By returning knowledge to form, Wood suggests that it may not be quite what we expect. This, in a sense, is the intuition of all those artists and writers who have ransacked the word 'form' to find out, not so much what it might be or mean, once and for all, but rather, more uncertainly, what it might continue to 'know or know of'.

* * *

What follows in this book is, like this chapter, neither comprehensive nor conclusive. It is not a one-way argument through history, with a clear destination, but a series of essays, attempts to read the ways in which the oblique relations of form and matter affect different texts. At the same time, it tracks an essentially aestheticist route through nineteenth- and twentieth-century literature, since that is the route which has brought the idea of form into prominence. Although often mocked and dismissed as a frivolity of late Victorian thought, aestheticism, which in fact is both older and younger than the Victorians, offers some of the most powerful and enduring accounts, not only of form, but of that sense of the literary as a kind of knowing—even if that includes a knowing nothing. The essay, Pater once wrote, 'came into use at what was really the invention of the relative'.[94] He thus associates the essay with modernity, agnosticism, uncertainty, and therefore with a kind of knowledge which does not easily reach conclusions or answers. Moreover, the essay is a personal genre. While not overtly autobiographical, he explains, it is a 'continuous discourse with one's self ... a part of the continuous company we keep with ourselves through life'. As such, it 'will have its inequalities; its infelicities; above all, its final insecurity'.[95] This is an apology, but it

---

[93] Wood, *Literature and the Taste of Knowledge*, 114.
[94] Walter Pater, *Plato and Platonism: A Series of Lectures* (London: Macmillan, 1910; first pub. 1893), 174.
[95] Ibid. 185.

is also a boast. The essay finally leads, not to a point proved but an 'insecurity' achieved. It is the critical genre which can, on the one hand, admit uncertainty, subjectivity, conditionalness, while also, on the other, putting its own shaped form into play as part of its matter.

In 'The Essay as Form', Adorno offers a brief but memorable definition of the essay as, indeed, an 'attempt', when he writes that it is 'an intention groping its way'.[96] The essay resists and delays answers. It is not an intention briskly written up, but 'an intention groping'—by implication, uphill or in the dark. This may be what makes the essay especially attuned to the idea of the aesthetic. Indeed, Adorno cheekily warns, it 'has something like an aesthetic autonomy that is easily accused of being simply derived from art'.[97] This fault, the sneaking desire for 'aesthetic autonomy', for a sense of pleasure that might also be simply pleasure for its own sake, makes the essay liable to all sorts of justified charges: that it is self-indulgent, opportunist, discontinuous. Nevertheless, it also entertains two elements which might, if nothing else, alleviate criticism's more serious purposes. 'Luck and play', Adorno writes, 'are essential to it.'[98] With those, it might be possible to catch at the notion of form, not in a philosophical nutshell, once and for all, but only along the way, in the part-gamble, part-guesswork which each singular, differently formed work inspires. The question of criticism's own form might thus become part of the story.

[96] Theodor Adorno, 'The Essay as Form', in *Notes to Literature*, vol.1, ed. Rolf Tiedemann, trans. Shierry Weber Nicholsen (New York: Columbia University Press, 1991; first pub. 1958), 3–23, 16.
[97] Ibid. 5.   [98] Ibid. 4.

How with this rage shall beauty hold a plea,
Whose action is no stronger than a flower?

William Shakespeare

whether all seeming, even the most beautiful, even precisely the beautiful, has not today become a lie.

Thomas Mann

2

Art for Art: On Pots, Crocks, Lyres, and Flutes

George Moore once suggested that if Walter Pater 'had lived to hear *L'après-midi d'un Faune,* he could not have done else but think that he was listening to his own prose changed into music'.[1] Debussy's piece was inspired by a steamy poem by Mallarmé about a lustful faun observing some playful nymphs. Cross-breeding between the arts was a fashionable ideal in the late nineteenth century, and one which could seem to protect artistic integrity by emphasizing the self-enclosed inviolability of art *on* art. At the same time, as Mallarmé's poem hints, cross-breeding might also involve strange relations between, say, fauns and nymphs. Art about art, while erecting a self-protective barrier against literal decoding, also allows all sorts of dreamy implications to float free. If Debussy's piece seemed to Moore the achieved musical condition of Pater's prose, this was also because that prose was always on the way to music. An innuendo, a lilt, a delaying, erotic sonorousness, the sense of music in Pater crosses and distracts from its sense of sense. It leaves an after-effect, as of something thinned into echo and rhythm. Music, it seems, may be all that remains when his words have run out.

---

[1] George Moore, *Avowals* (London: Heinemann, 1924; first pub. 1919), 187.

She is older than the rocks among which she sits; like the vampire, she has been dead many times, and learned the secrets of the grave; and has been a diver in deep seas, and keeps their fallen day about her; and trafficked for strange webs with Eastern merchants: and, as Leda, was the mother of Helen of Troy, and, as Saint Anne, the mother of Mary; and all this has been to her but as the sound of lyres and flutes.[2]

The well-known passage on the Mona Lisa, addictive, melismatic, secretive, progressively fades history, myth, and religious belief into the gentle piffling of 'lyres and flutes'. First published in the late 1860s, it still seemed to sum up the condition of modernity to Yeats when, in 1936, he versified it and made it the first entry of his Oxford anthology of *Modern Poetry*. Almost seventy years after its publication it might yet convey something of the ambiguous nature of the modern world. Wilde, who knew whole passages of Pater by heart, heard in it a manifesto for a new kind of criticism, one which would be 'more creative than creation'.[3] 'Who, again, cares,' he demanded, 'whether Mr. Pater has put into the portrait of Monna Lisa something that Lionardo never dreamed of? The painter may have been merely the slave of an archaic smile.'[4] He, like others, heard in Pater's prose the 'free play of the mind',[5] unconstrained by historical or documentary evidence. This was the theory and practice of a 'new aesthetics',[6] which would reveal 'all things under their conditions of beauty'.[7] Pater's work seduced generations of readers, who heard in it the distancing devices of a prose dedicated, it would seem, to the sound of sound. 'For art,' *The Renaissance* concludes, 'comes to you proposing frankly to give nothing but the highest quality to your moments as they pass, and simply for those moments' sake'.[8] As the final sentence rounds back on itself, enacting the short-circuit it ringingly advocates, 'moments ... for those moments' sake', it also slyly echoes the phrase which was already at this time a catchphrase for artistic affectation or dissent. Meanwhile, Pater lets his reader hear that 'proposing *frankly* to give nothing' is a proposition etymologically derived from the French.

[2] Walter Pater, *The Renaissance: Studies in Art and Poetry* (London: Macmillan, 1910), 125.

[3] Oscar Wilde, 'The Critic as Artist', in *Intentions* (London: Methuen, 1919; first pub. 1891), 93–217, 139.

[4] Ibid. 142.   [5] Ibid. 214.

[6] Oscar Wilde, 'The Decay of Lying', in *Intentions*, 1–54, 42.

[7] Wilde, 'The Critic as Artist', 202.   [8] Pater, *The Renaissance*, 239.

'*L'art pour l'art*' was a phrase by now well-established in France. Its first instance in print appears to have been in Benjamin Constant's *Journal Intime* (1804), which records a conversation with Henry Crabb Robinson, friend of Wordsworth and Coleridge: '*L'art pour l'art, sans but, car tout but dénature l'art.*'[9] (Art for art's sake, without purpose, because all purpose denatures art.) At about this time, too, both Coleridge and Leigh Hunt repeated the phrase, whether about beauty or poetry, 'for its own sake'.[10] In 1836 Victor Cousin published his *Cours de philosophie... sur le fondement des idées absolues Du Vrai, Du Beau, et Du Bien*, where he insists on the self-sufficiency of each: '*Il faut de la religion pour la religion, de la morale pour la morale, comme de l'art pour l'art.*'[11] (There must be religion for religion's sake, morality for morality's sake, as art for art's sake.) This squarely separates art from the ethical bent of the other two, and thus suggests that its place and purpose will be, perhaps, even irreligious or unethical. In 1850 Poe, in his essay on 'The Poetic Principle', advocated the dignity and nobility of 'this poem *per se*—this poem which is a poem and nothing more, this poem written solely for the poem's sake'.[12] By now the phrase is becoming a catchy and usable tautology, which will underlie the aestheticist thinking of half a century and more.

Its polemical and political edge, however, develops in France from the 1830s onwards, in the writings of Gautier and Baudelaire. In particular it is developed in Gautier's risqué, bisexual, transvestite novel, *Mademoiselle de Maupin* (1835)—a novel in which the goal of abstract beauty is pursued through various altogether unabstract sexual encounters, which thus help to flesh out a theory in practice. The aestheticist cult of beauty and art starts here, thirty or more years before Swinburne, Pater, and Wilde revive it in England. Although the phrase 'art for art' does not appear in the novel, it becomes indissolubly linked with it, as if the work were written to be a coded commentary on a

[9] Quoted in Andrew McNeillie, 'Bloomsbury', in *The Cambridge Companion to Virginia Woolf*, ed. Sue Roe and Susan Sellers (Cambridge: Cambridge University Press, 2000), 1–28, 21, note 4.

[10] See L. M. Findlay, 'The Introduction of the Phrase "Art for Art's Sake" into English', *Notes and Queries*, 218(July 1973), 246–8, 247. Also Nicholas Shrimpton, 'Pater and the "Aesthetical Sect"', in *Walter Pater and the Culture of the Fin-de-Siècle*, ed. E. S. Shaffer, *Comparative Criticism*, 17(1995), 61–84, 65–6.

[11] Victor Cousin, *Cours de philosophie... sur le fondement des idées absolues Du Vrai, Du Beau, et Du Bien*, quoted in Findlay, 247.

[12] Edgar Allan Poe, 'The Poetic Principle', in *Poems and Essays on Poetry*, ed. C. H. Sisson (Manchester: Carcanet, 1995; first pub. 1850), 91.

theme. Sex, here, is a metaphor for art, and art for sex. They double up, in a conspiracy of confusions which match all the other confusions the novel perpetrates. Meanwhile, the word 'beauty' is bandied from page to page by male and female characters alike, as that which defines and eludes sexual desire. As the hero D'Albert puts it: *'J'adore sur toutes choses la beauté de la forme;—la beaut' e pour moi, c'est la Divinité visible, c'est le bonheur palpable, c'est le ciel descendu sur la terre.'*[13] (I adore above all things beauty of form;—beauty to me is the Divine made visible, happiness made palpable, heaven come down upon earth.) So abstract beauty plumps into something visible and palpable, and the chocolate box phrases of the divine and the heavenly find their earthly place. As D'Albert insists: *'Tu sais avec quelle ardeur j'ai recherché la beauté extérieure, quelle importance j'attache à la forme extérieure, et de quel amour je me suis pris pour le monde visible.'*[14] (You know how ardently I have sought out external beauty, the importance I attach to external form, and the love I have for the visible world.) Material objects substitute religious and moral ideals, and 'beauty' rounds into the tangible 'form' of an object which can be appreciated by the senses. Paradoxically, however, the bisexuality and cross-dressing of the plot also ensure that 'beauty' remains somehow intangibly beyond materialization in things. The word takes on a curious, transgressive momentum of its own, evading capture as that neutral 'form' which changeably reappears in various human guises. The platonic flux of the word, which both abstracts its meaning from any object and also runs its hands down the outline of a body, encourages double meanings at every point. The beauty of form is that it nicely confuses body and soul, being both the object and the outline, the thing and its formal impression in the mind.

Mademoiselle de Maupin is one of those original books of secret knowledge which runs the gamut of aestheticist writing in the nineteenth century, till it peters out, as Linda Dowling points out, as a cheap cliché in pre-war 'pulp fiction'.[15] It also ensures that 'art for art', with its suggestion of studied withdrawal and absolute, artistic value, is permanently connected with illicit sex. The very homophonic symmetry of the phrase perhaps yields a homoerotic meaning which Gautier spells out at some narrative length. 'Art for art' is also art for pleasure, art for

---

[13] Théophile Gautier, *Mademoiselle de Maupin*, intro. Geneviève van den Bogaert (Paris: Garnier-Flammarion, 1966; first pub. 1835), 149.

[14] Ibid. 189.

[15] Linda Dowling, *Language and Decadence in the Victorian Fin de Siècle* (Princeton: Princeton University Press, 1986), 172.

scandal, art for sexual gratification. As a tautology it shuts into itself; as a *double entendre* it opens up to multiple possibilities. For Gautier the only end, not only of art but also of life, is beauty. Such a goal ostentatiously bypasses morality, person, emotional complexity, in order that the sexual object may be pursued as a work of art. The sense of the object, whether human or artistic, offers the pursuer a 'form' of beauty which might then assume a gratifying content. In his own declaration of artistic principle in the Preface to the novel, Gautier spells out his anti-utilitarian aesthetic: *Je préfère à certain vase qui me sert un vase chinois.*[16] (I prefer to a certain serviceable pot, a Chinese vase.) His chamber pot is useful, a china vase is beautiful. Between one vase and another there is an essential difference, as well as perhaps (at least in the French), an audible similarity.

Pater's famous Conclusion to *The Renaissance* thus goes out of its way to repeat, in its last two ringing sentences, the provocation of a phrase with a distinctly dubious currency: 'Of such wisdom, the poetic passion, the desire of beauty, the love of art for its own sake, has most. For art comes to you proposing frankly to give nothing but the highest quality to your moments as they pass, and simply for those moments' sake.'[17] As Denis Donoghue puts it, 'Pater loves to speak the phrase "for its own sake," as if to guard against violation some precious sentiment.'[18] There is a sense in which the phrase constructs its own 'precious' vase of sense, removed and untouchable, rounded up into nothing but itself. The echo of the French, however, also ensures that some sort of 'violation' is not entirely shut out, as the phrase touches on something all too desirably touchable. The sexual innuendo is brought out in another passage on Leonardo da Vinci, of whom Pater solemnly informs us, 'this solitary culture of beauty seems to have hung upon a kind of self-love, and a carelessness in the work of art of all but art itself.'[19] Between 'self-love' and 'art for art' there is a lingering, if repressed, connection. Both round back on themselves, in a stylistic closing which is somehow both demure and flirtatious. Even Pater, that shy, furtive aesthete, whose sentences seem to skirt every object as too dangerous to touch, ends up almost 'proposing frankly ...'.

Certainly, this hesitant, secretive prose haunted generations of writers for decades to come. If Pater in a sense goes underground in the

---

[16] Gautier, *Mademoiselle de Maupin*, 45.   [17] Pater, *The Renaissance*, 239.
[18] Denis Donoghue, *Walter Pater: Lover of Strange Souls* (New York: Alfred A. Knopf, 1995), 220.
[19] Pater, *The Renaissance*, 117.

twentieth century, he still does not altogether go away. Woolf's prose is soaked in him. Joyce's parody feeds on him. Yeats was haunted all his life by those 'wavering, meditative, organic rhythms' of the Nineties' cult of 'beauty',[20] even when, after 1916, 'beauty' had become 'terrible'.[21] Even T. S. Eliot, who vehemently denied his debt to Pater, blaming him, in a distinctly underhand circumlocution, for being 'not wholly irresponsible for some untidy lives',[22] might be seduced from time to time by a lyrical memory, enchanting 'the maytime with an antique flute'.[23]

So art for art's sake—to search for a legacy of that phrase in the twentieth century is to turn up only a quotation here and there. Yet interestingly, although the phrase would seem to go out of fashion with the advent of modernism, it does not entirely disappear. In fact, it is surprising just how much it continues to serve writers, sometimes defensively, sometimes apologetically, as a principle in opposition to use. In order not to be *for* anything—history, politics, or morality, for instance—art is for art. This short circuit fends off the very things literary criticism might want to bring in: argument, message, meaning, relevance. Such preciousness, however, works by stressing its own fragility. Against the force of everything outside, art for art might be a refuge of glass. The 'descendentalism', as Mark Edmundson calls it, of much twentieth-century criticism, the need to offer 'a quick transport to subterranean bedrock',[24] whether cultural, psychoanalytic, or political, drives art into purposefully workable ground. Perhaps, too, there is a hint of self-justification in the act. This is the work that criticism is made to do, thus overcoming its own anxiety of relevance. But the principle of irrelevance, of being 'for nothing', is ignored at peril. To acknowledge the 'nothing' at the heart of the literary is a way of starting to ask what the work knows, and therefore of seeking to modify the very terms of knowing. This is not the same as saying that ideological readings are irrelevant. It is rather to suggest that something constantly pulls against relevance, and reference. However it is described, form, style, beauty,

[20] W. B. Yeats, *Essays and Introductions* (London: Macmillan, 1961), 163.

[21] W. B. Yeats, *The Variorum Edition of the Poems of W. B. Yeats*, ed. Peter Allt and Russell K. Alspach (New York: Macmillan, 1957), 392.

[22] T. S. Eliot, 'Arnold and Pater', in *Selected Essays: 1917–1932* (London: Faber, 1932), 379–91, 390.

[23] T. S. Eliot, *Complete Poems and Plays* (London: Faber, 1969), 93.

[24] Mark Edmundson, *Literature against Philosophy, Plato to Derrida: A Defence of Poetry* (Cambridge: Cambridge University Press, 1995), 22.

music, it consists of finding what is 'for nothing' in the text—a kind of
lucky bargain. As Schiller once put it, in a passage which rings down the
nineteenth century from Shelley to Pater to Wilde: 'the agreeable, the
good, the perfect, with these man is merely in earnest; but with beauty
he plays.'[25] The importance of not being in earnest is precisely what
makes the play of literature important. It is *as* play, even as the playing
of 'lyres and flutes', that it might have something to say. Such play is
not a totally free play, but remains connected with ethical and political
values. But neither is it normatively identical with those values, so that
the one can be bedrocked in the other. Literature, perhaps, is the point
where the two meet, their hub and hold-off.

In his essay on 'Style', Pater at one point tries to account for the
musical surplus which nonplusses sense. He writes: 'the ornamental
word, the figure, the accessory form or colour or reference, is rarely
content to die to thought precisely at the right moment, but will
inevitably linger awhile, stirring a long "brain-wave" behind it of
perhaps quite alien associations.'[26] To seek 'the accessory form', the
surplus after-sense of pleasure or sound or colour, is at least to ensure
that criticism does not always go one way, 'trumping the aesthetic by
the ideological and political',[27] as Peter Brooks puts it. The point about
Pater's lingering 'brain-wave'—that lovely cross between a sound-wave
and an idea, which is also a very recent word, havering between figurative
and physical[28]—is that it refuses to be merely assimilated to thought.
It has a way of living on, posthumously, after the idea (vampires and
divers and all that) becomes uninteresting: 'as the sound of lyres and
flutes …'.

To go in search of art for art's sake may be a search for nothing
more than that sound. In the twentieth century such a search comes to
seem seriously compromised, not only by the element of late Victorian
silliness about it, but also, more importantly, by its apparent political
indifference. Walter Benjamin's resonant and troubling declaration that
twentieth-century fascism is the natural 'consummation of "*l'art pour*

---

[25] Friedrich Schiller, *On the Aesthetic Education of Man: In a Series of Letters*, ed. and
trans. Elizabeth M. Wilkinson and L. A. Willoughby (Oxford: Clarendon Press, 1967),
105–7.

[26] Walter Pater, 'Style', in *Appreciations* (London: Macmillan, 1910), 5–38, 18.

[27] Peter Brooks, 'Aesthetics and Ideology—What Happened to Poetics?', in *Aesthetics
and Ideology*, ed George Levine (New Brunswick, N.J.: Rutgers University Press, 1994),
153–67, 160.

[28] See Angela Leighton, 'Pater's Music', in *The Journal of Pre-Raphaelite Studies*,
14(2005), 67–79, 73.

l'art"',[29] was first made in 1936. Its prescient date might justify the horror of its point. But in retrospect that point is more polemical than persuasive. Martin Jay has suggested that such a summary position, like others of its kind, 'falls prey to the same homogenizing, totalizing, covertly violent tendencies it too rapidly attributes to "the aesthetic" itself'.[30] Benjamin's slip from aesthetics to politics, avowedly the fault of aestheticism itself, is actually reinstated in his brisk, verbal enactment of it: 'consummation' is achieved all too quickly, and artistic theory becomes political practice. Such rhetoric also depends on a highly simplified definition of nineteenth-century aestheticism. Another passage from Benjamin's essay declares, for instance, that in the nineteenth century 'art reacted with the doctrine of *l'art pour l'art*, that is, with a theology of art. This gave rise to what might be called a negative theology in the form of the idea of "pure" art, which not only denied any social function of art but also any categorizing by subject matter.'[31] The argument is carried by the force of that ' "pure" ', with all its highlighted religious, as well as political, connotations. The idea of 'pure' art in cahoots with 'theology' leaves out the extent to which Victorian aestheticism was almost always impure, unconformingly materialist and secular in its outlook, and beset by the very serious 'subject matter' it seems to avoid. As Jonathan Freedman argues, aestheticism is as political and complex as the avant-garde itself in the way that it 'comes to problematize the very art it would seem to erect as the locus of value; moreover, it problematizes that art by the same gesture with which it valorizes it'.[32] As a movement, Victorian aestheticism is inherently impure, sexually tainted by its association with the French, and ideologically compromised by its fondness for contradiction and wit. By comparison with Benjamin's, Pater's prose, especially in the Conclusion to *The Renaissance*, is reluctant and unconsummating in the extreme. Even in the final sentences, 'art for its own sake', far from being an assertion of pure artistic autonomy, is undercut by those repeated, passing 'moments'. Being 'simply for

[29] Walter Benjamin, *Illuminations*, ed. Hannah Arendt, trans. Harry Zorn (London: Pimlico, 1999), 235.
[30] Martin Jay, ' "The Aesthetic Ideology" as Ideology: Or What Does It Mean to Aestheticize Politics?' in *Force Fields: Between Intellectual History and Cultural Critique* (New York and London: Routledge, 1993), 71–83, 83.
[31] Benjamin, *Illuminations*, 218.
[32] Jonathan Freedman, *Professions of Taste: Henry James, British Aestheticism, and Commodity Culture* (Stanford, Ca.: Stanford University Press, 1990), 11.

those moments' sake', Pater offers art not for itself, but for its mere moment in some continuously passing history. It is 'for', but also of, the moment. As such, its hieratic object-ness is undermined by transience and subjectivity. 'Art for the moment' lets time, Pater's most hauntingly pervasive principle, into the picture. The time it takes for his sentences to reach their 'consummation', round obstacles and diversions of all sorts, is also the time it takes to undermine their meanings, moment by moment. By the end of *The Renaissance* art is no more than a momentary impression in the perception of the anonymous, briefly pleasured observer.

The essay form itself is chosen by Pater to express the hesitation, the relativism, the very temporary nature of this aestheticism. Like the dialogue, the essay is 'the instrument of dialectic',[33] made to express the sense of uncertainty and fallibility which characterizes knowledge in the modern world. Indeed, his are essays in, rather than on—the etymology of the word suggesting an audible reaching, even groping, for its subject, rather than a controlling hold on it. Far from being theological, then, the essay is an attempt at expressing modernity's refusal to settle for truth. The essay, Pater writes, is 'the literary form necessary to a mind for which truth itself is but a possibility'.[34] The perambulations and waverings of his style, like the essay form itself, offer an aestheticism constantly in the making, at odds with itself, reinventing itself at every sentence, every phrase. 'Pater's indifference to beginnings and endings, and his fascination with change,'[35] as Wolfgang Iser puts it, suggest constantly unfinished business, which is the business of time. In his work the nature of the aesthetic is a furtive, dialectical thing, riddled with double meanings and cautious of conclusions. Art 'simply for those moments' sake' is, therefore, the opposite of any pure doctrine or theology, celebrating, as it does, the secular moment in all its unredeemed insignificance.

Although Pater goes out of fashion, the phrase which he echoes like a mantra does not altogether disappear. Yeats, in 1905, attacked the overriding concern for 'practical reform' in Ireland, which, he declared, undermined 'disinterested contemplation' in the arts. 'Art for art's sake ... whether it be the art of the *Ode on a Grecian Urn* or of

[33] Walter Pater, *Plato and Platonism* (London: Macmillan, 1910), 188.

[34] Ibid. 175.

[35] Wolfgang Iser, *Walter Pater: The Aesthetic Moment*, trans. David Henry Wilson (Cambridge: Cambridge University Press, 1987), 79.

the imaginer of Falstaff, seems to [the Irish writer] a neglect of public duty',[36] he announced scornfully. His own preferences were with the opposite of duty, whatever that might be called. Virginia Woolf resorts to the phrase in the unlikely context of *Three Guineas*, her great manifesto against war and fascism, when she recalls at one point, on the rebound from her main argument, that the artist must work 'only for the sake of the art'.[37] In 1951 Forster began a lecture with the uneasy, apologetic confession: 'I believe in art for art's sake. It is an unfashionable belief.'[38] In 1946 the young Larkin worried over 'disparaging talk about "Art for Art's Sake" ', adding with irritation: 'It annoys me. For what other sake can art possibly be undertaken?'[39] Jeanette Winterson, in her collection of essays, *Art Objects*, insists throughout on the value of 'art as art (separate, Other, self-contained',[40] against art as ethics or art as entertainment. Derek Mahon, in his long poem 'The Yellow Book', announces at one point: 'The only solution lies in *art for its own sake*, | redemption through the aesthetic'.[41] The old tautology lives on. A cliché, a commonplace, an irrelevance, a pretext, it has nonetheless continued to be, in Steiner's words, 'a tactical slogan, a necessary rebellion against philistine didacticism and political control'.[42] Art objects, by a different stress, also *object*. The political purpose of purposelessness is never altogether out of hearing. As Larkin once ranted in a letter: 'Ah, beauty, beauty! What is truth? Balls. What is love? Shite. What is God? Bugger. Ah, but what is beauty? Boy, you got sump'n there. I should like to know.'[43] This is also, audibly, Larkin's jazz improvisation on a theme first summarized in a poem published in 1820:

> 'Beauty is truth, truth beauty,'—that is all
> Ye know on earth, and all ye need to know.[44]

[36] W. B. Yeats, *Explorations*, sel. Mrs W. B. Yeats (London: Macmillan, 1962), 197–8.

[37] Virginia Woolf, *Three Guineas* (London: Hogarth Press, 1938), 146.

[38] E. M. Forster, *Two Cheers for Democracy* (London: Edward Arnold, 1951), 98.

[39] Quoted in James Booth, *Philip Larkin: Writer* (London: Harvester, 1992), 15.

[40] Jeanette Winterson, *Art Objects: Essays on Ecstasy and Effrontery* (London: Jonathan Cape, 1995), 31.

[41] Derek Mahon, *Collected Poems* (Loughcrew: The Gallery Press, 1999), 233.

[42] George Steiner, *Real Presences: Is there anything in what we say?* (London: Faber, 1989), 143.

[43] Philip Larkin, *Selected Letters: 1940–1985*, ed. Anthony Thwaite (London: Faber, 1992), 16.

[44] John Keats, *Poetical Works*, ed. H. W. Garrod (London: Oxford University Press, 1970), 209–10, 210.

Keats's 'Ode on a Grecian Urn' ends as if it had solved the problem. In fact, as Larkin's 'I should like to know' suggests, it is only the start of a long excursion.

As early as 1882 Walter Hamilton, quoting Wilde, asserted that it is ' "in Keats that one discerns the beginning of the artistic renaissance of England" '.[45] In particular, as Yeats also noted, it begins with this poem, which supplies nineteenth- as well as twentieth-century writers with an art object they cannot forget. *'Je préfère, á mon pot de chambre, un pot chinois,'* Gautier declared fifteen years after the poem was first published. Keats's Grecian urn, like Gautier's china vase, stands for that artistic difference and indifference which will trouble and intrigue writers for two centuries to come. Beautiful and useless, the urn exists in an empty space. Apart from the chiming adjective 'Grecian', it is without context, history, origin, or destination. It is simply there, and the poem takes its shape. A precious exhibit in the *'Musée des Beaux Arts',* it also carries the clear warning: Do Not Touch.

> Thou still unravish'd bride of quietness,
> Thou foster-child of silence and slow time.
> Sylvan historian, who canst thus express
> A flowery tale more sweetly than our rhyme:
> What leaf-fring'd legend haunts about thy shape
> Of deities or mortals, or of both,
> In Tempe or the dales of Arcady?
> What men or gods are these? What maidens loth?
> What mad pursuit? What struggle to escape?
> What pipes and timbrels? What wild ecstasy?[46]

Timeless and well-wrought, the urn has always been considered the perfectly formalist form. It is there, for no reason, for its own sake only, and it refuses to answer human questions. Instead, it remains closed in its silence, or in the memory of some continuously unheard music: 'pipes and timbrels'.

Except, of course, this is not quite true. For a start the poem is a battery of questions. It breaks, quite violently, the rule of quiet in which it is imaginatively encased. The title, too, is a little surprising: 'Ode on a Grecian Urn', not 'Ode to a Greek Vase'. The objects Keats saw were all called vases: the Portland Vase, the Sosibios Vase, the Townley Vase, the Borghese Vase. The choice of 'Urn', recalling Thomas Browne's

45　Walter Hamilton, *The Aesthetic Movement in England* (London, 1882), 105.
46　Keats, *Poetical Works,* 209.

Urne-Burial or Thomas Gray's 'storied urn',[47] diverts the meaning to another context. A Greek vase is a self-contained artefact; a Grecian urn is an empty container. It therefore remembers a kind of use, a lost content. The empty space inside an urn presses for attention, offering an alternative to the flowery tale decorating the surface. This 'Cold Pastoral',[48] as Keats calls it, is indeed *dead* cold.

This, then, is an aestheticism with a catch to it. For all its beautiful indifference, its cool isolation, this art object bears the pressure of what it shuts out, or in: the pressure of context, content, reference, memory. An urn does not naturally stand on its own. It belongs among the dead and its empty hold recalls them. Cleanth Brooks ensured that *The Well Wrought Urn* became the symbol of formalism's concern with literature's uncontextualized inner workings, and drew on Donne's lines about the sonnet in 'The Canonization': 'As well a well wrought urne becomes | The greatest ashes'.[49] Keats's ode, however, uses a slightly different word. It is not so much 'well wrought' as subtly 'overwrought': 'with brede | Of marble men and maidens overwrought'.[50] This means, on the one hand, written or worked over; but it also means, on the other, breathless, emotional, and thus in some sense not perfectly worked into cool marble. The flush of being 'overwrought' hints at a workmanship perhaps not as finished or as formal as it might be: 'What mad pursuit? What struggle to escape?' The ornamental relief just hints at something out of proportion, out of artistic control.

If this depicted pursuit sometimes sounds, in its sweetness, like a game of tag, it only takes a little imagination (female imagination, perhaps), to hear in it a ravishment which the beauty of the decoration only stops in time. Behind such beauty there is force, specifically force against female objects: 'unravish'd bride', 'maidens loth', and later that 'heifer' which is led 'to the sacrifice', covered in another kind of disguising floweriness: 'with garlands drest'.[51] The urn only just holds off a deflowering which seems forever imminent. This may be a 'flowery tale', but beneath the flowers there is something unmentionable, which the rest of the poem only works 'over'. The famous last lines, then, far from resolving the

---

[47] Thomas Gray, 'Elegy Written in a Country Church-Yard', in *Gray and Collins Poetical Works*, ed. Austin Lane Poole (London: Oxford University Press, 1937), 91–7, 93.

[48] Keats, *Poetical Works*, 210.

[49] Quoted in Cleanth Brooks, *The Well Wrought Urn: Studies in The Structure of Poetry* (London: Methuen, 1968; first pub. 1947), 177–8, 178.

[50] Keats, *Poetical Works*, 210.   [51] Ibid. 209–10.

problem, only call attention to it. ' "Beauty is truth, truth beauty" '[52] goes both ways. It seems to offer a resolution in a nutshell, but ultimately exposes the sense of stress. For between beauty and truth there is a break, a crack. What we hear in that line, in spite of its dogmatic, quotable force, is the join. Keats seems to have known that a thing of beauty has a relationship with 'truth', with the world, human history, and human suffering, which is not necessarily a flawless match. Indeed, as Susan Wolfson puts it, there is a 'faint fissuring of everything well wrought'[53] in Keats's work, which will then become the tiny flaw that runs through aestheticism in the nineteenth and twentieth centuries. His, or the urn's, final syllogism protests too much to be *quite* true, or even truly beautiful. As if in commentary on the urn itself, that line comes apart in our hands.

When Oscar Wilde wrote in 1891 of a 'desire that we have not yet satisfied, the desire to know the connection between Beauty and Truth',[54] he was resuscitating an old, Keatsian problem. The 1870s and 1880s witnessed a flurry of texts about art objects: portraits, manuscripts, instruments, statues, as if art *about* art could ensure art *for* art, and thus eliminate the question of truth or life outside. It is Henry James who takes this subject of artistic inviolability and ironically unpacks the social violence it might contain. Art objects, in James, are spoils and trophies, buyable and collectible. They draw into their orbit the contextual problems of price, ownership, power, an aesthetic spoiling that is most intensely worked over in his last novel, *The Golden Bowl* (1904). The bowl is indeed worth 'frankly nothing', because the crystal under its gold veneer is cracked. The scene in the antique shop at the start sets the scene for a story which is all about the shop of values in which these rarefied characters—'so many distinguished ghosts'[55] Woolf called them—act out their tremulous, circumlocutionary affairs.

Practically the only thing that happens in this text is that the bowl is shattered, flung onto the floor and broken in three pieces. At this point Maggie says to her unfaithful husband: 'Its having come apart makes an unfortunate difference for its beauty, its artistic value, but none for anything else. Its other value is just the same—I mean that of its having

[52] Keats, *Poetical Works*, 210.

[53] Susan Wolfson, *Formal Charges: The Shaping of Poetry in British Romanticism* (Stanford, Ca.: Stanford University Press, 1997), 17.

[54] Wilde, 'The Critic as Artist', in *Intentions*, 116.

[55] Virginia Woolf, *The Essays of Virginia Woolf: 1904–12* , vol. 1, ed. Andrew McNeillie (London: Hogarth Press, 1986), 23.

given me so much of the truth about you.'[56] Very explicitly, James prises open the crack between beauty and truth. They are not identical, though the bowl has, until now, disguised the difference. It is as if James had taken Keats's Grecian Urn and smashed it at its weak point. However, the novel does not end with this shattered object. Soon after, Maggie tries to hold the pieces together. Cupped in her hands, 'the bowl might still quite beautifully ... have passed for uninjured'[57]—that 'uninjured' finely drawing into its orbit the hidden but distinct sound of human hurt. Beauty, James seems to be saying, might still survive the break with truth value, moral value, money value. In fact, it could be precisely the holding of those two things awkwardly together which constitutes beauty in the first place. If he starts by breaking aestheticism's mould, smashing the well-wrought bowl, he also tries to put it together again. If he trumps the aesthetic by the ideological, exposing the object as a cheat, a gimcrack, he also ends by trumping the other way: 'the bowl might still quite beautifully' come together, cracks and all.

Significantly, it is Maggie who performs this rescue. At one point her father, the wealthy art collector, looks at his daughter. She appears to him 'shyly mythological and nymph-like',[58] like 'a creature lost in an alien age and passing as an image in worn relief round and round a precious vase'.[59] Maggie has joined the other nymphs and maidens on Keats's classical pastoral. That phrase 'round and round' perfectly places her on a pointless circuit created by the movement of her connoisseur father walking round a 'precious' Greek vase. That 'vase' suddenly seems like a treadmill on which trapped, fleeing nymphs go 'round and round'.

The idea of the aesthetic, then, not only has a catch, but the catch might have something to do with women. Joyce, in a highly Paterian moment in *Ulysses*, seems to recall these same vase creatures. 'And yonder about that grey urn ...' he writes, 'you saw another as fragrant sisterhood, Floey, Atty, Tiny and their darker friend with I know not what of arresting in her pose'.[60] So who are all these 'arresting' (because arrested) women? these maidens, nymphs, this 'fragrant sisterhood'? Why is the aesthetic object by association female? One simple answer is that aesthetes are men. They are the connoisseurs, the collectors, the buyers of beauty, the ones with power and money. In a resonant

---

[56] Henry James, *The Golden Bowl*, vols. 23 and 24 (New York: Scribners, 1909), ii. 188–9.
[57] Ibid. ii. 182–3.   [58] Ibid. i. 188.   [59] Ibid. i. 187.
[60] James Joyce, *Ulysses*, ed. Jeri Johnson (Oxford: Oxford University Press, 1993), 401.

passage from *Mademoiselle de Maupin*, the aesthete D'Albert muses
on the creative incapacity of women: *'Il est vrai que les femmes ne
s'entendent pas plus en poésie que les choux et les roses, ce qui est très
naturel et très simple, étant elles-mêmes la poésie.'*[61] (It is true that women
have no more understanding of poetry than have cabbages or roses,
which is quite natural and obvious, since they themselves are poetry.)
George Eliot echoes just this point in *Middlemarch*, when Ladislaw,
who fancies himself a Bohemian aesthete, tells Dorothea: 'You *are* a
poem.'[62] However, in each case, the object answers back. Ladislaw's
naive insult rebounds on himself, and, far from being 'a cabbage or
a rose', Mademoiselle de Maupin, that lively predecessor of Woolf's
Orlando, goes on her own search for beauty, ending up in the beds of
both male and female lovers, after which she cheerfully goes off on her
own. In James's static bowl of a novel it is the women who act: it is
a woman who buys the bowl, another who breaks it, and it is Maggie
who tries to hold it together. The relation of women to the art object
becomes, in the nineteenth century, but also in modernism—Eliot's
'La Figlia Che Piange' beside her garden urn, for instance, and Stevens'
'Woman Looking at a Vase of Flowers'—a sign of unease, a disturbance,
even a 'breaking' point.

A short story by Alice Walker seems, at a distance, to recall James's
novel. 'Advancing Luna and Ida B. Wells' might be worlds away
from his delicate concerns. It is about interracial rape, specifically of a
white woman by a black man. The effort of confronting this morally,
historically confusing event leads to a kind of narrative breakdown, and
the story, instead of concluding, runs into various dead ends: second
thoughts, discarded notes, imaginary knowledge. The black woman
narrator cannot resolve her conflicting allegiances to a friend and to the
race, and therefore cannot turn her story into a nicely finished art object.
But there is one sentence which holds out the possibility, not only of
friendship, but of art's ability to hold together, in spite of its subject
matter. 'Several years later, she [the white woman] came to visit me
in the South and brought a lovely piece of pottery which my daughter
much later dropped and broke, but which I glued back together in such
a way that the flaw improves the beauty and fragility of the design.'[63]

[61] Gautier, *Mademoiselle de Maupin*, 206.

[62] George Eliot, *Middlemarch*, intro. W. J. Harvey (Harmondsworth: Penguin,
1965), 256.

[63] Alice Walker, 'Advancing Luna and Ida B. Wells', in *Any Woman's Blues*, ed. Mary
Helen Washington (London: Virago, 1980), 75.

Even rape, the rape which as a black woman the narrator does not want to confront, might be written as a story. Somehow, however, it depends on the 'pot' being smashed and put together differently. Walker, like James before her, seems to be trying to save the word 'beauty' from truth. That 'the flaw improves the beauty and fragility of the design' is like a last-ditch aestheticism, a holding together of the bowl of art, even when the truth seems too hard to write. 'What men or gods are these? What maidens loth?' Certainly Walker, like James, knows the flaw which lies at the heart of any aestheticism. But like him, she also wants to save something of that devalued bowl: 'the beauty and fragility of the design'. 'and all this has been to her but as the sound of lyres and flutes …'

Aestheticism from the start is troubled by 'her', that other art object. She, from Keats onwards, is a sign of beauty, unravished and untouched, but also a sign of what beauty holds off: ravishment and force. Thus, it seems, aestheticism brings into play the very ethical, sexual, economic questions it staves off. The crack which appears is like the sign of this strain. The solution, for both men and women writers, is not simple, and is not just a matter of throwing out the crocks. Something about the cracked vases and pots asks for a kind of mending, and a reassessment of value, or price.

Of all the modernists, the one who is perhaps the most indebted to, and exercised by, Victorian aestheticism is Virginia Woolf. This feminist modernist, who read Pater in defiance of her father,[64] who acknowledges his influence at the beginning of *Orlando* and who, in *Three Guineas*, recalls the artist's duty to work 'only for the sake of the art', in fact inherits and constantly reworks the aestheticist notion of formal beauty. A curious passage from *Jacob's Room* (1922), for instance, is typical in the way it uses the word 'beauty' to invite and repel physical objectification:

As for the beauty of women, it is like the light on the sea, never constant to a single wave. … Then, at a top-floor window, leaning out, looking down, you see beauty itself … beauty glowing, suddenly expressive, withdrawn the moment after. No one can count on it or seize it or have it wrapped in paper. Nothing is to be won from the shops, and Heaven knows it would be better to sit at home than haunt the plate-glass windows in the hope of lifting the shining green, the glowing ruby, out of them alive.[65]

---

[64] Perry Meisel, *The Absent Father: Virginia Woolf and Walter Pater* (New Haven and London: Yale University Press, 1980), 12–16.

[65] Virginia Woolf, *Jacob's Room*, ed. Sue Roe (London: Penguin, 1992), 100.

As the passage goes hunting for 'beauty itself' it runs into a tangle of contradiction. Beauty is something and nothing, there and not there, dead and alive. 'Nothing', Woolf declares, 'is to be won from the shops.' Yet the sentence ends up in the very place she rejects, imagining 'the shining green, the glowing ruby' behind 'plate-glass windows'. 'Nothing' turns out to be something after all, quite solid and buyable, as beauty, from being embodied in 'women', embodies itself in the emeralds and rubies of a long tradition. *Emeralds and Cameos* was the title of Gautier's 1850 volume of poems. However much she denies it, Woolf is back with the antique dealers and jewellers of the aesthetes, with the shops which sell beauty at a price. Yet she is also, audibly, trying to get out, 'in the hope of lifting the shining green, the glowing ruby, out of them alive'. In the hope of finding beauty 'alive', Woolf goes shoplifting. This nearly incoherent sentence, which tries to get free of the object it is stealing (the 'green' and the 'ruby' double-dealing between colours and precious stones), goes shopping, verbally, for something which cannot be 'won from the shops'. She summarizes, here, the contradiction of trying to remove the precious object from the conditions of its preciousness: its shop.

Woolf's fiction is haunted by shops, by their showy mix of beauty and price, purpose and purposelessness. When Rhoda in *The Waves* hears of Percival's death, she finds comfort in a shop: 'Here is the shop where they sell stockings. And I could believe that beauty is once more set flowing.'[66] The idea of price is raised, then denied, as beauty, instead of being bought, starts 'flowing'. While Woolf is haunted by shops: boot shops, stocking shops, jewel shops, flower shops, the shops of Mrs Dalloway's Bond Street,[67] those places where beauty comes in contact with money and women, it is also in the hope that beauty might go free of them in the end. That paradox runs through her work. At the beginning of *Mrs Dalloway* Septimus interprets the aeroplane's 'smoke words' as a form of 'inexhaustible charity and laughing goodness one shape after another of unimaginable beauty and signalling their intention to provide him, for nothing, for ever, for looking merely, with beauty, more beauty!'[68] This visionary Paterian moment, 'professing

---

[66] Virginia Woolf, *The Waves*, ed. Kate Flint (London: Penguin, 1992), 121.

[67] Rachel Bowlby, 'Walking, Women and Writing: Virginia Woolf as Flâneuse', in *New Feminist Discourses: Critical Essays on Theories and Texts*, ed. Isobel Armstrong (London: Routledge, 1992), 26–47.

[68] Virginia Woolf, *Mrs Dalloway*, intro. Elaine Showalter, ed. Stella McNichol (London: Penguin, 1992), 23.

frankly to give nothing', is richly, pointedly ironic. In fact Septimus, who is suffering from shell-shock, is entranced by the words of an advertisement spelling Blaxo, Kreemo, or is it toffee? If this is 'for nothing, for ever', it is also only the call of another shop, of something tackily sellable, of beauty at a price. Beauty is truth. Beauty is Blaxo. Beauty is also Gautier's chamber pot.

Aestheticism, then, is rarely 'pure' aestheticism. It is almost always impure, tainted by something else: pain, ethics, economics, ideology. Moreover, for women the play of beauty is complicated by its long association with themselves: 'As for the beauty of women ...' Woolf's attempt to throw off the association of beauty with femininity can be heard in the struggle of her sentences to escape from the place where goods and women might be shopped for. At the same time, she cannot forget that place, and the word 'beauty', to which she returns throughout her life, rarely comes free from the commodities of the sexual market place. Just such a struggle is theorized by Eavan Boland in her book about women writers in Ireland, *Object Lessons*. The 'woman poet', she writes, 'is in that poignant place ... where the subject cannot forget her previous existence as object. There are aesthetic implications to this, but they are not separable from the ethical ones.'[69] For Boland, the problem for the woman poet is to find a 'place' in a tradition which has tended to map desire for poetic expression too neatly onto desire for sexual possession. Sure enough, her argument returns to that familiar, founding text of the story of beauty: 'The young man in decorative chase on the side of the urn has the sexual perspective which seeks to possess; the maiden has the erotic task of being simply mute and beautiful.'[70] How to overcome being 'mute and beautiful' while still needing the idea of the beautiful for herself is the lesson to be learned by the woman poet. It is indeed a hard lesson *about* objects.

The event which summed up, for Boland, 'the stresses and fractures between a poet's life and a woman's'[71] was the suicide of Sylvia Plath in 1963. Plath, in an uncanny replay of the whole aestheticist tradition, repeatedly wrestles with objects which turn her back to stone or pot. It is as if she too cannot get free of the memory of that place on an urn, which goes round and round. 'The Lady and the Earthenware Head', a relatively early work, signals the dangers. Typically there are

---

[69] Eavan Boland, *Object Lessons: The Life of the Woman and the Poet in Our Time* (London: Vintage, 1995), 233.
[70] Ibid. 216.   [71] Ibid. 113.

two objects, not one: the 'Lady' and the 'Head', a two-headed hydra to wrestle with the poem's 'I'. Thus Plath begins: 'Fired in sanguine clay, the model head | Fit nowhere'. In that word 'sanguine' the exchange has already started. The dead calm matter of the clay becomes blooded with life. However, getting rid of the hated object proves difficult. The poet imagines how some boys might find the head which has been hidden in a tree, and enjoy a game of football at its expense. The idea is enough to 'waken the sly nerve up | That knits to each original its coarse copy.' That unnerving 'sly nerve' is exactly the thing Plath wakens so brilliantly in her poetry: a malicious, physiological connection between subject and object, self and poem, original and copy. Here it is woken by the imagined 'molesting' of 'Rough boys'.[72] Only a game of ball to be sure, but this woman poet is so transfused into the art object, into the 'sanguine clay' of this latest piece of pottery, that other ravishments come to mind. That 'sly nerve' is the key to Plath's scary mythologizing, to an imagination so haunted by the memory of 'a previous existence as object' that it cannot hold its ground as subject. The 'sly nerve' which connects poem to poet, head to speaker, is her special, frightening short-circuit; an electric shock of words which readily hostages self to an art object.

Ted Hughes wrote an answering poem in *Birthday Letters*. But his, by comparison, is safely sure of the differences between 'I', 'you', and 'it'. There are no eerie transactions between them. At one point, recalling how he lifted the head into its lodging tree, he wonders if:

> Perhaps
> It is still there, representing you
> To the sunrise, and happy
> In its cold pastoral, lips pursed slightly
> As if my touch had only just left it.[73]

That 'touch' is not a transfusion; it is a leave-taking. This poet can 'touch' his object, to the extent even of imagining a reaction to himself, 'lips pursed slightly', without being bound to do anything except abandon it. Meanwhile, the echo of Keats, that happy 'cold pastoral', is a kind of assurance of his own role, as well as the role of the poem in a long tradition—a tradition, among other things, of nymphs and maidens on their enduring cold vases. Certainly, the head which might

[72] Sylvia Plath, *Collected Poems*, ed. Ted Hughes (London: Faber, 1981), 69–70, 69.
[73] Ted Hughes, *Birthday Letters* (London: Faber, 1998), 57–8, 58.

be 'happy | In its cold pastoral' does not have, for Hughes, any sly nerves. Plath, however, comes from a different place. The earthenware head, a kind of debased art object, has a hold on her from far back. The last lines of her poem evoke an 'antique' thing, as if the idea of antiquity, literary as well as classical, had somehow got into the poem. This is an ancient artefact, older than the poem's narrative. It is also, significantly, too hard to smash:

> An antique hag-head, too tough for knife to finish,
> Refusing to diminish
> By one jot its basilisk-look of love.[74]

That stony 'look of love' (the poem's, not the poet's) finally wins out. This poet has lost her place as subject and is being turned to stone by the very object she has made: her own poem. The ugly clay head turns out to be, indeed, another all too well-wrought *urn*.

Plath, then, enters the aestheticist tradition with a vengeance. The art objects she invokes, in poem after poem, have a superstitious, traditional hold on herself, a 'look of love' which is likely to kill. The subject of these poems cannot withstand the assumption from the 'antique' that a woman belongs on a vase, or perhaps in a poem. Both in Hughes and Plath, the pottery head is haunted by a Keatsian precedent which shows the crack in its own aestheticist veneer. In Plath, however, the art object is 'too tough' to be broken, and she, the poem's 'I', remains somehow frozen in the gaze of that awful 'it'. This is the object lesson she repeatedly learns, in poems where the speaking subject relinquishes power, even life itself, to the formal other, to the perfectly self-contained statue, cast, head, effigy, which wins its place through a violent seduction, or blood-letting, of the woman herself. The poem is never quite separate or self-sufficient enough in Plath's brilliant, lifelong dicing with 'it'.

However, if at some level Plath wants to smash the poem's head because it contains her own lifeblood, she also, significantly, fails to do so. The head, like her other effigies, is horribly durable. Even if it figures a woman, it also remains inhuman, self-contained. The indifference of the art object is part of its artistic power. The Mona Lisa smiles through time, listening to 'the sound of lyres and flutes'. The stone dead woman in Plath's very late poem, 'Edge', similarly 'wears the smile of accomplishment'.[75] Both Pater and Plath relish the scandal value of that indifferent smile which expresses art's self-satisfied completion

---

[74] Plath, *Collected Poems*, 70.   [75] Ibid. 272.

and carelessness. Their rhetoric of inhuman artworks seems to drive out questions of humanity, relevance, identity, but only, it seems, in order to let us hear them all the more insistently offstage, edged out, or lying just on the other side of art's own 'Edge'. The scandal of aestheticism's precious, removed 'smile', its attention to 'lyres and flutes' at the expense of everything else, is part of its purpose. The art object's beautifully durable form betrays a profoundly ambiguous sense of finish.

It is that ambiguity and sense of scandal which Plath works so brilliantly as she carves art objects out of herself. The cost to the woman is high, but the thing is accomplished. The tension between those two gives her poems their charge, their mix of perfected craft and unscrupulously violated bodies.

The legacy of Victorian aestheticism in the twentieth century continues strong. Among men as well as women, the beautiful form of the work comes at a price. 'Aesthetics of Indifference' Fernando Pessoa subtitles a whole section of his avowedly aestheticist work, *The Book of Disquiet*. 'An adjective matters more to me than the real weeping of a human soul',[76] one of its heteronymic characters declares. Yet this ostentatious espousal of 'a refined Epicureanism', as he puts it, expressed by a life of 'aesthetic contemplation',[77] is wittily disproved by the title. To be as indifferently Epicurean as he proposes, devoted to style rather than to human souls, is paradoxically to admit the condition of 'disquiet'. 'I feel this because I feel nothing',[78] the speaker confesses, letting 'this' and 'nothing' jostle for attention as the object of feeling. Whether it is a feeling state or an unfeeling state depends on the precise angle of that 'nothing'. The sense of choice, however, incorporated in a stylistic riddle, is part of the aestheticist legacy Pessoa enjoys. Moreover, its calculated outrage might also be as honest a comment on political atrocity as any artistically espoused commitment. At least artistic expression is thus exposed for what it is: a lucky privilege of quiet (however disquieting) in the face of the world's pain.

In the twentieth century, such contradictions merely become more resonant and brittle. For instance, Adorno's contentious, repeated, then finally retracted statement, 'After Auschwitz, to write a poem is barbaric,'[79] is more convincing as a rhetorical contradiction than as

---

[76] Fernando Pessoa, *The Book of Disquiet*, ed. and trans. Richard Zenith (London: Penguin, 2001), 32.
[77] Ibid. 12.   [78] Ibid. 363.
[79] Quoted in John Felstiner, *Paul Celan: Poet, Survivor, Jew* (New Haven and London: Yale University Press, 1995), 139. See also 188, 225, and 232.

a literal injunction. When repeated by relatively profuse critics it can become suspect. George Steiner, for instance, declares at the end of 'Silence and the Poet': 'When the words in the city are full of savagery and lies, nothing speaks louder than the unwritten poem.'[80] This is fine rhetoric, but it is untrue. The 'unwritten poem' does not speak at all, however much the critic speaks on its behalf. The 'unwritten poem' says nothing to no one, and cannot help in any way. Writers and poets seem much less sure of this trope of shame than the critics who do not obey it. As Primo Levi points out, in answer to Adorno, poetry might be written not only *after* Auschwitz, but also ' "on" Auschwitz', even if it is 'a heavy, dense poetry, like molten metal, that runs away and leaves you gutted'.[81] He was probably thinking of the poet who did specifically write 'about Auschwitz', even if 'in some extremely obscure, not to say hermetic poems',[82] that is Paul Celan.

Of Celan's difficult and troubling poetry, Douglas Oliver once recalled that 'none wrote more beautifully post-war | of the perfection and terror of crystal.'[83] The poem which has been described as the '*Guernica* of post-war European literature',[84] originally titled 'Death Tango', quite shamelessly and shockingly, as John Felstiner puts it, 'foists music on killing'.[85] Celan's *'Todesfuge'* ('Death Fugue'), with its elaborate plait of repeats, its arresting, formal control, presses home the scandal of having to dance and play while Jews dig their graves. Set in the death camps, this fugue *of* death also expresses the lucky, guilty escape *from* death for those, whoever they are, who are allotted, instead, the role of dancing and playing. Though the poem rehearses the scandal of the proximity between art and barbarity, this is not Adorno's point proved. In fact, quite the opposite. Like the start of another of Celan's poems, 'Cello Entry | from behind pain',[86] the proximity of music to pain is a scandal, but it is a scandal to be voiced, not silenced. Against Adorno, Celan continues to speak, even sing. The cello, like the lyres and flutes, plays on. In *'Todesfuge'*, with its rudely designated pronouns which line up meanings and people in arbitrary groups of life or death,

[80] George Steiner, *Language and Silence: Essays 1958–1966* (London: Faber, 1985; first pub. 1967), 74.

[81] Primo Levi, *The Voice of Memory: Interviews 1961–1987* , ed. Marco Belpoliti and Robert Gordon, trans. Robert Gordon (Oxford: Blackwell, 2001; first pub. 1997), 10.

[82] Ibid. 42.

[83] Douglas Oliver, *Arrondissements*, ed. Alice Notley (Cambridge: Salt, 2003), 10.

[84] Felstiner, *Paul Celan*, 26.   [85] Ibid. 39.

[86] Paul Celan, *Selected Poems*, trans. and intro. Michael Hamburger (London: Penguin, 1990), 253.

the rhythmic beat is both the guard's shout and the poet's self-savingly performed music: '*stecht tiefer die Spaten ihr einen ihr andern spielt weiter zum Tanz auf*' ('jab deeper you lot with your spades you others play on for the dance'[87]). No other poem of the century similarly puts words into the reader's mouth which we ('you others') both sing and wish to spit out. This is poetry which makes the condition of music, that ghastly, jabbing playing on, almost too hard to bear.

If 'none wrote more beautifully post-war | of the perfection and terror of crystal', Celan also insists that the music of poetry cannot stop. Douglas Oliver titled his own volume about Celan's death, *The Shattered Crystal*. Crystal is a figure for poetry's precious, fragile, multifaceted jewellery, for Jewry itself (Paris's 'Jewish crystal quarter'[88]), but also, after *Kristallnacht*, for the glass-smashing terror of pogroms and death camps. There is a strong sense, throughout this volume, that history has caught up with the china vase. A direct reference to that vase occurs in Oliver's poem 'Between Celan and Heine', where he briefly recalls the figure of Prudhomme, the nineteenth-century Parnassian, who 'thought the poem's form a perfect crystal vase | knocked lightly, and so fissured insidiously'.[89] He thus situates Celan's work in a tradition of 'crystal' which goes back through nineteenth-century aestheticism to the Romantic Heine. The 'perfect crystal vase' of 'the poem's form' has always taken the knocks of something outside form: matter, history, context. The crack in the glass, the fissure in the crystal, was always there, as a reminder of the breakableness of form in the face of actual human violence. The shattered crystal of Celan's work belongs in that tradition, even if, in it, the light knocks have become the brutal blows of a subject which is almost, but not quite, unwritable. 'If art were a specialist human activity of purely aesthetic value it wouldn't matter to us',[90] Oliver writes elsewhere. That 'purely', as so often, is the key to the difference. A 'purely aesthetic value' would neither have matter, nor 'matter to us'. But an impure 'aesthetic value' might, and the word 'aesthetic' is thus, somehow, saved from meaninglessness. How it might still matter is summed up in a recent lecture, 'Poetry's Subject'. The poem, Oliver writes, 'by somehow encompassing both tradition

[87] Paul Celan, *Selected Poems*, trans. and intro. Michael Hamburger (London: Penguin, 1990), 60–1.

[88] Oliver, *Arrondissements*, 15.

[89] Douglas Oliver, *Three Variations on the Theme of Harm: Selected Poetry and Prose* (London: Paladin, 1990), 27.

[90] Ibid. 107.

and novelty will ... achieve its bedrock qualities: beauty, truthfulness, wisdom, prescience'.[91] Here the echoes of an old inscription resurface in the words of a poet who does not shirk from writing about the twentieth century's mass-realities of 'shattered crystal'.

Oliver's own personal tribute to Celan, in his poem 'The Weekend Curfew', replays a consciously aestheticist figure of containment and breaking, music and violence. He takes the older poet's *'Todesfuge'*, that 'urn carried in German | ceremonies of forgetfulness', and replays a shattering which Celan's own poem already suggests:

> For Nazi cruelty in its purist light
> had filled that lyric ...
> and when the hammer broke it
> musical fragments
> became shards,
> part of the song went hiding
> silent in stones ...[92]

The aestheticist 'urn' is always in danger of becoming a purely ceremonial container of the past, a bland appeaser of guilt and a museum-piece in the memory. However, the poet (or reader) can reject such ceremonies of innocence. Once again, the question turns on the problem of purity. The urn seems to contain all the horror of Nazism's 'purist light', as if the lyric itself perpetrated the very ideology associated with its content. The act of smashing the urn is thus an attempt to break the connection, but it is not an act of total destruction. The urn may become 'shards', the music become 'fragments', the song, at least 'part of the song', become 'silent in stones'. As with previous breakages, however, enough remains to carry on sounding, even if differently, in a new form: the mere fragments of an urn. Celan's sometimes violent rejection of his own poem, re-imagined by Oliver here, is a gesture which has always been implicit in the crystal vases of aestheticism. Too much crystal is likely to shatter at the touch of a heavy hand.

This, in a sense, is the logical culmination of art for art. The urn was always a container of death, though in Keats's poem at several removes. By the time Oliver comes to use it as a figure for poetry, the urn contains something unspeakable. After Auschwitz, as well as on Auschwitz, the lyric vessel must not only crack, but be broken in pieces, so that what it

---

[91] Oliver, 'Poetry's Subject', in *PN Review*, 105(1995), 52–8, 57.
[92] Oliver, *Arrondissements*, 11.

contains can escape the scandalous preciosity of being even containable. Yet, though the bowl may be cracked, the pot broken, the urn smashed, the shape which remains, even if just 'shards', will continue to express the sense of music, or beauty, set against the hard truth. Celan's poetry may increasingly, after *'Todesfuge'*, have consisted of 'musical fragments', broken bits of a vision which it can hardly bear to recall, but the music does not therefore stop. The cello comes in behind pain, just as, in that early, bitterly beautiful, guilty poem, *'Todesfuge'*, the death fugue goes on and on, the players unable to do anything else except 'sing now and play'.

to break through all the conditions of comely form,
recovering, touch by touch, a loveliness ...

Walter Pater

The only aristocracy is never to touch ...

Fernando Pessoa

3

Touching Forms: Tennyson and Aestheticism

'Art for Art's sake! Hail, truest Lord of Hell!' (III. 12. 1)[1] Tennyson's uninspired squib is a rare outburst on a subject which
engrossed many of his contemporaries. Between Victorian aestheticism and Victoria's Laureate there is a marked stand-off, a silence
broken only here and there by skirmishes on both sides. Tennyson
never refers to Pater in his letters, owned none of his books, though
he certainly read and marked some of his essays in journals.[2] Pater, for his part, is oddly circumspect about Tennyson. In the essay
on 'Style' he praises the poet's eclectic mix of 'savoursome' Latin
and 'Racy Saxon monosyllables' which are, significantly, 'close to
us as touch and sight'.[3] Otherwise, quotations from Tennyson are
dropped anonymously. 'The blot upon the brain | That *will* show it-
self without', from 'Maud', turns up unacknowledged in the essay

---

[1] All quotations from Tennyson's poetry are taken from *The Poems of Tennyson*, ed.
Christopher Ricks, 2nd edn, 3 vols.(London: Longmans, 1987), and are cited in the text.
[2] See *Tennyson in Lincoln: A Catalogue of the Collections in the Research Centre*,
compiled by Nancie Campbell, 2 vols. (Lincoln: Tennyson Society, 1971–3), ii. 38,
n. 4558. Gerhard Joseph discusses similarities between Tennyson and Pater in *Tennyson
and the Text: The Weaver's Shuttle* (Cambridge: Cambridge University Press, 1992).
[3] Walter Pater, 'Style', in *Appreciations* (London: Macmillan, 1910), 5–38, 16.

on 'Coleridge'[4] as an example of modern sceptical thinking, while
the two 'handfuls of white dust' from 'The Lotos-Eaters' are recalled
in *Marius the Epicurean*.[5] Some inhibition made Pater reticent about
Tennyson.

The same was not true of Swinburne, who pestered the Laureate
with copies of his own poems, as well as adulation and defamation. In
one place, in his reply to Buchanan's 'Fleshly School' article, he takes
a cheeky sideswipe at Tennyson, claiming that in 'Merlin and Vivien'
the Laureate far surpassed 'the author of *Mademoiselle de Maupin* or
the author of the *Fleurs du Mal*' in 'sensual immorality'.[6] Interestingly,
some thirty years before, Leigh Hunt had criticized the 1842 volume for
relying on feelings 'too sensual'.[7] If Swinburne relished the disreputable
association with Gautier and Baudelaire, Tennyson's own reported
comment on the sexual passages of his poem 'Lucretius', 'What a mess
little Swinburne would have made of this',[8] hints at a certain envious
rivalry with that self-proclaimed 'Lord of Hell'.

Tennyson's place in Victorian poetry has often been too monumental for its own good. An easy target for the *enfants terribles* of
his time, Swinburne and Wilde, he was, for modernist rebels, also a
mockable grandee: the stupidest poet, Lawn Tennyson, someone who'd
blundered. Nevertheless, the sound of Tennyson rings on in their ears
and their writings. Stephen Daedalus' wet-dream verse, '*Are you not
weary of ardent ways*',[9] mixes Tennysonian weariness—'My life is full
of weary days' (I. 383. 1)—with Nineties' lust. Stevie Smith is haunted
by his 'sea-sad, loamishly-sad'[10] sounds, which give all her work an
undertow of Victorian melancholy. Yeats, in 'The Tragic Generation',
attacks Tennyson for 'moral values that were not aesthetic', but in the
same paragraph recalls 'those islands' where 'beauty, certain forms of

---

[4] Walter Pater, 'Coleridge', in *Appreciations*, 65–104, 98.

[5] Walter Pater, *Marius the Epicurean*, 2 vols. (London: Macmillan, 1910), ii. 100.

[6] A. C. Swinburne, from *Under the Microscope* (1872), quoted in *Tennyson: The Critical Heritage*, ed. John D. Jump (London: Routledge & Kegan Paul, 1967), 318–21, 321.

[7] Leigh Hunt, review (1842), in Jump, ed., 126–36, 128.

[8] Quoted in Oscar Browning, *Memories of Sixty Years* (London: Bodley Head, 1910), 117.

[9] James Joyce, *A Portrait of the Artist as a Young Man* (Harmondsworth: Penguin, 1960), 223.

[10] Stevie Smith, *Novel on Yellow Paper* (Harmondsworth: Penguin, 1951), 19.

sensuous loveliness were separated from all the general purposes of life'.[11] Tennyson's sense of shorelines, of islands beyond or after life, might well have been in Yeats's mind alongside those of Spenser and Keats. 'I am haunted by numberless islands, and many a Danaan shore',[12] Yeats writes in 'The White Birds', echoing, perhaps not coincidentally, the metre of Tennyson's own Irish *imrama*, 'The Voyage of Maeldune': 'And we came to the Silent Isle that we never had touched at before' (III. 63. 11). To 'touch at' some island, with that little extra effort and reach of having to 'touch *at*' land, is a typically Tennysonian landing. It suggests the difficulty and delay of getting there, as if it needed a small final push: 'at'. If 'certain forms of sensuous loveliness' are similarly islanded in early Yeats, this is because Tennyson, as well as others, was there before. The paradox of Tennyson is that he managed to be both Victoria's Laureate, official and moral, and perhaps the most powerful, undeclared voice of English aestheticism at the same time. Listed along with Swinburne, Rossetti, Morris, and Wilde in one of the first books on the subject, *The Aesthetic Movement in England* by Walter Hamilton,[13] it is Tennyson who is also remembered, as late as 1950 by Richard Aldington, as 'for a time the chief master of the aesthetes'.[14]

The key to this unofficial reputation is, as critics like McLuhan and Bloom[15] have pointed out, Arthur Hallam. Hallam was there at the beginning, announcing Tennyson's place in 1831 as a 'Poet of Sensation'—a poet motivated by nothing more than 'the desire of beauty' or by 'the energetic principle of love for the beautiful'. For Hallam, 'Poems, Chiefly Lyrical' is an example of 'the spirit of modern poetry', which is marked by 'melancholy' and a 'return of the mind upon itself'.[16] The phrase 'art for art's sake', with its return of the idea on itself,

---

[11] W. B. Yeats, *Autobiographies,* ed. William H. O'Donnell and Douglas N. Archibald (New York: Scribner, 1999), 242.

[12] W. B. Yeats, 'The White Birds', in *The Variorum Edition of the Poems of W. B. Yeats*, ed. Peter Allt and Russell K. Alspach (New York: Macmillan, 1957), 122.

[13] Walter Hamilton, *The Aesthetic Movement in England* (London, 1882), 41.

[14] *The Religion of Beauty: Selections from the Aesthetes*, intro. Richard Aldington (London: Heinemann, 1950), 34.

[15] H. M. McLuhan, 'Tennyson and Picturesque Poetry', in *Critical Essays on the Poetry of Tennyson*, ed. John Killham (London: Routledge & Kegan Paul, 1960), 67–85; Harold Bloom, 'Tennyson, Hallam, and Romantic Tradition', in *The Ringers in the Tower: Studies in Romantic Tradition* (Chicago: University of Chicago Press, 1971), 145–54.

[16] Arthur Henry Hallam, *Remains in Verse and Prose* (London: John Murray, 1863), 294; 297; 302.

was not yet current in England, at least not in that precise formulation. Its first recorded use is in 1854, with the translation of Victor Cousin's *Lectures on the True, the Beautiful and the Good*, in which 'art for art's sake'[17] is separated from religion and morality. Hallam's advocacy of beauty for beauty's sake, and his definition of modernity as 'melancholy' and introspective, pitch the argument in exactly the key it will take later in the century. Pater's own account of modern poetry's 'inexhaustible discontent, languor, and home-sickness, that endless regret,'[18] might be echoing Hallam's self-returning 'melancholy'. Certainly, the continuing visibility of Hallam's review in the two main publications of the *Remains*, in 1834 and 1863, but also in that rare edition edited by Le Gallienne for John Lane in 1893, kept Tennyson's aestheticist reputation alive. It may have been this last edition that Yeats was remembering when he referred to 'what the younger Hallam called the Aesthetic School'.[19] In fact Hallam does not use the term 'Aesthetic', but the Paterian slip is a sign of the extent to which, by 1909, Hallam had been recruited to the aestheticist cause. Le Gallienne, for instance, praises his review as 'one of the early examples in England of that aesthetic criticism which is now so generally accepted amongst us'.[20] The continued publication of the *Remains* not only kept Hallam's death present, audibly in the very title of the book, but also, paradoxically, kept Tennyson, the aesthetic poet, alive.

A review which was almost as important as Hallam's was George Brimley's essay of 1855. This, interestingly, contains the first recorded use in English of the term 'aestheticism'. ' "The Lotos-Eaters" ', he remarks, 'carries Tennyson's tendency to pure aestheticism to an extreme point.' He is using the word in its relatively recent sense of a philosophy of the beautiful, separated from morality or use, rather than in the strict sense of sensuous perception. If 'The Lotos-Eaters' invites to a voyage which will soon become a cult expedition to the land of the senses, it is Brimley's description of it, as a type of 'pure aestheticism', which resonantly recruits the poem to a new cause. 'In some poems the artistic beauty seems given more for its own sake than for any moral', he helpfully explains. Hinting, here, at art for art's sake, he nonetheless ends up in a

[17] Quoted in L. M. Findlay, 'The Introduction of the Phrase "Art for Art's Sake" into English', *Notes and Queries*, 218 (July 1973), 246–8, 247.

[18] Pater, 'Coleridge', 104.

[19] Yeats, *Autobiographies*, 361.

[20] *The Poems of Arthur Henry Hallam, Together with his Essay on the Lyrical Poems of Alfred Tennyson*, ed. Richard Le Gallienne (London: Elkin Matthews, 1893), p. xxxiv.

roundabout way disparaging the early poems and praising *In Memoriam* for its human and moral interest: 'Poetry and passion are nobler and wiser than stoicism or Epicureanism', he concludes. Brimley offers an exposure and an apology at the same time. He exposes Tennyson's aestheticism and Epicureanism as youthful mannerisms, soon to be abandoned, but meanwhile lavishes attention on those poems which affect them. In particular, he indulges the sonorous effects of 'The Lotos-Eaters', writing, in one place, that its 'rhythmical language ... takes the formative impulse of the feeling, as falling water does of the forces that draw it into a flashing curve'.[21] In that one sentence he evokes Tennyson's formative emotional landscape: the Valley of Cauteretz, with its cataracts and streams, and makes it serve as the landscape of creativity, of that 'rhythmical language' which takes shape, or form, directly from feeling. Forming, falling, and flashing are words that Tennyson reworks throughout his life as if to unlock from them some secret source of meaning. The 'pure aestheticism' of 'The Lotos-Eaters' is connected, for Brimley, with that unforming form of the waterfall which, like rhythm, marks the physical 'impulse' of writing and connects it with feeling. The poem's echo-effects, its suspense of movement, its islanding self-containment and return of sounds on themselves, has something to do, Brimley seems to perceive, with a formative scene which is also the scene of artistic form.

> All along the valley, stream that flashest white,
> Deepening thy voice with the deepening of the night,
> All along the valley, where thy waters flow,
> I walked with one I loved two and thirty years ago.
>
> (II. 618. 1–4)

Thirty-one years later, to be precise, Tennyson was still returning to a remembered scene, with its flash of water which becomes, in retrospect, a sudden memory. 'In the Valley of Cauteretz', written more than ten years after the publication of *In Memoriam* and thirty-one years after that first visit with Hallam, is a reminder of just how formative a scene this was in Tennyson's life. Those 'waters that flashest white' have less to do with nature than with a human presence, loved and remembered. If the verbal echo is of Wordsworth's 'flash upon that inward eye | Which is the bliss of solitude',[22] it is noticeable that Tennyson's flashpoints of

---

[21] George Brimley, 'Alfred Tennyson's Poems', in *Cambridge Essays* (Cambridge: Cambridge University Press, 1855), 226–81; 237; 241; 279; 237.

[22] William Wordsworth, 'I wandered lonely', in *Poetical Works*, ed. Thomas Hutchinson, rev. Ernest de Selincourt (London: Oxford University Press, 1936), 149. The fact

memory are generally less tranquilly recollective. In *The Lover's Tale*, for instance, he writes: 'The very face and form of Lionel | Flashed through my eyes into my innermost brain' (I. 365. 93–4). Wordsworth's 'inward eye', a type of mental vision, has become Tennyson's much more literal-minded 'innermost brain' which, in spite of that flash, takes some getting 'into'. If this is poetic vision, it is oddly anatomical. Lionel's 'form' seems to have to push 'through' the corporeal eye to reach the 'brain', so that the flash of recognition is audibly slowed up by the obstruction of a body. Like the waterfall 'that flashest white', this flashing 'form' also somehow touches, through tactical delay, on a tangible presence. The metaphorical flash of memory is turned, by Tennyson, into a laborious effort, which touches on a lost, beloved body somewhere.

Brimley's review then quotes the whole section from 'Morte D'Arthur' where the word is used twice to describe the fall of Excalibur into the lake:

> And flashing round and round, and whirled in an arch,
> Shot like a streamer of the northern morn,
> Seen where the moving isles of winter shock
> By night, with noises of the northern sea.
> So flashed and fell the brand Excalibur
>
> (II. 12–13. 138–42)

Between 'flashing' and that last 'flashed' there is a long pause, as the Miltonic simile whirls into another time and place: 'the northern morn', the 'isles of winter'. The fall of the sword is held up, slow-motioned by something that lies between. Like the formative waterfall in 'The Lotos-Eaters', the lines can't quite let Arthur's sword fall. Some fifty-five years later, grieving the death of his son Lionel in the Red Sea in 'To the Marquis of Dufferin and Ava', Tennyson once again imagines something falling and flashing on water:

> When That within the coffin fell,
> Fell—and flashed into the Red Sea.
>
> (III. 201. 43–4)

Here, the flash happens only after the awful, unsynchronized bump of 'fell | Fell', as the poet characteristically feels, and feels *for*, the body 'within'. In 'Morte D'Arthur', similarly, the flash is delayed by a physical obstacle: 'Seen where the moving isles of winter shock | By night'. These

---

that Hallam quoted these lines in his review might have given them an extra resonance for Tennyson. See *Remains in Verse and Prose*, 297.

lovely lines (about touching islands again) express something which the flashing swift sword cannot: the sense of physical 'shock'; literally, the clash of icebergs below the surface of the water. Tennyson's placing of the word 'shock' at the end of the line lets the shock continue as the verb hangs, uncertainly, between transitive and intransitive senses. Do these 'moving isles' shock against something, or only shock, invisibly, in themselves? 'shock | By night' keeps both meanings in play. This 'shock' is grammatically intransitive, like a shiver that runs through the nerves. But it is also transitive because, as icebergs, what makes them 'shock' is the huge impact of physical bodies below the surface. The object of 'shock' is there, invisibly encountered as a shattering touch in another place. In parallel to the clean-cut fall of the sword, with its visionary flash, Tennyson gives us the after-'shock' of those unseen, unheard land masses, themselves supplying, at a distance, the missing object of the verb 'flashing'.

Such displaced touch is a defining characteristic of Tennyson's flashpoints. Again and again the moment of revelation, of spiritual or imaginative intuition, is slightly held up by the sense of a body. Even while the flash suggests instantaneous, visionary understanding, touching is harder, slower, and happens at a remove:

> So word by word, and line by line,
> The dead man touched me from the past,
> And all at once it seemed at last
> The living soul was flashed on mine
>
> (II. 413. 33–6)

The great moment of consolation in *In Memoriam*, which happens in a flash of revelation that the soul is 'living', is typically preceded by another kind of knowledge: 'The dead man touched me.' This touch should be figurative and intransitive. The poet, here, should simply be 'touched' by reading Hallam's letters, 'word by word, and line by line'. But the adjective 'dead' confuses the figure. Hallam was alive when the letters were written. He is now a 'living soul' when the letters are being read. Yet Tennyson writes: 'The dead man touched me from the past.' That death is in the past, certainly, but it is suddenly the subject of touch in the present. 'The dead man' as a result seems a more touching thing than either the words of his letters or his 'living soul'. Tennyson's displacement of the mystical flash into literal touch makes 'The dead man touched me' in fact the great, achieved revelation of this stanza—a revelation which carries the 'shock' of two bodies which have come into contact.

As in 'Morte D'Arthur' and 'To the Marquis of Dufferin and Ava', the poet cannot quite let go of the thing that must also disappear in a flash.

The collocation of touch and flash, the one a delayed reaction of the other, happens over and over again in his poetry. The Lady of Shalott comes down, like any fallen woman, at the mere flash of Sir Launcelot in a mirror. The betraying diamonds in 'Launcelot and Elaine', the mix of truth and lies in 'Balin and Balan', all flash with a light that somehow involves intimate, if illicit, touch. Guinevere's final farewell to Arthur at the end of the *Idylls of the King* returns, with the full emotional charge of that primal scene, to the same connection:

> Then she stretched out her arms and cried aloud
> 'Oh Arthur!' there her voice brake suddenly,
> Then—as a stream that spouting from a cliff
> Fails in mid air, but gathering at the base
> Re-makes itself, and flashes down the vale—
> Went on in passionate utterance

(III. 545. 602–7)

Guinevere's voice calling on Arthur takes Tennyson back to 'The Lotos-Eaters', the Valley of Cauteretz, and a poetry which holds off its own conclusion, event, purpose, in a pause, like held breath, before it 'flashes' into 'utterance' again. The extended simile of the stream separates Guinevere's longing to touch, 'she stretched out her arms', from the displaced impact of the flash which both realizes and loses the possibility of touch. The delay between them takes us back, for a moment, to the land of afternoon, the island of beauty, the valley where song returns endlessly on itself with no need to find moral or heroic purpose any more. In that aestheticist landscape of a valley, a stream, and a waterfall, Tennyson still hopes to find 'Arthur'.

'It may be we shall touch the Happy Isles, | And see the great Achilles, whom we knew' (I. 619. 63–4), the hero of 'Ulysses' declares. Here, touching land involves not only an end to heroic journeying, but also, characteristically, the other senses of touch. Touching 'the Happy Isles' is separated by one line only from Achilles, the delayed object of that verb. Tennyson always hears the sound of touching in landing, particularly when the land is an island, self-contained, removed, serene, where 'beauty, certain forms of sensuous loveliness were separated from … life'. It was Barrett Browning who once complained of Tennyson: 'He has not flesh and blood enough to be sensual … His representation of beauty … is rather the fantasma of beauty, than the thing. You can no more touch or clasp it, than beauty in a dream.'[23] In a sense she is right. Touching 'the Happy Isles' might lead to 'forms of sensuous loveliness', but it might also lead to nothing, where touching only breaks up on itself, like the sea in 'Break, break, break', which never seems to land in spite of touching land so often. In two lines of *In Memoriam* those breakers are set beside the old aestheticist landscape of Cauteretz, to suggest an object, invisibly present in both scenes, which may not be touched or clasped, however much it flashes: 'The cataract flashing from the bridge, | The breaker breaking on the beach' (II. 386. 15–16).

The criticism that Tennyson is either 'too sensual' or not sensual enough recurs throughout the nineteenth century, as if something about his poetry both rouses and thwarts the expectation of touch. The question is a formal one as much as it is thematic or emotional. 'I dread the losing hold of forms',[24] Tennyson himself once declared in relation to his poetry. The word 'hold', as Isobel Armstrong has pointed out,[25] carries a charge as strong as 'touch' in his work. 'And dream my dream, and hold it true' (II. 443. 10) is a 'hold' so pertinacious, desperate, sensuous, as to make the object not just a truth or dream, but something held for dear life. The word 'form' too, that great catchword of English aestheticism and one of its recurring ideals, pretexts, double entendres, is an object the poet dreads 'losing hold of'. 'It is not merely in art,' writes Wilde, 'that the body is the soul. In every sphere of life Form is the beginning of things.'[26] The beauty of the body etymologically haunts that word, while leaving it free to appear bodiless. Tennyson is as drawn to the physically forming potential of the word as Wilde and Pater. 'I dread the losing hold of forms' is a declaration loaded, not only with the sense of poetry's formal restraints and rules, but also with that other, human form which the poet also dreads 'losing'.

In *In Memoriam* Tennyson returns to the word 'form', as J. C. C. Mays points out,[27] with obsessive tenacity. So nature's 'hollow form with empty hands' (II. 321. 12) at the start is gradually replaced with

[23] Quoted in Robert Bernard Martin, *Tennyson: The Unquiet Heart* (Oxford: Clarendon Press, 1983), 266–7.

[24] Quoted in J. C. C. Mays, '*In Memoriam*: An Aspect of Form', *University of Toronto Quarterly*, 35(1965), 22–46, 24.

[25] Isobel Armstrong, 'The Collapse of Object and Subject: *In Memoriam*', in *Critical Essays on Alfred Lord Tennyson*, ed. Herbert F. Tucker (New York: G. K. Hall, 1993), 136–52, 148.

[26] Oscar Wilde, 'The Critic as Artist', in *Intentions* (London: Methuen, 1919), 95–217, 201.

[27] Mays, '*In Memoriam*', 23.

the form of Hallam, whose hand might fill the poet's own. Form, in *In Memoriam*, comes in many shapes and impels many kinds of action. It is something which divides, which might be worn, which is a formality of faith or custom, which is 'beauteous', 'seeming-random', 'ancient', which flows, which might be a 'first form', or an 'other form', or an 'after form'. As with so many of his key words, Tennyson rings the changes on 'form' as if, in his very language, acknowledging that words too 'flow | From form to form' (II. 443. 5–6). At the same time he admits that the dead man might only be touched and known as form. 'Come, beauteous in thine after form' (II. 409. 15), he begs, holding on to the physicality of 'form', even of the more distant 'after form', by means of an old association with beauty. Tennyson thus gives to English aestheticism a play on 'form' which indeed allows the soul to be the body, the spirit to be the letter, the flash of revelation to be the touch of the flesh. Form is one of those dream words which offers the dreamer an object he might literally '*hold* true', while knowing he might hold nothing at all.

The key lines about language as form appear, as critics have commented, in Section XCV: 'Vague words! but ah, how hard to frame | In matter-moulded forms of speech' (II. 413. 45–6). Armstrong argues that these lines justify an 'idealist'[28] reading of the poem, where language as living form triumphs over the dead meanings of words. Donald Hair, similarly, offers a Coleridgean reading, in which forms or moulds affirm language as a 'natural' or 'God-given capacity'[29] which itself transforms matter. Eric Griffiths, on the other hand, hears in it Tennyson's attention to the printed body of the text, and therefore to the body itself, 'the physique of his intellection'.[30] Both idealist and materialist interpretations find room to manoeuvre in that packed phrase: 'matter-moulded forms'. To these I would add a little extra focus on 'moulded'. This, as well as carrying idealist overtones of shaping and creating, also sets up a sympathetic resonance with 'matter'. This may be the 'matter' of speech, the purpose and sense of it, which stops this too being 'a tale of little meaning'; or it may be 'matter' itself, the material basis or body of all form. The word 'moulded' inevitably recalls earth itself, the grave of the poem's 'Dark Yew' sections: 'Thy roots are wrapt about the bones' (II.

---

[28] Armstrong, 'The Collapse of Object and Subject', 150.

[29] Donald S. Hair, *Tennyson's Language* (London: University of Toronto Press, 1991), 20.

[30] Eric Griffiths, 'Tennyson's Breath', in Tucker ed., *Critical Essays*, 28–47, 36.

319. 4). It is that very sense of mould which Pater will unearth and toy with throughout his curious story 'Duke Carl of Rosenmold', where the roots of words and trees dig down into the earthy mould or matter of the world, however many 'roses' grow from it: 'the higher informing capacity, if it exist within, will mould an unpromising matter to itself',[31] he punningly and ambiguously suggests. Tennyson himself, with his keen ear for etymology, must also have registered the materialist meaning of 'matter-moulded forms'. Language, too, is made up of physical matter, which moulds its forms, transitively, into shape and life, but also moulds, intransitively, back to earth. The materialist–idealist debate is played out in the very stuff of Tennyson's language, specifically in the curious shiftiness of his verbs. Flash, shock, form, mould, touch, all have a flickering play about them, a restless, objectless palpability, as if feeling for both the empty and full possibilities of their own forms.

I am suggesting, then, that Tennyson, consciously or unconsciously, offers the nineteenth century one of its most memorable, sensuous, aestheticist voices. It is he who pushes language almost as far as it will go into music, whose rhymes and echoes ring on the other side of sense, who uses refrains and returns like audible embodiments of the tautology of art for art's sake. This musical compulsion is not a search for metaphysical self-validation, but a feeling for form as a thing to be held as literally as possible against the threat of formlessness. The strain of 'pure aestheticism' in his work does not stop, however, with the earthly paradises of 'The Lotos-Eaters' and 'The Palace of Art'. It runs all through his writing, turning up in those islanded moments when beauty, for its own sake, becomes separated from the moral and narrative action of the poem. 'And we came to the Silent Isle that we never had touched at before', he writes as late as 1880. Touching at, or on, islands is something he has been doing all his life.

This aestheticism is not, however, just a matter of sound and sensuousness. Like Pater's, it has an ancient and powerful philosophical rationale. Brimley, in his concern to exempt *In Memoriam* from the charge of aestheticism, for instance, ends by declaring that 'Poetry and passion are nobler and wiser than stoicism or Epicureanism.' Tennyson, he proposes, abandoned his 'all serene'[32] style in the later work in recognition of that superiority. In 1885, Pater published *Marius the*

---

[31] Pater, 'Duke Carl of Rosenmold', in *Imaginary Portraits* (London: Macmillan, 1910), 119–53, 129.

[32] Brimley, 'Alfred Tennyson's Poems', 279; 261.

Epicurean, in which he gives a semi-novelistic account of the philosophy which underlies the whole aesthetic movement—a philosophy which, he writes, reinforces 'the deep original materialism or earthliness of human nature itself, bound so intimately to the sensuous world'.[33] By the 1880s Pater was riding a high tide of interest in Lucretius, mainly as a result of the perception that Lucretian atomic theory intriguingly paralleled contemporary scientific developments. Lucretius, as Frank Turner[34] points out, was only taken seriously by the Victorians in the 1870s, after the publication of Munro's great edition of *De Rerum Natura* in 1864, as well as after the first important article on 'The Atomic Theory of Lucretius' in 1868. It was in 1868 that Tennyson published his dramatic monologue 'Lucretius'. He already owned Munro's edition, along with several others, and indeed had consulted Munro on the accuracy of the poem's detail, much of which comes out of Lucretius' poem.

However, as Brimley hints, Lucretius was always deeply embedded in Tennyson's imagination. The opening of 'The Lover's Tale' is drawn from the famous opening of Book 2, on the sweetness of watching a storm at sea from a safe distance, while in 1842 Tennyson added the whole last section of 'The Lotos-Eaters', based on Lucretius' account of the serene contemplation of the Epicurean gods: 'On the hills like Gods together, careless of mankind' (I. 476. 155). The interest, as one might guess from its prominence in this poem, goes back to the years with Hallam. And indeed, Hallam's essay 'On Sympathy'[35] is full of references to Lucretius and Epicurus, while in a letter he specifically compares Tennyson's 'manner of delineation' to, among others, 'the divine passage about the sacrifice of Iphigenia in Lucretius'[36]—the passage which shows, in Munro's translation, 'So great the evils to which religion could prompt!' (3)[37] Throughout his life Tennyson included Lucretius among his favourite classical poets, and once declared himself, laughingly, a potential convert to the Roman poet's 'heart-crushing atheism'.[38] References to Lucretius in Tennyson's work abound, as Paul

[33] Pater, *Marius the Epicurean*, i. 146.

[34] Frank M. Turner, 'Lucretius Among the Victorians', *Victorian Studies*, 16(1973), 329–48, 335.

[35] Arthur Hallam, 'On Sympathy', in *The Writings of Arthur Hallam*, ed. T. H. Vail Motter (London: Oxford University Press, 1943), 133–42.

[36] *The Letters of Arthur Henry Hallam*, ed. Jack Kolb (Columbus, Ohio: Ohio State University Press, 1981), 401.

[37] Titi Lucreti Cari, *De Rerum Natura*, with a translation and notes by H. A. J. Munro, vol. 1 (Cambridge: Deighton Bell and Co, 1864), 5.

[38] Quoted in Paul Turner, *Tennyson* (London: Routledge, 1976), 122.

Turner[39] first noted and as Christopher Ricks has widely footnoted. Between Tennyson and Pater, Lucretius is the missing link. *In Memoriam*'s sense of the disintegrating atomism of nature leads, through Lucretius, to Pater's sense in the Conclusion to *The Renaissance* of the human form as 'but the concurrence, renewed from moment to moment, of forces parting sooner or later on their ways'.[40] Lucretius' account of a world from which the gods have been removed to a faraway calm, a world which is made up of nothing more than a fortuitous concourse of atoms, gives to Tennyson his 'dust of continents to be' (II. 352. 12) and to Pater his 'perpetual flight'[41] of impressions. The materialist basis of aestheticism, not in the Marxist but the Lucretian sense, could be said to start with Tennyson, who, in the words of Huxley, was 'the first poet since Lucretius who has understood the drift of science'.[42]

It is not exactly 'science' that Tennyson takes from Lucretius, but a materialist or 'matter-moulded' perspective on the world which remained with him to the end. There may be nothing more, as Tennyson's own Lucretius chants, than 'atom and void, atom and void' (II. 719. 257).[43] By the law of bodies, the soul is too thin to survive its parting from matter, and is thus lost in the air. Tennyson's own lovely rendering of '*dispersa per auras*' is 'the soul flies out and dies in the air' (II. 720. 273). Such thinness of matter also marks the nature of the gods. As he puts it:

> If all be atoms, how then should the Gods
> Being atomic not be dissoluble,
> Not follow the great law?
>
> (II. 714. 114–16)

The proof of everything that is not void, then, is touch. Everywhere in Lucretius the definition of matter, of body, *corpora*, is its tangibility. So, for instance, in Munro's translation, 'nothing but body can touch and be touched' ('*tangere enim et tangi, nisi corpus, nulla potest res*'),[44] or, later from Book 2, 'touch, touch … is feeling of the body' ('*tactus*

---

[39] Quoted for Turner, 122.

[40] Walter Pater, *The Renaissance* (London: Macmillan, 1910), 234.

[41] Ibid. 235.

[42] *Life and Letters of Thomas Henry Huxley*, ed. Leonard Huxley, 2 vols. (London: Macmillan, 1900), ii. 338.

[43] For a less positive reading of Tennyson's debt to Lucretius, see Helen Small, 'Tennyson and Late Style', *The Tennyson Research Bulletin*, 8(2005), 226–50, 230–1.

[44] Titi Lucreti Cari, 14.

enim, tactus ... corporis est sensus').[45] This leads to the logical conclusion, in Book 3, that 'when we see that none of these effects can take place without touch nor touch without body, must we not admit that the mind and the soul are of a bodily nature?' (*'corporea natura animum constare animamque?').*[46] In Book 5 he writes that, since the fine nature of the gods 'has ever eluded the touch and stroke of the hands, it must touch nothing which is tangible for us; for that cannot touch which does not admit of being touched in turn' (*'tangere enim non quit quod tangi non licet ipsum').*[47] Tennyson's Lucretius calls on the goddess Venus: 'Nay, if thou canst, O Goddess, like ourselves | Touch, and be touched' (II. 712. 80–1). The untouchableness of the Lucretian gods proves either their non-existence, or else their sheer indifference, in a realm of 'eternal calm', to storms and troubles below. They cannot 'Touch, and be touched' because they have no physical reality, no atomic structure which proves their presence or interest in human affairs.

Instead, in their 'tranquil abodes,' Munro translates, the gods 'laugh with light shed largely round' (*'et largo diffuso lumine rident').*[48] In 'Oenone' Tennyson similarly imagines how they 'Rest in a happy place and quiet seats | Above the thunder' (I. 428. 129–30). In 'Lucretius' he writes: 'Nor sound of human sorrow mounts to mar | Their sacred ever-lasting calm!' (II. 713. 109–10). In 'Morte D'Arthur', 'the island-valley of Avilion' (II. 18. 259), to which Arthur journeys after death, is, as Tennyson himself noted, the place of the Epicurean gods: 'Deep-meadowed, happy, fair with orchard-lawns' (262). Throughout his life he falls back on certain words: touch, calm, serene, happy, far away, which are never quite the innocently cheerful words they seem. Instead, they carry the darker, or lighter, connotations of Lucretius' view of a universe where everything that is not sensed and touched is dismissed to an outer space of godly irrelevance. There, they might 'laugh with light'—a laughter that sounds as empty as bright air. In Tennyson, too, the word 'happy' carries overtones of that purposeless content. The 'Happy Isles', 'the happy dead', the 'happy ... orchard-lawns', 'the happy Autumn fields', are all examples of a happiness which is nearer to Lucretius' place where the gods 'laugh with light' than to the Christian land of the Blessed. The problem that runs through Tennyson's accounts of such sunny lands is that, in Lucretius' scheme, their inhabitants are also immaterial, untouchable, thin, out of reach.

---

[45] Titi Lucreti Cari, 14. 70.   [46] Ibid. 111.   [47] Ibid. 217.
[48] Ibid. 105.

It is possible, then, to read *In Memoriam* as a poem deeply troubled, but also inspired, by that Lucretian materialism which will become the basis of Victorian aestheticism. As Pater puts it in *Marius*: 'The various pathetic traits of the beloved, suffering, perished body of Flavian, so deeply pondered, had made him a materialist.'[49] Materialism, for Pater and his contemporaries, is a philosophy based on the materiality of the body. For Tennyson too, the attempt to recover the body of Hallam, 'Sweet human hand and lips and eye' (II. 449. 6), involves him in a long, tormented drama of touch, precisely because touch is the Lucretian touchstone for being there at all. By ranging Hallam among the classical gods almost to the end of the poem, Tennyson's language goes on begging for physical communication, in defiance, but also in subtle justification, of the Lucretian universe:

> O, therefore from thy sightless range
> With gods in unconjectured bliss,
> O, from the distance of the abyss
> Of tenfold-complicated change,
>
> Descend, and touch, and enter; hear
>
> (II. 410. 9–13)

That Miltonic 'sightless' does double duty: Hallam is blind to, but also invisible to, the living. The 'distance of the abyss' is somehow too far for either side to see across. This invisible distance is then emphasized by the phrase 'unconjectured bliss', which puts 'bliss' firmly beyond conjecture, itself the most unreliable of sense perceptions. This, once again, is a Lucretian scene, with Hallam set among the unimaginable 'gods', in a place beyond sight or conjecture. The extraordinary line which then follows: 'Descend, and touch, and enter; hear', must win its force from the blocking distances of the previous lines. Across 'the distance of the abyss' comes the body of Hallam, with all its capacities, of course, for 'touch'. Interestingly, Tennyson leaves those verbs: 'Descend, and touch, and enter', intransitive, as if still casting for their object. Rather like the trees that 'Laid their dark arms about the field' (II. 412. 16), the desired object of this embrace is missing, and the verbs engage in shadow play. For 'nothing but body can touch and be touched', Lucretius insists.

As late as Section CXXVII Tennyson is describing a self-evidently Epicurean scene of storm and tumult, a scene from which the dead are safely immured:

---

[49] Pater, *Marius the Epicurean*, i. 125.

> While thou, dear spirit, happy star,
> O'erlook'st the tumult from afar,
> And smilest, knowing all is well.
>
> (II. 448. 18–20)

That smile unnervingly recalls the gods who 'laugh with light', whose happiness is an indifference to 'the tumult' rather than a concern for it, and who remain untouched by human invocations. Once again the word 'happy' evokes calmness 'from afar', from a place or condition with a sense of being *untouched* about it. Set above the storm of human and natural life, Hallam has returned to that first scene of bliss—the one which, according to Brimley, marked the 'extreme' point of Tennyson's aestheticism: the Lotos land where gods recline together, 'careless of mankind' (I. 476. 155), and 'smile in secret' (159). Whatever biographical event originated this scene, it seems that *In Memoriam* cannot get free of it. Tennyson cannot relinquish the idea of a touch which on the one hand assures Hallam a kind of afterlife among the gods, and on the other puts him at an eternal remove.

This trouble of touch is then often signalled by Tennyson's nervous, intransitive verbs. Even when they should grasp something, as in 'Laid their dark arms', they seem to cast 'about'. There is something unfinished, unsatisfied about them, a sense of touch missing its object. This is true, for instance, of the lines: 'Break, break, break, | On thy cold gray stones, O Sea!' (I. 24. 1–2). Here, the strategically placed last comma changes the meaning of 'break', from 'break on' to 'break,' which thus, visibly and aurally, curtails its arrival on the shore as well as its arrival at the real object of breaking: 'the touch of a vanished hand' (11). This is the 'break,' both of not reaching the happy isle, but also, perhaps, of breaking on it with such force that there is a breaking-up shock involved in the touch. 'Break, break, break,' Tennyson writes, as if, not being able to reach his object and touch the 'hand', he can only repeat the effort, leave the verb curbed by its comma, and save at least his intransitive heartbreak. Something similar is going on even at the very end of *In Memoriam*: 'Until we close with all we loved' (II. 452. 11), the poet writes. To 'close with' ought to mean to finish, bring to completion, to close the book. But it also means, of course, to meet, touch, embrace, whether in love, with its hint of sexual climax, or perhaps, as with an enemy or angel, in combat. Tennyson, once again, silently slips the idea of a body beside a verb which both yearns for, yet cannot quite reach it. 'Until we close with' fails to 'close' its meaning quite as quickly as it should.

The proverbially famous "'Tis better to have loved and lost' (II. 345. 15) plays a similar game of absent objects. The collocation of loving and losing suggests that something, other than just love, is the object of loving and losing. After all, the poet has not 'lost' love—he goes on loving after Hallam's death—but he has lost the loved body which is not there. Once again, the sense of a body, palpably lovable, lies somewhere in the vague reaches of those verbs. Something that is 'loved and lost' is not just love; it is also a presence, an object. Tennyson thus makes verbs work hard to find the transitive sense of an intransitive loss. Displaced, unknown, far away, the idea of an object remains obliquely connected with those Tennysonian verbs: flashing, shocking, breaking, casting, loving, losing, which seem to assert an objectless activity.

The phrase 'far, far away' was, as is well known, a favourite with Tennyson since childhood. He wrote that it 'had always a strange charm for me' (III. 197 note). The charm of sound for its own sake, that condition of music, meant that his ear showed certain addictions to the lotos-fruits of words. Towards the very end of his life he wrote a short poem, specifically for music, called 'Far—Far—Away', in which the repeated phrase mimes its own musically distancing effect. But two deleted lines also point to an old, autobiographical pain: 'Ghost, do the men that walk this planet seem' and 'Ghost, can you see us, hear us? do we seem' (III. 198 note). The self-sufficient sonority of the phrase 'far, far away' is also, these lines tell, a call to be heard by one who may always be too far to hear. 'He is not here; but far away' (II. 326. 9), Tennyson writes in *In Memoriam*. There the phrase doubles back, to qualify, not the place where Hallam might be, but the too near 'noise of life' (l. 10) which shuts him out. At some point in Tennyson's life the romantic distance of the past became confused with the distance of the future, as ghosts and gods came to be ranged on the other side of that 'far away'. For as Lucretius puts it, in a passage which Tennyson marked heavily in his own copy, the 'gods must … enjoy immortality together with supreme repose, far removed and withdrawn from our concerns' (*'semota ab nostris rebus seiunctaque longe'*).[50] The Latin *'semota'*, 'far removed', gives Tennyson a phrase for a distance both unmeasurable and beyond 'our concerns'.

At the start of *In Memoriam*, for instance, the poet uses this phrase in a passage which asks to find, like a profitable reward, 'The far-off interest of tears' (II. 318. 8). Here 'interest' also punningly expresses

[50] Titi Lucreti Cari, 80.

the fear that such 'tears' may not be interesting any more to the 'far-off' dead, who may, after all, be smiling about something else. If the gods are 'far removed and withdrawn from our concerns', they will not answer tears. The same contradiction emerges in Section LXXXII. At first the old profit motive, sprung from a grave imagery of roots and flowers, seems to offer hope:

> Nor blame I Death, because he bare
> The use of virtue out of earth:
> I know transplanted human worth
> Will bloom to profit, otherwise.

> (II. 394. 9–12)

However, in the next stanza that hope fails, and the argument from 'use' and 'profit' collapses before the old clamour to be heard:

> For this alone on Death I wreak
> The wrath that garners in my heart;
> He put our lives so far apart
> We cannot hear each other speak.

> (II. 394. 13–16)

Once again the Lucretian perspective, 'so far apart', opens up an incommunicable distance—a distance to make all speech simply unprofitable and useless; it may be, to make all speech 'a lamentation and an ancient tale of wrong, | Like a tale of little meaning though the words are strong' (I. 476. 163–4). The Epicurean gods or sailors in 'The Lotos-Eaters' are deaf to ancient wrongs, having gone too 'far' across the sea to hear them. ' "Our island home | Is far beyond the wave" ', they sing, that 'far' going in both directions, so there is no knowing which 'island' is 'home'. Without the use and profit of the Christian resurrection, speaking to the dead might indeed be a useless lamentation, a 'pure aestheticism' perhaps. Tennyson's great poem wrestles, not only with doubt and faith, grief and consolation, body and soul, but also with a classical perspective which, in its blithe indifference to gods and ghosts, both too thin to touch, also acknowledges that void, that far-awayness, which might turn speech back on itself, into a useless if beautiful art for art's sake. 'Ghost, can you see us, hear us?'

Interestingly, the final stanza of *In Memoriam*, which seems to resolve the poem into a prayer of hope, catches, for one last moment, on that old perspective. The lines, as Ricks points out, lovingly echo one of Hallam's own poems: 'The Love | Toward which all being solemnly doth move' (II. 458 note). This, in its turn, echoes the last line of

Dante's Paradiso: 'The Love that moves the sun and the other stars'. But Tennyson's version differs slightly from both:

> That God, which ever lives and loves,
> One God, one law, one element,
> And one far-off divine event,
> To which the whole creation moves.

(II. 459. 141−4)

Dante, of course, puts love at the centre of his universe, and makes it the moving lever of the whole system. Hallam still centres 'Love', but the movement is creation's towards it. Tennyson adds two new ingredients to divine love: 'one law, one element', with their hint of scientific, elemental matter rather than spiritual purpose. He then adds the tiny labour and distance of his own favourite phrase: 'far-off'. After a poem which has so turned on the calm and happy indifference of things 'far-off', it is strangely disconcerting to find, at the end, that the poet is still, covertly, asking, 'how far' the point 'To which the whole creation moves'?

To end the poem, thus, with another intransitive verb, leaves its object still unreached, untouched. The verb 'moves' both closes and refuses to close. Its 'event' is no nearer, after all, but still 'far-off'. So Tennyson ends, not with God's or Hallam's love reached, but with the long effort to move towards it, possibly even to move it at all, through the thing he has so touchingly celebrated in all its forms: 'the whole creation'.

The strong sunlight, the wind from the sea,
all the conditions of its existence,
may have flaked off the paint ...

Elizabeth Bishop

Every aesthetic ... comes down to this question: Under what
conditions does the work, the text, find a *taker?*

Roland Barthes

4

Aesthetic Conditions: Pater's Re-forming Style

The notion of the aesthetic has, by and large, been defined as the product of a historical moment: the mid-eighteenth century. It is, writes Eagleton, 'a bourgeois concept in the most literal historical sense, hatched and nurtured in the Enlightenment'.[1] Specifically, the concept was first 'hatched', at least in its modern sense, by Baumgarten in 1750. Although Kant rejected Baumgarten's definition, of the aesthetic as 'the science of sensitive knowing'[2] or the critique of artistic taste, this sense of the term survived and was introduced into England in the early 1830s. In 1832 an article in the *Philological Museum* noted that 'some writers used "aesthetic" to designate the principles of beauty and ugliness upon which taste depends.'[3] By the late 1850s this new sense of the term was widely established. Thus, at about the same time as the first recorded use of 'aestheticism' in Brimley's 1855 review of

---

[1] Terry Eagleton, *The Ideology of the Aesthetic* (Oxford: Blackwell, 1990), 8.
[2] Quoted in Nicholas Davey, 'Alexander (Gottlieb) Baumgarten', in *A Companion to Aesthetics*, ed. David E. Cooper (Oxford: Blackwell, 1992), 40–2, 40.
[3] Quoted in T. J. Diffey, 'A Note on Some Meanings of the Term "Aesthetic"', *British Journal of Aesthetics*, 35(1995), 61–6, 63.

Tennyson,[4] the philosophical association of '*the* aesthetic' with art and its appreciation was also becoming current. This fruitful, if sometimes over-rich, concoction of literary and philosophical ideas only needed the extra ingredient of 'art for art's sake' to produce the heady mix of Victorian aestheticism proper.

The connection between Baumgarten's definition of 'the aesthetic' and the idea of the art object as isolated from use is not specifically dated by those theorists who nonetheless insist on its founding importance. Thus Eagleton, with a twist of the old Paterian phrase 'for nothing', asserts: 'Once artefacts become commodities in the market place, they exist for nothing and nobody in particular, and can consequently be rationalized, ideologically speaking, as existing entirely and gloriously for themselves.'[5] Gadamer, similarly, invokes a founding historical moment, though more through wishful grammar than from a sense of specific dates. 'As soon as ... the work of art began to stand on its own,' he writes, 'divorced from its original context of life, only then did art become simply "art" in the "museum without walls" of Malraux.'[6] The question of when, precisely, this divorce from life started is less important than the alienating dualism which it initiates.

Certainly, from Kant to Gadamer, the philosophical tradition of 'the aesthetic' raises the prospect, even if deprecated, of a continuing separation between art and life, art and history. As Peter de Bolla puts it, Kant's 'so-called disinterested thesis ... has been taken to imply that aesthetic judgments are absolutely distinct from ethical, social, or political considerations'. This line of argument, which is not, de Bolla insists, a true account of Kant's own position, 'leads to the notion that the artwork is beyond or outside the realm of politics or ethics'.[7] The supposed divorce between disinterested art and interested politics is, others claim, a product of the very bourgeois ideology which created the notion of 'the aesthetic' in the first place. Adorno's subtle and troubled account of the social relations of the art work in *Aesthetic Theory* remains caught in the well-worn dualisms it sets out. Thus he writes: 'beauty

[4] George Brimley, 'Alfred Tennyson's Poems', in *Cambridge Essays* (Cambridge: Cambridge Univ. Press, 1855), 226–81, 237.

[5] Eagleton, *The Ideology of the Aesthetic*, 9.

[6] Hans-Georg Gadamer, *The Relevance of the Beautiful and Other Essays* (Cambridge: Cambridge University Press, 1986), 19.

[7] Peter de Bolla, 'The Discomfort of Strangeness and Beauty: Art, Politics, and Aesthetics', in *Politics and Aesthetics in the Arts*, ed. Salim Kemal and Ivan Gaskell (Cambridge: Cambridge University Press, 2000), 204–20, 211.

establishes a sphere of untouchability; works become beautiful by the force of their opposition to what simply exists.'[8] At the same time the opposite is true. As he writes later on: 'Without historical remembrance there would be no beauty.'[9] Beauty is implicated in history and the aesthetic in the ideological, even if at a distance, oppositionally or reminiscently. As Isobel Armstrong glosses: 'Adorno uses the paratactic method of exposition, juxtaposing contradictory ideas without telling us they are contradictory.'[10] The contradiction, however, seems to belong to the very subject at issue: 'the aesthetic' knows itself by what it is not. It is not life, history, ideology, production, but something that opposes them. The dualisms by which 'the aesthetic' is described, though often meant to undermine its idealized status, in fact also reassert it. It thus remains, even if negatively, an object of philosophical or theoretical attention. Even Eagleton's 'ideology of the aesthetic' does not entirely run the aesthetic out into ideology, but keeps it linguistically in play, in a game of opposites which never seems to end. Thus the abstract noun holds its own, for at least as long as the thrill of desecrating its imaginary sacredness remains strong.

Curiously, however, neither Eagleton's *Ideology of the Aesthetic* (1990), nor Armstrong's *The Radical Aesthetic* (2000),[11] nor Joughin and Malpas' *The New Aestheticism* (2003),[12] mention the name which might be regarded as one of the aesthetic's major theorists: Walter Pater. This may be, in part, a sign of the extent to which aesthetics and aestheticism have parted company since the 1850s, leaving aestheticism, at least the older one, stranded without evident succession in a by-way of literary history. Yet Pater's is the voice which, more than any other, gives to later generations of writers an account of art which then becomes a founding style or music. Evidently there is something about his work which resists the conceptual dualisms underpinning philosophical aesthetics. It is interesting, for instance, that he himself almost never invokes 'the aesthetic' as an abstract noun. Less a theorist than a practitioner of his theory, aesthetic qualities are, for him, attributive, adjectival,

    [8] Theodor W. Adorno, *Aesthetic Theory*, ed. Gretel Adorno and Rolf Tiedemann, trans. Robert Hullot-Kentnor (London: Athlone Press, 1997), 51.
    [9] Ibid. 65.
    [10] Isobel Armstrong, 'And Beauty? A Dialogue: Debating Adorno's *Aesthetic Theory*', *Textual Practice*, 12 (1998), 269–89, 274.
    [11] Isobel Armstrong, *The Radical Aesthetic* (Oxford: Blackwell, 2000).
    [12] John H. Joughin and Simon Malpas, eds., *The New Aestheticism* (Manchester: Manchester University Press, 2003).

a matter of aesthetic poetry, aesthetic criticism, aesthetic beauty. The word, as a result, suggests something which transfuses readily into other things. Its outlines are more permeable than the abstract concept of 'the aesthetic', which can be set up to be knocked down, but somehow keeps its consistency like any other bogey. It is a comment on Pater's very understanding of aesthetics generally that he avoids both the metaphysical–philosophical reification of 'the aesthetic' and the potential coterie badge of 'aestheticism'. Although, as Billie Inman has pointed out, 'no single work had a more profound influence than Hegel's *Ästhetik*'[13] on Pater's thinking, he himself rarely theorized his subject as a noun. This difference may leave him in a backwater as far as the philosophical tradition is concerned, but it is a backwater which then feeds most of the mainstreams of literary writing in the twentieth century.

To write about Pater's aesthetics, then, is in some ways to have a problem of subject matter. He is not a theorist with a subject to be honed and defined. Moreover, since he does not deal in the nominal form of 'the aesthetic', it is sometimes not clear what he is writing *about*, though his style goes round about enough. This absence of definable matter may be the very reason why he is so influential a literary voice. The aesthetic, for him, is not a subject on which to discourse; it is of the nature of literary discourse itself. It is something that remains at work, and at play, in his style. It is an effect of writing, an elusive, ghostly effect perhaps, rather than an object of contention. Carolyn Williams, in her book on Pater's *Aesthetic Historicism*, points precisely to the consequences of this for the reader, when she suggests that the assumptions in his work must be approached 'not as ideas or simple content, but as forms, as habits of organization, as relations through which figures are implicated with one another to compose narratives'.[14] Form, a word Pater loves, helps shift 'content' to 'narratives'. It distracts from the search for a subject and emphasizes, instead, the passage of meaning, the sense of a style. Such a style, in the words of Leon Chai, is marked by 'a consciousness of form within the movement of time'.[15]

[13] Billie Andrew Inman, *Walter Pater's Reading: A Bibliography of His Library Borrowings and Literary References, 1858–1873* (New York and London: Garland Publishing, 1981), 49.

[14] Carolyn Williams, *Transfigured World: Walter Pater's Aesthetic Historicism* (Ithaca and London: Cornell University Press, 1989), 7.

[15] Leon Chai, *Aestheticism: The Religion of Art in Post-Romantic Literature* (New York: Columbia University Press, 1990), 87.

Time, historical time as well as clock time, runs through form, making it, as in so many previous formulations, an idea on the move. Whether in Williams's 'relations' or Chai's 'movement', form is a way of thinking in time, not outside it. The very fluidity of Pater's prose, its wandering openness to suggestion and affect, its provisional extendedness, ensure that ideas and concepts rarely harden against the flow. Instead, it is the flow itself which defines, for him, the nature of 'the aesthetic'.

This sense of flow and passage is the key to Pater. Temporality and a temporizing instinct make his writing seem almost neurotically evasive. He undermines statements and assertions by subjecting them to the whoozy sway of his sentences and the punning etymologies of his words. To write about Pater is, in the end, to write about style, about the sinuous musicality of his sentences, which might make sense locally in passing, but rarely add up to a creed. His work may have provided generations of writers with a manifesto for art, but that manifesto remains lodged in the sound, the form, sometimes the merely purple memorability of his prose. He is, above all, a writer of conditions, of principles which are temporary and subject to revision. The fact that the word 'conditions' is one of his favourites signals the extent of his caution. Both founding principles and provisional characteristics, conditions qualify everything he writes. They represent the way that the foundational, in his work, becomes relative, meaning becomes transient, and hard matter becomes provisional form. By subjecting all his statements to the hesitations and prevarications of his exquisitely timed and time-conscious style, he makes conditionality itself the basis of his aesthetic creed.

The origin of this creed lies in the classics. In March 1873, soon after the publication of the first edition of *Studies in the History of the Renaissance*, Pater received a letter from his fellow colleague, the theologian John Wordsworth, which summarizes a sense of dismay:

> But after a perusal of the book I cannot disguise from myself that the concluding pages adequately sum up the philosophy of the whole; and that that philosophy is an assertion, that no fixed principles either of religion or morality can be regarded as certain, that the only thing worth living for is momentary enjoyment and that probably or certainly the soul dissolves at death into elements which are destined never to reunite.[16]

Art for the moment's sake is only, the writer points out, a reformulation of the Epicurean philosophy of 'momentary enjoyment'. That 'the soul

---

[16] Lawrence Evans, ed., *Letters of Walter Pater* (Oxford: Clarendon Press, 1970), 20.

dissolves at death' is not something Pater explicitly states in the Conclusion, but its audible echo of Lucretius' assertion that the soul is dispersed in the air, *'dispersa per auras'*, shows that John Wordsworth recognized the main classical influence on Pater's thinking. The 'philosophy' which the Conclusion advocates, while naming no names, is Lucretian materialism: that without the touch of the senses, there can be no authority for the immortality of the soul. 'This elegant materialism',[17] Margaret Oliphaunt dubbed it in a hostile review later that year. Just at the time when Lucretian atomic theory was very much in the air, in the 1860s and 1870s, Pater's Conclusion makes a connection which will run through his writing. Art for art's sake, or, in his version, for the *moment's* sake, asserts a philosophical world view which draws on the ancients to assert a strikingly modern position. Although the epigraph to the Conclusion is from Heraclitus, the moving spirit behind Pater's lyrical description of 'physical life' as a matter of far-flung 'elements' briefly brought together, of a 'concurrence, renewed from moment to moment, of forces parting sooner or later on their ways',[18] is Lucretius. Much more than Hegel, it is he who gives Pater, as he does Tennyson, the rationale for an aesthetic of flux and disintegration without metaphysical or religious consolations. Classical atomic theory offers Pater the basis of an Epicurean world view characterized by the meeting and dispersal of the purely physical 'forces' of matter.

The Conclusion is one long hymn to matter, which slips human beings into its story only as small items among material forces. Like Lucretius, Pater then resorts to the one temporary solution to this atomic flux, which is, not to abstract from it unseen spirits or gods, but to try to touch the material world itself: 'gathering all we are into one desperate effort to see and touch'.[19] The intransitive mode of 'see and touch' betrays the 'effort', but hides the object. In his understated way, and in the space of a few pages, Pater brings a whole philosophical and classical argument to bear on art for art's sake. For if, as he concludes, the only purpose of art is to give 'the highest quality to your moments as they pass, and simply for those moments' sake',[20] this is also because nothing exists beyond the moment. The gods are invisible and untouchable, and all that remains is the moment. 'This elegant materialism', which

[17] Quoted in Linda Dowling, 'Walter Pater and Archaeology: The Reconciliation with Earth', *Victorian Studies*, 31(1988), 209–31, 209.

[18] Walter Pater, *The Renaissance* (London: Macmillan, 1910), 233–4.

[19] Ibid. 237.   [20] Ibid. 239.

dissolves into dispersing particles not only the soul but all the stuff of which life is composed, suggests a world in which the best that can be hoped for is, briefly, 'to see and touch'.

Pater, then, brings to the catchphrase of art for art's sake a profoundly materialist–scientific perspective. He undermines, long before twentieth-century theory does, the timeless transcendence supposed to inhere in the art object. Far from being in a timeless preserve, art belongs precisely to 'the moment', and the moment snatched, by passionate attention, from universal flux and disintegration. Such a moment is as likely to be found in the 'work of the artist's hands' as in 'the face of one's friend'.[21] It slips readily from art object to human object, from creation to love, binding them both into the same universe of matter and the rule of time. Pater's 'historicism',[22] as Peter Dale summarizes, is thus deep-set in his aestheticist thinking. The whole of the Conclusion is a celebration of art, not as a work *of* art, but as a work of perception, which rescues, for nothing but its own enjoyment, the moment as it passes. More important than the object, for Pater, is the time that makes it passingly precious. He offers a variation on 'art for art' which, dwelling less on the sense of artistic permanence in it, asks instead: what remains from history and time? The answer seems to be 'the moment' only, which is the one certain uncertainty on which the Conclusion comes to rest. Art is for 'your moments as they pass, and simply for those moments' sake'.[23]

Certainly, Pater's habit of recruiting writers to the aestheticist cause can be cavalierly unhistorical. Plato, he declares, 'anticipates the modern notion that art as such has no end but its own perfection, — "art for art's sake" '.[24] The poems of William Morris, similarly, offer a pretext for elaborating a kind of poetry which, not necessarily having much to do with Morris, shows 'artistic beauty of form to be an end in itself'.[25] That aesthetic ritornello, shorting the argument about what art is *for* into its being for *itself*, allows Pater to round up almost any congenial writer into that bracket. Meanwhile 'form' in Pater, though recalling the Platonic essential Forms, is far from fixed, either as an eternal verity or as a timeless art form. In fact he is not really interested in the

---

[21] Pater, *The Renaissance*, 237.
[22] Peter Allan Dale, *The Victorian Critic and the Idea of History: Carlyle, Arnold, Pater* (Cambridge, Mass.: Harvard University Press, 1977), 171 ff.
[23] Pater, *The Renaissance*, 239.
[24] Pater, *Plato and Platonism* (London: Macmillan, 1910), 268.
[25] Pater, 'Poems by William Morris', *Westminster Review*, 34(1868), 300–12, 309.

form of art *objects* at all, and there are relatively few of them in his writing. Instead, form, even 'artistic beauty of form', is conditional on the perceiver, and therefore on the moment of perception caught in the passing flux of time. Like his contemporaries, Pater loves the way that 'form' is itself a conditional word that can touch on abstractions, like 'beauty', as well as on beloved bodies. At one point in the Conclusion, it is greeted specifically as the latter. 'Every moment some form grows perfect in hand or face', [26] he writes. For Pater, as for Gautier (whose *Maupin* he certainly owned and read, though reticent about the fact),[27] 'form' easily interchanges artistic and physical beauty. Here, the syntax typically lets form hold off, but only just, from the 'hand or face' it grows '*in*'. It is a curious phrase. Perception, which is the etymological origin of the word 'aesthetic', keeps 'form' touching on the matter of the body, while not being fully identified with it. That 'form grows perfect' is a strange extrapolation, a kind of halo almost, from the object in question. It also, typically, takes time: 'Every moment'. This devious sentence ensures that 'form' mediates between desirer and desired, perceiver and perceived, but the mediation, the sense of movement to and from, is also of the essence of the argument. Form, writes Barthes, 'is what is *between* the thing and its name, form is what delays the name'.[28] Certainly, in Pater's sentence, form is an extra to the sense, a delaying tactic which lets us hear how long 'Every moment' might be. It is not quite a 'hand or face', though it is also, evidently, nothing else.

While the word provides Pater with an aestheticist banner, a way of turning life into art, it may be that it also owes something to recent, scientific writings, specifically evolutionary theory and wave theory. In *The Origin of Species* (1859) Darwin invokes the word 'form' on almost every page. It is that which survives and evolves, but is not necessarily definable as species or genus. Thus forms may be 'improved', 'ancestral', 'extreme', 'perfect', 'doubtful',[29] to take just a few early examples. The word offers him a way of explaining those physical features which suffer and survive evolutionary time. The form is an extrapolation from the particular, but not yet a general category. Darwin ends the whole work by repeating this word which helps bring together, before the ending

[26] Pater, *The Renaissance*, 236.　　　[27] See Evans, *Letters of Walter Pater*, 23 n. 3.
[28] Roland Barthes, *The Responsibility of Forms: Critical Essays on Music, Art, and Representation*, trans. Richard Howard (Oxford: Blackwell, 1986; first pub. 1982), 234.
[29] Charles Darwin, *The Origin of Species*, ed. Gillian Beer (Oxford: Oxford University Press, 1996), 6, 14, 18, 27, 44.

asserts the rights of his evolutionary theory, both religious and scientific perspectives:

There is grandeur in this view of life, with its several powers, having been originally breathed by the Creator into a few forms or into one; and that, whilst this planet has gone cycling on according to the fixed law of gravity, from so simple a beginning endless forms most beautiful and most wonderful have been, and are being, evolved.[30]

The evolutionary potential of 'forms', which have gone on changing in the time since 'the Creator' first gave them life, is thus tactfully emphasized. With or without the Creator, however, form is a time-bound word. John Tyndall's accounts of light and wave theory, which Pater also knew,[31] may have encouraged his own emphasis on the temporary properties of form. In *Six Lectures on Light* (1873), for instance, Tyndall explains wave motion in terms of a form crossing and surviving its material substance: 'The propagation of a wave is the propagation of a *form*, and not the transference of the substance which constitutes the wave.'[32] The physics of form, in both Darwin and Tyndall, may have encouraged that materialist perspective in Pater which already found congenial matter in Lucretius.

When, for instance, he writes in the Conclusion that 'This at least of flamelike our life has, that it is but the concurrence, renewed from moment to moment, of forces parting sooner or later on their ways', he may be echoing, not only Lucretius' concourse of atoms, but also contemporary scientific accounts of, as he puts it, 'light and sound—processes which science reduces to simpler and more elementary forces'. Certainly, his image of the 'flamelike' represents not just a moment of isolated individual consciousness, but belongs in a larger picture of elements composing the matter of the world as it wastes and renews itself perpetually. 'Like the elements of which we are composed, the action of these forces extends beyond us: it rusts iron and ripens corn',[33] he writes. So Pater, quietly and poetically, puts the human in the same temporal category as 'iron' and 'corn'. Elementally, there is no difference. The hedonism of his Conclusion is thus yoked to a scientific perspective, both classical and modern, which reduces all life to the same 'elements', the same basic matter of

---

[30] Darwin, *The Origin of Species*, 396.
[31] Inman, *Walter Pater's Reading*, 104–5.
[32] John Tyndall, *Six Lectures on Light* (London: Longmans, Green & Co., 1873), 53.
[33] Pater, *The Renaissance*, 234.

the world, out of which forms merely grow and die. As this passage makes clear, however, it is as a writer rather than a theorist that Pater survives. Whatever scientific perspectives underpin his aestheticism, it emerges less as a worked-out theory than as a working language. Form, that wonderfully capacious word, which crosses so many disciplinary boundaries, also carries with it a sense of the alternatives: of those objects which form delays or recalls. In particular Pater repeats and enacts the aestheticist sense of form as opposed to content. There is in his work, as Williams proposes, a 'crisis...in the notion of "content," which is no longer something "held" in the mind but something that passes through it'.[34] The container-model of form and content, mind and object, does not work for Pater because it leaves out the movement of time, the constantly altering relativity of every moment.

Pater's aestheticism, then, sneaks into the sanctuary of 'art for art' not only the condition of matter, in the scientific sense, but also the conditionalness of 'the moment'. It is difficult to extract theoretical propositions from the narcotic sway of his prose because propositions themselves are always conditional on a process of historical, and stylistic, temporizing. Nevertheless, for instance, the famous passage about music in 'The School of Giorgione', which is often taken out of context as an unequivocal absolute, in fact depends for its meaning on the subsequent play on form and matter which it generates:

All art constantly aspires towards the condition of music. For while in all other kinds of art it is possible to distinguish the matter from the form, and the understanding can always make this distinction, yet it is the constant effort of art to obliterate it. That the mere matter of a poem, for instance, its subject, namely, its given incidents or situation ... should be nothing without the form, the spirit, of the handling, that this form, this mode of handling, should become an end in itself, should penetrate every part of the matter: this is what all art constantly strives after, and achieves in different degrees.[35]

To quote only the opening sentence is to miss the way it is quickly qualified. Not only is '*the condition of music*' an object of constant aspiration merely—the very condition of the proposition being aspirational *movement*—but the rest of the passage then enacts the struggle it involves. Unlike Wilde, whose epigrams flagwave a proposition achieved—the artist 'gains his inspiration from form, and from form purely', for

instance, or 'Form is everything. It is the secret of life'[36]—Pater sets
form and matter in an extended, syntactically wrestling combat which
is not resolved into a conclusion. Meanwhile, he also cunningly decon-
structs the spirit–body binary that traditionally supports the dualism of
form and matter. Form is, indeed, 'the spirit' here, but only momen-
tarily. A rhetorically placed comma lets 'the spirit,' avoid its corollary
by a hair's breadth. The 'spirit, of the handling' cunningly allows 'handling' to sound like an afterthought; but it also ensures that the 'spirit'
definitely has a hand in its management of matter.

Hands in Pater are found everywhere. Here, as so often, 'handling'
brings a surprise touch to an abstract argument. It hints at a sexual movement at work in the prose, as those implied hands might 'penetrate every
part of the matter'. Pater is adept at such grammatical undercurrents of
desire. But even without explicit decoding, the word 'handling' ensures
that form itself becomes as much matter as matter. The double, or
quadruple, meaning of 'matter', as material, fact, content, and import,
is stolen by that 'handling' hand, which reclaims the physical authority
from matter and gives it to form. Pater may be echoing here, as he does
in *Plato and Platonism*,[37] Schiller's formulation of the same dualism in
The Aesthetic Education of Man. Schiller writes, in a translation perhaps
closer and more congenial to Pater's own:

In a truly beautiful work of art the content should do nothing, the form
everything ... However sublime and comprehensive it may be, the content
always has a restrictive action upon the spirit, and only from the form is true
aesthetic freedom to be expected. Therefore, the real artistic secret of the master
consists in his *annihilating the material by means of the form.*[38]

Schiller's point is simple: a triumph of form over content, spirit over
matter. The religious hierarchy of soul and body remains firmly in
place, even if transposed to the realm of the aesthetic. The spirit gains its
freedom from matter by *'annihilating'* it and living on, alone. In Pater,
the metaphor is dialectical rather than hierarchic, sexual rather than
religious: 'matter' does not perish, but yields itself to the penetrating
hand of 'form'. As usual, he wants it both ways: 'this form, this mode
of handling, should become an end in itself; should penetrate every part

[36] Oscar Wilde, 'The Critic as Artist', in *Intentions* (London: Methuen, 1919; first
pub. 1891), 95–217, 201.

[37] Pater, *Plato and Platonism*, 8.

[38] Friedrich Schiller, *On the Aesthetic Education of Man, in a Series of Letters*, trans.
Reginald Snell (London: Routledge & Kegan Paul, 1954), 106.

of the matter.' Crudely, form handles only 'itself'; but it also wants to enjoy 'every part of the matter'. Pater's aesthetic of form is deeply reluctant to let go of the matter of the body. For form too has its hands, and those go roving beyond its own pleasure to handle something more tangible and substantial. Pater's sense of the pun in 'matter' resources his own profound materialism, as well as his nervous, yearning wish for a body somewhere, which form will not annihilate, but restlessly seeks.

This crucial passage may be muddled philosophy, but it is suggestive writing. Wary of the religious underpinnings of Idealist philosophy, Pater opts, instead, for a peculiarly tortuous, contradictory rhetoric, which ensures that 'matter', the presence of physical reality, remains in play. Meanwhile, the whole passage points to the fact that *the condition of music*, pure, singular, immaterial, is never reached. The other arts, in particular poetry, are subject to rather different conditions.

It is a sense of conditions, meaning context, cause, or foundation, but also manner, quality, or character, which governs many of Pater's crucial statements. For instance, in the 'William Morris' review, he writes that:

Here, under this strange complex of conditions, as in some medicated air, exotic flowers of sentiment expand, among people of a remote and unaccustomed beauty, somnambulistic, frail, androgynous, the light almost shining through them.[39]

Here, he extracts from Morris's poetry a scene of lotos-loving torpor. Those 'exotic flowers of sentiment', which are the main subject of the sentence, hover precariously between fact and rhetoric, between flowers and *fleurs du mal*. They set the scene for a description of 'the clear crystal nature' which, from the paper on 'Diaphaneitè' onwards, allows a transfusion of inner and outer, soul and body. Here, Pater insists on a 'beauty' so diaphanous that it can diffuse and invite penetration at the same time. These thin-skinned androgynes are 'almost' transparencies—as if, somewhere between air and angels, their edges contradictorily receive and rebuff the idea of touch. Pater, however, insists on a restriction, almost a safeguard: 'under this strange complex of conditions'. The beautiful dream-people of Morris's poetry, sleepwalking in a mist of ambiguous sexuality, only exist under certain 'conditions'. Not on condition, but 'under' conditions, as if conditions themselves weighed heavily on the mind. What might have remained a merely descriptive account of Morris's poetry, however far-fetched,

---

[39] Pater, 'Poems by William Morris', 302.

becomes an account of some imagined historical moment. That 'strange complex of conditions' is mysteriously, suggestively extrinsic to the poetry. It hints at external forces: weather, dates, places, on which intrinsic 'beauty' itself might be dependent.

'Forms of intellectual and spiritual culture sometimes exercise their subtlest and most artful charm when life is already passing from them',[40] Pater begins his essay on 'Coleridge'. His sense of form, artistic or intellectual, is indeed peculiarly complex and elegiac. Form is not some commanding, spiritual authority, but part of a dialectic or process. Here, losing life is kept visibly, or audibly, in play: 'when life is already passing from them'. Since the very condition of life, Pater constantly reminds us, is to be 'passing', this 'when' is always already now, in a continuous 'passing' present signalled by the participle. It turns out, as the essay develops, that this 'passing' is of the very nature of modernity. In defining that modernity, Pater circles obsessively round the word 'conditions', as if it might contain the clue to this endlessly present, yet culturally backdatable, moment. 'To the modern spirit nothing is, or can be rightly known, except relatively and under conditions',[41] he declares. This is Pater the agnostic speaking out. The relative spirit of the modern world embraces 'conditions' as an insurance against absolutism. To be 'under conditions', like the people in Morris's poetry, is to accept that there are no absolute truths, only the relativity of the passing moment. A few sentences later Pater worries at those conditions again, as if he had not quite finished with their possibilities:

Man's physical organism is played upon not only by the physical conditions about it, but by remote laws of inheritance, the vibration of long-past acts reaching him in the midst of the new order of things in which he lives. When we have estimated these conditions he is still not yet simple and isolated; for the mind of the race, the character of the age, sway him this way or that through the medium of language and current ideas. ... It is the truth of these relations that experience gives us, not the truth of eternal outlines ascertained once for all, but a world of fine gradations and subtly linked conditions.[42]

That first simple condition of the 'physical organism', a kind of deterministic baseline, is soon overrun by the vast, plural influences of race, the age, language, and ideas. These, too, are all conditions on which the nature of the self depends. As a result, that self loses its clear outline,

[40] Walter Pater, 'Coleridge', in *Appreciations, With an Essay on Style* (London: Macmillan, 1910), 65–104, 65.
[41] Ibid. 66.   [42] Ibid. 67–8.

its essential core, and lets in a rain of external social forces. Self is indeed constructed of language and ideas, physical and ideological inheritances. But 'constructed' is not quite the right verb for Pater's fluid, atomistic prose, which attempts, in the very writing, to atomize structures, to propose and enact a Lucretian fluidity by which the boundaries between spirit and matter, self and race, are broken down.

Not even 'conditions', then, survive this intellectual and stylistic breakdown. Even those are subject to 'relations' and 'fine gradations', thus challenging all 'eternal outlines', whether self, truth, or, covertly of course, God. By the end of the essay Pater's advocacy of the 'relative spirit' depends on recognizing 'fugitive conditions'[43] as the basis of knowledge. Far from being reliable bases or substructures, 'conditions' have joined the atomistic flow of matter. They too express a world that is 'passing', a world conditioned by the physics of light waves or atomic particles. Pater's is an aestheticism which builds its theories, not in an empty museum space removed from historical process, but on the shifting, moment-by-moment conditions of that process.

He might, then, be called a modernist before his time. He is also an aesthete whose sense of the aesthetic cannot ever shake off history. History remains entrammelled with 'conditions', not as explanatory foundations of the aesthetic, but rather as 'fugitive', 'complex', constantly altering pressures on it. The most influential passage in Pater, for example, the Mona Lisa section in *The Renaissance*, is more about time than it is about a picture in an art gallery. Pater's bizarre reading of da Vinci's portrait, far from setting it apart in a museum space of untouchable preciousness, in fact takes the painting out of the gallery and loads it with unlikely contextual references: Helen, Leda, St. Anne, 'the return of the Pagan world, the sins of the Borgias'.[44] What passes through the picture is a movie of history and myth, even if reduced to fairly random scenes. Pater is less concerned with the painting itself than with the ways in which it might evoke a panorama of passing time, with creeds, moralities, and myths caught up in an egalitarian flux. 'Without historical remembrance there would be no beauty', writes Adorno. It is 'historical remembrance' which the Mona Lisa elicits, to the extent that it is riddled, almost defaced, by other stories and histories from the past. This is an aestheticism, not in conflict with extrinsic conditions outside the picture frame, but deeply confused with them. The way that Pater reads the Mona Lisa almost unframes it altogether, marking no division

---

[43] Ibid. 103.   [44] Pater, *The Renaissance*, 125.

between the art object and the swimmingly impressionistic memories which it inspires. 'Who, again, cares whether Mr. Pater has put into the portrait of Monna Lisa something that Lionardo never dreamed of?'[45] Wilde once asked. What Pater has put into it is his own sense of the moment, of the historical and physiological processes which undermine absolutes, which secularize and relativize creeds, and reduce even the most timeless of artworks to the conditional interpretations of time.

Thus time, and time passing, give to Pater's aestheticism its idiosyncratic, if imprecise, originality. In *Plato and Platonism* he defends at one point what he calls 'the historic method' of criticism. Though published twenty years after *The Renaissance*, it is interesting that he is still, here, harping on conditions. The historic method, he explains, looks 'as far as possible in the group of conditions, intellectual, social, material, amid which [a work] was actually produced'.[46] Pater, the aesthete, sounds for a moment like Marx, searching for the 'intellectual, social, material' context of a work, the means of its production. The word 'conditions' occurs three times in the same paragraph, as if he were wrestling with a difficult but insistent concept: 'in every age there is a peculiar *ensemble* of conditions which determines a common character in every product of that age',[47] he writes. Such conditions, though they are a common determinant of an age, are not fixed but changing, however. They are, he continues, aspects of 'the never-resting "secular process" '.[48] This is an interesting phrase, in which the older sense of 'secular', meaning of the centuries or centuries-old, jostles with its very recent, contemporary meaning of 'secularist'. This second meaning was first advocated in the 1850s by Holyoake, and promoted by a number of newly emerging 'secular societies' in the provincial towns. While referring ostensibly to Hegel,[49] Pater also sneaks the modern sense, with its associated anti-religious message, into the innocuous-sounding process of historical time. The principle of continuous time, of motion and restlessness at the heart of things, is one which, for Pater, keeps criticism itself secular, in both senses of that word.

This ' "secular process" ', with its emphasis on continuous change and motion, then leads to a discussion of Heraclitus, the philosopher who, much more than Plato, emphasizes the physical flux of life. Paraphrasing Heraclitus, but also elaborating his own aesthetic relativism, he writes: 'The principle of disintegration, the incoherency of fire or flood ... are

---

[45] Wilde, 'The Critic as Artist', 142.   [46] Pater, *Plato and Platonism*, 9.
[47] Ibid. 9–10.   [48] Ibid. 10.   [49] Ibid. 19.

inherent in the primary elements alike of matter and of the soul ... But the principle of lapse, of waste, was, in fact, in one's self.'[50] That nature is a Heraclitean fire needs no redeeming, here, by the Christian Resurrection. Unlike his one-time pupil Hopkins, Pater relishes the unredeemable 'disintegration' of nature, its general wastefulness, and sees it at work everywhere, including finally in 'the soul'. He makes no bones about that last connection. Both 'matter' and 'soul' are formed of 'primary elements', and as such are bound by the law of 'disintegration'. As Lesley Higgins points out, throughout *Plato and Platonism* Pater quietly subverts Jowett's translations of Plato by emphasizing, by contrast, the transient physicality of 'the body'.[51] He also constantly challenges Platonism by discussing at some lyrical length the work of Heraclitus. It is Heraclitus, not Plato, who offers Pater the principle of 'lapse' and 'waste' which underlies his own writing. Nothing is permanent; not even the sentence itself, which tries to hold a meaning to account but in fact lets it go. As he summarizes: 'the Heraclitean flux, so deep down in nature itself—the flood, the fire—seemed to have laid hold on man, on the social and moral world, dissolving or disintegrating opinion, first principles, faith, establishing amorphism, so to call it, there also.'[52] Lighting on that crucial word 'amorphism', as if casually by chance, Pater quietly undermines any doctrine of permanent forms, whether Platonic or aesthetic. Form is no more permanent than matter. It too, whether as forms of art or spirit, of society or morality, is subject to the de-formation, the inevitably unforming 'amorphism' of nature's timely process.

Even the self is part of this universal process of undoing. The 'principle of disintegration' is at work every moment, altering the forms of things, whether bodies or ideas. Far from protecting the self and self-identity, Pater devotes some of his most searingly lyrical passages to describing the self's disintegration. 'But the principle of lapse, of waste, was, in fact, in one's self.' While Hopkins anxiously defends the 'immortal diamond'[53] against the Heraclitean flux of nature, Pater's own Heracliteanism refuses to let the self harden. Instead, he subjects it to a grammatical erosion, even a vanishing, as he explores its all too permeable borders.

[50] Ibid. 15.
[51] Lesley Higgins, 'Jowett and Pater: Trafficking in Platonic Wares', *Victorian Studies*, 37(1993), 43–72, 53.
[52] Pater, *Plato and Platonism*, 21.
[53] Gerard Manley Hopkins, *The Poems of Gerard Manley Hopkins* (London: Oxford University Press, 1967), 106.

Quoting the famous line from Heraclitus, 'No one has ever passed twice over the same stream', he then adds a gloss which tellingly slips into the present tense: 'Nay, the passenger himself is without identity.' Echoing Keats, but generalizing this identity-lessness into a universal condition, he finds the word which sums up the reasons for that loss: 'the passenger'. What passes in Pater is not only time, but the very self itself. Being a 'passenger' on the stream of time means that the self is conditional on each new moment. This is a radical kind of amorphism. Since the stream has always already changed under our feet, no 'identity' can survive its flow. And as with 'identity', so with 'knowledge', which is thus made, if not 'impossible', then 'wholly relative'.[54] So Pater has found his way back to a recurrent position. There is no 'diamond' value in the world—nothing so certain or immortal that the stream of time, or history, will not alter its form. From Heraclitus it is but a short step to a view of human nature as 'without identity', as it suffers the conditional, and conditioning, movement of time.

Pater's real gift lies not so much in what he says, however, which is often second-hand paraphrase, but in the way he says it. His own style flows like the stream he describes, taking the subject away from itself, on a journey of shifting, wandering clauses, which end up, not saving but losing the thing in question. The Heraclitean flux is not only a congenial theory of life; it is a practised style. Long, passenger-like sentences carry their meaning, moment by moment, turn by turn, in an elaborate formal reproduction of the matter they disclose. So when Pater describes the passenger-self on its stream of time in the famous passage from the 'Conclusion', his style rises to the challenge of an idea that lies at the heart of all his work:

Every one of those impressions is the impression of the individual in his isolation, each mind keeping as a solitary prisoner its own dream of a world. Analysis goes a step farther still, and assures us that those impressions of the individual mind to which, for each one of us, experience dwindles down, are in perpetual flight; that each of them is limited by time, and that as time is infinitely divisible, each of them is infinitely divisible also; all that is actual in it being a single moment, gone while we try to apprehend it, of which it may ever be more truly said that it has ceased to be than that it is. To such a tremulous wisp constantly re-forming itself on the stream, to a single sharp impression, with a sense in it, a relic more or less fleeting, of such moments gone by, what is real in our life fines itself down. It is with this movement, with the passage and dissolution of impressions, images, sensations, that analysis leaves off—that continual vanishing away, that strange, perpetual weaving and unweaving of ourselves.[55]

For all its familiarity, the ways in which this passage mimes 'the passage and dissolution' of its own meaning are astounding. The subject is the self, 'the individual', but more than any modernist destabilizing, Pater enacts a dissolving of the ego which leaves almost nothing. The carrying effect of his own prose, as it journeys away from each analysable noun: 'impressions', 'the individual', 'a wisp', 'a relic', has the effect of 'vanishing away' its very object, till all that remains is a verb, apparently unattached to any subject: 'weaving and unweaving'.[56]

This passage begins with a stark, existentialist assertion of intractable loneliness: 'each mind keeping as a solitary prisoner its own dream of a world'. Whether the 'solitary prisoner' relates to the mind or to the dream—the ambiguity only adding to the sense of mental lock—the self is a creature in a padded cell of dreams. It is as if, at first, Pater is trying to protect the idea of 'the individual', that etymologically undivided thing, by locking it up in a special place of its own where it seems unaffected by external influences. He repeats the word, as if nervously holding on to something that threatens to get away. However, as the passage continues, the identity of that solitary prisoner starts to break down—or rather, out: 'those impressions of the individual mind ... are in perpetual flight.' The 'infinitely divisible' nature of time gets to work on the 'individual', in an etymological game which means that the mind breaks into 'flight' from itself. Thus the whole notion of self is lost in a rain of 'divisible' impressions, as Pater's highly impressionist prose enacts the atomizing of the very self it defines. This strangely dehumanizing passage scatters the core self in pieces while paradoxically liberating it from prison. The prose whittles away its object, till all that remains is a tiny item of physical being.

Hence, the diminishing returns of that penultimate sentence: 'To such a tremulous wisp constantly re-forming itself on the stream, to a single sharp impression, with a sense in it, a relic more or less fleeting, of such moments gone by, what is real in our life fines itself down.' This,

[55] Pater, *The Renaissance*, 235–6.

[56] In fact, in the original 'William Morris' version, Pater drove the point home even more clearly: 'Struggling, as he must, to save himself, it is himself that he loses at every moment' ('Poems by William Morris', 311). For another close reading of this, and the preceding passage, see Denis Donoghue, *Walter Pater: Lover of Strange Souls* (New York: Alfred A. Knopf, 1995), 50–4.

in the long flight of impressions, might be, at last, a stopping place. The
end of the sentence seems to reach some ultimate reality: 'what is real in
our life'. However, there is an element of the absurd about this. Pater
is not claiming that the self is a will-o'-the-wisp on the stream of time,
though that is how it appears on a first reading. He is suggesting, rather,
that the self is a 'relic', albeit paradoxically still sensitive, 'with a sense
in it', of moments already 'gone by' and therefore no longer sensed. As
if being reduced to a relic of one's own physical matter were not loss
enough, even this supposedly durable object is then on the way out,
like the moments which it tries to commemorate: 'a relic more or less
fleeting'. That earlier 'perpetual flight' is still in action in 'fleeting'. The
contradictions which mass into this sentence, between the sentient and
the insentient, the wispy and the durable, the fleeting and the fixed, turn
the whole thing into a prolonged, nerve-racking clutching at straws. The
object flees as quickly as those Paterian 'moments' on which it depends
for its very realization.

It seems, then, that the passage out of the prison of self leads simply
to disintegration. In the end all that is left of the individual mind in its
solitary dream is a faint flicker of memory: the idea of 'moments gone
by'. The whole passage mimes its losses, being a passage (in both senses)
out of essential identity into a fallout of momentary impressions. The
centre cannot hold against this dispersal, as each clause undoes the brief
securities of the previous one, and offers its own revision of what went
before. Even that 'tremulous wisp constantly re-forming itself on the
stream' adds its own small amorphism, from moral 'reform' to literal
're-form'. Meanwhile, 'more or less fleeting' might be a manner of
speaking, but it might also be a sly alternative, to keep even 'fleeting'
hesitantly unsure of its way. The wisp's 're-forming' goes, like Pater's
own sentence, in and out of fixed form.

Meanwhile, typically, he withholds till the very end the main subject
of the proposition: 'what is real'. This ought to be the end of the
flight: 'what is real in our life fines itself down.' The verb 'fine' might
mean refine, the holding on to some finer preciousness or aesthetic
irreducibleness at the heart of life. But it might also carry the other
meaning, whereby the metal of 'what is real' is literally fined down into
even smaller parts, or shavings. In this second case, Pater is snatching
back even the last reassurance of what is 'real' or precious. For it
too disperses into a fine atomic dust at the end. His favourite, and
aesthetically rarefying word, 'fine', is thus subjected to a wordplay
which includes the possibility of a continuous verbal–physical decay.

It is not so fine as not to be fined down further. This is both a description and an example of Pater's own 're-forming' style. His sentences do not form their content once and for all. They re-form it, as the flux of (also grammatical) time undermines purpose, identity, certainty. In the end, the whole passage enacts that 're-forming', not as a philosophical proposition which might be summed up, but as a mysterious performance of language, which has to be read again.

*   *   *

It was Max Beerbohm who once complained that Pater 'laid out every sentence as in a shroud'.[57] If he does, and there is a sense in which precise meaning is always shrouded in his work, what is laid out is also never quite dead. It stirs unnervingly. Like that 'relic' there is 'a sense in it'. And that sense, the shifting of possible meanings below the surface, is what makes his work so subversive, so difficult to pin down into theoretical positions. Those long, constantly adjusting sentences, with their veiled suggestions, delayed gratifications, and etymological subplots, express the restlessness of a world where nothing can be saved, spiritually or physically, from the stream of time. There is, however, something deathly going on. The obsession with relics, with those things saved from the past, traditionally body parts of the saintly dead, is an obsession which also accounts for his attitude to language. Pater goes digging for meaning, excavating etymologies, as if that ground were some resourceful place which releases unexpected objects. This archaeological instinct involves, as Linda Dowling puts it, an 'etymological digging [which] brings us closer to the material earth itself'.[58] Relics are, of course, essentially just pieces of matter. They are sensuous in that they have a remembered sense in them, of the body, of the living being, even if what they symbolize are bodiless saints. But relics are also, for all their religious overtones, etymologically just that which remains. Pater's fondness for the word is a sign of how much, for him, is remaindered from the past, recovered from history. This includes language itself, which recalls longingly, elegiacally, an object which time has altered for good. The passage of time ensures that nothing is so formed as not to be de-formed or re-formed, whether by the archaeological years or by grammar's own time.

[57] Max Beerbohm, *The Works of Max Beerbohm* (London: Macmillan, 1922), 129.
[58] Dowling, 'Walter Pater and Archaeology: The Reconciliation with Earth', 219.

To turn at this point to some of his short stories is to find the idea of the past embodied, or reliqued, in a strange afterlife. In 'Duke Carl of Rosenmold' and 'Denys L'Auxerrois', for instance, the relic itself brings back a character from the past, but also reflects art's deep-mired engrossment in the past. As in so much of Pater's writing, the drive of the plot gives way to a digging down into language and its buried meanings. As a storyteller he is better at stirring dull roots than telling a rollicking tale. Indeed, 'Duke Carl' starts with the uprooting of a tree in a storm, which then reveals the relics, literally, of two buried people. For the rest of the story, the Duke's ambitions to bring about a Renaissance of art by recovering the lost art treasures of the past is grotesquely entwined with an imagery of unearthed corpses. The most innocuous sentence seems unable to get free of them:

> In art, as in all other things of the mind, again, much depends on the receiver; and the higher informing capacity, if it exist within, will mould an unpromising matter to itself, will realise itself by selection, and the preference of the better in what is bad or indifferent, asserting its prerogative under the most unlikely conditions.[59]

This seems to be a straightforward comment about the subjective nature of perception and interpretation: 'much depends on the receiver.' Here, too, the idea of form is invoked: the 'informing capacity' which shapes 'matter' to its own ends. Form and matter once again play out their old struggle for superiority. The sentence, however, then returns to the very thing which resists the 'prerogative' of form: 'conditions'. Something external to the mind, 'under' which it labours, asserts its awkward resistance. Those 'most unlikely conditions' exert their pressure even on art's 'higher informing capacity'.

Other obstacles are created by the puns in the sentence. The passage ought to be a defence of something like the Romantic imagination, which shapes and creates, forming the object in its own likeness. But instead it insists on the material nature even of the forming: 'will mould an unpromising matter to itself'. This moulding echoes the 'mold' of Duke Carl's name, which is also the mould of the earth in which dead 'matter' is discovered—specifically of course the matter of the body. The name Rosenmold contains the unresolved antithesis of roses, the florid, baroque art which appeals to the Duke, and the

---

[59] Walter Pater, 'Duke Carl of Rosenmold', in *Imaginary Portraits* (London: Macmillan, 1910), 129.

mouldy earth which changes bodies to matter and, in the long run, to relics. The phrase 'mould an unpromising matter to itself' earths Pater's meaning, as so often elsewhere, in an unredeemed, physiological process of decay. The body lies at the bottom of it, insisting on a materialism of perspective which affects, not only nature in its perpetual Lucretian flux, but also language, as sentences disintegrate into puns and etymologies, and 'mould' rounds into 'matter'. The lapse and waste of the material world are at work, both in the 'informing' faculty and in the matter which is formed. The passage thus starts to mean the opposite of what it says. Arguing the case for the subjective power of the individual to understand and interpret art, it then punningly subjects the individual to the grotesque etymology of words and names. Duke Carl's rosy, youthful appearance is only matter which the earth will mould, as it did the unearthed bodies at the start. Matter is the condition of everything, and 'the higher informing capacity' is, textually at least, re-formed by it.

Relics, in Pater, then, are not a sign of the afterlife, but a reminder of the earth. Such a memory runs through his writing, grounding it in a sense of the past and in the process of decay. 'Denys L'Auxerrois' is similarly preoccupied with what might be dug out of the ground: bits of stained glass, a Greek coffin, the relics of a saint, the skeleton of a Roman child, the body of Denys's own mother. The story imagines a return of the god Dionysus in the Middle Ages, and replays the dismemberment he suffers in the classical myth. Denys, his modern re-embodiment, is torn limb from limb by a carnival mob, and his heart, all of him that remains intact, is buried in the cathedral aisle. As usual, in Pater, the storyline does not matter much. What matters is something going on underground. The narrative takes shape from the 'relics, old glass and the like,'[60] which the narrator finds in the shops and pieces together into an imaginary portrait. But it is one relic in particular which brings Denys back to life in the story. The Greek coffin which, we are told, had been reused at a Roman funeral, contains not a body but something else: 'an object of a fresh and brilliant clearness among the ashes of the dead—a flask of lively green glass, like a great emerald'.[61]

Emeralds have a long tradition in aestheticist writing, going back at least to Gautier's *Emeralds and Cameos* (1852). Whatever the intertextual significance, the discovery of this 'lively green glass' in a coffin is what marks the return of Denys from the dead. A recovered gem or art work, like all the other curious relics in the story, this is buried treasure

---

[60] Pater, 'Denys L'Auxerrois', in *Imaginary Portraits*, 51.   [61] Ibid. 56.

come to light. It figures an art for art's sake, recovered from history, a beautiful object removed from the conditions of its production and use, but still slyly reminiscent of those conditions: 'the ashes of the dead'. Whether 'green glass' or 'emerald', its jewelled beauty survives intact, but has also been close to the death it commemorates. Like the Grecian Urn, it too is a historian, of 'ashes'. Characteristically, this old flask, or whatever it is, has a transparency, a 'brilliant clearness', which lets in the light of the present day. It is not sealed within itself, but reflects, reciprocally, the new temporal context in which it comes back to life, in a 'fresh' and 'lively' resurrection. Pater's relic, then, is a figure for the aestheticist puzzle of art itself: it is irrelevant and inhuman, but it is also remaindered from life which it recalls and commemorates. Its beauty survives time, as Denys himself does, but only because it registers a history of time: Greek, Roman, Medieval, all levelled into a ' "secular process" '. These weird and narratively incoherent stories point to the ways in which Pater's prose has to be read archaeologically, with a view to what lies buried in the ground of its double meanings and literary echoes.

The double meanings and echoes of 'Denys L'Auxerrois' may, in their turn, have inspired Virginia Woolf's curious short story, 'Solid Objects'. In it, one of two men on a beach, burying a hand in the sand, finds 'a full drop of solid matter' with 'a green tint'. Woolf writes that 'it was impossible to say whether it had been bottle, tumbler or window-pane; it was nothing but glass; it was almost a precious stone.'[62] This object, like Pater's, is ambiguously either precious or worthless, significant or random, opaque or transparent. An imaginary emerald, it is also only a bit of old glass. However, for this increasingly obsessive searcher after objects, almost anything will do: 'Anything, so long as it was an object of some kind, more or less round, perhaps with a dying flame deep sunk in its mass, anything—china, glass, amber, rock, marble'.[63] Pater's 'gemlike flame'[64] goes on flickering in Woolf's work, appearing here and there in her prose like a sign of her continuing aestheticist yearning. 'Look! What a beauty!' cries Eleanor in *The Years*. 'A flame danced on top of the coal, a nimble and irrelevant flame.'[65] Beauty, that 'irrelevant flame', can still get a 'nimble' footing on the coals in the twentieth

---

[62] Virginal Woolf, 'Solid Objects', in *The Complete Shorter Fiction of Virginia Woolf*, ed. Susan Dick (London: Hogarth Press, 1985), 96–101, 97.

[63] Ibid. 98.   [64] Pater, *The Renaissance*, 236.

[65] Virginal Woolf, *The Years*, ed. Hermione Lee, notes by Sue Asbee (Oxford: Oxford University Press, 1992), 31.

century. The echo of Pater, as Perry Meisel points out, is even clearer in Woolf's essay 'Reading': 'We want something that has been shaped and clarified, cut to catch the light ... yet sheltering as in a clear gem the flame which burns.'[66] The 'hard, gemlike flame', durable and transient, fixed and elusive, offers a figure which unsettles, even as it tries to consolidate, the aesthetic moment. It is a cliché with enough life in its condensed dialectic, in its 'interpretive conundrum',[67] to continue to figure in Woolf's imagination, as she too goes digging, metaphorically, for the jewel of aesthetic value in the rubble.

In 'Solid Objects', a kind of deranged, modern Huysmans, who has abandoned his political career, fills his house with bits of broken glass, stone, and china picked up on the waste lands of London. The aesthetic allure of stones, pots, and crocks: 'some piece of china or glass curiously marked or broken',[68] undermines the title's matter-of-fact solidity as well as the sanity of the principal character. Woolf, too, it seems is haunted by the broken china vase, or jewel, from the past. Meanwhile her prose, like Pater's, tests the ludicrous combination of something solid liquefying into flame or water. That 'full drop of solid matter', as she puts it, contradictorily comes in the form of what falls and disperses by the minute. Matter, in Woolf, is certainly as richly permeated by the physics of breakdown as it is in Pater. The relics which both writers dig up out of the earth, hoping for jewels, are also only momentary drops, falling to nothing, bound by the condition of time which streams through them. For all their apparent hardness and durability, these relics are as changeable as water or flame. In the end, they represent no more than the impressionistic choice, faith, or simple madness, of the treasure seekers themselves.

> 'Worthy of a jewel,' they say of beauty,
> Uncertain what is beauty
> And what the precious thing.[69]

So Laura Riding, in her poem 'Echoes', points to the element of indecision at the heart of aestheticism's favourite simile. Jewels, or

---

[66] Quoted in Perry Meisel, *The Absent Father: Virginia Woolf and Walter Pater* (New Haven and London: Yale University Press, 1980), 73.

[67] Jonathan Freedman, *Professions of Taste: Henry James, British Aestheticism, and Commodity Culture* (Stanford, Ca.: Stanford University Press, 1990), 19.

[68] Woolf, 'Solid Objects', 100.

[69] Laura Riding, 'Echoes', in *The Poems of Laura Riding* (Manchester: Carcanet, 1980; first pub. 1938), 71–5, 74.

the 'gemlike' generally, figure readily as images of artistic beauty in the nineteenth century. But such objects also show the limits of the comparison, and the uncertainty of knowing beauty at all. Woolf's fictional commentary on Pater's 'gemlike' relics hints at the madness which might lie that way, but also enjoys the play of form against matter, beauty against thing, which his own work so often opens up. Bits of china and glass may be precious jewels, figuring an unfathomable beauty in the eye of the observer, but like the 'gemlike flame', the figure is temporary, uncertain, even just downright maddening. 'Pretty stones',[70] is the last word of the bemused friend in the story, who can't wait to return to the *more* solid world outside.

Pater's sense of temporariness, then, whether as history or style, means that 'the aesthetic' does not exist in his work as a thing apart, protected, and immutable. Instead, it is known only in time, and is therefore subject, like everything else, to the stream's undermining. The relic, the imaginary emerald from the past, is not a lucky talisman against the stream; it is only a reminder of the passage of matter itself. The relic is of the earth, and its mould, however well-wrought, recalls the mouldering physical body it has survived. So form, that banner of Victorian aestheticism, rarely gets free, in Pater, of the matter which keeps it close to something tangible, desirable, and perishably human. Form's matter, then, matters almost as much as form. Certainly Pater keeps them jostling dialectically, throughout his writing, as he tentatively establishes the materialist basis of an aestheticism full of caution and conditions.

[70] Woolf, 'Solid Objects', 101.

ᐩ

Some lovely glorious nothing I did see.

John Donne

All the forms of art come to us in their own ways and allow us to
make more forms, and to make this exchange.

Muriel Rukeyser

5

Seeing Nothing: Vernon Lee's Ghostly Aesthetics

'By the way, talking of literary fame, the only two creatures who seemed
to have heard of me as a writer were Wm. Rossetti & Oscar Wilde!'[1]
So wrote the twenty-five-year-old Vernon Lee, author of *Studies of
the Eighteenth Century in Italy* (1880) and a collection of essays on
'Aesthetical Questions', *Belcaro* (1887). Some fifty years, and more than
forty volumes later, soon after the publication of *Music and Its Lovers*
in 1932, she answered an admiring letter from Roger Fry with similar
despondency: 'But what your letter does make up for is the incurable
disappointment (even at seventy-six) of finding all my work on aesthetics
utterly wasted.'[2] The reputation of Vernon Lee has always been a puzzle.
She felt snubbed or neglected throughout her life, yet her work was
read and admired by many of her famous contemporaries, not only
Rossetti and Wilde, but Pater, James, Stephen, Schreiner, Wharton,
Wells—and indeed not only by eminent Victorians, but also by the
modernists: Huxley, Smyth, Bell, Fry, Strachey, Woolf. Yet by the
time Peter Gunn published the first official biography of Lee in 1964,

---

[1] Vernon Lee, *Vernon Lee's Letters*, with a Preface by her Executor (Privately printed:
1937), 66.
[2] Quoted in Peter Gunn, *Vernon Lee: Violet Paget, 1856–1935* (London: Oxford
University Press, 1964), 230.

he was writing, almost apologetically, about a forgotten author. The short stories, the dialogues and essays on aesthetics, the studies of music, language, place, the pacifist polemics and plays had mostly gone out of print, and out of mind. When, in 2003, Vineta Colby published a new biography of Lee, she too registered the silence of literary history. 'It is a small company who read Vernon Lee today',[3] she begins.

Yet the story is not simply one of neglect and silence. Edith Wharton, for instance, recalled in 1933 that the three authors who had influenced a whole generation were 'Pater, Symonds and Vernon Lee'.[4] The same trio turns up, less flatteringly, in the excised Fresca passage of *The Waste Land*: 'Fresca was baptised in a soapy sea | Of Symonds—Walter Pater—Vernon Lee.'[5] Lee's misfortune, perhaps, was to outlive many of her contemporaries, and therefore to suffer in her lifetime the reaction of a generation all too ready to consign the Victorian past to the realms of the irrelevant. 'We belong to a generation which has—to be blunt—passed away',[6] Edmund Gosse wrote to her in 1906. That same year she wrote rather sadly in her journal: '(I know my writings tend more and more towards the soliloquy.) It gives, perhaps, a certain freedom and decency, but sometimes, not often, it makes one feel a bit lonely, as if one were the vox clamans, not in the desert, but inside a cupboard.'[7] Nevertheless, contemporaries like Lytton Strachey, Roger Fry, and Desmond McCarthy continued to hear and appreciate the voice from the cupboard, and to defend its eccentric, sometimes unfashionable opinions. Bernard Shaw, in particular, found occasion to praise Lee's pacifist and internationalist outlook in the 1920s: 'I take off my hat to the old guard of Victorian cosmopolitan intellectualism, and salute her as the noblest Briton of them all.'[8]

To the modernists, Vernon Lee presented the puzzle of an eminent Victorian who, not only had not quietly passed away, but was sometimes, in her sheer formal inventiveness, as avant-garde as they. Certainly the mixed media of *Satan the Waster* (1920), with its 'splicing' from 'film and

---

[3] Vineta Colby, *Vernon Lee: A Literary Biography* (Charlottesville and London: University of Virginia Press, 2003), p. xi.

[4] Edith Wharton, *A Backward Glance* (New York: Scribner's, 1964; first pub. 1933), 141.

[5] T. S. Eliot, *The Waste Land: A Facsimile and Transcript*, ed Valerie Eliot (London: Faber, 1971), 41.

[6] Quoted in Colby, 270.   [7] Ibid. 308–9.   [8] Ibid. 307.

gramophone' as Gillian Beer notes, is more 'beyond the *pale*'[9] of what it is possible to write than many a contemporary modernist experiment. Lee's 'cupboard' may have seemed lonely, but it was neither stuffy nor antiquated. Throughout her life she wrote with a sense of formal invention, mixing history and fiction, philosophy and autobiography, story and theory, often in ways which are quite unique. The very antipathy shown towards her work, by T. S. Eliot, Wyndham Lewis, and I. A. Richards for instance, is also a sign of her ability to provoke and antagonize. Certainly, the 'cupboard' did not shut her up.

Lee's writing does not lend itself to summary, partly because it is so prolific and varied, and partly because, like Pater's, it enjoys the dialectic of altering points of view. Her understanding of the aesthetic is in some ways more ambiguous and morally inflected than his. She rejected 'art for art's sake' as trivial: 'art without root, without organism, without logical reason or moral decorum, art for mere buying and selling',[10] she wrote, and advocated in its place 'art for the sake of life'.[11] Meanwhile, she continued to probe the question of the aesthetic, forging in the process a description of form which is peculiarly flexible and original, as well as more influential than the grudging footnote given to it by later commentators. That Vernon Lee is probably best remembered today for her ghost stories is not a contradiction of this influence. In fact, it is in the ghost stories that her aesthetic theory comes most persuasively and memorably into play.

There is a telling anecdote in Katherine Mix's *A Study in Yellow* which recalls how Lee, on a visit to the Paters, arrived too late for dinner. As a result, Mix claims, 'the self-sufficient young woman decided to forage for herself and descending to the kitchen late at night was met by her host, who took the floating white form for a ghost, to their mutual discomfort.'[12] The idea of a 'floating white form' which turns out to have a hungry appetite, enough to steal provisions from the kitchen, is nicely appropriate. Apocryphal or not, the story resonates with something of that witty irony, that interchangeability of flesh and

[9] Gillian Beer, 'The Dissidence of Vernon Lee: *Satan the Waster* and the Will to Believe', in *Women's Fiction and the Great War*, ed. Suzanne Raitt and Trudi Tate (Oxford: Oxford Clarendon Press, 1997), 107–31, 109.

[10] Vernon Lee, *Laurus Nobilis: Chapters on Art and Life* (London: John Lane, 1909), 260.

[11] Vernon Lee, *Renaissance Fancies and Studies: Being a Sequel to Euphorion* (London: Smith Elder, 1895), 259.

[12] Katherine Lyon Mix, *A Study in Yellow: The Yellow Book and Its Contributors* (London: Constable, 1960), 255.

spirit, material and immaterial, which runs through so many aestheticist texts. This ghost, true to form, is driven by distinctly fleshly needs. As a metaphor of the relationship of host and guest, it is also quietly pointed. Vernon Lee helps herself to what she needs from Pater, while he, for his part, might well feel unnerved by her furtive self-sufficiency.

Ghosts are in the air of Victorian aestheticism. Though Pater himself does not write about them, preferring more literal relics and reincarnations, there is some reason why Lee, like Wilde, is drawn to the ghost story, with all its tricky business of seeing things. Perhaps the very nebulousness of aestheticist positions, with their emphasis on style rather than content, form rather than matter, suggests a world of shifting outlines and effects. This is certainly the gist of I. A. Richards' attack on them in the first chapters of *Principles of Literary Criticism*. 'That paralysing apparition Beauty, the ineffable, ultimate, unanalysable, simple Idea, has at least been dismissed and with her have departed or will soon depart a flock of equally bogus entities',[13] he asserts triumphantly. Banishing ghosts is part of the enterprise of modernism—in particular, banishing the distinctly female 'apparition Beauty'. That Richards has a particular 'apparition' in mind is suggested by the name which occurs twice on previous pages: that of Vernon Lee. With a lordly wave of his hand he dismisses the aestheticist ghosts of the past, those fuzzy abstract nouns, capitalized as objective presences. Beauty and other bogeys, among them 'form', 'design', and 'rhythm',[14] are sent packing, along with the aesthetes who promoted them. In defence of his own ' "moral" theory of art', Richards then rounds on 'Art for Art's sake' as, in 1924, 'a doctrine definitely and detrimentally dated'.[15] Unfortunately, the ghosts of beauty, form, and aestheticism, far from being banished for good, have the uncanny knack, as ghosts do, of coming back.

Victorian aestheticism is haunted by varieties of revenants from the past. This is odd because, as a movement, it is generally sceptical and agnostic, materialist, in the sense of being concerned with the matter of the body, and commodity-minded, in its concern with the value of artefacts. It may be, however, that these are precisely the reasons why. The purpose of a ghost, after all, is to set something floating, to offer itself as conditional, ambiguous. Without necessarily commanding belief, the ghost offers itself for interpretation or evaluation. It is

<hr />

[13] I. A. Richards, *Principles of Literary Criticism* (London: Routledge & Kegan Paul, 1960; first pub. 1924), 12.
[14] Ibid. 14.   [15] Ibid. 54.

therefore, essentially, a pivot in a relationship between the ghost-seer and the original body that the ghost represents. Seeing a ghost, after all, involves choice and need, options which reflect as much on the seer as on the ghostly object. Ghosts do not exist for themselves, and have no purpose without an object to haunt. At the same time they recall some original version of themselves, some living presence, with a story and motive identifiable from the past. The ghost shifts between the two. It is a figure from history and historical time, come back perhaps on unfinished business; but it is also just an outline, emptied of its body, something the ghost-seer dreads or expects. The impressionable uncertainty of the ghost, disembodied yet recalling a body, empty yet full of itself, gives it an uncanny similarity to the word which also best expresses it: form. What else is the ghost but a form, let loose from its body?

The year before Richards published his *Principles*, Lee published her own work of literary criticism: *The Handling of Words* (1923). The title, like so much Victorian aestheticism, enjoys the material satisfactions of touch while also hinting at the lost body beyond touch. The very *effort* of touch in the word 'handling', with its overdetermined physicality, tells how difficult such grasping might be. If a sense of the body gets everywhere in Lee, it also, in another sense, gets nowhere. There may be biographical–sexual reasons for this, but there are also, perhaps, aesthetic ones. Indeed, *The Handling of Words* offers an account of literary meaning which depends precisely on what might be called material ghostliness. Before the formalist challenge to intentionalist fallacies, Lee challenges the authority of authorship by seeing the work as a body (of words) which lends itself to strange transactions of touch. Those transactions are caught in the recurrent, insistent, yet elusive word 'form'. The writer, she argues, has no greater knowledge of the work than anyone else, for the 'work, when complete, is just that various, fluctuating, inscrutable form which owes its being to the Reader as much as to himself, and which is hidden from him by the impenetrable wall of flesh separating one soul from the other.'[16] Pater's isolated dreamer from the Conclusion to *The Renaissance* is clearly remembered here, as Lee argues for a separateness not only of consciousness but also of artistic control. The art form presents an 'impenetrable wall of flesh' to both writer and reader as it rounds into a completed life of its own. At the

---

[16] Vernon Lee, *The Handling of Words, and other Studies in Literary Psychology* (London: John Lane, 1927; first pub. 1923), 81.

same time Lee, like Pater, cannot resist the contradictory possibilities of 'flesh', which, if not penetrated can at least be 'handled'. Even while she argues against fallacies of intention, she fleshes out the 'inscrutable form' of the artwork into something which asks to be touched.

Paradoxically, then, it is precisely 'when complete' that the work leaves its writer to become a 'form' for the reader. This movable, abstracted category gives Lee a way of accounting for the renunciations of authorship and the inventions of reading. Form, which is 'various, fluctuating, inscrutable', is that transmissible aspect of the work which goes between writer and reader, varying and evading the control of each. By being 'complete', the work starts to escape from the intention of its author, and becomes a 'fluctuating' category, able to haunt its reader or perceiver. It thus achieves this specific, ghostly dimension, as of an appearance, a moving apparition, which lends itself to ever new sightings.

Although associated with metaphors of sight, *seeing* form is rarely easy, however. In an early essay, 'Beauty and Ugliness' (1897), co-written with Lee's close companion, Kit Anstruther-Thomson, the idea of form as a visible fixed object is clearly under question. Here, they write: 'it is we, the beholders, who, so to speak, *make form exist* in ourselves by alteration in our respiratory and equilibratory processes.'[17] Beholding form, far from being proof of its external existence, comes close to an imaginary projection: we make it '*exist* in ourselves'. The sentence has almost snatched '*form*' from the view of 'the beholders' in order to give it back as an inner imagining. It comes to exist by being seen, but invisibly, 'in ourselves'. The sentence mimes the transaction which is its definition. Form goes from here to there, from author to reader, from being a projection of physical breath and balance to a kind of independent existence. As psychology, this is probably laughable. But as an account of artistic form, it proposes a movable quality, a transaction between consciousness and object, which is peculiarly rich and freeing. Certainly, it wholly disproves I. A. Richards' criticism that the aesthetes treated form, and other abstractions, 'as though they stood for qualities inherent in things outside the mind'.[18] His misreading of Lee is a carelessness almost amounting to wilful blindness. In many ways, her definitions of form are even more dependent on subjectivity,

---

[17] Vernon Lee and C. Anstruther-Thomson, 'Beauty and Ugliness', *Contemporary Review*, 72(1897), 544–69 and 669–88, 686.
[18] Richards, 14.

on mental or physiological impressions, than his. Far from being an 'inherent' quality of the artwork, form is elicited by the need, effort, even invention of the observer. Like a ghost, its floating identity requires an exchange of views.

This sense of ghostly movement is Lee's great contribution to aestheticist thinking. Although there is something comical about her practical experiments in artistic perception—the way she and Kit went round art galleries humming to themselves in order to sample pictures through tunes[19]—the theory of subjective interplay or 'empathy' which they developed from Theodor Lipps's '*Einfühlung*', or 'feeling into',[20] is peculiarly dynamic and modern. It is not pure subjectivity which Lee advocates, but an empathic meeting, 'more than half way', of reader and writer, beholder and artist. The idea which figures this meeting point is, of course, 'form'. Like so many abstract nouns in her work, the word refers less to a thing than to the temporally or spatially moving appearance of a thing. It is thus a word which rejects ethical or empirical fixities, and which, instead, foregrounds difficulty, context, interpretation. If form exists, it is less as an object than as a drama or event. It involves, as Lee puts it, 'the larger or smaller dynamic dramas of effort, resistance, reconciliation, cooperation'.[21] These 'dynamic dramas' of form precede by almost a hundred years Derek Attridge's formulation in *The Singularity of Literature* (2004), which argues for 'the eventness of the literary work, which means that form needs to be understood verbally—as "taking form," or "forming," or even "losing form".'[22] The aestheticist history of the word has long set form moving, away from its Platonic sense of God-given essence or identity, towards an event of interpretation. The complexities of such interpretation are something Vernon Lee explores with peculiar conviction and imagination.

In particular, she does so by mixing the genres she uses. She forces us into 'dynamic dramas' of reading in part by confusing our expectations of the prose-form itself. So, for instance, her book *Renaissance Fancies and Studies* (1895) contains historical essay, biography, autobiography, and pure story. One piece, called 'A Seeker of Pagan Perfection,' is a pseudo-biography of a Renaissance humanist, Domenico Neroni.

[19] C. Anstruther-Thomson, *Art and Man: Essays and Fragments*, intro. Vernon Lee (London: The Bodley Head, 1924), 38–9.

[20] Vernon Lee, *The Beautiful: An Introduction to Psychological Aesthetics* (Cambridge: Cambridge University Press, 1913), 66.

[21] Ibid. 133.

[22] Derek Attridge, *The Singularity of Literature* (London: Routledge, 2004), 113.

Like her contemporaries, Lee uses 'humanist' to mean a Renaissance intellectual who defies the moral laws of church and state, and whose wit and curiosity are classical and pagan in perspective. Neroni, we are told, is a 'fanatical lover of human form' who, in his attempt to understand its workings, would often be found 'handling horrible remains'.[23] That 'handling', once again, suggests an effort to touch the ambiguous object of desire: the 'remains' or relics of 'human form'. Form here, as so often, lets the body in and out of its frame of reference. It is, and is not, that which can be handled. A little later we are told that the decorative artists of the Renaissance, in copying the classical style, 'laid hold of it as merely so much form, joining sirens, griffins, garlands, rams' heads, victories, without a suspicion that they might mean or suggest anything. They do, in fact, mean nothing'.[24] Here form is *mere* form, a kind of empty pattern, devoid of matter or meaning, except, of course, that by being 'laid hold of' it also seems to be peculiarly substantial. The sentence dramatizes form, filling and emptying it at the same time, offering it as something and nothing to the touch. These motley 'sirens, griffins' and the rest 'in fact, mean nothing'. They are classical figures which have lost their religious, social, or ethical relevance, and have become merely decorative. Nonetheless, 'so much form' also lends itself to the artist's purpose, in being, handily, shapes 'merely' for shape's sake, and therefore for nothing. The word 'nothing' haunts 'form', in Lee as in others. Like two ghosts circling each other, the apparent emptiness of form draws towards it the emptiness of nothing. By being '*merely* so much form', these creatures retreat from meaning. Their matter is a mere materiality, a *given*. It is not a subject matter. Like Pater, Lee invokes the tautological thing for its own sake, form for form's sake, in order to dramatize the paradoxical substance and emptiness of the art *form* itself.

Her many studies of the visual arts, particularly Renaissance art, continue to tap the rich pickings of the word 'form'. In one place, she points to Botticelli's 'deficient knowledge of anatomy and habit of good form'. That 'good form' keeps an ethical resonance. Botticelli's art, by implication, is bad form, almost bad manners. She then launches into a passage of aestheticist prose which enjoys every fashionable adjective of the time. Botticelli's desire for 'delicate form' becomes 'a most persevering and almost morbid research'. She continues, referring to the ugliness of his models:

[23] Lee, *Renaissance Fancies and Studies*, 177.   [24] Ibid. 182.

For grace and distinction, which are qualities of movement rather than of form, do not strike us very much in a figure which is originally well made. ... Whereas, in the case of defective form, any grace that may be obtained affects us *per se*. It need not have been there; indeed, it was unlikely to be there; and hence it obtains the value and charm of the unexpected, the rare, the far-fetched. This, I think, is the explanation of the something of exotic beauty that attaches to Botticelli: we perceive the structural form only negatively, sufficiently to value all the more the ingenuity of arrangement by which it is made to furnish a beautiful outline and beautiful movement; and we perceive the great desire thereof. If we allow our eye to follow the actual structure of the bodies, even in the Primavera, we shall recognise that not one of these figures but is downright deformed and out of drawing. Even the Graces have arms and shoulders and calves and stomachs all at random; and the most beautiful of them has a slice missing out of her head. But if, instead of looking at heads, arms, legs, bodies, separately, and separate from the drapery, we follow the outline of the groups against the background, drapery clinging or wreathing, arms intertwining, hands combed out into wonderful fingers ... we recognise that no pattern could be more exquisite.[25]

In a sense, this is a string of Nineties' clichés, a weirdly elongated prose mannerism to match Botticelli's artistic equivalent. Pushing and pulling at the word 'form' — 'delicate form', 'defective form', 'structural form', 'deformed' — the passage worries at something which will not be pinned down into a single definition. Form may be the human figure of the model, but it is also something added by the artist which, echoing the old round of art for art, 'affects us *per se*'. The passage, which sounds careless in its formulation, in fact succeeds in communicating the bizarre dehumanization of Botticelli's painting, which can 'furnish a beautiful outline and beautiful movement' out of 'deformed' figures. The word 'furnish' swings the argument in the direction it must go: towards mere material fact. Meanwhile Lee, like Pater, milks the etymological senses of words. Those 'qualities of movement' which characterize Botticelli's art also trouble her own language: 'research', 'far-fetched', 'exquisite', 'abstracted'. We are meant to hear the effort of recovery in them: 'research' is harder and more prolonged than a search; 'far-fetched' carries what it has fetched from far back; 'exquisite' comes from a seeking it still recalls; 'abstracted' refers less to a concluded abstraction than to something still being drawn out of something else. All these words contain a historical drag from the past, an effort of meaning which is not quite finished. They thus help to describe Botticelli's own

[25] Ibid. 99–101.

imperfect sense of form as something which opens up to, rather than closes down, a sense of movement.

Clearly, there is a familiar aestheticist agenda here too. Form provides Lee with a way of talking about the body as mere material stuff. Botticelli, she writes, 'uses the human form as so much pattern element, mere lines and curves'.[26] Like Pater's Mona Lisa, the form of the body offers a reduction to the absurd of matter itself. Botticelli's women have 'arms intertwining, hands combed out into wonderful fingers'. That 'combed out' leaves hands as insentient as hair or fringes. The 'pattern element' of form turns bodies into mere accessories and furnishings. However, form is not quite so simple either. It keeps a residue of human meaning—of what has been left behind or fetched from far back. The idea of movement, of time, and therefore of something 'various, fluctuating, inscrutable', troubles the notional fixity of form, giving it a kind of lost or forfeited life. Botticelli's Graces were once women, however 'combed out' into mere design. The conflict between the two, like the shiftiness of the word 'form', keeps a movement between human and inhuman troublingly visible. This will be the movement of Lee's own ghost stories. The ghost, after all, is a form from which the original life or meaning has gone, but which it still uneasily recalls. Conversely, form is a ghost: a ghost of the body, or a ghost of intention, message, meaning. It has been 'abstracted' from all of those, but it also draws on them like a distant reminiscence.

Abstraction, for Lee, as for Wallace Stevens after her, is not a hardened philosophical category, exemplified by the abstract noun. If it must be abstract, this only means that art or form, or whatever it is, must still be drawing away from an original point of departure. The etymology of the word is still live, still at work in it. This is clear in an intriguing passage about music in Lee's introduction to Anstruther-Thomson's posthumously published *Art and Man* (1924). There she writes that the feeling aroused by music is not a human feeling but its '*ancestor*'. She then pauses on the word '*ancestor*', and continues: 'for the feeling thus awakened by music, the movement thus attributed to visible shapes, is like the infinitive of our verbs, an abstraction, what modern mental science identifies as a MEMORY-IMAGE; it is the ghost of concrete experience.'[27] Once again, the word 'abstraction' helps to describe this thing which is not so much an achieved feeling, but a feeling abstracted

[26] Lee, *Renaissance Fancies and Studies*, 100.
[27] Anstruther-Thomson, *Art and Man*, 83–4.

from, drawn out from, the past. It carries the movement of time in itself. Such a feeling has the outline of something, of an *'ancestor'*, of something alive and experienced in the past. Such a feeling is also, however, a go-between, the shape of its return is a 'ghost of concrete experience', which depends as much on the listener as on the composer who set it moving. The 'ghost' is an abstraction because, like form, it is the still fluid memory of something else.

Far from being a frivolous or conventional figure, then, the ghost is crucial to Lee's aesthetic theory. Her fictional ghosts are abstracted forms, semi-inventions of their beholders, go-betweens, uncertain, ancestral presences, dependent in part on the desires of the ghost-seers. This may also be why her ghost stories don't quite work. They are as much about aesthetics, about beauty and desire, as they are about human revenge or terror. These 'culture ghosts', as she called them, are part of a ghostly aesthetics of interaction and interplay which she was working out throughout her life. They are about the psychological effects of obsession or desire, but they are also about interpretation and artistic meaning. At about the same time as Lee published her later works, Ortega y Gasset wrote, in 'The Dehumanisation of Art' (1925), that the majority of people 'are unable to adjust their attention to the glass and the transparency which is the work of art'. They try to see through it, to the object represented beyond. He then compares the nature of art to a transparency of which most people would say that 'they see nothing in it.'[28] Of course, seeing nothing in it is precisely what they should see. This is Wilde's point too, when he explains of the common complaint that some new poet 'has "nothing to say"', that that is exactly what he should say. To have '"nothing to say"' is a sign that 'He gains his inspiration from form, and from form purely, as an artist should.'[29] The old association of form and nothing continues its rhetorical dance.

Lee's own interest in form, and the ways in which it abstracts from but does not deny feeling, content, or human import (author's and reader's), is her version of this 'nothing' which is still, somehow, 'in it'. The ghost is a form, a kind of 'glass' or 'transparency', which activates a story of perception and interpretation that is not a simple seeing *through*. Instead, it dramatizes its own diverted visibility and purpose. Behind

[28] Quoted in Susanne K. Langer, *Feeling and Form: A Theory of Art Developed from Philosophy in a New Key* (London: Routledge & Kegan Paul, 1953), 54.

[29] Oscar Wilde, 'The Critic as Artist', in *Intentions* (London: Methuen, 1919; first pub. 1891), 152–217, 201.

the ghost there is nothing. At the same time, the ghost comes from somewhere, or from someone, and is thus related, ancestrally, to reality. It shifts between something and nothing, finding in the space between them the drama of the literary itself: a drama of diversion, obliquity, choice, play. If this is nothing, it is also, transparently, something by which one might nevertheless be haunted.

*   *   *

It is in her short stories that Lee puts the ghost to work as a figure for this ambiguous, aesthetic emptiness. These stories, with their tongue-in-cheek wit and surreal non sequiturs, are hardly the traditional, heart-stopping tales we might expect. Yet in their way, they are as gripping as any. In one of her early essays, Lee suggests that 'To raise a real spectre of the antique is a craving of our own century.'[30] The nineteenth century is an age of ghost stories. Sceptical of the supernatural yet nostalgic for it, the age turns to ghosts in reaction, perhaps, to the encroaching secularization and 'materialism'[31] of the modern world. The ghost story not only indulges the unstable order of fantasy at the expense of 'naturalistic art and the materialist philosophies of which it is an expression';[32] it also indulges the wish to believe in another, more fearful world beyond the material order of things. Lee, however, appears to deviate from this sentimental tradition. Her two collections of stories, *Hauntings* (1889) and *Vanitas* (1892), contain ghost stories which largely reject the Gothic mode of terror and vengeance. 'To raise a real spectre of the antique' hints at this difference. Spectres by their very nature are figures for what is dead and gone; but a 'spectre of the antique' has an impersonal, historical specificity normally lacking in the run of Victorian family spooks. The idea of 'the antique' not only sets up the possibility of a '*real* spectre,' ironically casting the others into the shade, but also of a 'craving' for spectres which considerably alters their aspect. Lee's are the ghosts of a historical perspective largely untroubled by supernatural design. They figure, not the terror of the unknown, but the seductive, desirable return of the past. They are located *in* history, not extraterrestrially out of it.

[30] Vernon Lee, *Belcaro: Being Essays on Sundry Aesthetical Questions* (London: W. Satchell, 1880), 104.

[31] Julia Briggs, *Night Visitors: The Rise and Fall of the English Ghost Story* (London: Faber, 1997), 24.

[32] Glen Cavaliero, *The Supernatural and English Fiction* (Oxford: Oxford University Press, 1995), 7.

Thus, whether the ghost is 'Dionea', a reincarnated Venus whose physical beauty destroys her sculptor, or 'Medea', a Renaissance beauty in a portrait who brings about the death of her nineteenth-century admirer, or the phantom Elizabethan lover of 'Oke of Okehurst' who returns from the past to kill the woman who is infatuated with him, the point is not terror of disembodiment but desire for the flesh. The ghost affords a pretext for cravings which, if illicit and decadent, are also, in their flagrant unreality, often also ironic and witty.[33] Henry James, on receiving a copy of *Hauntings*, praised 'the bold aggressive, speculative fancy'[34] of it, as if recognizing that its ideas drove well beyond the usual requirements of the popular market. A 'real spectre', for Vernon Lee, is a substantially physical speculation. The irony of it, dissipating belief but insisting on a simple matter-of-fact, is the key to the odd tone of many of her stories. Their ironic literal-mindedness may be partly due to the author's own 'Voltairian'[35] atheism. She once castigated her old friend Maurice Baring for his 'Catholic other worldliness', adding: 'I abominate such making light of life and its ... well! *uniqueness*.'[36] She herself was pleased to be dubbed 'only a poor materialist'[37] by a French cousin and, in an article on 'The Responsibilities of Unbelief', assessed the advantages of being, as she put it, 'emancipated, free, superior ... a thorough materialist'.[38] Such materialism has no time for ghosts except, precisely, as objects of unbelief. This is the point Lee makes in *Belcaro* when she writes that 'we have a form of the supernatural in which, from logic and habit, we disbelieve, but which is vital; and this form of the supernatural is the ghostly.'[39] Her own fictional ghosts have no designs on their readers' or victims' beliefs; rather, it is the readers and viewers who have designs on the ghosts. Objects of strange, anachronistic desire, they are figures for a beauty as palpable as it is imaginary, as seductive as it may be unreal. By dispensing with the conventions of fear, Lee

[33] See Catherine Maxwell, 'Vernon Lee and the Ghosts of Italy', and Angela Leighton, 'Resurrections of the Body: Women Writers and the Idea of the Renaissance', in *Unfolding the South: Nineteenth-Century British Women Writers and Artists in Italy*, ed. Alison Chapman and Jane Stabler (Manchester: Manchester University Press, 2003), 201–21, 222–38.

[34] Henry James, *Letters*, 4 vols., ed. Leon Edel (London: Macmillan, 1974–84), iii. 276.

[35] Gunn, 16.

[36] Quoted in Ethel Smyth, *Maurice Baring* (London: Heinemann, 1938), 331.7;

[37] Vernon Lee, *For Maurice: Five Unlikely Stories* (London: John Lane, 1927), p. xvii.

[38] Vernon Lee, 'The Responsibilities of Unbelief: A Conversation between Three Rationalists', *The Contemporary Review*, 43(1883), 685–710, 700.

[39] Lee, *Belcaro*, 93.

clears the way for a story which enjoys the aestheticist possibilities of ghosts, and thus, also, the unaccountable, ghostly nature of the aesthetic itself.

That inverting connection is particularly evident in the ghosts which emerge from art works: from portraits, books, or pieces of music. It is as if the ghost story literalizes the formal metaphors of Lee's aesthetic theory: for instance, that the feeling 'awakened by music' is 'the ghost of concrete experience'. These rhetorical or fictional ghosts hover in an atmosphere of insistent physicality and verbal nuance, which is the atmosphere of her own writing style. It is a style in which meaning itself tends to be a ghostly affair. The condition of music, in particular, lends itself to that separation of form and content which allows a ghost to flit dangerously free. Lee was always fascinated by music. Her first book, *Studies of the Eighteenth Century in Italy* (1880), is about early Italian opera, and carries a preface in which she recalls the months spent copying out forgotten airs in a dusty attic of the Bologna music school. There, she writes, a 'passion for actually seeing and touching the things of that time'[40] turned into an obsessive love affair with the music of the past: 'my many love passages with various composers, my infidelities and remorseful returns'.[41] Just as Pater cannot resist turning the scholar–connoisseur Winckelmann into a toucher-up of statues—'he fingers those pagan marbles with unsinged hands'[42]—so Lee punningly imagines 'passages' and 'returns' of an amorous as well as musical nature. The touch of old manuscripts not only rouses her craving for the past, but also then releases its ghostly presences. Without the 'life-blood of attention', she explains, those lost musicians, like 'ghosts flocking hopelessly round the sacrificial trench of Odysseus,' can 'never speak to posterity nor lay their hands on its soul'.[43] The handling, it seems, goes both ways, as the immaterial ghosts become blooded with desire to touch the soul of posterity. Nearly fifty years later, recalling one of those old singers, she reminded Maurice Baring, her fellow haunter of attics, 'what would we not have given if some supernatural mechanism had allowed us to catch the faintest vibrations of that voice!'[44]

---

[40] Vernon Lee, *Studies of the Eighteenth Century in Italy* (London: Fisher Unwin, 1907; first pub. 1880), p. xxi.

[41] Ibid. p. xxiv.

[42] Walter Pater, *The Renaissance: Studies in Art and Poetry* (London: Macmillan, 1910), 222.

[43] Lee, *Studies of the Eighteenth Century in Italy*, p. xlv.

[44] Lee, *For Maurice*, p. xxix.

That 'supernatural mechanism' is, in a sense, the ghost story itself. Imagined as a kind of stenograph, a machine to catch voices, the ghost story provides the only means, mechanical and unbelievable, with which to manage the supernatural. Lee wrote at least four variations of the same story: the first in about 1874 when she was still researching her book on Italy; a second, 'A Culture Ghost: or, Winthrop's Adventure', appeared in *Fraser's Magazine* in 1881; a third, French version, entitled *'Voix Maudite'*, in *Les lettres et les arts* in 1887 and, finally, 'A Wicked Voice', the best of them, in her collection *Hauntings* in 1889. It is indeed a text which is thus itself full of echoes and returns. For more than twenty years Lee toyed with the idea of hearing a voice from the past—a voice which would give body to its lost music. Such a recovery is conceived, appropriately enough, as a kind of play, starting with those first rummaging researches in the Bologna attic: 'the play instinct let loose in a lumber-room', [45] she calls it. That 'lumber-room' is both the origin and the narrative destination of the story. Not only the literal attic of old manuscripts, it is also the jumbled idea of the past itself: 'the hay-loft, the tool-house, the remote lumber-room full of discarded mysteries and of lurking ghosts'.[46] In addition, this is the place of fiction. It is a storehouse of things, useful and useless, which may be brought back into play. And playing, both in Schiller's sense, of an instinct essential to all artistic work,[47] and in the musical sense, is the art and trick of this ghost. For all her distrust of the 'vital lies' perpetrated by such 'professional prophets' as Nietzsche,[48] Lee

---

[45] Lee, *Studies of the Eighteenth Century in Italy*, p. xxi.   [46] Ibid. p. xvi.

[47] Schiller's conclusion that 'With beauty man shall only play, and it is with beauty only that he shall play' (*On the Aesthetic Education of Man: In a Series of Letters*, ed. and trans. Elizabeth M. Wilkinson and L. A. Willoughby (Oxford: Clarendon Press, 1967), 107) is repeated with variations by both Pater, specifically in connection with music (*The Renaissance*, 151–2), and by Lee, when she asserts, for instance, that 'All decent human work partakes ... of the quality of play' (*Laurus Nobilis*, 219–20). If, as Denis Donoghue has forcefully argued, Pater is the founder of modernity in his aestheticist separation of art as 'commodity' from art as 'play' (*Walter Pater: Lover of Strange Souls* (New York: Alfred A. Knopf, 1995), 319), that separation has its roots in Romanticism, and in Schiller's influential proposition that 'beauty ... accomplishes no particular purpose, neither intellectual nor moral; it discovers no individual truth, helps us to perform no individual duty' (147).

[48] Vernon Lee, *Vital Lies: Studies of Some Varieties of Recent Obscurantism*, 2 vols. (London: John Lane, 1912), ii. 205. Against the various 'hoodwinking' (ii. 182) myths of her own day, among them, the Freudian Unconscious and the Nietzschean Will, Lee asserts art's more modest purpose: 'The difference between art on the one hand and religion and philosophy on the other, lies just in this, that in order to commend itself to our acceptance, art does not (need not) pretend to be more than a pleasure and a

acknowledges the Nietzschean point that 'music is beyond (or outside) Good and Evil.'[49] The question of an aesthetic purity, beyond moral and social responsibility, is never far from her thoughts when writing about music, that '*condition*'[50] which Pater famously put beyond the aspiring reach of all the other arts. Yet if music is unconditionally beyond morality, a 'play' of the imagination set free in a lumber-room, it is still not absolutely removed from what lies outside. That Paterian and Nietzschean 'beyond' is itself a measure of the distance dividing, but not altogether disconnecting, art from good and evil. A 'lumber-room', after all, is a place full of stuff which has lost its relevant use, but has not therefore forgotten it. 'A Wicked Voice', as the title itself suggests, opens up the space between beauty and morality, between the disembodied voice and the wickedness of the singer, which is Victorian aestheticism's special playroom.

Even at the age of thirteen, Lee understood the physical origin of the haunting sound she sometimes heard in the churches of Rome, gleefully reporting to her father an awkward conversation with a family friend about whether such a singer could be 'a woman dressed up'.[51] The physical machinery of the human voice is obviously and closely implicated in its sound. The voice, she explains, in an essay on 'An Eighteenth-Century Singer', 'is the close neighbour of human nerves, mind, and heart'; it is 'played upon by the performer residing in the very fibres of its mechanism'.[52] This confusion of flesh and mechanism, the performer denatured into pure instrument, gives the song an inescapable and pervasive body. Music, she writes, penetrates to 'the soul's vague viscera';[53] it 'imitates what no words have ever imitated ... the languors and orgasms within the human being'.[54] Such organic, even orgasmic, proximity to flesh means that music touches all too intimately on the body's nervous system, thus riddling the means and ends, the material and immaterial properties of art. The aesthetic purity of music lies not so much 'beyond' the body, and all its potential for good and

refreshment, leaving its deep utility to individual and race to be deduced or guessed (or neither) just from this modest, venerable fact of pleasantness' (ii. 154).

[49] Vernon Lee, *Music and Its Lovers: An Empirical Study of Emotional and Imaginative Responses to Music* (London: George Allen & Unwin, 1932), 553.

[50] Pater, *The Renaissance*, 135.   [51] Lee, *Letters*, 12.

[52] Vernon Lee, 'An Eighteenth-Century Singer: An Imaginary Portrait', *Fortnightly Review*, 56(1891), 842–80, 845.

[53] Lee, *Laurus Nobilis*, 141.

[54] Quoted in Carlo Caballero, '"A Wicked Voice": On Vernon Lee, Wagner, and the Effects of Music', *Victorian Studies*, 35(1992), 386–408, 394.

evil, as deep within it. Such riddling acknowledges the commodifications of aestheticism, its impure associations, its physiological realities, while celebrating its capacity to evoke beauty, or music, for its own sake.

'A Wicked Voice' is a haunting story, if inconsistent as allegory. The narrative is raw, and the cracks in its construction are often visible. Yet nevertheless, its ghost is eerily convincing. The idea of a contemporary Norwegian composer in Venice who is haunted by the ghostly voice of an eighteenth-century castrato, to the extent of being unable to compose his own northern, Wagnerian music, opens up for Vernon Lee a 'lumber-room' of connections as untidy and odd as those of her own researches. The 'play instinct' thrives in such a room. As Schiller puts it: 'the agreeable, the good, the perfect, with these man is merely in earnest; but with beauty he plays.'[55] The importance of not being in earnest carries with it the sound of what must be discounted, particularly goodness. 'And thus,' claims Vernon Lee, 'the world of the physically beautiful is isolated from the world of the morally excellent: there is sometimes correspondence between them, and sometimes conflict ... most often there is no relation at all.'[56] 'A Wicked Voice' sets wickedness and the singer's voice in an opposition which is almost 'no relation at all'. Whatever is wicked about the voice, its physical manufacturing, its hinted sexual deviancy, its overwhelming seductiveness, remains at odds with its art. Those odds are the main point of the story.[57]

It opens with the haunted Norwegian composer, Magnus, recalling the event which precipitated his enthrallment to the past. In a boarding house in Venice, surrounded by his rowdy fellow lodgers and the debris of a shared meal—he recalls at one point seeing 'huge hard peaches which nature imitates from the marble-shops of Pisa'[58]—he is given an engraving by one of the company of an eighteenth-century singer

---

[55] Schiller, *On the Aesthetic Education of Man*, 105–7.   [56] Lee, *Belcaro*, 207.

[57] Vernon Lee rarely wavered from her early belief that beauty and morality, or beauty and truth, are different and not necessarily reconcilable principles. 'Beauty ... is not in the least the same thing as Goodness, any more than beauty (despite Keats's famous assertion) is the same thing as Truth' (*Laurus Nobilis*, 10), she wrote. Caballero's assertion that 'she claimed for aesthetic beauty a specifically *ethical* role within daily life' (' "A Wicked Voice" ', 386) is not quite correct. Even in so late a work as *Music and Its Lovers* (1932) she concludes by declaring that art's 'aesthetic playground' is set apart from the 'right and wrong' (555) of real actions and moral choices. The ethical value of art comes only from that apartness, that short freedom to play.

[58] Vernon Lee, 'A Wicked Voice', in *Hauntings: Fantastic Stories* (London: John Lane, 1906; first pub. 1890), 193–237, 198. All subsequent references to this story are taken from this edition and will be cited in the text.

known as Zaffirino, which means Sapphire.[59] The portrait shows an 'effeminate, fat face ... almost beautiful, with an odd smile, brazen and cruel' (206). His fellow guests then force him to tell the story of the singer, and to sing some of the songs for which he was famous. This prompts one of the listeners, an old Venetian count, to tell another story: that of Zaffirino's legendary power over the ladies, in particular over the count's own aunt who, it is asserted, died listening to the irresistible '*Aria dei Mariti*', the air of the husbands, well-known for its killing effects. The count's improbable, long-winded narrative is at first dismissed by Magnus as 'a hopelessly muddled story ... full of digressions'. However, he finds himself becoming drawn into it in spite of his contempt. It 'becomes more intelligible, or perhaps,' he acknowledges, 'it is I who am giving it more attention' (202). This is that very 'life-blood of attention' which, according to Lee, gave the dusty ghosts of her musical researches 'bulk' and 'voice'. Her own, indeed 'hopelessly muddled story' has a similarly transfusive effect on its reader. The count's 'cock-and-bull story of a vocal coxcomb and a vapouring great lady' (206) becomes 'intelligible' because Magnus brings to it the subjective measure of his own desire. To pay attention is to enter the 'lumber-room' of meanings, and to start to order them after one's own heart. Magnus does so in a catastrophically literal way.

'That night,' he remembers, 'I dreamed a very strange dream' (208). This is the traditional gateway to ghostliness. Yet the dream-frame, like most frames in Lee, fails to do what Ruth Robbins calls its 'framing work'.[60] Instead of taking us through into another place, it bumps us back into the present, where Magnus is lying, still awake, on a sofa in the big Venetian drawing room that was the scene of the after-dinner storytelling. He notices a scent of white flowers, the watery white moonlight playing on the walls, and then he goes over the story of his Nordic opera, about a knight who returns home to find that hundreds of years have passed, and only a song, sung to him by a minstrel, recalls his life and exploits. It is from this vague waking state, in a present already rendered uncertain by that time-lapsed story from the antique, that he lapses into the vivid reality of a dream. He is looking down

[59] The meaning of Zaffirino's name plays on the ambiguity associated with jewels throughout aestheticist and decadent literature. A symbol of beauty beyond price, the jewel is also, of course, commercially valuable.

[60] Ruth Robbins, 'Vernon Lee: Decadent Woman?', in *Fin de Siècle/Fin du Globe: Fears and Fantasies of the Late Nineteenth Century*, ed. John Stokes (Basingstoke: Macmillan, 1992), 139–61, 155.

on a ballroom, with yellow sofas and theatrical boxes, from where he hears the sounds of a voice, an 'exquisite vibrating note', and then the awful 'thud of a body on the floor' (210). He immediately wakes in horror, realizing that he has dreamed the tale of the count's aunt, and encountered, meanwhile, the voice belonging to the portrait. This dream contains its own small joke-reminder of reality. In it, Magnus becomes aware of 'a heavy, sweet smell, reminding me of the flavour of a peach' (210). The dream thus orientates itself around a dream-memory of those artificial peaches on the boarding house table which set the scene for the first telling of stories about Zaffirino. Where Magnus *is*, is in a story, which is also where we, the readers, are—although the fact that those original peaches were a trick against nature suggests that reality, in this story, in true aestheticist style, takes its bearings from art. In any case, dream peaches seem more appetizingly real than marbly, real-life ones. The frustrated desire to eat them then displaces into the stranger appetites of dream.

These two initial scenes: the first, of storytelling, the second, of story-dreaming, set the pattern of events to come. Magnus hears the voice of the dead singer everywhere. Searching desperately for the original melody of his own northern knight, he finds instead the laughing, virtuoso voice of Zaffirino. Lee's descriptions of this voice become the leitmotifs of a story which comically trounces the self-important, nationalistic mythologizing of the Wagnerian Magnus with the light, cosmopolitan, sexually ambiguous voice of an eighteenth-century castrato. Not only is Magnus 'a figure for Wagner'[61] as Caballero points out, and for a kind of music Vernon Lee once described as leaving the reader 'devitalised as by the contemplation of a slug',[62] but he also embodies something of that racial (and masculine) consciousness which the cosmopolitan Lee denounced wherever she saw it, and against which she launched her later pacifist work. On a gondola, one night, the ghost-voice comes clear: 'a thread of sound slender as a moonbeam, scarce audible, but exquisite, which expanded slowly, insensibly, taking volume and body, taking flesh almost and fire, an ineffable quality, full, passionate, but veiled, as it were, in a subtle, downy wrapper' (214). It becomes evident at this point that this is a story, not about a ghost haunting his victim, but about a victim haunting his ghost. That ghost takes 'volume and body,' the two ideas of sound and flesh coming together, as they do in

---

[61] Caballero, ' "A Wicked Voice" ', 401.
[62] Quoted in Smyth, *Maurice Baring*, 209.

many of Lee's descriptions of music, to evoke an art built up by desire. Metaphors intended merely to describe the voice, start to embody it. The notes which 'swell,' a word repeated with almost embarrassing frequency, fill out a spectral into a corporeal presence. The ghost starts to inhabit his own body, the voice its own instrumental flesh. The play of meaning between 'volume and body' returns the idea of the voice to the 'vague viscera', the physiological 'fibres' of its own ghostly sound. For the voice, as Magnus frequently expostulates, is a 'violin of flesh and blood' (195), drawing into art the material imprint of the body, and specifically, of course, of a body unnaturally tuned to give forth that particularly haunting sound. The 'downy' quality, repeatedly associated with Zaffirino's voice, also shifts unnervingly from an immaterial meaning—veiled, blurred, soft, feathery—to a suggestion of puberty physically stopped in time.

Thus the ghostly voice snags, by way of puns, on these troubling other senses. Its artistry and beauty, so ethereally out of this world, catch from a long way off on the facts of life. To give body to that ghostly sound, as the story does, is to acknowledge, however discreetly, that its aesthetic power is connected with bodies all round. Those nervous mechanisms, which may be touched, maimed, or even, we are given to believe, killed by beauty, cannot explain, exonerate, or condemn beauty's power, but neither are they irrelevant to its production. Lee's punning awareness of the body in this story makes the condition of music, for all its pure play, a matter also of some harsh physical conditions. But those are remembered at a distance, in a wordplay, a kind of dream-wit, which makes the song's 'killing' effects, on both singers and listeners, no bar to pleasure. The moral of the narrative, that such music is harmful and enervating, goes athwart a style which makes nothing so desirable as just hearing the music once again.

Tormented, then, by Zaffirino's voice, and finding that his own 'heroic harmonies' of masculine exploits are being undermined by 'voluptuous phrases and florid cadences' (216), Magnus tears up the mockingly effeminate portrait which seems to have started all this mischief. He throws the pieces out of his bedroom window into the canal, though one 'scrap,' he notices, is caught in the 'yellow blind below' (217). Eventually, in desperation, he seeks a doctor, and receives the salutary advice to stop work and take a break in the country. Evidently the problem is a psychological disturbance, induced by the unhealthy atmosphere of Venice. The count, on hearing the advice, immediately suggests that Magnus go and stay at his son's villa on the mainland and help with the maize harvest. The name of the place, Mistrà, is recognized by Magnus, in a delayed reaction, as the place where the count's old aunt met her death at the 'hands' of Zaffirino. He accepts the invitation 'with gratitude and pleasure' (222).

The third section of the story, at Mistrà, should mark a return to normality and sanity after the wavering light of Venice and its moonlit hallucinations. The villa is dull and ordinary. The maize harvest is in full flow, and Magnus is forced out of his creative nightmare into attending to the practicalities of cereal farming. By the end of the day he is exhausted. But before retiring to bed, he opens the shutters onto the garden and becomes aware of 'a sudden whiff of warm, enervating perfume, a perfume that made me think of the taste of certain peaches, and suggested white, thick, wax-like petals' (229). The scent of peach flowers and the associated taste of peaches once again become the dream-cue for another repetition, a déjà vu driven inexorably, not by ghostly machinations but by internal desire, indeed appetite: 'And with this odd impression of naturalness was mixed a feverish, impatient pleasure. It was as if I had come to Mistrà on purpose, and that I was about to meet the object of my long and weary hopes' (231). The word 'feverish' makes the pleasure at once willed and still sick, while 'naturalness' remains a principle under severe strain. The moment that Magnus is able to acknowledge his craving for the ghost-singer is also the moment which sets in motion another take of the story. The fever is for 'pleasure', at once a sickness and a purpose, a natural and an unnatural goal, a supernatural nonsense and a supreme inspiration.

Indeed, the narrative drives with undeterred, if unreal, logic towards the place that was first heard in a story and then dreamed in a dream: the ballroom. Magnus, unable to sleep, wanders through the villa's half-derelict passages, and suddenly comes out into a little theatrical box above a ballroom, with its chandeliers, its frescoes, its yellow sofas and, in the corner, a harpsichord. This time he is awake, but the difference is hardly relevant anymore. There is a woman on the sofa surrounded by other people, and, as he watches from above, a man sits down at the instrument and starts to sing:

The voice wound and unwound itself in long, languishing phrases, in rich, voluptuous *rifioritaras*, all fretted with tiny scales and exquisite, crisp shakes; it stopped ever and anon, swaying as if panting in languid delight. And I felt my body melt even as wax in the sunshine, and it seemed to me that I too was turning fluid and vaporous, in order to mingle with these sounds as the moon-beams mingle with the dew. (234)

Magnus suddenly realizes 'that this voice was what I cared most for in all the wide world' (234). The unashamed sensuality of the voice, which has become more of a solid body than the bodies of the living, is caught in the 'languishing phrases' of Lee's prose. This is the 'pleasure' for which the whole story has been impatient. From tall tale, to dream, to waking reality, it makes a return journey through various unstable frames to find the 'real spectre of the antique' at last. While repetition baffles the sense of progress, desire creates the impression of a natural destination: the sound of Zaffirino's voice, 'languishing', 'voluptuous', 'panting'.

But there is a catch. Characteristically, the danger is signalled by a trick of words: 'it seemed to me that I too was turning fluid and vaporous.' The word 'vaporous' harks back to the misty moonlight of Venice and the sickly dreams which it induced. Magnus is himself becoming insubstantial as a shade. But the word also echoes an earlier reference, when the composer had dismissed the whole story of Zaffirino's musical prowess as a 'cock-and-bull story of a vocal coxcomb and a vapouring great lady' (206). Immediately, there is a distracting sound from the sofa, and he hears, as he had in his dream, the death throes of the old countess. The 'vapours', like all the other insubstantial, ghostly notions in this story, have come real, and the woman falls down dead, presumably with pleasure. Such breathtaking beauty has literally taken the breath of its hearer.

At this point reality cracks, and Magnus finds himself in a bare room, stacked with lumber, including heaps of yellow maize and a broken harpsichord. Both singer and victim have gone. Instead, there are 'pools of moonlight', which appear to him 'cold, blue, vaporous, supernatural' (236). The whole event collapses into moonshine, into a supernatural gimmick, though the lingering look of light on the ballroom floor still hauntingly recalls the 'vaporous' condition of the woman and the composer, both of whom dreamed on a sofa and found the beauty of Zaffirino's voice too exquisite to bear. To decode this death either as a re-enacted castration scene,[63] or as a displaced form of the sexual double,[64] is perhaps to miss the element of play in the story, the crazy paving of its language in which patterns, for no moral or emotional reason, repeat themselves like dreams. Indeed, the story itself ends

---

[63] Caballero, ' "A Wicked Voice" ', 404.

[64] Catherine Maxwell, ' From Dionysus to "Dionea": Vernon Lee's Portraits', *Word & Image*, 13(1997), 253–69, 262.

up where it all began, in the place where Vernon Lee herself became obsessed with the music of the past. The vaporous moonlight, the yellow corn, the broken harpsichord are indeed, literally, in a 'lumber-room', a place full of the broken pieces of a story to which desire briefly gave life. Those objects in the deserted ballroom have become the imagination's bric-a-brac again, rubbish left in decay, but from which the voice of the past, seductive and beautiful, might be fleshed and blooded once more. The final scene in the ballroom reveals that, far from being cured, Magnus is only more sick. He has caught the fever which, he was warned, lingered in the night air. 'Airs', like 'vapours' in this story, circulate maddeningly through several meanings, playing literal against metaphorical, ghosting their own common sense. The 'air' of Venice is a miasmal, unhealthy atmosphere, and that sickliness becomes literal at Mistrà where, as Caballero points out, the 'bad air' is etymologically a 'mal-aria' which kills. By some weird logic of etymologies, the bad air is also the '*Aria dei Mariti*', which induces another, but equally mortal fever,[65] so that music, particularly the long-lost airs of the past, are contaminated by these other meanings. The imagination itself plays fast and loose with these references, collapsing the frames which should keep them apart, so that language itself is haunted by spectral other meanings which threaten to revive.

Related to these airs and vapours is that recurring yellow. The 'scrap' of paper which catches in the 'yellow blind' also catches in a network of references: the 'yellow satin sofas' (210) of the dream, the 'yellow, reflected light' (215) of the miasmal lagoon, the 'yellow' (224) plaque on the statues in the church, the 'yellow light' (226) of the acacia hedges on the mainland, culminating in the malarial 'yellow faces of the peasants' (230) at Mistrà. Thus malaria pervades the text, textually cued by that little 'scrap' of paper which will not be destroyed, but insists, like any ghost, on coming back. Just as cholera runs through Thomas Mann's *Death in Venice* (1912), another text which asserts the aestheticist creed of being 'indifferent to good and evil',[66] so malaria gives Lee an imagery, not only of a sickness long associated with Venice, but also of that decadence which spawned so many infectiously risky yellow books. Airs, vapours, and moonlight transmute, readily, from sense to sense, as the text plays out the ghosts in what should be safe and sane meanings.

---

[65] Caballero, ' "A Wicked Voice" ' 402.

[66] Thomas Mann, *Death in Venice*, trans. H. T. Lowe-Porter (1912; Harmondsworth: Penguin, 1955), 18.

One other connotation of this skidding associationism may have come from Lee's own original researches. The particular singer who was her model for Zaffirino, at whose singing, it was said, 'people remained silent and breathless, and occasionally fainted and went into hysterics',[67] was Farinelli, the Italian castrato, friend of Metastasio, Hesse, and Handel, whose fame spread all over Europe in the mid-eighteenth century. Farinelli, however, abandoned all his fame when he moved to the Spanish court and agreed to sing the same four songs every night for the melancholic Philip V. The name Farinelli may have derived from 'farina', or flour, denoting that his family or patrons were millers or sellers of flour. The stacks of yellow corn which fill the derelict ballroom at the end of 'A Wicked Voice' thus suggest, at a distance, one last piece of imaginative lumber, a long lost pun brought back to life. Fiction itself is a room in which author and reader both agree to play, in the hope of being inspired by the mechanism, however creaky, which might bring back beauty's ghosts.

'The genuine ghost?' asks Vernon Lee. 'And is not this he, or she, this one born of ourselves, of the weird places we have seen, the strange stories we have heard?' (p. x). 'My ghosts', she adds, 'are what you call spurious ghosts (according to me the only genuine ones)' (p. xi). 'A Wicked Voice' haunts us, not so much by its events, or even its misty atmosphere of derangement, but by its repetitions and puns, which stir threateningly or seductively in the text. They thus slip the frames of reference set up, just as stories, dreams, and waking life slip the hierarchies of their respective convictions. Puns have a fruitful afterlife in this story, returning to haunt the narrative, even to lead it to illogical destinations. The narrative takes its direction from them, as if pegged to the dream wishes of language itself. Ultimately, the fun of the whole story is that Lee can give us a 'spurious' ghost in whom, like fiction, we do not need to believe, but whose beauty is cravingly desired and pursued. By comparison, the moral substructure of the narrative is unconvincing. Magnus's last action in the ballroom is to try to retain the 'unfinished cadence' of the voice he has lost. But when he tries to play it on the harpsichord, there is only a 'jingle-jangle of broken strings' (236). This is his Faustian fate. He recovers from his fever only to find that he is doomed to compose a jangle of little airs, while suffering a 'hell-thirst' to hear the lost voice again. It is that 'thirst', that 'craving' of a whole age, maybe, which has the last word: 'May I not hear one note,

[67] Lee, *Studies of the Eighteenth Century in Italy*, 184.

only one note of thine, O singer, O wicked and contemptible wretch?' (237) Against this morally cautioning indictment, the idea of those lost notes still sings out.

Music, Vernon Lee repeats in several places, is 'a riddle'; [68] it is 'a spell of our own devising which we cannot decipher'.[69] The idea of art as a sphinx has a longer history than its obvious fashionableness in the *fin de siècle*. 'All artworks—and art altogether—are enigmas',[70] Adorno points out, adding that 'Artworks fall helplessly mute before the question "What's it for?" '[71] At the same time, this muteness is not a final refusal, an insistence on the enigma for its own sake. Works cry out to be understood, and thus differ from the muteness of ordinary objects. Like riddles and enigmas, they 'await their interpretation'.[72] In 'A Wicked Voice' the structure of the narrative cries out for the ghost which might satisfy its want, and explain the meaning of the voice which haunts Magnus. But it is of the nature of both art and ghosts, even spurious ones, to refuse to solve the riddle once and for all. The figure in the carpet, as Henry James's nearly contemporary short story acknowledges, cannot be unravelled from its pattern.[73] What remains is the pattern, the form, the structure which seems to be a riddle, calling for an answer. However, while the critic is doomed to circle that structure, hoping to give the explanation of its puzzle, the ideology of its aesthetic, it is the condition of want which, like Pater's other supreme condition of music, is calculated to make us go on wanting it. Vernon Lee has struck on that keynote of pleasurable desire which rings, loud and clear, beyond all moral or ideological solutions to her text: 'May I not hear one note, only one note of thine...?'

Literature then, one might argue, is neither an unreferential pure play nor an ideologically coded impure play. It is a play between the two, in a place, a lumber-room perhaps, in which things are not obviously quite useful or known, and where their meanings might not be quite what we expect—which is not to say that there is no meaning at all. Hence, writes Lee, 'that confusion in all save form, that indifference to

---

68 Vernon Lee, 'The Riddle of Music', *Quarterly Review*, 204(1906), 207–27.

69 Lee, *Belcaro*, 107.

70 Theodor W. Adorno, *Aesthetic Theory*, ed. Gretel Adorno and Rolf Tiedemann, trans. Robert Hullot-Kentnor (London: The Athlone Press, 1997), 120.

71 Ibid. 121.   72 Ibid. 128.

73 The point about the figure in the carpet, of course, is that the critic who must search for extractable tricks, clues, messages will never find it. In the story only another writer (interestingly a woman) discovers the secret by writing her own, equally secretive, version of it. That way, the riddle is transmitted but not solved.

all save beauty, which characterises all the great epochs of art ... which we, poor critics, would fain reduce to law and rule, to chronological and ethnological propriety.'[74] There is a sense in which criticism will always be a church, establishing proprieties and laws, whether traditional or new, of the left or the right. But the figure in the carpet, the ghost in the machine, is lost if taken out of play, that is, out of the indifferent, formal pattern of the work itself. It is that pattern which ultimately demands attention, as something that sets itself against the many explanatory systems, social, political, or historical, within which art plays.

A 'great picture', writes Pater, 'has no more definite message for us than an accidental play of sunlight and shadow ... caught as the colours are in an Eastern carpet'.[75] If this is the origin of James's 'Figure in the Carpet', it also tells that 'play' is not a totally free play; it figures, after all, in a carpet, specifically an 'Eastern' one, the ideological, marketable implications of which the *fin de siècle* relishes. But it is nonetheless a 'play,' a disturbance, a resistance of form to message, 'accidental' or indefinite as it might be. Pater, like Lee, and indeed all the twentieth-century writers who follow in their wake, makes a space for the aesthetic, for the condition of music or beauty which works, not exactly as a transcendence beyond reference, but as a different stress within it.

'A Wicked Voice' may be a relatively raw and eccentric example of the delights and anxieties of Victorian aestheticism. But it does expose, in the form of an embodied ghost, the tension between beauty, for its own sake, and moral, sexual, ideological messages. Those messages are thrown into confusion, indeed into 'a hopelessly muddled story', by the sound of a voice which simply insists, across history, dream, and narrative inconsequence, on the condition of its own music. In the end we read the story, not to be frightened or to find out what it's about or for, but because we want to hear that voice. The craving to 'hear one note, only one note of thine, O singer' is the keynote of what makes art worth playing, and also worth interpreting, in the first place.

---

[74] Lee, *Belcaro*, 127.   [75] Pater, *The Renaissance*, 133.

ᔅ

Give beauty back, beauty, beauty, beauty, back ...
Gerard Manley Hopkins

The concept of beauty in 'l'art pour l'art' is at once strangely
empty and content-laden ...

Theodor Adorno

6

Just a Word: On Woolf

Woolf is a novelist with a poet's sense of the word. It is not just that
she writes poetically, with a feel for verbal colour and affect, but that
she finds in words, certain words in particular, a structuring device
which is part of the story. Words, for Woolf, can have the poetic
tangibility of solid objects. Her prose turns them over and over, till they
ring unfamiliarly in the ear. She can thus, through repetition, make a
word sound resistant and palpable, not a clear opening to sense which
allows a meaning to pass, but thick with its own shape—indeed, *just* a
word. Such words remain set against representation, their object to miss
their object (in both senses of 'miss') and to call attention to themselves
instead. This, of course, is what all writers do to a greater or lesser degree.
They intensify language, so that the route to pure meaning is delayed,
sometimes blocked, and the reader comes back to the word or words with
a sense of savoured unfamiliarity. In Woolf, this intensity of language is
often achieved through repetition. Certain words are reiterated, so that
a rhythm or pulse starts up which interferes with the impulse of the
narrative. It is in moments like these that she turns the primary, forward
drive of the story into something else: elegiac recollection.

Elegy, of course, was the term Woolf once imagined she might
substitute for that of the novel. 'I have an idea that I will invent a new
name for my books ... But what? Elegy?'[1] By the early 1920s she was

---

[1] *The Diary of Virginia Woolf*, 5 vols., vol. iii: 1925–30, ed. Anne Olivier Bell, ass.
Andrew McNeillie (London: Penguin, 1982), 34 (27 June 1925).

pushing at the boundaries of the novel, pressing towards a new kind of fiction in which the conventions of chronology, character, and event would be challenged. Woolf's modernist experiments in the work of her middle years are deeply implicated with the nature of the elegiac. Not only was she at some level writing elegies to commemorate members of her own family, but she was also pressing towards a kind of fiction which reduced narrative interest to a minimum. These two aims lead to the great, if somehow unsurpassable, achievements of *To the Lighthouse* (1927) and *The Waves* (1931)—works in which writing itself seems to loosen its hold on literal events in order to express a different kind of relationship with the dead. Elegy, after all, is writing bereft of its object, form missing its content. It thus, thematically, corroborates the gap which lies at the heart of all literary writing generally. Form and content do not quite match up. The dead are far off, out of reach, absent, and thus leave language feeling its formal purposelessness, its failed relevance.

Elegy, as a genre, also therefore chimes with certain aspects of the new formalisms developed by Clive Bell and Roger Fry. Bell's definition of 'significant form', as form abstracted from subject matter, underlies much of Woolf's own thinking about art. His proposal, for instance, that 'lines and colours combined in a particular way, certain forms and relations of forms, stir our aesthetic emotions',[2] gives her a language for describing how modernist art might resist the simple directions of realism. Roger Fry, too, though he modifies Bell's view of 'significant form' at the end of *Vision and Design*, nevertheless continues to probe 'the value of the aesthetic emotion' as something which is 'as remote from actual life and its practical utilities as the most useless mathematical theory'.[3] While this seems rather unspecific, it does reveal how much the modernists look to another language, to abstract art, mathematics, or geometry, in order to describe non-utilitarian aesthetic values. For Fry, as for Bell and Pound, 'the aesthetic' is that which pulls away from representation, and all its ethical–pictorial props. Quite how far may be debatable, but the point is the pull. Woolf's own attitudes to writing largely draw on Bell's and Fry's definitions of form, and thus constantly hover round metaphors drawn from the visual arts: 'lines and colours', 'forms and relations of forms'. Thus she writes, for instance,

---

[2] Clive Bell, *Art* (London: Chatto & Windus, 1914), 7–8.

[3] Roger Fry, *Vision and Design* (London: Chatto & Windus, 1925; first pub. 1920), 302.

recalling Fry's influence on a whole generation: 'Cézanne and Picasso had shown the way; writers should fling representation to the winds and follow suit.'⁴ Flinging 'representation to the winds' is an ideal which might characterize the aims of the visual arts in the early twentieth century, but its reproduction in writing is harder to achieve. Like many of her contemporaries, Woolf finds ways to loosen the bonds of form and matter, thus challenging the conventions of realism and asserting the rights of the novel to 'aesthetic values' which are not life's. At the same time, the elegiac strain in her fiction complicates these formal experiments. In spite of the anti-representational impulse of her work, it is also haunted by recollection. Something, or someone, is remembered, and the legacy of the past, mixed as it is with the legacy of her own family, tends to come back. Elegy, after all, plays with tropes of distance, difficulty, even of unreclaimable absence, but it does not simply forget.

Both *To the Lighthouse* and *The Waves* are narratives interrupted by a death. The deaths of Mrs Ramsay and of Percival divide each novel in half, into before and after, innocence and experience, but also throws into relief the question of how those deaths are to be described. If 'representation' must be flung 'to the winds', how are the dead to be recalled or named? This seems to be the question that troubles Bernard in *The Waves*, when, musing on the death of his brother, he struggles to find the right language of recall:

Mercifully these pictures make no reference; they do not nudge; they do not point. Thus they expand my consciousness of him and bring him back to me differently. I remember his beauty.

Woolf finished writing the novel with a sense of overwhelming relief, but also in tears. She was remembering, among other things, her dead brother Thoby, and wondered if she might put his name on the first page. But that, she decided, was impossible. Her novel must make 'no reference' to him. Reference, that pointing, nudging thing, the simple naming function of language, in fact obstructs the act of remembering. In particular, this passage tells, it obstructs something which might come back to memory 'differently': 'I remember his beauty.' The struggle against reference, against pictorial literalism, leads to the surprise of 'beauty', that achieved obscure object of desire. The word recalls something, even someone, but obliquely, expansively, without drawing any pictures or naming any names. It might be the verbal

⁴ Virginia Woolf, *Roger Fry: A Biography* (London: Hogarth Press, 1940), 172.

equivalent of a line, a colour. 'Lines and colours',[5] not accidentally perhaps, are the first words of the next line, as if Woolf were specifically aiming to fulfil Clive Bell's abstracting account of 'significant form'. Meanwhile, the word 'beauty', which she invokes over and over again, in worry-bead repeats throughout the novel, is a strange alternative, banal and imprecise. 'I remember his beauty', for all its vagueness, insists on something which challenges the modernist experiment in anti-realism: that is, elegiac recall, the sense of something missed and remembered. The aestheticist charge of the word 'beauty' keeps the memory of him, but brings it back, 'differently'.

As a word, 'beauty' is hardly either new or neutral. It is redolent of the rich preciosity, the extravagance, the fashionable camp naughtiness of the Nineties. Moreover, its increasingly chocolatey meanings, in the early decades of the twentieth century, was probably one of the reasons for its brisk dismissal in 1924 by I. A. Richards. He waved off the 'paralysing apparition Beauty', a silly, female gorgon, and all her 'bogus'[6] companions, as examples of an outmoded and meaningless rhetoric. Yet Woolf, at the height of her powers in the 1920s and 1930s, is obsessed by the word. It appears everywhere in *To the Lighthouse*. It turns up in *The Waves*, in odd places: in the sand, in a stocking shop, in the smoke of a phrase. In *Orlando* it is the constant inconstant which suffers and survives all other historical or sexual changes, as it does in the novel which inspires it: *Mademoiselle de Maupin*. Throughout her works Woolf chooses to reiterate a word which might, by now, be weary with over-use.

Even towards the end of her life, she returns to the word as if it were a charm. Perhaps it is precisely *as* a charm, a word emptied by constant repetition, that she cherishes it. In *A Letter to a Young Poet* (1932), for instance, there is a suggestive passage in which she tries to identify the missing ingredient of much contemporary poetry. As she listens, she hears 'the repetition in the bass of one word intoned over and over again by some malcontent': the word is 'beauty'.[7] It is indeed just 'one word', and not so much defined, as heard. It might be a note in music, a rhythm, something intoning below the level of sense. It is also, however, a disturbance, a restlessness, the word of a 'malcontent'. The sentence

---

[5] Virginia Woolf, *The Waves*, ed. Kate Flint (London, Penguin, 1992), 118. All subsequent quotations will be taken from this edition and cited in the text.

[6] I. A. Richards, *Principles of Literary Criticism* (London: Routledge & Kegan Paul, 1960; first pub. 1924), 12.

[7] Virginia Woolf, *A Letter to a Young Poet* (London: Hogarth Press, 1932), 23–4.

intones what it desires, letting the abstract noun empty into a rhythmic ground 'bass' which insists without explaining. That 'one word intoned over and over' becomes the sound of beauty itself, missing and desired, meaningless and essential. It is a chant or pulse, an idea functioning below the level of consciousness, but indispensable, nevertheless. 'I am writing *The Waves* to a rhythm not to a plot',[8] Woolf once asserted, pointing to a feature of her writing, a quality of 'over and over again', which is crucial to her style. Beauty, here, has something to do with poetry, rhythm, repetition, with the seduction of a sound, of a shape in the ear. It is almost *just* a word for the word's sake.

Like Pound and Yeats, Woolf cannot relinquish this word. For all its aestheticist overtones, perhaps even because of them, she needs and repeats it. 'I remember his beauty', Bernard concludes, in an elegiac formula which saves the memory of the dead while refusing to picture them. Beauty is a word which functions as a refrain in her writing, as an idea which refuses to adjust, perfectly, to the object in hand, and thus remains resourceful, mysterious, unsatisfied. At another point in *The Waves*, Jinny also muses on the dead, on how people 'are so soon gone', and adds:

That man there, by the cabinet; he lives you say, surrounded by china pots. Break one and you shatter a thousand pounds. ... Hence the pots, old junk found in lodging-houses or dug from the desert sands. And since beauty must be broken daily to remain beautiful ... (132)

That awkward non sequitur, 'And since beauty', is charged with a connection Woolf continually probes. There are objects, 'solid objects' (as in the short story of that name which the passage recalls), which signal the idea of beauty. Moreover, those 'pots, old junk' carry more than a whiff of aestheticism's fascination with bric-a-brac, with shopped-for, cracked golden bowls. Like James, Woolf also knows that shattering the bowl is part of the point, part of what allows 'beauty', which 'must be broken daily', to separate itself from mere price: that 'thousand pounds'. So, 'beauty' is associated with something adrift from use, value, history. Though she remembers the price, she also knows that the object must be shattered. This is 'old junk', the breakages of which are what make it beautiful, and strangely commemorative. In addition, it is associated with a particular place: 'dug from the desert sands'. The sea shore, that

---

[8] *The Letters of Virginia Woolf*, 6 vols., ed. Nigel Nicolson and Joanne Trautmann (London: Hogarth Press, 1978), iv. 204.

founding childhood scene for Woolf, is the place where 'beauty' may be found, like leftovers of a life. As in 'Solid Objects' the sands are where, through luck or chance or just sheer madness, something may be recovered which might be precious. Woolf's version of the spoils of aestheticism is one that toys with broken objects in the sand.

'Being poetry, they roll along, wave upon wave, solemn, majestic, no matter what poor drift and drivel they leave behind for disappointed treasure-seekers.' This quotation is not by Woolf, but it catches the atmosphere of the novel which is full of waves and treasure-seekers. In *To the Lighthouse*, things lost and found on the beach make up an incidental imagery, like musical motifs, on which the plot depends. For instance, most pointedly, Minta on the night of her engagement loses her brooch in the sand.[9] But this seems to set off a series of similar events, as one character after another loses something. Lily imagines being drowned 'looking for a pearl brooch on a beach' (191). She also buries 'the perfection of the moment ... like a drop of silver' (187) in the sand. In the 'Time Passes' section, the impersonal voice imagines something durable and precious, 'some crystal of intensity ... something alien to the processes of domestic life, single, hard, bright, like a diamond in the sand' (144). 'They had all their little treasures' (66), Mrs Ramsay says of her children. Treasure-seeking and treasure-losing go on throughout the novel, connecting the shore to the emotional rhythms of the plot. These treasures, whether pearls, silver, or diamond, like Jinny's 'pots' and 'old junk', have the value of the preciously haphazard, the lost and found, winnings and losings. Such treasures pinpoint whatever has been emotionally invested in them, as well as nothing at all, for they are mostly worthless, imaginary. At some level, too, they figure the very workings of the novel, the way that its incidents and characters are caught up in a wave which 'bore one up with it and threw one down with it, there, with a dash on the beach' (53). What happens in this novel is like a random find on a beach, which also has behind it the large sweep of a totalizing wave. Characters, like bits of junk, may be lifted and then dashed. The impersonal wave will take them or leave them, like the rhythms of Woolf's own prose, which has also often left its readers (those looking for a story, perhaps), like 'disappointed treasure-seekers'.

---

[9] Virginia Woolf, *To the Lighthouse*, ed. Stella McNichol, intro. Hermione Lee (London: Penguin, 1992), 110. All subsequent quotations will be taken from this edition and cited in the text.

'But then I'm one of those people who want beauty, if it's only a stone, or a pot.'[10] This is not Jinny, but the speaker of the penultimate fragment in the short story, 'Portraits'. The pathos and preciosity are audible, but the point is the same: 'a stone, or a pot' might mean treasure, beauty. The satirical tone, a little like Eliot's in 'Portrait of a Lady', sounds at first like modernist mockery, an uneasy contempt for women who go talking of Michelangelo. But behind the satire there is a plea. Woolf's story, itself a fragment broken off from any context, speaker or history, keeps rounding back to the word 'beauty', as well as to the name which seems to be associated with it: 'I never spoke to her. But in a sense, the true sense, I who love beauty always feel, I knew Vernon Lee.'[11] Knowing Vernon Lee, that author of innumerable works on aesthetics, is a memory by association, repeated in this story with fretful insistence. Loving beauty leads to knowing Vernon Lee, in a wish-fulfilling connection which is never developed or resolved. It may be, however, that that connection, which biographies of Woolf have tended to ignore, lurks elsewhere in Woolf's pleading, baffled repetitions of that one word. Beauty, she acknowledges in this story, does not come out of an abstract void, created by modernism; it comes out of nineteenth-century aestheticism's long, pretentious, rebellious history of seeking beauty of form. And one of the voices associated with that search is, of course, Vernon Lee's.

During her life Woolf reviewed several of Lee's books, though they caused her some bother. 'I am sobbing with misery over Vernon Lee, who really turns all good writing to vapour, with her fluency and insipidity',[12] she laments in 1907. Although enraged by Lee, she nonetheless uses her as a yardstick for comparison: 'My writing makes me tremble; it seems so likely that it will be d—d bad ... after the manner of Vernon Lee.'[13] She is infuriated by Strachey's praise of Lee: he 'jumps up and seizes withered virgins like Vernon Lee'.[14] But her attitude in later life softened. She was intrigued, for instance, by Roger Fry's praise for Lee's book on *Music and Its Lovers*,[15] and when Ethel Smyth condemned Lee's pacifist views in 1933, Woolf rallied to her defence: 'Why do you

[10] Virginia Woolf, 'Portraits', in *The Complete Shorter Fiction*, ed. Susan Dick (London: Hogarth Press, 1985), 236–40, 239.
[11] Ibid. 240.
[12] *The Letters of Virginia Woolf* (To Violet Dickinson, December 1907), i. 320.
[13] Ibid. (To Violet Dickinson, 15? October 1907), i. 315.
[14] Ibid. (To Vanessa Bell, 15 July 1918), ii. 261.
[15] Ibid. (To Ethel Smyth, 22 December 1932), v. 137.

think Vernon Lees views on the war detestable? What would you say to mine?'[16] Then, hearing of Lee's death in 1935, she admitted a sense of missed opportunity: 'I'm sorry old Vernon is dead. I had hoped rather to see her.'[17] Woolf's vehemence, antipathy, puzzlement, and then simple regret hint, somehow, at an unfinished story. 'I who love beauty always feel, I knew Vernon Lee', her inconclusive portrait concludes.

There is one comment, from a letter of 1922, which makes the possibility of knowing Vernon Lee resonant beyond mere biographical facts. 'Oh yes,' Woolf writes, 'I remember Vernon Lee, in the dining room at Talland House, in coat and skirt, much as she is now—but that was 30 years ago. She was a dashing authoress. She gave my father her books, which were in the dining room too.'[18] The specifics of that location go beyond personal anecdote, suggesting, as they do, the novel which takes its main inspiration from them. 'It was all dry: all withered' (164), Lily Briscoe laments of her art. In one place she describes herself as 'a peevish, ill-tempered, dried-up old maid presumably' (165). At another, looking at her own painting, 'She could have wept. It was bad, it was bad, it was infinitely bad!' (54). Being 'd—d bad ... after the manner of Vernon Lee' hints at an anxiety of influence which is also, covertly, an anxiety of self-identification. 'I who love beauty' is an I who might have learned more from Lee's books about beauty than she cared to admit. The intoning repetition of the word throughout *To the Lighthouse* draws, by association, on the memory of a presence at Talland House which is not only Julia Stephen, the original for Mrs Ramsay, but also the writer who wrote numerous books about beauty, about the difficulty of defining it or assessing its relation to ethics and history. Both Lee herself and her books figure at some level, however subconsciously, in that novel's 'dining-room'.

In 1908, Virginia, Vanessa, and Clive Bell took a trip to Italy, visiting Siena, Perugia, and Milan. Although the scant journal entries for the time make no mention of it, the letter of 1922, which mentions Talland House, also recalls a visit to Florence and a meeting with Vernon Lee. 'I saw her 10 years later, at Florence, when she fell in love with Nessa',[19] Woolf recalls. Writing to Violet Dickinson four years later, she asks: 'Do you remember taking us to see her at Florence?'[20] It seems very likely

[16] *The Letters of Virginia Woolf* (To Ethel Smyth, 6 January 1933), v. 146.
[17] Ibid. (To Ethel Smyth, 15 February 1935), v. 369.
[18] Ibid. (To Katherine Arnold-Forster, 23 April 1922), ii. 550.   [19] Ibid. ii. 550.
[20] Ibid. (To Violet Dickinson, 26 July 1926), iii. 283.

that Lee would have extended her customary hospitality to the Stephen girls, whom she had met both in London and, it seems, in Cornwall. Whether or not they stayed with her in Florence, it is interesting that, returning to England via Perugia, Woolf wrote a long journal entry about the frescoes of Perugino. In it, she is evidently working out a theory of writing for herself, but the language rings with echoes of Lee's, as well as Clive Bell's, insistence on the abstract forms of art:

I looked at a fresco by Perugino. I conceive that he saw things grouped, contained in certain & invisible forms; expression in faces, action—&c. did not exist; all beauty was contained in the momentary appearance of human beings. ... His fresco seems to me infinitely silent; as though beauty had swum up to the top, stayed there, above everything else ...

A group stands without relation to the figure of God. They have come together then because their lines & colours are related, & express some view of beauty in his brain.

As for writing—I want to express beauty too—but beauty (symmetry?) of life & the world, in action. Conflict?—is that it?

If there is action in painting it is only to exhibit lines; but with the end of beauty in view. Isn't there a different kind of beauty? No conflict.

I attain a different kind of beauty, achieve a symmetry by means of infinite discords, showing all the traces of the minds passage through the world; & achieve in the end, some kind of whole made of shivering fragments; to me this seems the natural process; the flight of the mind.[21]

Woolf's understanding of 'beauty', a word repeated no less than eight times in this short passage, shifts constantly from subjective to objective, visible to invisible, static to conflicting. Beauty might be an idea in the brain, but also a 'symmetry' of artistic effect. It might be contained, expressed, viewed, attained, but it also swims clear, rising, like Tennyson's Kraken, to an imagined surface 'above everything else'. The muddle, and the mixed metaphors—'symmetry' of 'infinite discords'—suggest a working out, and through, of an idea Woolf cannot leave alone, but also cannot settle. The passage is intriguing for letting us hear how 'one word intoned over and over' can become Woolf's method of thinking and writing. She circles round the word 'beauty', finding it everywhere, but at the same time abstracting it from the context as, she claims, Perugino himself does. So it seems to have 'swum up to the top ... above everything else', an object in its own right. 'As

---

[21] Virginia Woolf, *A Passionate Apprentice: The Early Journals 1897–1909* , ed. Mitchell A. Leaska (London: Hogarth Press, 1990), 392–3.

for writing—I want to express beauty too', she asserts, but admits that painting cannot be translated simply into writing, and that hers must be 'a different kind of beauty', full of life, conflict, discord. Already, however, 'beauty' is a word which spoils the picture, or rather, makes the picture, even Perugino's, more design than representation, more a matter of 'forms' than of 'expression'. As Woolf repeats it, she pulls it out of the picture, and gives it an ambiguous, shifting place of its own, 'above everything else'. So she begins a long translation of the visual arts, of 'lines & colours'—that favourite phrase which runs through Pater, Bell, Fry, and Pound—into an aesthetic of writing.[22] The word 'beauty' is already, at this early date, a refrain in her thinking—something which, far from being pinned down and defined, is elusively on the move, in, through, and from the represented object in question.

A year later, in 1909, Woolf reviewed Lee's new volume of essays on aesthetics, *Laurus Nobilis*. Here she asks the question which lies at the heart of her own work, as well as Lee's: 'who is going to say what aesthetic beauty is?' She then adds, ambiguously: 'Here, at any rate, is Vernon Lee's definition: "Beauty is that mode of existence of visible, audible, or thinkable things which imposes on our contemplating energies rhythms and patterns of unity, harmony, and completeness." '[23] Neither human nor moral, beauty is a formality of art, which abstracts itself, as rhythm or pattern, from the object in question. Woolf might, however, have quoted any number of loosely related definitions from the same work: 'Beauty ... is not in the least the same thing as Goodness, any more than beauty (despite Keats's famous assertion) is the same thing as Truth',[24] Lee asserts. But later she also claims that the 'essential character of beauty is its being a relation between ourselves and certain objects'.[25] The young Woolf is rather dismissive of Lee's attempts at aesthetic theory. Nevertheless, the older writer's prolonged, if inconclusive accounts of the idea of beauty, as rhythm, pattern, design, form, come close to her own. What 'aesthetic beauty is' remains a question which tantalizes Woolf as much as it does Lee, even if her own search for that elusive

[22] See Andrew McNeillie, 'Bloomsbury', and Sue Roe, 'The Impact of Post-Impressionism', in *The Cambridge Companion to Virginia Woolf*, ed. Sue Roe and Susan Sellers (Cambridge: Cambridge Univ. Press, 2000), 1–28, 164–90.

[23] Virginia Woolf, 'Art and Life', in *The Essays of Virginia Woolf 1904–12*, vol. 1, ed. Andrew McNeillie (London: Hogarth Press, 1986), 277–80, 277.

[24] Vernon Lee, *Laurus Nobilis: Chapters on Art and Life* (London: John Lane, 1909), 10.

[25] Ibid. 53.

abstraction happens in fiction rather than in essays. Certainly, the word never runs out of steam for her. That 'one word' rings its changes throughout her writing, as if its resources were not yet, after almost a century, used up. Even in the early Perugino passage, beauty is the real object of attention, goading her to try a new sentence, rephrase a point, as she struggles to work out how it might be relational, a moving affect, as well as a pictorially static and visual effect. Her own style will always be haunted by the notion of beauty, as of some ulterior object at odds with what can be merely seen.

Given Woolf's long apprenticeship in the visual arts, in particular the writings of Lee, Bell, and Fry, it is not surprising that it is a painter, Lily Briscoe, who represents the artist in *To the Lighthouse*. It is Lily, in this novel, who struggles against the domestic allure of Mrs Ramsay in the first half, and who is the main reason for the powerful, elegiac recovery of her in the second. This happens, in part, through a painting, specifically a modernist or post-impressionist one, which bravely substitutes form for content, formality for feeling, 'lines & colours' or just 'a purple shadow' for the figure of a woman at the window. As Lily insists to Mr Bankes, 'the picture was not of them.' It is not a representation of mother and child, as he expects, but 'a shadow here and a light there, for instance. Her tribute took that form' (59). Lily, who is a mix, perhaps, of Vernon Lee, the Victorian spinster 'at Talland House', and Woolf herself, is the means by which content, feeling, and real life are exchanged in this novel for the abstract lines of a work of art. One of the ways in which this is achieved, in writing, is through an intoning, over and over, of the word which has always been connected in Woolf's mind with the flight from representation.

That word is also associated, however, with something that Bell and Fry would not countenance: the physical beauty of Mrs Ramsay. Not only a formal abstraction, a matter of shadows and lights, beauty is also a human attribute. It is as if Woolf has returned to the ambiguous double meaning that runs through aestheticist texts. Far from being safely abstracted into geometrical and mathematical principles, beauty of form can still mean beauty of body, and therefore the desirable, touchable fact of the human object. So at one point, she writes of Mrs Ramsay: 'What was there behind it—her beauty, her splendour? ... Or was there nothing? nothing but an incomparable beauty which she lived behind, and could do nothing to disturb?' (34) Mrs Ramsay's beauty, like Julia Stephen's, is an object of fascination and distrust. The dance of two words in this passage, both of them repeated, form a connection which will run through the novel. Here 'beauty' carries with it the charged negative of 'nothing', though the passage also contradicts itself, since the 'nothing' that lies 'behind it—her beauty'—then becomes quite distinctly a 'she' who lives 'behind' beauty, which she 'could do nothing to disturb'. The first 'nothing' is an emptiness, a mere absence; the second 'nothing' is a presence, suggesting instead the impotence of the woman who would get out from behind the bars of beauty. The passage repeats the word till it starts to yield a human story out of 'nothing'. Woolf the feminist certainly has enough distrust of women's beauty to want to probe the real woman 'behind it'. But Woolf the modernist is also fascinated by a 'nothing' which might be all that is left over from 'beauty'. Beauty and nothing will circle round each other, with variations, for the rest of the novel.

Mrs Ramsay's physical beauty, then, is the central subject of the first part. It is a magnet, a lure, a holding of everything together. At the same time, it is a sentimentality, a coercion, an artistic obstacle. This is the lesson that Lily must learn. When, in a moment of rare intimacy at the start, she leans her head on Mrs Ramsay's knee, she finds that 'Nothing happened. Nothing! Nothing!' (57) The word recharges with repetition. All Lily's emotional desire and frustration can be heard in it, as her gesture of need or love is somehow unreciprocated. Later, a similar rejection takes place, and a similar association made between human beauty and waste and unresponsiveness. William Bankes, suddenly wanting to get back to his work, thinks with irritation that 'now, at this moment her presence meant absolutely nothing to him: her beauty meant nothing to him; her sitting with her little boy at the window—nothing, nothing' (97). This is partly boredom, partly pique. But it is also a recognition of the conditions for work. Like Lily, Mr Bankes finds physical beauty a distraction, a trivial irritation. He longs for it to mean nothing so that he can escape the emotional tie of that old sentimental picture of mother and child which Mrs Ramsay embodies. This 'nothing, nothing', like Lily's earlier nothings, hammers away at 'beauty', as if the two words were conjoined at some level, but also as if 'nothing' might break the cloying emotional hold of that picture, and substitute something that has, like 'nothing', 'no reference'. Woolf, the poet, understands how a word can toll its meanings below the level of conscious narrative. This particular repetition works like a worry at the heart of her prose. Behind human beauty there is nothing; or else human beauty leads to a mere desire for nothing. Either way, the two words modify and haunt each other, as if unable to let go of the ambiguity between them.

However, if in the first half of the book, beauty is a human attribute which imprisons and distracts, in the elegiac second half the sheer absence of death is imaginatively reconfigured as a kind of beauty. This change starts in the 'Time Passes' section, where the empty house seems to come to life without human beings. This is the novelist's equivalent to Lily's modernist painting. It is a writing which almost dispenses with plot, character, chronology, those things which, Woolf believed, had cluttered the Victorian novel with irrelevancies and needed to be exorcised. So here she writes as if with the abstract brush of the contemporary painter: 'So loveliness reigned and stillness, and together made the shape of loveliness itself, a form from which life had parted' (141). With the death of Mrs Ramsay, something impersonal and formal appears, a 'shape' which is not the shape *of* anything. For 'the shape of loveliness itself' is 'a form from which life had parted'. So 'shape' is realized as 'form', by an old transaction, but one which leaves little to see or identify. This ought to be the human 'form' of Mrs Ramsay, whose death has occurred, without warning between understated brackets. But instead this is 'a form from which life had parted'. That life has 'parted', rather than 'departed', keeps the form abstract. There is a detachment about 'parted' which lets the notion of 'form' get free of mere physical shape and beauty, and round up, abstractly, into itself. Woolf's play on 'form' points to an object which, while recalling the lost 'life' of Mrs Ramsay, also parts company with that life and becomes the self-involved 'shape of loveliness itself'. It is as if Woolf wins back to the aestheticist position, of art for art, form for its own sake, *through* elegy. Form is what remains, but it is also all there is.

Mrs Ramsay's death, then, becomes crucial to Lily's art as it is crucial to the emotional as well as narrative structure of the novel. If there was 'nothing' in the living woman's beauty, there is another kind of nothing after her death. A few pages later, at the start of the third section, Lily, having returned to the house, thinks of her old love: 'For really, what did she feel, come back after all these years and Mrs. Ramsay dead? Nothing, nothing—nothing that she could express at all' (159). Just as she had met with 'nothing' when leaning her head against Mrs Ramsay's knee, so now the sense of 'nothing' returns like another failure of feeling. The repetition, however, insists too much. 'Nothing, nothing—nothing' starts to sound, in spite of what it says, like something after all: dissatisfaction, desire, anger, grief. Woolf, by reducing everything to just a word that pounds like a rhythm, also hints at the sound of a fist, hammering at what it cannot say. So this is not feeling 'nothing', perhaps, but only 'nothing that she could express at all'. Somewhere behind the beat of 'nothing' are Lily's undisclosed, confused feelings of love.

Then, in a moment of witty and surprising comedy, Lily does find beauty again, not in Mrs Ramsay's reappearance but, of all things, in Mr Ramsay's 'beautiful boots!' The moment is light, and loaded:

'What beautiful boots!' she exclaimed. She was ashamed of herself. To praise his boots when he asked her to solace his soul; when he had shown her his bleeding hands, his lacerated heart, and asked her to pity them, then to say, cheerfully, 'Ah, but what beautiful boots you wear!' (167)

Refusing to be caught in a Pietà, in Mr Ramsay's exaggerated self-martyrdom, Lily keeps her cool. And Woolf, in a moment of suddenly forgiving acceptance of her tyrannical father, with his expeditionary boots and emotional demands, wins the object of beauty for herself. The surprise, and the joke, is that Lily, by refusing to sympathize, in fact consoles: 'Mr. Ramsay smiled' (167). Like Jinny in the stocking shop or Septimus seeing the aeroplane, Lily recognizes beauty in an unexpected place, ordinary, commodified, trivial, and inhuman. Her quirky epiphany is detached from any human relationship. By feeling precisely nothing, except the arresting delight of those 'beautiful boots!' she saves herself both *from* Mr Ramsay's emotional demands, and *for* her art. For it is after this cheery exchange that she can turn to the 'difficult white space' of the canvas, and start to fill it with 'her first quick decisive stroke', 'a running mark', 'a dancing rhythmical movement', and 'brown running nervous lines' (172). She begins, suddenly, to paint. The confidence comes from having rejected sympathy, humanity, fellow feeling, for the sake of those merely formal strokes, those marks, rhythms, lines. She has 'thrown representation to the winds' and begun her post-impressionist work.

However, Lily has not finished with Mrs Ramsay. The novel does not conduct a simple exorcism of her presence, of her beauty and assuaging femininity. Nor does it simply exchange her for a vision of boots and art. Instead, she has to come back. Lily must win her artistic confidence also from Mrs Ramsay's magnetic beauty, not by rejecting but by recalling the dead. Her painting, after all, is *of* Mrs Ramsay. For all its abstract marks, rhythms, and lines, it remembers something, someone. Lily's painting is an elegy, which recalls the presence of the dead in their absence. It is a tribute to them, as well as a way of remembering them, 'differently'. The pull of the past, of that human beauty which once seemed so empty and controlling, now exerts its power.

Then, just as Lily starts to paint, she encounters a sense of presence—one which can hardly be described as a ghost, but could be described, in that usefully equivocal substitute, as a 'form':

> For what could be more formidable than that space? Here she was again, she thought, stepping back to look at it, drawn out of gossip, out of living, out of community with people into the presence of this formidable ancient enemy of hers—this other thing, this truth, this reality, which suddenly laid hands on her, emerged stark at the back of appearances and commanded her attention. ... It was an exacting form of intercourse anyhow. Other worshipful objects were content with worship; men, women, God, all let one kneel prostrate; but this form, were it only the shape of a white lamp-shade looming on a wicker table, roused one to perpetual combat ... (172–3)

This wrestle with the angel of 'form' is a secular diversion from other kinds of 'worship'; it is 'exacting' and 'formidable', a losing combat with an 'enemy', but also a necessary lonely struggle which draws Lily away from 'gossip', 'living', and 'community'. Meanwhile, Woolf herself wrestles with a word which means something and nothing, which is full and empty, there and not there. The pun may be unwitting, but between 'form' and 'formidable' the prose fiddles with an idea which will neither free into visible representation nor disappear as pure wit. The presence of Mrs Ramsay lies somewhere behind it, like the sense of ordinary living that Lily forfeits. The 'exacting form' is without life, without intention. It may be 'only the shape of a white lamp-shade looming'. The passage marvellously intimates the idea of an appearance, perhaps only the appearance of things as they are—although, like more forceful ghosts, this invisible appearance has suddenly 'laid hands on her'. Lily, it seems, has indeed found the 'form' of her art, the thing for which she has abandoned the human community. But she has also found the 'form' of a presence, with sudden 'hands' to command her attention. Form, as so often in Vernon Lee, is a strange, secular ghost, shifting between objects which cannot quite hold it: 'this form, were it only the shape of a white lamp-shade looming on a wicker table'. Were it, indeed.

This passage prepares us for a later one in which Mrs Ramsay is again encountered by Lily. In the meantime, in the last twenty pages or so of the novel, 'one word' is 'intoned over and over again': 'all her being, even her beauty, became for a moment, dusty and out of date' (190). 'Did she not admire their beauty?' (291) William asks, puzzled at Lily's resistance to the mother-and-child icon. 'She was astonishingly beautiful, William said. But beauty was not everything. Beauty had this penalty … It was simpler to smooth that all out under the cover of beauty' (193); 'for this was Mrs. Ramsay in all her beauty' (196); 'her beauty took one's breath away'; 'Also her beauty offended people probably' (212). 'Among them, must be one that was stone blind to her beauty' (214). So Mrs Ramsay's 'beauty' goes on calling, calling, to the end. It is an irritant, a plea, a cliché, a cover-up. But it is also the call of the human, coming through 'that abstract one made of her' (194), as Lily puts it. Her own abstract painting, made of shapes, colours, lines, and forms, has been gained through a rejection of human beauty, not to deny it wholly but to remember it, differently. The 'form from which life had parted' also recalls its human loss.

So Lily's last ambiguous encounters with Mrs Ramsay play round a sense of absence and return. In the end it is not exactly a ghost which appears, but a shape, which is also, still, just the shape of things as they are:

Oh Mrs. Ramsay! she called out silently, to that essence which sat by the boat, that abstract one made of her, that woman in grey, as if to abuse her for having gone, and then having gone, come back again. It had seemed so safe, thinking of her. Ghost, air, nothingness, a thing you could play with easily and safely at any time of day or night, she had been that, and then suddenly she put her hand out and wrung the heart thus. Suddenly, the empty drawing-room steps, the frill of the chair inside, the puppy tumbling on the terrace, the whole wave and whisper of the garden became like curves and arabesques flourishing round a centre of complete emptiness. (194)

This, like so much of Woolf's writing, falls back on abstractions, on those summary 'curves and arabesques' which empty out the 'centre'. Like Vernon Lee's, Woolf's forms take shape around 'emptiness'. Specifically, the form here is of a 'wave' (a sea-wave as well as a sound-wave [26]), but it is also the form of a visual diagram or doodle, mere lines which flourish in the place of the flowers and the life they outline.

[26] Gillian Beer, *Virginia Woolf: The Common Ground* (Edinburgh: Edinburgh University Press, 1996), 107. Beer points to both the Darwinian and Tyndallian emphasis on 'form' as something through which a movement passes. Tyndall, in *On Light*, writes: 'The propagation of a wave is the propagation of a *form*, and not the transference of the substance which constitutes the wave.'

However, although the paragraph ends by abstracting everything into empty flourishes—'flourishing' puns quietly between a living and an empty gesture—it does so as a result of a surprising human contact: 'then suddenly she put her hand out and wrung the heart thus.' This touch of a hand that is dead recalls the earlier 'hand', and comes like a human response to Lily's invocation: 'Oh Mrs Ramsay!' Something, as well as nothing, has happened. Something as well as nothing has been recognized. What remains may be 'complete emptiness', which art's 'curves and arabesques' contain, but it is an emptiness touched by real life. While Pater and Lee touch the cold forms of aestheticism's abstract properties with the 'hand' of sexual desire, Woolf, like Tennyson, longs for the hand of the beloved, the remembered dead. Whether or not this is anything more than 'Ghost, air, nothingness' does not matter. The point is that Lily can draw it. Without representation or reference, this is an elegy for the beauty that has gone, and left nothing but 'the whole wave and whisper of the garden'.

At the end of *To the Lighthouse* Lily confronts once again this same scene of 'empty' steps, and draws her final 'line' (226). Negotiations between emptiness and the lines of art have gone on throughout the novel. Her famous last line may reproduce the line of the lighthouse which has marked the horizon throughout. By the end, however, it is only 'a line', abstract and singular, detached from everything that has happened. 'I meant *nothing* by The Lighthouse', Woolf once insisted in a letter, adding, with weighty *sprezzatura*: 'One has to have a central line down the middle of the book to hold the design together.'[27] This sounds very like Fry's assertion in his 'Essay in Aesthetics' (1909) that 'unity is due to the balancing of the attractions to the eye about the central line of the picture.'[28] Meaning nothing, however, is, by the logic of elegy (as well as of grammar), also *something*. It is the thing from which Woolf, like Lily, wins the 'line' of her design. As Gillian Beer puts it: 'The serenity with which Mrs Ramsay materialises owes everything to art in its fullest sense.'[29] As an elegy for Mrs Ramsay, *To the Lighthouse* searches for the ways to write about her death in terms of a failure of reference which is the point of modernist painting, or writing, at all. At the same time, that failure of reference lets her come

[27] Woolf, *Letters* (To Roger Fry, 27 May 1927), iii. 385.
[28] Roger Fry, 'An Essay in Aesthetics', in *Vision and Design* (London: Chatto & Windus, 1925), 11–25, 21.
[29] Gillian Beer, 'Revenants and Migrants: Hardy, Butler, Woolf and Sebald', *Proceedings of the British Academy*, 125(2004), 163–82, 173.

back, differently, as the mere look of things, a 'white lamp-shade' or the wave-like flourishing of a garden—as well as, more traditionally, that hand from the past which touches the living, suddenly and painfully.

If Lily's abstract 'line' is a sign of Mrs Ramsay's absence and return, a similar abstraction is won by Rhoda in *The Waves*: 'Percival, by his death, has made me this gift, let me see the thing. There is a square; there is an oblong', she asserts. This curious object, a mere geometrical shape, or just the toy blocks of a child at play, nevertheless then becomes sheltering and consoling. She goes on:

The players take the square and place it upon the oblong. They place it very accurately; they make a perfect dwelling-place. Very little is left outside. The structure is now visible; what is inchoate is here stated; we are not so various or so mean; we have made oblongs and stood them upon squares. This is our triumph; this is our consolation. (123)

This is Rhoda's monument, her useless, formal construction which is set against the conditions outside, 'inchoate' and death-dealing as they are. In the end, this modernist 'structure' does not save her from her own death, but it provides a 'dwelling-place' for a time. An empty house, or perhaps a Cubist sculpture, its purpose is merely to signify, to state. Like Clive Bell's 'significant form', or Woolf's other peculiar 'solid objects', it is in itself nothing at all, of no use or value, bearing no relation to the uses of real life. But it stands in memory of something, or someone, and thus offers its own kind of 'triumph' and 'consolation'. The gift of death, bequeathed by Percival, is to reveal an object as merely itself, 'a square', 'an oblong', a mere abstraction of grief. But as an abstraction, it allows the dead to be brought back nonetheless, to be remembered in a different form, and thus to give life to the modernist text which recalls them: 'I remember his beauty.'

Both *To the Lighthouse* and *The Waves* are structured as elegies. They take shape round a character who dies in the middle of the story and provides a kind of absent centre. That centre then focuses the problem of beauty, both human, physical beauty, and the beauty of artistic form which might be won from it. The tolling of that one word in Woolf's work suggests the extent to which her experimental modernism is yoked to an aestheticist creed. She cannot let go of 'beauty'. At the same time, she allows the word to ring on repetitively, till it seems both obtrusively present, an object of constant yearning, and nonsensically empty to our ears. The word 'beauty', which tolls like a rhythmic puzzle through *To the Lighthouse*, means almost nothing, but that 'almost nothing' is also the thing to which Woolf is drawn. This may be just a word, but it is one that has not yet given up its resources for meaning, which are also, of course, the resources for not meaning anything at all.

That Woolf worries so much over this word might also, in part, be a tribute to that Victorian aesthete, the eccentric, stubborn, prolific writer about beauty and the aesthetic, whom Virginia at some level knew. The modernist Woolf takes her bearings from that memory, to which she makes almost no overt reference, but which gives to her writing the charge of yet another elegiac recall. 'Oh yes, I remember Vernon Lee, in the dining room at Talland House, in coat and skirt.'

'Being poetry, they roll along, wave upon wave, solemn, majestic, no matter what poor drift and drivel they leave behind for disappointed treasure-seekers.'[30] This quotation about the workings of poetry comes from a short pamphlet published in 1926, the year before *To the Lighthouse*, by the Hogarth Press. It was written by Vernon Lee. If 'disappointed treasure-seekers' is a temptingly appropriate description of something that Woolf, too, knows—that the pleasures of reading have to do with listening to the waves, rather than searching the 'drift and drivel' of the seashore—it is also true that Woolf, like Lee, recognizes the rich mis-connections of form and content, rhythm and matter, waves and drift, which literary writing throws up. That one word, 'beauty', continues to stand for this absurd and troubling divergence in her work. Woolf, the experimental modernist, thus offers her own version of how 'wave upon wave' of rhythmic prose is never altogether congruent with what readers might seek: the 'poor drift' of meaning. 'But in a sense, the true sense, I who love beauty always feel, I knew Vernon Lee.'

[30] Vernon Lee, *The Poet's Eye* (London: Hogarth Press, 1926), 18.

Rhythm begins, you see. I hear.

James Joyce

The field of moral choice affords man's
Feet crackling ice
To tread, and feet are
A sensational device.

Marianne Moore

7

Yeats's Feet

Yeats's esoteric beliefs caused some discomfort to the writers who succeeded him in the war-torn 1940s. His apparently naive faith in what George Orwell called 'a hocus-pocus of Great Wheels, gyres, cycles of the moon, reincarnation, disembodied spirits, astrology and what-not'[1] seemed, in 1943, if not downright 'Fascist',[2] at least laughable. MacNeice, in a grudgingly honest revaluation of Yeats's gifts in 1941, found himself reconsidering his own generation's 'reaction against Pure Form, against Art for Art's Sake'.[3] Although 'Pure Form' was an irritant to the generation for whom 'a poem must be *about* something',[4] Yeats's poetry drove MacNeice back to the old, aestheticist distinctions between form and matter. 'Form', he writes, 'must not be thought of as a series of rigid moulds. All matter is to some extent *informed* to start with; and the very selection of matter is a formalistic activity.'[5] The problem of Yeats's subject matter, his eccentric pursuit of magic and astrology, sent MacNeice back to the importance of form as the immaterial force which

[1] George Orwell, 'W. B. Yeats', in *W. B. Yeats: A Critical Anthology*, ed. William H. Pritchard (Harmondsworth: Penguin, 1972), 187–93, 189.

[2] Ibid. 190.

[3] Louis MacNeice, *The Poetry of W. B. Yeats* (London: Oxford University Press, 1941), 2–3.

[4] Ibid. 2.   [5] Ibid. 4.

renders matter almost insignificant. Such a force may not be exactly 'Pure', but it stands apart from the 'hocus-pocus' of whatever poems are merely about. The word 'form', in the 1940s, may sound poetically retrograde and politically suspect, but even MacNeice needs its ghostly, verbal energy when trying to account for the puzzle of Yeats's gifts.

Two years before, in 1939, Auden similarly wrestled with what he regarded as the poet's political and personal silliness: his belief 'in fairies' and in 'the mumbo-jumbo of magic'.[6] However, in the imaginary court case to which he brings the poet, the defence lights on a phrase which will yield its own poetic riches: 'the fallacious belief that art ever makes anything happen'.[7] As is well known, Auden's elegy, 'In Memory of W. B. Yeats' (1939), takes the phrase and turns it inside out. 'For poetry makes nothing happen', he writes, adding, a few lines later: 'It survives, | A way of happening, a mouth.'[8] That 'poetry makes nothing happen' is an axiom which has irked poets ever since, not only MacNeice, but Jarrell, Hill, Heaney, and Muldoon.[9] However, the phrase also turns, by a tiny inflection, a redistribution of its stresses, into its opposite: 'poetry makes nothing háppen'. By this accentual difference, 'nothing' shades into a subject, and happens. This is an event,[10] and its 'happening' sums up the ways of poetry. Intransitive and tautological, nothing is neither a thing, nor no thing, but a continuous event: 'a way of happening, a mouth'. The present participle and the unstopped 'mouth' ensure that 'nothing' remains a kind of unfinished speech. Auden thus adds his own little conundrum to the ongoing story of how form informs matter: it turns matter to no account in order to show the accounts of 'nothing'. If Yeats forced him into a reluctant, admiring

[6] W. H. Auden, 'The Public v. the Late Mr William Butler Yeats', in *W. B. Yeats: A Critical Anthology*, 136–42, 139.

[7] Ibid. 142.

[8] W. H. Auden, *Collected Poems*, ed. Edward Mendelson (London: Faber, 1976), 197–8, 197.

[9] Peter Robinson, *Poetry, Poets, Readers: Making Things Happen* (Oxford: Clarendon Press, 2002). Robinson's argument that 'poetry makes things happen in the reader. People wouldn't read poetry if it didn't do *something* for them' (28) works by turning Auden's 'nothing' into 'things' and then into '*something*'. These positives, while concealing a multitude of differences between large historical events and merely personal affects, lack the playfulness of Auden's 'nothing', with its push-and-pull sense of alternatives.

[10] John Lyon, 'War, Politics and Disappearing Poetry: Auden, Yeats, Empson', in *Twentieth-Century War Poetry from Britain and Ireland*, ed Tim Kendall (Oxford: Oxford University Press, 2007), forthcoming. Lyon adds his own twist to this 'most discussed and interpreted' phrase, by pointing to the nonsensical element of 'contradiction' in it, rather like Keats's final teaser in the 'Grecian Urn'.

admission of poetry's 'nothing', he was also enough of a poet to know that 'nothing' has many ways 'of happening'. Indeed, being a 'way' turns the focus of poetry from what to how. 'A way of happening, a mouth' has the curious effect of making us watch the mouth and listen to its 'happening', even if no objective event occurs.

To turn to Yeats at this point is to turn to a poet whose sense of things makes no distinction between reality and myth, event and vision, between life and the life of the dead.[11] Anything is matter for poetry, and 'form' is a word which serves, interchangeably, for fact or fiction, body or spirit, as if the usual differences did not apply. Thus the very things which unnerved Orwell and Auden, the 'Gyres' and the 'fairies', are as much part of his poetry's 'happening' as are Irish politics or personal love affairs. So, in January 1912 for instance, Yeats made the following comment on a remark by the Cambridge Platonist, Thomas More, which seemed to corroborate his own opinions:

I am deep in my ghost theory ... I have now found a neoplatonic statement of practically the same theory. The spirit-body is formalist in itself but takes many forms or only keeps the form of the physical body 'as ice keeps the shape of the bowl after the bowl is broken' (that is the metaphor though not quite the phrase).[12]

In a lecture given by the poet two years later, it is a jug rather than a bowl which holds 'the soul of the dead man'. That soul, a listener reported, 'would keep the form of the jug after the vessel that had contained it was destroyed'.[13] In both, however, the soul is like frozen water, holding, at least for a while, the shape of its original container: the body as bowl or jug. The 'spirit-body' thus keeps the form, or forms, of 'the physical body', so that 'body', with its sense of substance, transfers effortlessly from life to death. The broken bowl, even if 'not quite the phrase', hints at James's golden bowl, which also keeps its crystal veneer in spite of being cracked. Form crosses from bowl to ice, from living to dead, physical to spiritual, without losing its essential contours or substantiality. Yeats's 'ghost theory' is thus hardly about

[11] Peter McDonald, 'Yeats and the Life of the Dead'. Although not specifically on form, McDonald's essay takes seriously, in a way few others have, 'the blurred boundary between the natural and the supernatural in Yeats's thought and writing'. Typescript of a lecture given at the 2005 Yeats International Summer School.

[12] Quoted in R. F. Foster, *W. B. Yeats: A Life*, 2 vols. (Oxford: Oxford University Press, 1997 and 2003), i. 464.

[13] Quoted in Peter Kuch, ' "Laying the Ghosts?" —W. B. Yeats's Lecture on Ghosts and Dreams', *Yeats Annual*, ed. Warwick Gould, 5(1987), 114–35, 130.

ghosts at all. Instead, the posthumous creatures it promotes inhabit new forms or bodies with an ease and purpose which seem almost comically routine. Whether the spirit-body 'keeps' its bowl-like shape or 'takes many forms', it carries those active verbs over the border of life itself into the life of the dead. The spirit keeps or takes forms, as if they were bodily shapes to be changed at will.

This neoplatonic sense of form supplies Yeats not only with a theory of the afterlife, but also with a fairly idiosyncratic view of language. It is a word he associates with the transformability of bodies, and therefore with an almost free adoption of states of being, whether 'physical body' or 'spirit-body', in life or after. Form, as a word, of course, has always gravitated towards both substance and emptiness. On the one hand it suggests a tangible object with a determined shape, but on the other it suggests an outline, a shadow, a way of appearing, particularly as a ghost after death. To be a form is to be both inside and outside an object, both shaped and free. In the *Sleep and Dream Notebooks*, those diary writings which George Yeats sometimes co-wrote with her husband, she proposes at one point an almost mechanical system of embodiment after death. The spirit at various stages adopts a form. It might at first be the shape in which the shade 'last remembers itself'. Later, the shade might 'select among forms it had during life'. Eventually, it might become 'that form by which it was known to the largest number of people'.[14] Form, here, is a visual habit taken by the spirit at various points on its onward journey. George rationalizes what was probably for her husband a more haphazard system. In both, however, the word is associated with a 'ghost theory' which depends on a willed or deliberate metempsychosis. The dead transmute into forms, and thus continue to appear, bodily, to the living. The crossover from one world to another is made, by caprice or choice, by the constantly migrating spirit.

Even when Yeats is not primarily thinking of neoplatonic theories, form has a curious solidity in his imagination. He writes, for instance, in 'The Symbolism of Poetry', that form is a way to 'give a body to something that moves beyond the senses'.[15] Whether dead or alive, that extrasensory thing needs a 'body' through which to be perceived. Ideas or theories must be invested with physical matter in order to be realized.

[14] *Yeats's Vision Papers*, 3 vols., *Sleep and Dream Notebooks, 'Vision' Notebooks 1 and 2, Card File*, ed. Robert Anthony Martinich and Margaret Mills Harper (London: Macmillan, 1992), iii. 106.
[15] W. B. Yeats, 'The Symbolism of Poetry', in *Essays and Introductions* (London: Macmillan, 1961), 153–64, 164.

Form thus involves a kind of physics of the imagination, whereby invisible entities, ghosts or thoughts, are realized as facts. When, in 1907, Maud Gonne offered Yeats a kind of compensatory, imaginary sex life, she invoked a transaction dear to his heart: 'You had taken the form I think of a great serpent', she assured him, as a result of which 'We melted into one another.'[16] She could thus appropriate his own sense of the exchangeable 'spirit-body' to further her own, if not his, sexual advantage. As a 'great serpent' he was welcome; as a man, less so. Yeats's own fundamental and erratic beliefs in the transformability of form could be as weirdly literal as this visionary coition. Form, in the sense of body or matter, offers a world of effortlessly exchangeable identities. As the mere dress of perception, it answers to any subjective need or wish. By the time Yeats came to write 'Per Amica Silentia Lunae' (1917), this easy interchangeability had become a hermetic creed: 'all our mental images no less than apparitions (and I see no reason to distinguish) are forms existing in the general vehicle of *Anima Mundi*',[17] he wrote. There is no difference, here, between 'mental images' and ghostly 'apparitions'. Both exist as permanent 'forms' in the mind or spirit of the world. As a result, the self takes shape, whether as a broken bowl or a lusty serpent, driven by nothing less than its own desire or will.

This mystical understanding of form as real yet infinitely adaptable has a curious effect on Yeats's language. It means that, for him, similes and metaphors are less figures of speech than figures of literally acted desire. Comparisons are not drawn, they happen; likenesses are not descriptions, but events. Since transformation is in the nature of all perception, spiritual apparitions are neither more nor less real than strong mental images, and both depend on the imagination's wishes. This means that the poet can make the most outlandish comparisons sound matter-of-fact. The soul is a bowl or a jug. It is not 'like' those objects, but takes their forms. If George, by the end, had wearied of her husband's eccentric theories—'Willie talking poppycock'[18] she would mutter under her breath—he himself remained undaunted and credulous.

It was this streak of literal-minded visionariness which irked Empson, and led him to propose, for instance, that the last stanza of 'Sailing to Byzantium' (1927) is simply 'funny': 'one sentence of continually

16 Quoted in Foster, *W. B. Yeats*, i. 387.

17 W. B. Yeats, 'Per Amica Silentia Lunae', in *Mythologies* (London: Macmillan, 1959), 319–69, 352.

18 Quoted in Foster, *W. B. Yeats*, ii. 380.

delicious hesitating rhythm, full of the lilting flipness of the comic prose of Oscar Wilde'.[19] Such a 'rhythm', however po-faced the tone, is, for Empson, a piece of aestheticist provocation, a shruggingly camp gesture thrown off for fun:

> Once out of nature I shall never take
> My bodily form from any natural thing,
> But such a form as Grecian goldsmiths make
> Of hammered gold and gold enamelling ... [20]

If this is a *fin-de-siècle* pose 'against nature', it is also, however, a neoplatonic shape-shifting which depends for its effect on the flexibly reincarnating possibilities of the word 'form'. The lines come straight out of Yeats's ghost theories. Form is associated with an afterlife, with being 'out of nature', and with something the spirit might actively 'take'. Its 'bodily form' will be a bird 'form'. The word tracks the development of the soul as it takes on the ambiguously literal form *of* something: a golden bird, for instance. However, the poet is not definitively a bird, but only 'such a form as Grecian goldsmiths make'. To take 'such a form as' is to keep other forms, other potential similes, in waiting. This transmogrification has the flippant appeal of a likeness caught on the hoof—a golden bird, why not?—as if the soul might take another any time. Meanwhile, the combination of something both formed and 'Grecian' brings into the poem, alongside its weirdly mechanical bird-body, the memory of Keats's 'Grecian Urn'. That first aestheticist object gives Yeats a figure for art which is as coolly mandarin as it is also haunted by what it has lost. Although the bird is a silly artefact—'one of those clockwork dickey-birds, in a gilt cage',[21] Empson called it—and although utterly removed from the 'sensual music' (407) of life's sea, it is also, for those very reasons, able to sing about the sea. Like Keats's urn, the bird sings of everything its protected, inhuman condition shuts out.

The form of the bird, then, is on the one hand a neoplatonic option for the afterlife; but it is also, on the other, a figure for art's self-contained expressiveness. If Yeats's neoplatonism gives him a wild freedom with

[19] William Empson, 'Mr Wilson on the Byzantium Poems', in *W. B. Yeats: A Critical Anthology*, 288–94, 290.
[20] *The Variorum Edition of the Poems of W. B. Yeats*, ed. Peter Allt and Russell K. Alspach (New York: Macmillan, 1957), 408. All further references to Yeats's poems are taken from this edition and cited in the text.
[21] Empson, 'Mr. Wilson on the Byzantium Poems', 290.

language, an ability to turn simile into fact, his debt to aestheticism gives him his sense of art's separate sphere. That debt was lifelong. As late as 1917, for instance, he re-read Pater's *Marius the Epicurean*, 'expecting to find [he] cared for it no longer', but discovered to his surprise that it still seemed 'the only great prose in modern English'.[22] Whatever its effect on the tragic generation, the style of *Marius* still seemed unique. Towards the very end of his life Yeats reasserted the importance of Pater by placing him first in his *Oxford Book of Modern Verse* (1936). In its introduction he traces a line of descent from the 'revolutionary importance'[23] of the Mona Lisa passage to 'a poetry, a philosophy, where the individual is nothing, the flux of *The Cantos* of Ezra Pound'.[24] It was Pater's rhythm, his cautious haltings and deliberations, his counterpointed avoidance of subject matter, which still haunted Yeats. 'Pater', he declares, 'was accustomed to give each sentence a separate page of manuscript, isolating and analysing its rhythm.'[25] Although untrue, the point is revealing. It was not the sense but the rhythms of the Mona Lisa passage which Yeats heard and versified in 1936, emphasizing Pater's role as the first singing-master of the moderns. That nineteenth-century legacy goes back, through Pater, Tennyson, and Hallam, to Keats.

While Hallam's essay on Tennyson is an example, in Yeats's phrase, of 'the Aesthetic School',[26] it is Keats, of course, who stands at its head: 'Keats, who sang of a beauty so wholly preoccupied with itself that its contemplation is a kind of lingering trance'.[27] Keats bequeaths to the later poet, as he does to Pater, Woolf, Pound, and Stevens, a word which somehow never loses its savour. In *Autobiographies*, for instance, Yeats recalls that in Spenser's islands 'certain qualities of beauty, certain forms of sensuous loveliness were separated from all the general purposes of life' as they would not be again 'till Keats wrote his "Endymion" '.[28] The isolation of 'beauty' or 'loveliness' from 'all the general purposes of life' is an ideal revived by Keats and passed on to the moderns. 'Beauty' is a word Yeats cannot leave alone. 'Beauty is the end & law of poetry. It exists to find the beauty in all things ... & in so far as it rejects beauty it destroys

---

[22] W. B. Yeats, *Autobiographies*, ed. William H. O'Donnell and Douglas N. Archibald (New York: Scribner, 1999), 235.
[23] *The Oxford Book Of Modern Verse: 1892–1935*, chosen by W. B. Yeats (Oxford: Clarendon Press, 1936), p. viii.
[24] Ibid. p. xxx.   [25] Ibid. p. viii.   [26] Yeats, *Autobiographies*, 361.
[27] W. B. Yeats, 'Edmund Spenser', in *Essays and Introductions*, 378.
[28] Yeats, *Autobiographies*, 242.

its right to exist',[29] he wrote in 1900. He returns to the word in poems and their titles, as if to some self-justifying, entrancing object which will not be divested of its essential magic. From 'He Remembers Forgotten Beauty' (1899) to 'Beautiful Lofty Things'(1939), the word troubles his writing like the sign of something which will indeed not be forgotten. To remember 'forgotten beauty' nicely summarizes modernism's ambiguous recollections of the past. What is forgotten must be remembered again, with an extra will and determination, as if recovering the repressed. Keats, who first separated 'beauty' from 'life', is the acknowledged originator of this aestheticist tradition. In 1905, castigating his own countrymen's emphasis on political purpose in the arts, Yeats declares that: 'Art for art's sake ... whether it be the art of the *Ode on a Grecian Urn* or of the imaginer of Falstaff, seems to [the Irish writer] a neglect of public duty. It is as though the telegraph-boys botanised among the hedges.'[30] He thus pinpoints in Keats both the beginnings of art for art's sake, and the poetic exploitation of delay associated with it. Instead of running to deliver, 'the telegraph-boys' are distracted, waylaid. In that one word, 'botanised', the sound of their running feet stops still, and a deviating pause begins. The difference between running and pausing can be heard everywhere in Yeats's poetry, marking the difference between 'public duty', getting messages to their destinations, and the diversionary tactics of botanizing. Behind this quotation lies something that is central to the poet's artistic aim. What can be heard in the abrupt change of 'the telegraph-boys botanised among the hedges' is the altered pace of their feet.

Indeed, this poet, who claimed to be tone deaf, had an extraordinarily complex and subtle sense of rhythm. It is the rhythms of Pater, Tennyson, and Keats which ring in his ears, and it is rhythm which is invoked when he tries to account for his own art. Rhythm, writes Derek Attridge, 'is the apprehension of a series of events as a regularly repeated pulse of energy, an experience which has a muscular as well as a mental dimension'.[31] The fact that both 'muscular' and 'mental' dimensions are present gives rhythm a physiological as well as emotional purpose, connecting it to both the nerves and feelings. 'Footbeats for the metre and heartbeats for the rhythm',[32] Robert Frost once insisted, similarly

[29] *The Collected Letters of W. B. Yeats*, ed. John Kelly, vol. II, 1896–1900, ed. Warwick Gould, John Kelly, Deirdre Toomey (Oxford: Clarendon Press, 1997), ii. 522.
[30] Yeats, *Explorations*, sel. by Mrs. W. B. Yeats (London: Macmillan, 1962), 197–8.
[31] Derek Attridge, *The Rhythms of English Poetry* (London: Longman, 1982), 77.
[32] Robert Frost, *Collected Poems, Prose, and Plays* (New York: The Library of America, 1995), 847.

putting rhythm close to the heart, while highlighting a contrast like that of Yeats's telegraph-boys: metre tramps, but rhythm has a varying, divergent pulse. 'Poetry', he explains, 'plays the rhythms of dramatic speech on the grid of meter.'[33] The association of rhythm with the body, and the body's wavering, feeling pulses, makes it personal and unpredictable. As Ronald Schuchard explains of Yeats: 'the rhythms of his poetry are founded upon the relation of cadence to metrical structure.'[34] Yeats, as a poet, works within fairly regular metres, but his rhythms, surprising and counterpointing, carry the sound of his own poetic voice.

The sense of that voice was associated from the start with rhythm. Yeats once recalled that 'The Lake Isle of Innisfree' was 'my first lyric with anything in its rhythm of my own music. I had begun to loosen rhythm.'[35] Just as it is Pater's rhythm which he hears and reproduces in *Modern Verse*, so here it is a looser rhythm which conveys his 'own music'. Something of what Yeats meant can be heard in his own extant reading of 'Innisfree': 'I will arise and go now, and go to Innisfree' (117), he half-chants. The sheer slowness of the poem's hexameters, modulating at the end of each stanza into tetrameters, is made even more pronounced by the extra emphases, the wavering line-ends, and the almost diphthonged pronunciation of the last vowels. Everything conspires to arrest the lilting upbeat of 'I will arise and go now'. Already, the second 'and go' slightly stalls, as if something blocked the way ahead, forcing the poet to take it again. Even without Yeats's eccentrically slow voice, the pace of the poem runs contrary to its intentions. After the initial energy, we are rhythmically marooned in a lotos-eating island-time which beautifully enacts the place that is imagined. The long, slow lines, shifting between hexameter and heptameter, suggest just how far it might be, so that by the end it is not surprising that the poet has gone nowhere. The Lake Isle is lost in the drawn-out pause of its own writing, as if, indeed, 'separated from all the general purposes of life', while the poet remains where he was at the beginning, 'on the roadway, or on the pavement grey'. In some ways, this is a poetic enactment of those telegraph-boys who should 'arise and go', or even run, but are diverted, instead, into imagining, dallying, dreaming.

---

[33] Frost, *Collected Poems, Prose, and Plays*, 809.
[34] Ronald Schuchard, ' "As Regarding Rhythm": Yeats and the Imagists', *Yeats: An Annual of Critical and Textual Studies*, vol. ii, ed. Richard J. Finneran (Ithaca and London: Cornell University Press, 1984), 209–26, 210.
[35] Yeats, *Autobiographies*, 139.

It was just such a sense of the poetry's rhythm that affected James Joyce when he heard Anna Mather, in 1899, chant the lyric 'Who Goes with Fergus?' Soon after, he tried to set the poem to music; then, many years later, remembered it in both *Portrait of the Artist* and the 'Proteus' section of *Ulysses*.[36] John Masefield, similarly, could not forget the sound of Yeats reading: 'He stressed the rhythm until it almost became a chant; he went with speed, marking every beat and dwelling on his vowels. That wavering ecstatic song ... was to remain with me for years.'[37] Once again it is rhythm, a sound capable of unexpected 'wavering', which haunts the listener. For rhythm can change the stress of the beat without necessarily changing the metre. Unlike metre, it is internal, variable, affected by subject matter and feeling. Rhythm is the ligament of poetry, connecting the outward tap of the metre with a pulse which follows the two imponderables of sense and voice. 'That wavering ecstatic song' catches the pace of something which cuts across metrical regularity, metrical control. Metre never misses a beat, but rhythm can let you hear the heart stop.

Yeats is a master of such contrary speeds. Their counterpoint is connected to others in his writing, those between beauty and work, dream and duty, the call of the aestheticist past, with its islands of lost time, and the call of Ireland here and now, demanding action. This cross current is audible in the poem which ends the second volume of 1893: 'To Ireland in the Coming Times'. Written '*to sweeten Ireland's wrong*' (137), it takes its energy and metrical time from Blake's 'The Tyger', as if thereby harnessing that poem's revolutionary drive. Certainly, it sounds at first as if it were all on the side of political action. But in fact, no sooner does Yeats touch on Ireland and its wrongs than the language starts to circle round a particular word:

> *The measure of her flying feet*
> *Made Ireland's heart begin to beat;*
> *And Time bade all his candles flare*
> *To light a measure here and there;*
> *And may the thoughts of Ireland brood*
> *Upon a measured quietude.* (138)

[36] Ronald Schuchard, '"The Countess Cathleen" and the Chanting of Verse, 1892–1912', *Yeats Annual*, ed. Wayne K. Chapman and Warwick Gould, 15(2002), 36–68, 40–1.

[37] John Masefield, ibid. 65, note 29.

These three references to '*measure*' in the first stanza hint at a back-tracking almost from the start. The '*measure of her flying feet*' suggests a waking up of Ireland's Blakean heart, to arise and go into a new life. Very quickly, however, this becomes the different '*measure*' of a stately, candlelit dance under the aegis of '*Time*'. Finally it turns into that '*measured quietude*', which might recall Keats's own 'Cave of Quietude'. This last is a measure which is neither '*flying*' nor dancing, but so constrained and inward that it is hardly a movement at all. So the one word, '*measure*', charts an altering rhythm, a change of footstep through the poem, from the '*flying feet*' of a newly awakened Ireland to the '*measured*' sense of quiet brooding. By the end, the word has reined in the footbeat and heartbeat of an Ireland bent on action and change. The very word is an alternative, internal '*measure*', delaying the urgent tetrameter of the verse.

So the measure, though not the metre, of things changes. It slows up, pivoting on a word which can mean footstep, tempo, dance, limit, as well as measurement and moderation. Then, in the final stanza, yet another imaginary beat lets itself be heard: '*For God goes by with white footfall*' (139). This is an eerie line, which starts a new pulse altogether, and one calculated to alter the story of '*Ireland's wrong*'. What speed is a '*white footfall*' and how heavy is its tread? Yeats is still hearing the feet of what passes, as if measuring out the sound of his content, the music of his matter. Like the '*elemental creatures*' that go about his '*table to and fro*' (138) in a nearly inaudible patter, here he catches a footfall so light, or '*white*', that it is almost silent. The drumbeat of Ireland's '*flying feet*' is thus subdued to a strangely different foot, which still goes walking, however lightly, in four stresses to the line. '*I cast my heart into my rhymes*', the poet declares, as if God's '*footfall*' gave him a new, lighter measure of making the heart go. This inwardness finally turns away from the feet that run, purposefully and noisily. And yet, although the poem heads for a place almost free of footfalls altogether: '*In truth's consuming ecstasy*' (139)—a place that heralds the later 'artifice of eternity' which will 'Consume my heart away' in 'Sailing to Byzantium'—it also cannot quite relinquish the idea of '*measure*'. As in the later poem, the sound of the heart beating, however subdued or internalized, can still be heard. Both poems end by recollecting the race of feet in time, the rush of something to be done, the pounding heart of a purpose that is still *not* completely consumed away. In 'Byzantium', 'what is past, or passing, or to come' (408) keeps the heart-pace of life still moving, even in the mechanical song of the bird. In 'To Ireland' the poet ends by recollecting how, in spite of eternity and its political quietism, '*my heart went with them*' (139). The slowed-up measure of artistic escape still recalls, at a distance, the pounding measure of action.

So within the same metre Yeats lets us hear rhythms, whether of sound or sense, crossing its path. Throughout his life, when he thinks about poetry he thinks about rhythm, about the sound of something flying, dancing, wavering, or staying almost perfectly still. Footsteps are a sign of it. The connection between steps and rhythm goes back to his early days, when he was marking out a tempo of poetry to reflect his aestheticist sympathies. In 'The Symbolism of Poetry', for instance, he remembers those who, like himself:

> would cast out of serious poetry those energetic rhythms, as of a man running ... and we would seek out those wavering, meditative, organic rhythms, which are the embodiment of the imagination, that neither desires nor hates, because it has done with time, and only wishes to gaze upon some reality, some beauty. [38]

This 'man running', with the determined energy of the metronome, recalls the 'telegraph-boys' with their proper 'public duty'. To change the 'running' of a man for a different rhythm, a 'wavering, meditative, organic' rhythm, is not only to throw off the shackles of high Victorianism, as Yeats saw it, but also to throw off the 'energetic' purpose of political grievance. Of course, however, grievance returns to haunt the poet, as it has always returned in the aestheticist tradition. The sound of 'a man running', or of Ireland flying, disturbs his verse, filling it with the menace and duty of public action. As a result, those 'wavering, meditative, organic rhythms', with their connection to 'beauty', timeless and self-sufficient, quarrel with something else. And it is the quarrel which matters. If this is, thematically, a quarrel with oneself, it is also a quarrel of sounds, of something in the poetry which, whatever else it is about, beats out a variation to the ear. This is not a metrical innovation, but a sound-sense variation, which offers itself like an odd, insistent footwork, heard against the grain.

Even at the end of his life, Yeats was insisting on the requirements of the ear. In 1937, two years before his death, he noted that 'I have spent my life in clearing out of poetry every phrase written for the eye, and bringing all back to syntax that is for ear alone.'[39] Although he might abandon his early opinions about symbolism, he does not abandon his

---

[38] Yeats, *Essays and Introductions*, 163.   [39] Ibid. 523.

concern 'for ear alone'. As he writes, also in 1937, 'the rhythm is old and familiar, imagination must dance, must be carried beyond feeling into the aboriginal ice.' He then adds, in a moment's uncertainty: 'Is ice the correct word?'[40] It may be that some memory of the 'ice' which keeps the shape of the bowl after it has broken, or perhaps of the similar 'ice burned and was but the more ice' (316) of 'The Cold Heaven', hovers in the thought of being 'beyond feeling'. In that unfeeling place, the icy coldness must keep the pulse of the rhythm live and dancing. To be 'carried beyond feeling into the aboriginal ice' does not mean simply to die. It means to take on another form, consciously and coldly; even to 'dance' into one by a rhythm which is indeed 'old and familiar'. By the end of his life, whatever feelings must be sloughed off, rhythm remains and 'must dance'. The sense of feet at work, even at work in the ice, is crucial to Yeats's greatest poetry.

It is interesting, then, to notice how often that poetry imagines feet: the feet of the runner, the lover, the dancer, of horses and birds. It is as if the poetry projected its own technical variety into the subject matter, projecting the sound of its own rhythm as a kind of content. As the feet of various creatures beat into the language, they register something which is elemental, essential. In the early sonnet, 'He Bids His Beloved Be at Peace' (1899), for instance, the shadowy horses' hooves drum through the poem, in a sound that refuses peace and contradicts the bidding of the title. Whether those horses are figures of nightmare, desire, or restlessness, their beating makes a continuous ground bass, a rhythm which keeps, if not the beloved, at least the speaker and reader awake. 'Their hoofs heavy with tumult' that 'plunge in the heavy clay' (154) are still audible and working in the last words of the poem: 'their tumultuous feet'. That confusing and overwhelming onslaught drowns out the other, quieter beat: 'your heart beat', which must win its rest from the horses of nightmare or disaster. Yeats, as if to catch the ambiguity of these creatures, slightly varies the metrical time of the lines. 'And hiding their tossing manes and their tumultuous feet' may stress the second 'their', drawing the line out to a conforming hexameter, or else 'their' may be elided for a final, solving pentameter. In fact, throughout, pronouns may either be emphasized or not: 'Beloved, let your eyes half close, and your heart beat | Over my heart, and your hair fall'. The weight of the poem falls heavily or lightly, in hexameter or pentameter, depending on whether 'your' is stressed or not. Thus,

40 Yeats, *Essays and Introductions*, 523

indeed, the loaded irony of the title, and the question whether anyone at all is at peace in this poem, are made audibly clear in the rhythmic choices a reader must make. 'He Bids His Beloved Be at Peace' is a title with hard work to do against the 'tumultuous feet' which 'plunge' so relentlessly in the strange soil of its meaning.

The later, but comparably nightmarish love poem, 'On a Picture of a Black Centaur by Edmund Dulac' (1928), similarly plays hexameter against pentameter. 'Your hooves have stamped at the black margin of the wood' (442), it begins, in a line which sounds unequivocally like pentameter. Two lines later, it is echoed by 'My works are all stamped down into the sultry mud', which wavers, depending on whether 'into' is emphasized or not. Then follows: 'I knew that horse-play, knew it for a murderous thing', which similarly pauses on the edge of hexameter, leaving the reader to decide whether to emphasize 'play' or not. Each line which remarks on the centaur's hooves is indecisive, its stamp irregular. It hovers between two metres, as if uncertain of its movements. The rest of the poem, however, is mostly in hexameters, thus reasserting Yeats's metrical regularity. In the end, it is hard to tell if the centaur is a creature of rigid, violent actions, whose 'hooves have stamped' through time to murder the poet's desires and works, or if it is a more variable stamper, whose destructive urges are perhaps, ultimately, not as terrible as those of the other nightmare figures of the poem: the 'horrible green parrots'. Even while being 'murderous', the centaur's movements might, after all, only be 'horse-play', a childish game, indulged for fun. Meanwhile, as in 'He Bids His Beloved', the speaker stays awake, attentive to the hoof-rhythms of something he cannot altogether control or shut out. Although he would keep the sound at bay, he also does not wish to escape or sleep, but stays awake, alert to the cross-rhythms, as well as to the puzzling cross-senses, of these horses. Whatever they are, destructive or playful, murderous or desirable, the poet is listening.

This intermediary role of listener and guardian is important. Horses, in Yeats's poetry, are generally associated with violence and tumult, with the call of action and revolt. Yet in order that the poem might settle into its quieter artistic pace, the poet fends off that row, that nightmare of reality coming too close. 'Violence upon the roads: violence of horses ... Thunder of feet, tumult of images' (432, 433), Yeats writes in Section VI of 'Nineteen Hundred and Nineteen'. Here, the old threatening figure returns: 'the nightmare | Rides upon sleep' (429). External and internal horses are rife. They bring with them the beat of action, danger, even of civil war, and the sound is not one that the poem can altogether shut out. The poet must listen, even at a distance, to the gong-driven dancers and the 'violence of horses'. Those horses tramp through his poems, their feet insisting on what is urgent, purposeful. Their clatter must be heard, even if heard against the slower feet of dreaming, brooding, meditating, of the imagination let loose from the sound of running. At the end of Yeats's life this doubleness persists. In a gesture of peace, indifference, or it may be continuing attention, the poet in 'Under Ben Bulben' demands: '*Horseman, pass by!*' (640) This might mean, I have done with horses and all their noise. But it might equally mean, that the poet after death intends to lie still within earshot of them. A touch of ambiguity makes it uncertain how near or how far that '*pass by!*' might be.

The sound of feet, then, is everywhere audible in Yeats. They tread, measure, pace, plunge, wander, dance, pass. Their movements characterize his figures, as if these communicated not by talking but walking. 'Tread softly because you tread on my dreams' (176), the poet tells his beloved in 'He Wishes for the Cloths of Heaven'. The idea of feet treading on 'dreams' pivots ambiguously between destruction and creation, presumably depending on how 'softly' she goes. In 'He Gives His Beloved Certain Rhymes', the poet asserts that stars and sky 'Live but to light your passing feet' (158). The Shelleyan figure of the beloved, walking on the poet's work, may destroy or inspire, darken or lighten them. This is in part just an old trope of desire, hovering between the abject and the lusty. But it is also a trope for poetic rhythm, for the sound of a tread which lies deep in the language of the poem itself. Yeats may be addressing his beloved, but the figurative double meanings of tread, beat, measure, suggest that the beloved's feet, or any other creature's feet, are only a visualization of the sound and speed of the poem itself.

The importance of this image is underlined by an intriguing account of Yeats's compositional methods given by James Cousins. In 1912, while staying in the same house as the poet, he recalled hearing 'a queer monotonous murmur' from a back room. 'Its constant repetition of the same sounds in similar order had the eeriness of the inaudible made audible', he wrote. This sound, continuing for up to 'three hours', was then ascertained to be 'the Yeats method of composing verse, making a sound-scheme into which words were fitted after much trial and alteration'.[41] This suggests that the poet would start with the rhythm, and through its repetition, 'trial and alteration', would find

---

[41] Quoted in Schuchard, ' "As Regarding Rhythm": Yeats and the Imagists', 223–4.

words to match. Perhaps it was the same sound that Pound recalled in the *Cantos*, 'as it were the wind in the chimney', but 'in reality Uncle William | downstairs composing'. That wuthering noise then comes clear in the elongated chanting of 'made a great Peeeeeeeacock'.[42] Yeats's strangely obsessive sense of feet, then, grew out of that 'murmur', that chanting 'sound-scheme', which is the poem in formation. Without meaning or matter, such a chant would only later metamorphose into words, and so into the poem's dancing of feet, trample of hooves, tread of birds. Feet, for Yeats, modulate from the simple rhythm in his head, a counting of beats, to the feet of creatures moving, somehow, on the surface, in time to the time already set. Feet are not primarily a subject matter, but a 'measure' of his verse. They represent, not something literal happening, but the divergent beats or pulses at which it happens. Like those 'rhythms which are the embodiment of the imagination', they carry the sound of an event, which may be only the beat of an idea as it drums or dances in the head.

The 'sound-scheme' or sound-sense of Yeats's poetry thus propels its writing, dictating its imagery, keeping the originating 'murmur' still audible within it. In 'The Cat and the Moon' (1919), for instance, he writes:

> Minnaloushe runs in the grass
> Lifting his delicate feet.
> Do you dance, Minnaloushe, do you dance? (378)

In the later play of the same name, the cat's 'delicate feet', by a weird transaction, cure the Lame Beggar. It does not matter what or who the Lame Beggar is. What matters is the dancing that affects his feet, the music which makes something happen. In Yeats any creature, whether horse, cat, bird, or man, may be no more than an investment of imaginary impressions, an embodiment of something that 'moves beyond the senses.' The cat dances and the Lame Beggar walks. Like the much-disputed peahens,[43] these are not precise descriptions, subject

---

[42] Ezra Pound, *The Cantos of Ezra Pound* (London: Faber, 1987), 547–8.

[43] Christopher Ricks, 'Literature and the Matter of Fact', in *Essays in Appreciation* (Oxford: Oxford University Press, 1998), 304. Ricks's point that Yeats failed to be concerned 'with the poultry yards' in his dancing peahens has been answered by Peter McDonald, in *Serious Poetry: Form and Authority from Yeats to Hill* (Oxford: Clarendon Press, 2002), 47–9. To McDonald's call for more discrimination of poetic facts, I would add that Yeats's whole attitude to poetry and metaphor in fact accepts metaphors as literal matters of fact. The peahens, like the cat or any number of creatures, do not look *as if* they are dancing, correctly or incorrectly; they do literally dance, believe it or not.

to anatomical proof, but a fait accompli. The sound of their feet on the ground is the point and end of the play, as perhaps it was also its beginning: 'a queer monotonous murmur' in Yeats's head.

Everywhere in these poems, then, there is a kind of tapping, usually of feet marking their time, or perhaps expressing a dispute with time. In 'The Symbolism of Poetry' the poet suggests that the 'purpose of rhythm ... is to prolong the moment of contemplation'.[44] In 'Mythologies', similarly, he declares that 'a vision, whether we wake or sleep, prolongs its power by rhythm and pattern.'[45] To 'prolong the moment' is not necessarily to alter the metre, but to alter the tempo within it. This is evident in a poem like 'Meditations in Time of Civil War' (1928). As the title suggests, this is a poem of prolonged meditation or contemplation, but contemplation harassed by the thought of war. The two conditions are imagined as rhythms, as feet. In the first section we hear the peacock's 'delicate feet upon old terraces,' the nearly inaudible and Keatsian 'slippered Contemplation', and the 'pacing to and fro on polished floors' (418) of ancestral feet. All of these suggest an aristocracy under threat. There is something closeted and hushed about these paces, even if 'to and fro' hints at underlying anxiety. Then, in the second section, there is the surprising intrusion of the 'stilted water-hen' and 'the splashing of a dozen cows' (419), as if an indifferent nature crashed into the scene. Finally, in the wonderful counterpoint of the seventh section, the running of the 'rage-hungry troop, | Trooper belabouring trooper' suddenly gives way to the eerie calm of 'Their legs long, delicate and slender, aquamarine their eyes, | Magical unicorns bear ladies on their backs.' All of these references subtly affect the tempo, drawing out the time it takes to read, making the feet in fact beat time against the metrical time. The hurrying, repetitive rage of the troopers, trundling, plunging, crying for vengeance, meets the sudden slowness, with no metrical alteration, of those slender-legged unicorns and the women thinking of 'Nothing but stillness' (426). The power of this poem comes from its many feet, all in their different ways insisting on their own time: aristocratic, animal, revolutionary, magical. The poet, too, is caught up in this pedometrical subtext. He turns at one point 'towards my chamber' (424), then climbs 'to the tower-top', leans 'upon broken stone' (425), and finally shuts it all out: 'I turn away and shut the door, and on the stair | Wonder' (427). Although they are more muted, he too has his steps. He goes halting, listening to the

---

[44] Yeats, *Essays and Introductions*, 159.
[45] Yeats, 'Per Amica Silentia Lunae', 341.

riot outside, his turning indoors and inwards marking a necessary turn
if he is to catch 'the cold snows of a dream' (424). His feet climb, pause,
wonder. These rhythms are different from either the precious footsteps
of section one or the tramping rage of the rebels outside. Although Yeats
listens with increasingly troubled and bitter attention to the sounds of
civil war, he also returns to the quiet of meditation, and to the birds and
beasts whose feet tap out another sense of time and dance to other, more
careless routines. His poems, at their best, catch this conflict, playing
out its tensions in the odd footwork of his human and animal figures.

By the middle period of Yeats's life there are fewer women tramping
in his imagination, and more birds. The emphasis is thus lighter, more
oblique. A bird, after all, may simply fly away. At the same time, the
sounds of bird-step and bird-flight are as prominent as those many calls
which 'beat, wheel, cry, hover, keen through Yeats's poems'.[46] That feet
and wings have a sound has less to do with facts of nature, however,
than with the hidden emotional pulses of these poems. Birds are neither
just symbolic nor decorative. They are more like percussive instruments
which set the pace of feeling in a work. So, in 'The Wild Swans at
Coole' (1919), Yeats writes:

> All's changed since I, hearing at twilight,
> The first time on this shore,
> The bell-beat of their wings above my head,
> Trod with a lighter tread. (322–3)

Here, the poet remembers a cheerful consonance between the swans
and himself, as the 'bell-beat of their wings' echoes his 'lighter tread'.
Once they went together, in a match that sounds in step, doubling what
happens 'above his head' with his 'tread' below. But now 'All's changed'.
However, instead of projecting this change, the poem postpones it, and
continues the theme of contented doubleness set up at the beginning:

> Unwearied still, lover by lover,
> They paddle in the cold
> Companionable streams or climb the air ... (323)

Contrary to the autobiographical misery of the speaker, who recalls
the swans of nineteen years before (and the woman they recall),
these continue the rhythm of togetherness, paddling in companionable

---

[46] *A Concordance to the Poems of W. B. Yeats*, ed. Stephen Maxfield Parrish, programmed James Allan Painter (Ithaca, New York: Cornell University Press, 1963), p. v.

twosomes. The poem's great arch of time, which looks back nineteen years and forward to a possible new loss, in fact settles for the prolonged pulse of the present, where the swans, in twosomes, 'drift on the still water, | Mysterious, beautiful'. The slow 'paddle' becomes, by the final stanza, the swans' almost motionless 'drift'—a movement without feet, continuing as if forever. This poem about lost love and emotional failure is also, if we listen to its rhythms, about a moment of companionship which seems endless, as the swans' feet bring everything almost to a standstill, slowing down to a perfect, unrunning 'drift'. The story of nineteen years, with its awesome, even politically charged 'All's changed', is thus opposed by this other rhythm, of continuity and quiet. By the end, the sense of change and loss is postponed into a future fear that 'some day' they might 'have flown away?' But in the time of the poem there is only now, with the swans' feet going quieter and quieter, as if touching on the poet's own stiller, underwater emotions. The sheer slowness of those feet is more than a naturalist's accident and less than an allegorist's message. It is, instead, the emotional pace at which the poem is set.

When, in 'Coole Park and Ballylee, 1931' (1933), Yeats returns to these old haunts, he ends by imagining another change and swans from the past:

> But all is changed, that high horse riderless,
> Though mounted in that saddle Homer rode
> Where the swan drifts upon a darkening flood. (492)

In these three lines he brings together ideas which have been accumulating for years. The 'all is changed' recalls the political change of 'Easter 1916' as well as the 'All's changed' of the first 'Wild Swans at Coole'. But by a freak association the 'sudden thunder of the mounting swan' (490) has changed into the riderless Pegasus of Homer. Thus 'mounting', with its faint recollection of 'Leda and the Swan', turns into the different 'mounted' of this one-time Homer. The word turns on its puns, and brings into the poem one of those horses that trouble Yeats elsewhere. This one too goes galloping on, though 'riderless'. Meanwhile, in a line that also gathers into itself the force of previous use, 'the swan drifts upon a darkening flood.' That 'drifts', though a little darker than the earlier drifting 'on still water', still prolongs the present, keeping the possibility of something unchanged in spite of what has changed and gone: the house, the woman, and all 'the last romantics'. At the end, contrary to the story of the poem with its deaths and sense of defeat, both horse and swan continue, their feet defying the sense of an ending.

Against the warning sign that 'all is changed', something disputes that political marker and continues unchanged, leaving the almost no-sound of its paddle on the 'darkening', but not yet dark, 'flood'.

These creatures on the whole are expressive as imaginary sound effects. They carry the emotional charge of the poem, their movements replicating a beat which cuts through, or crosses, the human story of loss or mourning. As a result, there is a disjunction between the narrative and the poem's rhythmic dance. It is the dance, the movement of wing or foot, which is really the poem's emotional centre. The swans and the horses come closer to the heartbeat than the speaker's plain words. Ezra Pound once tried to define the idea of a rhythm which is not just supernumerary technique. He wrote: 'I believe in an "absolute rhythm," a rhythm, that is, in poetry which corresponds exactly to the emotion or shade of emotion to be expressed.'[47] It is interesting that Yeats is among those named by him when he tries to define this absolute rhythm of art. He writes that 'fewer still feel rhythm by what I would call the inner form of the line. And it is this "inner form," I think, which must be preserved in music; it is only by mastery of this inner form that the great masters of rhythm—Milton, Yeats, whoever you like—are masters of it.' The idea of some 'inner form', which is neither 'quantity' nor 'stress'[48] but somehow corresponds to 'the emotion or shade of emotion to be expressed', is intriguing. Form, here, is a musical idea, a rhythm or sound-shape; but at the same time it carries the expressivity of the work. Often, in Yeats, there is another rhythm at work, which is neither metrical nor narrative, but might be imagined as an alternative heart at work. Rhythm is not just a preset clock; it is a variable emotional effect, and affect, too.

This profound sensitivity to the pace of a poem starts with Yeats's debt to the wavering, botanizing evasions of aestheticism, but continues to the end of his life. It is both the mainspring of his verse and its after-effect, a first knocking, perhaps, and a sound that lingers after the poem has been read. Very often it is figured as the sound of feet, trampling, paddling, drifting, dancing, like a notation from a different score. In the late poems, this same figure continues with variations. For instance, in 'Long-Legged Fly' (1939), each stanza resolves into the refrain: *'Like a long-legged fly upon the stream | His mind moves upon silence'* (617). Like

---

[47] Quoted in *Ezra Pound and Music: The Complete Criticism*, edited with commentary by R. Murray Schafer (London: Faber, 1978), 469.
[48] Ibid. 471.

the 'long-legged bird' of 'Lapis Lazuli', flying over the heads of 'Two Chinamen' (566), this one too might just touch on what lies, literally or metaphorically, below those long legs skimming the water. Somehow 'long-legged' seems superfluous unless some touch were hinted at. With the lightest of movements the fly's legs drag, just dipping, it seems, *'upon the stream'*. Meanwhile, the connection between the fly and the abstract tenor of a mind which also moves *'upon'* something is made by those unmentioned, but working feet.

As in so many of Yeats's similes, the word *'Like'* is ambiguous. Caesar, Helen, and Michael Angelo are not very much like each other; yet all, being dreamers, or seen at the moment of dreaming, are like the fly. Caesar is caught in a thoughtless moment, his mind 'fixed upon nothing', which, as Dennis Haskell points out, is 'quite different from, is in fact the opposite of, not being fixed upon anything'.[49] That 'nothing' makes of the active man, the man who runs or delivers telegrams, the one who, instead, gazes 'upon some reality, some beauty'—indeed some point of 'nothing'. The old rhythms of botanizing, of gazing for its own sake, catch even the 'master Caesar' in the subtle fixation of 'nothing'. In Helen, the child-woman, Yeats gives another example of mindless diversion: 'her feet | Practice a tinker shuffle.' Unthinking, irrelevant, careless, her feet dance *'Like a long-legged fly'*. There is no reason or direction to this 'shuffle', but the feet are a reminder, once again, of the rhythmic basis of Yeats's ear. This too is a kind of nothing, a concentrated, unthinking dance, a meaningless pattern. Finally, Michael Angelo's 'hand moves to and fro. | *Like a long-legged fly* ... ' (618). In each of these, the visual or intellectual likeness is abandoned, and instead there is movement, a pulse or repetition. Yeats still seems to be opposing to 'those energetic rhythms, as of a man running', some other rhythm: 'a tinker's shuffle', a movement 'to and fro', the movement of 'nothing' or of feet going nowhere, hand brushing up and down. They each, however, implicitly tap out a beat, as does the imaginary, long-legged fly *'upon the stream'*. That word *'upon'* brings into the poem the touch and pulse of something so light it is almost inaudible, but not altogether irrelevant.

'Long-Legged Fly' thus suggests the extent to which similes, in Yeats, draw on an aural as much as a visual similarity. What makes them

[49] Dennis Haskell, ' "Long-Legged Fly" and Yeats's Concept of Mind', *Yeats Annual*, 10(1993), 250–6, 254–5.

'like' can be heard. The sheer delicateness of the touch of the fly, as it barely touches '*upon the stream*', is a reminder, too, of how different it is to the trampling horses of action or nightmare. Both, however, are attempts to express an idea as a sound, a figure as a rhythm. It may be, too, that in the 'general cistern of form',[50] which is Yeats's reusable depository of poetic images, the long legs of the fly re-emerge as the stilts of 'High Talk'. For this figure too is a 'Daddy-long-legs' (623). Malachi Stilt-Jack goes with a halting, toppling stride, a sway and a laugh, and the tacky sound of those 'timber toes' finding where to land. Yeats might be recalling too the 'stilted water-hen' from 'Meditations in Time of Civil War', which also walked with an awkward gait, making its own imaginary sound-pattern on the ground. In 'High Talk', those stilts have to be worked to sound their tune. While, on the one hand, they may represent the unrelinquished, high-talking pretensions of the 'Decadent'[51] past, as Linda Dowling suggests, they also recall all the other odd walkers of these poems. Walking is a funny business in Yeats. He perceives it with the keen eye, or rather ear, of the musician, hearing a sound even where a sound is inaudible. It is as if, from his earliest poems, he is listening to the 'inner form' of a work, a form at odds with its story and traced obliquely on the ground or water. In the late poems, that story has almost disappeared. Malachi, after all, never gets down because his stilts have become his feet. Practised, artificial, off-the-ground, he goes gaily on and on into another cold dawn. Those stilts are the sound of a rhythm which, uneven and odd, take the poem out of literal or allegorical messages and into the reader's remembering ears. That 'stalk on, stalk on' is Yeats's last injunction to his poetic high walker.

In poem after poem, then, he drums out this 'inner form' of the rhythm, sometimes noisily, sometimes so softly it can only be inferred. It is there in the legwork of his verse, the way that he transmutes his creatures' feet into a beat, a movement, a refrain, and so counters the human narrative with something perhaps indifferent and gay. His own lifelong concern with rhythm, with a ground bass of meaning from which his poems start, is preserved in these references to feet. For these are the measure of something happening which is at an angle, indifferent to logic: a tinker's shuffle or a stilt-jack's procession.

[50] Yeats, 'Per Amica Silentia Lunae', 351.

[51] Linda Dowling, *Language and Decadence in the Victorian Fin de Siècle* (Princeton: Princeton University Press, 1986), 283.

Moreover, to listen to the rhythm is to hear how Yeats also imagines form. Form is, simply, the shape that is taken, likeness embodied, metaphor adopted. 'The spirit-body is formalist in itself but takes many forms or only keeps the form of the physical body "as ice keeps the shape of the bowl after the bowl is broken".' This is a world in which taking 'forms' is literal and changing. Yeats does not deal in rhetorical figures, but in incarnation, reincarnation, a taking of forms, in or out of nature. This means that the horses, birds, dancers, circus animals, are not simply projections of the self; they are projections of a rhythm which goes below, or sometimes across, the sense. 'They came like swallows and like swallows went' does not mean that the scholars and the poets of 'Coole Park, 1929' are 'like swallows'. Instead, the swallows, with their coming and going, ply a rhythm which renders human regret, loss, and memory unimportant. They 'cut through time or cross it withershins' (489), leaving in the poem a cross current of tempo, a pulse which will go on, whatever else is lost.

There is one other figure which seems to repeat the transforming literalness of Yeats's theory of form. 'How did it follow,' he asks in 'Per Amica Silentia Lunae', 'that an ignorant woman could, as Henry More believed, project her vehicle in so good a likeness of a hare that horse and hound and huntsman followed with the bugle blowing?'[52] The Cambridge Platonist, More, once again offers a figure which reverses the roles of literal and figurative. That the woman might 'project her vehicle in so good a likeness of a hare' justifies Yeats's hermetic theory of forms. Those can be given or taken at will. Though 'vehicle' and 'likeness' suggest a metaphor, in fact the 'horse and hound and huntsman' turn likeness into fact. In true neoplatonic fashion the 'ignorant woman' takes the form of a hare, and runs with it. This is not a simile or an allegory; it is a radical, if idiosyncratic understanding of the nature of bodily form, as something into which it is possible to 'project' one's identity. For 'our mental images no less than apparitions ... are forms existing in the general vehicle of *Anima Mundi*'. Both image and apparition can be recycled by the mind strong enough, or 'ignorant' enough, to take what is needed and run. There is a similar, capricious self-projection in the short story 'Red Hanrahan', where, we are told, 'a hare made a leap out from between [Hanrahan's] hands, and whether it was one of the cards that took shape, or whether it was made out of nothing in the palms of his hands, nobody knew, but there it was running on the floor

---

[52] Yeats, 'Per Amica Silentia Lunae', 350.

of the barn, as quick as any hare that ever lived.'[53] Hanrahan's bare
hands then release a pack of hounds, till the hare 'doubled and made a
leap over the boards',[54] escaping into the night. This might be a figure
for all the forms in Yeats. Nobody knows if it is made of cards, or of
nothing. But it is 'quick', as if the fact of running gives it life, substance,
even if it started as a mere wish in the mind. Yeats's ability to think
unallegorically, to turn a woman into a hare 'as quick as any hare that
ever lived', is the key to his poetry's peculiar power. He uses animals to
suggest an estranged, yet essential rhythm into which the human might
slip. Hanrahan's hare, whether made of cards or 'made out of nothing',
is 'quick' enough to be chased.

In autumn 1918, Yeats sent Iseult Gonne 'Two Songs of a Fool'. In
the first, the Fool guards his 'speckled cat' and 'tame hare' by the fire, but
suffers from a crippling sense of 'responsibilities' (380). The word recalls
the volume of 1914, with its anonymous epigraph: 'In dreams begins responsibility.' But it also recalls the responsibilities Yeats himself felt about
Iseult's mother, Maud. In a passage from *Autobiographies* he toys with the
word, remembering how, during a violent march led by her, he lost his
voice and was unable to give a speech, being therefore 'freed from responsibility'. Then, finding in the next day's newspapers 'that many have been
wounded', he is drawn back to a sense of responsibility, wondering if he
should 'count the links in the chain of responsibility, run them across my
fingers, and wonder if any link there is from my workshop'.[55] Although
'Two Songs of a Fool' is for Iseult, it is riddled with Yeats's feelings
about his poetic responsibilities in relation to Maud Gonne's politics.
The prayer to be eased of 'My great responsibilities' at the end of Part
I is answered, in Part II, when he imagines how the hare might escape:

> Who knows how she drank the wind
> Stretched up on two legs from the mat,
> Before she had settled her mind
> To drum with her heel and to leap? (381)

If the hare is Maud—'even at the starting-post, all sleek and new, | I saw
the wildness in her' (619), he writes in 'A Bronze Head'—the woman's
bid for freedom is a solution as well as a loss. In a rather complicated
reassessment of his love for her, the poem frees her, and the poet is eased

---

[53] *The Secret Rose, Stories by W. B. Yeats: A Variorum Edition*, 2nd edn revised and
enlarged, ed. Warwick Gould, Phillip L. Marcus, and Michael J. Sidnell (Basingstoke:
Macmillan, 1992), 88.
[54] Ibid. 89.   [55] Yeats, *Autobiographies*, 277.

of his 'responsibilities'. But even without this autobiographical reading, the hare, which is also a woman, goes the way of all hares. Its leaving is dramatic, powerful—the emotional point of the poem. Who knows if it was a hare or a woman? Who knows where it went? What is clear is that drumming of heels and then the 'leap'. As the hare escapes, it is the feet that we hear, the rhythm of its drumming on the ground, the last thud before the 'leap'.

In the same volume, the short poem 'Memory' also recalls a hare, but here the creature has already gone, leaving only its imprint behind: 'the mountain grass | Cannot but keep the form' (350) of it. Here form doubles up on its other meaning: the hare's lair. Such a 'form' stays in the memory, though the hare has gone, and all the poet can do is keep the impression of it, its warmth or after-shape. The word not only hints at the verse-form from which the subject has escaped, but also at the neoplatonic sense of something wilfully inhabited, or abandoned. When, at the very end of his life, Yeats asked: 'Which of her forms has shown her substance right?' (618), he was acknowledging the difficulties of his own view of form. The hare is perhaps no more Maud Gonne than the horses or swans are. Yet its relation to her is like that of a 'form'—something she has chosen, taken, and then left. 'Memory' is the title of a poem in which the triple sense of 'form', neoplatonic body-form, poetic verse-form, and literal lair, is both what is left over from the 'mountain hare' and all that is left of it. The 'form' was taken, and then abandoned. Moreover, the form is a simile for the hare, as the hare is a simile for the woman. At the same time, inhabiting forms may be all we have. If nothing else, 'Memory' is the form of an elegy for whatever it is that has gone.

*   *   *

When Michael Longley, Andrew McNeillie, and David Harsent write about hares in their poetry, they recall at some level 'the form' Yeats bequeathed them. In Longley's four-line poem called 'Form', the speakers' two pairs of hands mislay 'the hare and the warmth it leaves behind'.[56] It is as if they are feeling at one remove for something that Yeats also lost. McNeillie's poem, 'Hare', acknowledges Yeats's implicit division of form and content, but puts them together again: 'Form and

---

[56] Michael Longley, *The Ghost Orchid* (London: Cape Poetry, 1995), 1.

meaning so snug together'.[57] In David Harsent's 'The Woman and the Hare (1)' the bleakness of Yeats's poem, its uncanny failure of direct comparison, is recalled:

> I have come to come
> to nothing, or less than nothing if nothing
> is absence and absence nothing more than a face or name
> gone missing.[58]

Something in this poem, as in all the others, is 'missing': both the 'hare' and 'a face or name'. Yeats's 'Memory', with its controlled heartbreak and play on 'form', gives to these later poets a perfect miniature: of 'form' as something left over when the creature has gone. To 'keep the form' is the poet's loss, but also, in the end, his gain. The hare has gone, and with it, content, matter, story, emotion. But the form remains. For form is simply the rhythm of what came and went, and was saved in the various forms of language itself, as well as in the sound of all those wandering, beating, escaping feet.

[57] Andrew McNeillie, *Now, Then* (Manchester: Carcanet, 2002), 74.
[58] David Harsent, *Legion* (London: Faber, 2005), 53.

What is a poem? A poem is nothing.

Laura Riding

And saying so to some
Means nothing; others it leaves
Nothing to be said.

Philip Larkin

8

Wallace Stevens' Eccentric Souvenirs

In 1899, the year that Yeats published his third volume, *The Wind Among the Reeds*, the nineteen-year-old Wallace Stevens wrote in his journal:

Art for art's sake is both indiscreet and worthless. It opposes the common run of things by simply existing alone and for its own sake ... Beauty is strength. But art—art all alone, detached, sensuous for the sake of sensuousness, not to perpetuate inspiration or thought, art that is mere art—seems to me to be the most arrant as it is the most inexcuseable rubbish.[1]

Four months later he jotted down an account of an afternoon at home:

I sat in the piano room reading Keats' 'Endymion', and listening to the occasional showers on the foliage outside. ... The thought occurred to me that it was just such quick, unexpected, commonplace, specific things that poets and other observers jot down in their note-books. It was certainly a monstrous pleasure to be able to be specific about such a thing.[2]

Eight years later, the opportunity to view the original copy of 'Endymion' at Columbia University could still fill him with excitement. 'You know the beginning—', he enthusiastically reminded his correspondent: ' "A thing of beauty is a joy forever." '[3] These extracts point to a difficulty, or at least a complexity, in Stevens' attitude to aestheticism. On the one hand, as early as 1899, he rejected the still fashionable mantra of art

---

[1] Wallace Stevens, *Letters of Wallace Stevens,* ed. Holly Stevens (London: Faber, 1967), 24.
[2] Ibid. 28–9.   [3] Ibid. 110.

for art's sake. Its self-indulgence, its tendency to mean 'sensuous for the sake of sensuousness', occasions an abrupt moral outburst in the young poet: 'the most arrant ... the most inexcuseable rubbish'. Like Eliot's revulsion against untidy lives, Stevens, whose life will be super-tidy, is quick to reject the hint of moral laxity in the whole movement. Art must not be an immoral indulgence of mere 'sensuousness'. However, the incongruous, headmasterly tone at the end has a false ring to it. Some other, perhaps paternal presence has entered the sentence, and its heavy thump puts an end to the debate. Meanwhile, however, something escapes censure. Beauty, that traditional associate of art for art, is not routed by the moral voice, but stays intact, assured of its importance. 'Beauty is strength,' Stevens declares. While art for art sounds like self-indulgent hedonism, beauty remains strong and still workable.

The reason, as the second extract makes clear, is Keats. The first line of 'Endymion' is a proposition not easily thrown out. In particular, a *'thing* of beauty' has its own special appeal to the young poet. The sense of 'things' can be heard in both journal passages: 'the common run of things' and 'commonplace, specific things'. He might be recollecting Yeats's *'common things that crave'*[4] in *'To the Rose upon the Rood of Time'*. However, the ultra-aesthetic pose of reading 'Endymion' by an open window suggests that these 'things' are also intrinsically Keatsian. The famous first line of 'Endymion' gives Stevens a word which will insist on its importance throughout his work. 'A thing of beauty' is this or that common object: raindrops, foliage, a piano. Having rejected art for art's sake, he ends up advocating a sense of beauty focussed on common things, and the lazy pleasure of sitting 'in the piano room reading Keats'. Unlike Keats, however, who sets an imaginative alarm clock in his poems, to wake and break the dream of beauty, the young Stevens finds no interruption of 'pleasure' in the sound of 'showers on the foliage'. The scene of reading might go on and on. And indeed, in 1906, he posed himself a question which would be pertinent throughout his life: 'May it be that I am only a New Jersey Epicurean?'[5]

The legacy of Keats may be diverted from its connection with art for art, but for Stevens it is not diverted very far. The aestheticist past shapes and directs his work throughout life, encouraging, as Milton Bates puts

---

[4] *The Variorum Edition of the Poems of W. B. Yeats*, ed. Peter Allt and Russell K. Alspach (New York: Macmillan, 1957), 101.
[5] Stevens, *Letters,* 87.

it, a 'deep and abiding sympathy with the very [Paterian] program he thought he was rejecting'.[6] Certainly, the vehemence of his rejection of art for art in the first journal extract contradictorily announces the importance to him of Keats, and of the word which, still untainted by its long use, is associated with Keats. Like Woolf and Yeats, Stevens cannot reject either the word, or the idea associated with 'beauty'. It is as if he finds a way of obeying the authoritative voice which booms 'inexcuseable rubbish' at art for art, while also ensuring that he stays attentive to things of beauty, in Epicurean detachment in the solitude of 'the piano room'.

When, in 1901, Stevens wrote to his father proposing to resign from journalism and 'spend [his] time in writing', the suggestion, whether literally or metaphorically, was returned to him 'torn to pieces'. This rejection set him musing: 'If I only had enough money to support myself.'[7] Money, which seemed the problem, then became the solution. In the reverse story of innumerable nineteenth-century lives, both fictional and real, Stevens obeyed the voice of his father, undertook a training in law and settled for a lifelong career in insurance. He became, as Roger Kimball puts it, 'the ultimate aesthete who was also a hard-nosed legal adviser for the Hartford Accident and Indemnity Company'.[8] 'Money', he was able to write years later, 'is a kind of poetry.'[9] Certainly, it was money which allowed 'the dandyish, awkward, epicurean, intensely private Stevens' to buy all the 'exotic fruits, fine wines and costly book-bindings'[10] in which he took such delight. The Huysmans-like state of mandarin detachment associated with art for art's sake was thus bought by the very means advocated by his disapproving father. Money allowed Stevens to live the life of a connoisseur, collector, hermit, and poet, while seeming to reject the anti-bourgeois scandalizing of nineteenth-century aesthetes. With

---

[6] Milton J. Bates, *Wallace Stevens: A Mythology of Self* (Berkeley, Los Angeles: University of California Press, 1985), 31.

[7] Stevens, *Letters,* 53.

[8] Roger Kimball, 'A Metaphysical Loss Adjustor', *Times Literary Supplement* (16 January 1998), 25.

[9] *Wallace Stevens: Collected Poetry and Prose,* sel. Frank Kermode and Joan Richardson (New York: The Library of America, 1997), 905. All subsequent references to Stevens' poetry and prose will be from this edition and cited in the text.

[10] Mark Ford, 'The Insurance Man', *Times Literary Supplement* (29 November 2002), 8–9, 9.

money, Longenbach quips, 'he visited Paris by mail-order',[11] amassing a collection of precious souvenirs from places he never visited. Under the guise of a quiet normal life, Stevens could indulge the very sensuous pleasures he once derided as a folly of art for art's sake.

Stevens' high modernist style, like Woolf's and Yeats's, thus comes out of a sly re-routeing of aestheticist ideas. His uneasy shifting can be heard in a letter of 1935, written in answer to the accusation that his verse might be merely formal and decorative. Stevens starts in the negative, but then adds:

there was a time when I liked the idea of images and images alone, or images and the music of verse together. I then believed in *pure poetry*, as it was called.

I still have a distinct liking for that sort of thing. But we live in a different time, and life means a good deal more to us now-a-days than literature does. In the period of which I have just spoken, I thought literature meant most. Moreover, I am not so sure that I don't think exactly the same thing now, but, unquestionably, I think at the same time that life is the essential part of literature .... here people who speak about the thing at all speak of my verse as aesthetic. But I don't like any labels.[12]

He is still, here, hedging his denials with affirmation. He acknowledges that 'life' may be more important, and that the idea of *'pure poetry'* may, in 1935, be either passé or politically provocative, but he will not relinquish the term. Even if 'that sort of thing' now seems historically jejune (the paternalistic voice of moral disapproval once again audible), he cannot altogether forgo it. After the crucial pause of the paragraph break, Stevens confesses his 'distinct liking' for the term. So much did he like it that, a year later, he repeated it on the jacket of *Ideas of Order* (1936): 'The book is essentially a book of pure poetry' (997), he claims. It is interesting that he should thus so publicly affiliate himself with the aestheticist aims of the French tradition. Paul Valéry, in his essay *'Poésie Pure'*, claimed that, like Pater's condition of music, the phrase marks an impossible aspiration rather than an achievement: *'un objet impossible à atteindre'.*[13] He also, however, acknowledges that the term is widespread and attributes its origins to that early promoter of art for art: Edgar Allan Poe.[14] The term 'pure poetry' is repeated by Baudelaire, Gautier,

---

[11] James Longenbach, *Wallace Stevens: The Plain Sense of Things* (Oxford: Oxford University Press, 1991), 124.

[12] Stevens, *Letters*, 288.

[13] *Modern French Poets on Poetry*, arr. and annotated by Robert Gibson (Cambridge: Cambridge University Press, 1961), 149.

[14] Ibid. 138.

Mallarmé, as well as Pater and Moore, and becomes as much a badge of aestheticist thinking as art for art. In espousing it, Stevens also issues a defensive challenge just at a time, as Alan Filreis points out, when 'radicals like Max Eastman were reasonably attacking modernism as "The Tendency toward Pure Poetry".'[15] By invoking it, Stevens audibly disclaims political or social purpose in his poetry, letting the word 'pure' stand for the opposite of life itself. The phrase serves him, on the one hand, as a modesty trope (almost a synonym for '*mere* poetry'), and on the other as the badge of an aesthetic marked by the self-involved apartness of art. Far from being a response to the ominous political context of the 1930s, Stevens' second volume is thus marketed as poetry for its own sake, untouched by political responsibilities. Stevens is still, in 1936, finding refuge in the distant piano room of the imagination.

'Poet, be seated at the piano' (107), is the opening injunction of 'Mozart, 1935'. The poem expresses, Stevens once explained, 'something that I have very much at heart, and that is: the status of the poet in a disturbed society, or, for that matter, in any society'.[16] The status of the poet is that of the musician. Stevens, like his predecessors, finds the condition of music to be the ultimate model for poetry, even, or especially, 'in a disturbed society'. It is that disturbance which makes the stance all the more challenging and politically assertive. The poet must not only *be* seated at the piano, but *remain* seated, against menacing odds: 'If they throw stones upon the roof' or 'carry down the stairs | A body in rags' (107). So Stevens shuts his poet in the room of art, immune to disturbance. More than thirty years after he self-consciously read 'Endymion' in the piano room, he still finds poetry, or music, in the place of aesthetic enclosure. The poet's task is to play on and on, even if practising 'arpeggios' seems shockingly trivial beside those awful clatters and bumps outside. 'Be seated', the poem repeats, hinting that someone at the piano might be nervously trying to get up.

Simple and repetitive as it is, this is also a truly scandalous and deeply political poem. As the title tells, history is hard on the heels of the aesthete, and is even about to kick open the door. That carefully placed comma in the title[17] gives to Mozart an anachronistic afterlife, as well as a date which jars with his name. A year before Benjamin's attack on art for art's sake in 1936, Stevens published this dogged,

[15] Alan Filreis, *Modernism from Right to Left: Wallace Stevens, the Thirties, and Literary Radicalism* (Cambridge: Cambridge University Press, 1994), 8.
[16] Stevens, *Letters*, 292.   [17] Filreis, *Modernism from Right to Left*, 212.

desperate, perhaps ambiguously satirical defence of 'the status of the poet'. Whatever revolt or pogrom is going on outside, the poet must play. He must even play, with Mozartian serenity, that 'lucid souvenir of the past, | The divertimento' (107). Both a 'play'-time and a diversion, the 'divertimento' is, as the very name suggests, a form of evasion. It is an artistic fiddling while Rome burns. It is also, instead of an attention to the present, a 'lucid souvenir' of the past. Drawn from the vocabulary of trivial tourism, the phrase suggests not only a clear memory, but also a cheap trinket or memento. A 'lucid souvenir' is something to be recalled, but also held onto with those playing hands.

This poem might be a simple satire of the aesthete in 1935, except that the Shelleyan exchange of voices, 'Be thou ... Not you', hints at a transaction which gives the player or poet an authority that is not his own. In the music room someone else speaks, a loftier, archaic 'thou'. Yet it is out of this impersonal voice that the poem also speaks *for* the other sounds outside: the 'fear' and 'pain' and 'cries' (108) in the streets. 'Mozart, 1935' is as outrageous, in its way, as Celan's *'Todesfuge'*. The poet survives the disturbance and must play, but is also, therefore, able to express the disturbance outside, obliquely, differently. Getting up is not an option. The Mozartian music room, apparently immured from cries, is at the same time the place from which cries might be re-played. As Stevens writes elsewhere, the 'ivory tower' would be intolerable if it did not have 'from the top, such an exceptional view of the public dump and the advertising signs of Snider's Catsup, Ivory Soap and Chevrolet Cars' (770). 'Our rowdy gun-men', he suggests, 'may not appreciate what comes from that tower. Others do' (717). Perhaps the only difference between the ivory towers of the aesthetes and those of the modernists is that the 'gun-men' lurk very audibly outside the latter. The sound of war or revolution comes right up to the poet's door, conflicting with the sounds of the piano. Stevens, like his fellow modernists, stays in his tower, but sees and hears what is going on outside: the 'public dump' and the 'advertising signs'. The walls of the tower may lean and the doors be no longer barred, so that to stay seated and playing in such a fragile structure takes, perhaps, an extra artistic courage. 'Mozart, 1935' does not disguise the date of its absurd, aestheticist withdrawal, but insists, nonetheless, on its necessity. The cost of that necessity, to the player as to the people outside, is also audible.

In a later poem, 'Of Modern Poetry' (1942), Stevens acknowledges that the theatre of action has changed, the modern world is different, and that the past is therefore no more than one of those memory-trinkets he loves to recall:

> Then the theatre was changed
> To something else. Its past was a souvenir. (218)

If all is changed utterly, and the theatre of modern life become much more dangerous than before, this also means that the past is nothing more than a 'souvenir', a trinket from a lost country. Yet souvenirs were things Stevens acquired throughout his life, and their elegiac recollection of another country was important to him. Words, too, can be 'souvenirs', trading on nostalgia and the exotic. This most aestheticist of modernists toyed all his life with words made fashionable by a previous generation: words like 'exquisite', 'porcelain', 'epicure', 'rose', 'bouquet', 'artifice', and 'abstract', which give his poetry the flavour of the Nineties, its knowing, cultivated sensuousness. Stevens recycles and metamorphoses words saved from the past rather than those belonging to the changed theatre of the modern. His idiom is not contemporary-vernacular, like Eliot's; it is removed, recherché, and full of things. He is an aesthete collector in poetry, his language packed with delicately cherished and unusual objects. The 'souvenir'—the very word a Paterian toying with French etymology for the sake of a richer mix of memory and thing—might itself signal the extent to which this poet remembers the music of a previous age, and plays divertimenti on it.

Stevens is quintessentially, then, the poet of objects, of things which catch the attention but seem devoid of human reference. For instance, in his early play 'Three Travelers Watch a Sunrise' (1916), he knowingly sets a precious object, a porcelain or glass bottle, in full view, and then considers how it catches the candlelight, which 'shines, perhaps, for the beauty of shining' (604). In the words of the Second Chinese:

> Such seclusion knows beauty
> As the court knew it.
> The court woke
> In its windless pavilions,
> And gazed on chosen mornings,
> As it gazed
> On chosen porcelain ...
> It never woke to see,
> And never knew,
> The flawed jars,
> The weak colors,
> The contorted glass ... (604–5)

These lines might be taken as an expression of the poet's rejection of aestheticist isolation and his preference for the 'flawed jars' which recall human violence. But in fact, like Yeats's Byzantium, the 'windless pavilions' of the mandarin court, where the candle-flame is not disturbed or blown out, are more attractive to his imagination than the invasion which the play then enacts. As the Third Chinese proposes, repeatedly and indifferently, 'Let the candle shine for the beauty of shining' (606). That candle, out of date, secluded from the weather of the contemporary, will figure throughout Stevens' life as the object and subject of art. It is, as the echo suggests, an art for art's sake by another name, shining 'for the beauty of shining'. It is of no use to anyone, but casts a kind of self-regarding, objectless light. By the time Stevens came, at the very end of his own life, to write the poem called 'A Quiet Normal Life' (1954), that candle is still shining well into the age of electricity. In the last two lines, which are full of Yeats's own oriental-aestheticist escapism, he concludes:

> There was no fury in transcendent forms.
> But his actual candle blazed with artifice. (444)

This is 'Byzantium' rewritten, but from a more homely place. Stevens replaces Yeats's 'artifice of eternity' with the candle of poetic attention by which the poet works. The lines are pure Stevens in their audible filching from another poet (and Yeats is one of his favourites), but also in their recycling of poetic terms. The 'candle' is like a souvenir of art for art, there merely for 'the beauty of shining', while 'artifice' recalls, via Yeats, the whole cult of the artificial in the aesthetes' manifesto against nature. Rejecting Plato's 'transcendent forms', Stevens opts for the form of a *thing*, an 'actual candle', but one which has also somehow become too artificial to be quite itself.

These two lines might contain, in miniature, the story of his own derivative, yet unique aestheticism. His poetry is full of objects which are consciously turned into art objects by being set apart, and attended to. They function less as things in the narrative than as complex souvenirs. The porcelain bottle in 'Three Travelers', for instance, which stays centre stage in spite of disturbances and deaths, seems to represent the legacy of aestheticism, while being, itself, a literary souvenir of that legacy's key poem: 'Ode on a Grecian Urn'. Stevens' debt to Keats, particularly in his many poems about jars, pots, cans, bottles, and urns, was profound.[18] 'Secretary for Porcelain' (228) is a title which suits this poet who saw himself, in some ways, as the last keeper of the museum in which urns, and other precious things, survive. 'Three Travelers' plays round the porcelain bottle which keeps the imagination's candle focussed, and which, in spite of everything, survives the play's sudden, violent denouement.

Two late poems, both published in the 1950s, suggest the depth of Stevens' indebtedness to Keats, as well as the originality of his rewritings of him. The first is 'Someone Puts a Pineapple Together' (1951):

> If he sees an object on a table, much like
> A jar of the shoots of an infant country, green
>
> And bright, or like a venerable urn,
> Which, from the ash within it, fortifies
> A green that is the ash of what green is,
>
> He sees it in this tangent of himself.
> And in this tangent it becomes a thing
> Of weight, on which the weightless rests: from which
>
> The ephemeras of the tangent swarm, the chance
> Concourse of planetary originals,
> Yet, as it seems, of human residence. (694)

If, as the title tells, the pineapple has to be put together again, it must have fallen apart. Stevens is well aware of the origins of this 'wholly artificial nature' (693). The pineapple, he asserts, is the 'double fruit of boisterous epicures' (695), of those who, like himself, delight in the exotic, the far-fetched, the foreign. From the imaginary breakages of the title it is not, then, a far step to the fruit as urn. This bizarre comparison carries the logic of the title's brittle contradiction, so that a jar of green shoots, or an urn of green's ashes, seem like apposite extensions of a pineapple. A pineapple that has to be put together again is as fragile as a jar or urn. Breakableness runs deep in Stevens' sly appropriation of Keats's 'venerable urn'. It is as if he were holding the object up to the violence, implicit or explicit, of the contemporary world. Meanwhile, he is alert to the death motif that lurks in all urns, and which recalls their lost ashes. But such is the play of words that what is ash and what is green can barely be separated. The urn 'fortifies | A green that

---

[18] See Helen Vendler, *Wallace Stevens: Words Chosen Out of Desire* (Cambridge, Mass.: Harvard University Press, 1986), 45, and *On Extended Wings: Wallace Stevens' Longer Poems* (Cambridge, Mass.: Harvard University Press, 1969), 89.

is the ash of what green is'. This is Stevens taking the container model of art, and finding almost nothing in it, or something so riddling that it fails to yield any clear object at all. 'A green that is the ash of what green is' is just about visible, as an ashier sort of green—but, if fortified, does it then become greener than green? This is a juggler's trick of meaning, which in the end does what Stevens so often enjoys: it tricks us out of meaning. The pineapple-urn contains as many green shoots as ashes within, as much life as death, as much something as nothing.

The object of the poem, then, is not inside the jar, but rather goes between. It is a 'tangent'. Stevens repeats the word three times as he tries to discover what the 'object on a table' is. Watching himself see, he writes about the process as a movement between himself and things which start to metamorphose through words. This shifting, of ash into green, for instance, is then associated with the Epicurean worldview upheld by so many nineteenth-century aesthetes. The 'chance | Concourse of planetary originals' is Lucretius' fortuitous concourse of atoms. This swarming of minutiae deranges the fixed focus of objects and meanings. It is not the specific thing, pineapple, jar, or urn, which matters, but 'the tangent' which affects those objects when looked at. Neither ash nor green, but the curious unfinished slippage between them is what constitutes the urn. Finally, within the larger swarm of atoms there is, Stevens admits, something 'of human residence'. However residual, there is a home for the human in this inhuman sufficiency of things in their atomic drift. So this most Epicurean of poets, who seems more concerned with porcelain than with people, feels the pressure from human disturbance, and includes it, tangentially, in the strange, verbal interactions which constitute a poem—or pineapple.

The fact that something put together must also have fallen apart might sum up the curious dynamic of Stevens' work. He is a poet of objects, even the most collectible, recherché objects, but he does not let them stay still. They are affected by those tangents of attention which set everything moving in a kind of absurd, Lucretian drift of language. An urn may be a pineapple and ash may be green. The 'object on a table' (694) sets off a process of verbal invention which might be called metaphor, except that, for Stevens, metaphors are all vehicle without tenor. This object, after all, is only 'much like | A jar' or 'like a venerable urn', each of these being ephemera or chances in the game of language they release. The pineapple, the title tells, is already not a pineapple at all, but a breakable artefact, evoking 'Someone' who might or might not be able to mend it again. The *objet d'art,* from the start, is not a thing in itself, but a likeness, a thing by a 'tangent' of seeing or thinking, and it comes with cracks.

The second poem, 'The Bouquet' (1950), was published the previous year, and repeats a situation which is dear to Stevens. There is, to start with, an object on a table. The whole poem, as Justin Quinn points out, 'conjures up a dandyish, effete nineteenth-century atmosphere; the old category of the aesthetic in all its fragility and irrelevance'.[19] Stevens, it seems, has never finished with that 'old category':

> The bouquet stands in a jar, as metaphor,
> As lightning itself is, likewise, metaphor
> Crowded with apparitions suddenly gone
>
> And no less suddenly here again, a growth
> Of the reality of the eye, an artifice,
> Nothing much, a flitter that reflects itself. (384)

Once again the jar, the container, is there not to disclose its contents but to set 'metaphor' loose. It is an occasion for poetry, which means an occasion for 'apparitions', 'artifice', as well as 'Nothing much'. Stevens might indeed be answering the critic who points out aestheticism's 'irrelevance'. This is, he modestly agrees, a 'Nothing', a 'flitter'. But it is also 'much'. Being 'Nothing much' points both ways, like so many verbal plays on nothing. This poem, like others, is full of Nineties words, fetched from abroad and from the literary past: 'farouche', 'choses', 'argentine', 'Regarded', 'mille-flored', 'dulce', 'debris', 'appanage', as well as the 'bouquet' itself. They are culled from the hothouses of Huysmans, Pater, and Wilde, and are audibly exotic, as if they came loaded with foreign memories. The jar, like Stevens' own jar in Tennessee (60), both reflects its object transparently and also distorts it. It is as if the play of form and content were set in motion by this ambiguous relationship. The transparent jar ought to be the invisible container of the flowers. In fact, it distorts them, confusing what we see, which is both 'Crowded with apparitions' but also 'Nothing much, a flitter'. The form–content game set off by Stevens' many jars, bottles, vases, and urns is a game in which language flies free of reference into proliferating metaphors. So the line: 'As lightning itself is, likewise, metaphor' tells us, jokingly, that being 'likewise', or wise in likeness, is the name of the game.

[19] Justin Quinn, 'How to live. What to do', *PN Review*, 121(1998), 26–31, 29.

In Section III, Stevens confronts the memory-element in this prolif-
eration of metaphors. He writes:

> The bouquet,
> Regarded by the meta-men, is quirked
> And queered by lavishings of their will to see.
> It stands a sovereign of souvenirs
> Neither remembered nor forgotten, nor old,
>
> Nor new, nor in the sense of memory. ...
> A sovereign, a souvenir, a sign ... (386)

So he fusses round his 'bouquet', which reminds him of something
'Neither remembered nor forgotten'. Once again, he is drawn to the
word 'souvenir', as to an object which has almost dropped its memory-
function in English. Although not 'in the sense of memory', the bouquet
recalls 'souvenirs' that are not 'forgotten'. This devious discomfort about
memory is interesting. Stevens, it seems, wants neither memory nor
forgetting, but something which might be both. Thus the bouquet,
distorted by 'their will to see' (even the subject here is meta-phorized
into a meta-presence), stands not *for* something, but simply 'stands a
sovereign of souvenirs'. So in an irresistible etymological consonance,
Stevens has his memory and loses it. Like Mozart's divertimento,
this is a 'souvenir of the past', as all souvenirs are, but it is also 'a
sovereign'—almost a tangible coin of souvenirs, or a supreme souvenir,
or a royally powerful one. All those meanings are set moving in that odd
phrase, which might be memory, but is also a mere lucky charm of sound.

The bouquet, with its 'eccentric twistings' (386), thus sets off the
work of the imagination as a dealer indeed in things, but things already
become 'meta' or 'para' ('the thing | Turned para-thing' (387)). There is
no controlling gaze in the poem; only a kind of disembodied eye, at best
the regard of 'the meta-men', with their quirky and queer need to see.
Everything about the bouquet is already metaphor. The one line which
evokes a sort of haunted presence, 'One remembers a woman standing
in such a dress' (386), is only a memory from another poem: Eliot's
'Prufrock'. There ought to be some emotional connection between the
bouquet and the woman, but it has been lost in the peculiar twists and
turns of this meta-language. Human presence is almost an irrelevance in
this poem, which shapes itself beyond subject and object as a 'souvenir'
of something 'Neither remembered nor forgotten'. The idea of a love
story, of a 'Woman Looking at a Vase of Flowers' (223) as another
poem puts it, lies almost hidden in this poem of meta-meanings and

meta-men; of metaphor running out of control. Somewhere, however, the fixation on memory, on strangely recurrent souvenirs, suggests that 'Nothing much' is also not quite nothing.

After the tensely dramatic equilibrium of the first four sections, the entry of the soldier in Section V is as poetically clumsy as the figure himself: 'He bumps the table. The bouquet falls on its side' (387). Here, evidently, is the dramatic denouement. Stevens allows the gunman to enter the ivory tower, the stone-thrower the piano room. The fact that it is a 'soldier, an officer' (387) is a shocking specific in this poem of semi-realities. The poet's sense of guilt, perhaps at his own luxurious seclusion from a war which claimed the life of his sister, suddenly breaks the illusion, and by implication the golden bowl once again. Beyond the games of language, the political intrusion asserts its crude demands, its human drama, and rough violence. For Stevens, more than thirty years after 'Three Travelers', the invasion of humanity knocks the porcelain or glass jar of his aesthetic musings, and brings the poem to an abrupt end. While the poet himself has no wish to break out of the aesthete's room, he does, throughout his life, acknowledge the force of what might, at any moment, break in.

*   *   *

In 1936, in a lecture on 'The Irrational Element in Poetry', Stevens returns to the question which exercised his younger self: the relevance of 'pure poetry' in the twentieth century. It is, he claims, 'a term that has grown to be descriptive of poetry in which not the true subject but the poetry of the subject is paramount' (786). Instead of sounding silly and outdated, 'pure poetry' might thus suggest a complication of subject matter, in which the 'true subject' is substituted by that odd thing: 'the poetry of the subject'. It is useful to Stevens to define poetry as offering some kind of interference with 'the true subject', as if bare truth were part of the problem. What remains when truth is subtracted is 'pure poetry'. Fifteen years later he has not essentially changed his position. The lecture on 'Two or Three Ideas' (1951) starts baldly: 'My first proposition is that the style of a poem and the poem itself are one' (839). The example offered is from a century before: one of Baudelaire's *Fleurs du Mal*. From this identity of poem and style, Stevens continues, 'it follows that ... the poets who have little or nothing to say are, or will be, the poets that matter' (840). Thus the old aestheticist tags, that 'style is the man' and that 'nothing' expresses the purpose of art better than something, are repeated in the mid-twentieth century, by the modernist still defending a threatened patch.

In fact, the refrain that 'style is the man' was never given as proof of personality, but rather of escape from personality. Pater, in his essay on 'Prosper Mérimée' (1890), for instance, summarizes a well-established axiom when he writes of 'Mérimée's much-praised literary style ... impersonal in its beauty, the perfection of nobody's style—thus vindicating anew by its very impersonality that much worn, but not untrue saying, that the style is the man'.[20] The insistence on style was always, for the aesthetes, a way of emphasizing the 'impersonality' of art, its distance from self-expression as well as its distance from simple intention. Style has no natural connection either with the author or with the age. It is, indeed, a pose, an empty and emptying thing, 'nobody's style'. Stevens returns to the notion again and again. In 'Two or Three Ideas' he circles back to it when he writes: 'A man has no choice about his style. When he says I am my style the truth reminds him that it is his style that is himself' (845). As in Pater, this reverse analogy works to obliterate the centrality of the self. Self is style, and in the poet's case there may be nothing else. In 'Effects of Analogy' (1948) he repeats the point that 'a poet manifests his personality ... by his style', and adds: 'This is too well understood to permit discussion' (718). He himself has not substantially altered his poetic affiliations since the 1890s. If anything, his later poetry becomes even more purely concerned with style, with 'the poetry of the subject' at the expense of all 'true' subjects in the world outside. Some notion of 'pure poetry', however much menaced by invasion or interruption, continues to direct his thinking about verse.

He does, however, discover a new purpose in a word, and in a book, which was first published in English in 1942. Stevens probably read Henri Focillon's *The Life of Forms in Art* soon after its English appearance. He refers to it in 'The Figure of the Youth as Virile Poet' (1944) as 'one of the really remarkable books of the day', and quotes a passage which he will repeat frequently:

Human consciousness is in perpetual pursuit of a language and a style. To assume consciousness is at once to assume form. Even at levels far below the zone of definition and clarity, forms, measures and relationships exist. The chief characteristic of the mind is to be constantly describing *itself*. (671)

---

[20] Walter Pater, 'Prosper Mérimée', in *Miscellaneous Studies* (London: Macmillan, 1910), 36.

The word 'form', which lies at the heart of Focillon's understanding of art, gives Stevens a word which connects 'style' with human 'consciousness'. Although Focillon's emphasis is hardly new—he himself quotes Balzac at the start of his book: 'everything is form, and life itself is form'[21]—it does add a twist to the story. By attributing form to consciousness, he reaches a new short-circuit by which the mind itself is a form in search of form, and thus is always describing '*itself*'. Although he takes his bearings from the visual arts, and in particular from the spatial structures of architecture and sculpture, his account of form is the opposite of static. Form enacts an idea, or rather, it enacts an action. It is art as process.

Certainly, the whole legacy of art for art's sake is still audible in Focillon's prose, in his sentence constructions, which tend to round up into that familiar magic circle of the thing for its own sake: 'whereas an image implies the representation of an object, and a sign signifies an object, form signifies only *itself*,'[22] he declares. Thus external cause and effect are removed from the self-perpetuating life of forms. As Focillon moves from assertion to assertion, his prose enacts an account of form as self-justifying process. Form, he writes, 'is born of change, and it leads on to other changes'. Particularly in geometric Muslim art, it 'sparkles with metamorphoses'.[23] He continues, 'primarily form is a mobile life in a changing world. Its metamorphoses endlessly begin anew.'[24] The force of the word 'life' is indeed the life force of the whole book. Forms are not objects removed from human life; they almost come to generate life themselves. 'Forms tend to manifest themselves with extraordinary vigor', he writes, as language, for example, may 'become the mold for many different interpretations, and, having attained form, experience many remarkable adventures'.[25] This energy, change, and variation make form not only essentially mobile, but also infinitely interpretable. Form provokes meaning, it does not contain it. By thinking, or rather feeling, in forms, the artist becomes part of this interaction of forces, rather than their cause or source. Focillon thus insists on the vitality of form and on the adventure of its transmission from work to reader, artist to work, or just work to work. In a last ringing sentence he offers, not a conclusion but a kind of envoi to the object of his discussion: 'form, guided by the play and interplay of metamorphoses, [goes] forever

---

[21] Henri Focillon, *The Life of Forms in Art*, rev. and trans. Charles Beecher Hogan and George Kubler (New York: George Wittenborn, Inc., 1948; first pub. 1934), 2.
[22] Ibid. 3.   [23] Ibid. 6.   [24] Ibid. 7.   [25] Ibid. 5.

forward, by its own necessity, toward its own liberty.'[26] It goes 'forward' by a dynamic which has been at work throughout the book, as sentences themselves construct and reconstruct the movement of its necessity and liberty, its sense and senselessness.

Focillon's lyrical meditation is fascinating for the way it can make the word work, rather than mean. Rather like Pater, he offers something approaching a prose poem, the shifts of which are of more interest than any conclusion. While the frisson of sexual beauty has gone from the word 'form', its openness, its somehow available emptiness and multi-significance, remain. The very title, *The Life of Forms*, comes to life in the course of the book, emphasizing, as it does, change, interplay, metamorphosis, experiment, adventure. Form is what happens in art, which includes the formal act of making and the formal nature of interpreting. It is a word which invokes an act of attention to those movements, and thus participates in what is going on.

Stevens echoes Focillon whenever he writes about form, which he does with increasing emphasis in the later years of his life. In a poetry review of 1948, 'The Shaper', he summarizes: 'This constant shaping, as distinguished from constancy of shape, is characteristic of the poet' (818). The slip from noun to verb, 'shape' to 'shaping', is typical of his thinking about art. In the same year, a piece on 'The State of American Writing' concludes with a long paragraph on the true and false meaning of form: 'So, too, experiment in form is one of the constants of the spirit', he writes. Form is not 'the appearance of the poem on the page'; it 'is not a question of literary mode'. These are 'trivialities'. For this poet, who seems to epitomize strictly traditional verse-forms, form, in fact, is neither the fixed pattern of a poem nor a set of rules to be followed, but the sense of experiment which the poem undertakes as part of its 'constant shaping'. As in Focillon, form is a movement within the work which commands another kind of knowledge. 'Poetic form in its proper sense', writes Stevens, 'is a question of what appears within the poem itself' (824). One way or another, form is a word which goes to the heart of what makes poetry poetic. It is, on the one hand, the thing 'itself', withdrawn from parallel explanations or appropriations; but on the other, it is an ongoing act of language, a forming or appearing, which needs the reader, and is never finished.

Six years later the question of form is still at the forefront of his mind. In a lecture entitled 'The Whole Man' (1954), he writes:

[26] Ibid. 64.

I suppose it is true that nothing keeps painting alive from one time to another except its form. What is true of painting is no less true of poetry and music. Form alone and of itself is an ever-youthful, ever-vital beauty. The vigor of art perpetuates itself through generations of form. (875).

Thus form is the energy, vigour, and life-force of art. For Stevens, however, the style of Focillon is crossed with Keats. The 'forever young' figures on the Grecian Urn haunt the rhythm of his prose, as 'beauty' comes with its Keatsian charge of being 'ever-youthful, ever-vital'. 'Beauty is strength' the young Stevens had written, in an effort to save it from the moral disapprobation caused by 'art for art'. As he continues to try to define form at the end of his life, as an 'energy' and 'life-force' which will not be simplified into content or reference, and which will not harden into formal rules, it is Keats who comes to mind. The aestheticist basis of the word 'form' can still be heard here, in a reference to that first art object, with its still moving figures ranged round the sides.

So Stevens develops from his early Keatsian reveries a theory of the poem as something exploratory, changing, appearing, full of its own tangents and quirks: 'The instant of the change that was the poem' (303), he writes in 'Two Tales of Liadoff'. The nice friction of 'instant' and 'change' expresses the complexity of it. A poem is both a finished 'instant', and still changing. Increasingly dispensing with viewpoints, speakers, places, and emotions, Stevens achieves within his mostly traditional stanza-forms a poetry which radically undermines what we expect language to do. His later work in particular moves towards an emptiness of reference, an evasion of identity or event, and a reliance instead on what Vendler has called 'depth and breadth of internal reference'.[27] Such reference seems almost impervious to paraphrase, to explanation or analysis. Certainly, Stevens himself was neurotically allergic to explanations of his work. 'A paraphrase like this is a sort of murder',[28] he once expostulated to a correspondent who had sent a list of questions on 'The Man with the Blue Guitar'. 'A poem of symbols exists for itself. ... The poem is the poem, not its paraphrase',[29] he insisted. The late poems in particular show him resisting representation and paraphrase almost successfully.

It is as if, in these, the snowman's 'mind of winter' has finally come to dominate Stevens' thinking. Games of nothing were always of interest. 'Nothing that is not there, and the nothing that is' (8), the famous

---

[27] Vendler, *Wallace Stevens*, 54.   [28] Stevens, *Letters*, 360.   [29] Ibid. 362.

last line of 'The Snow Man', switches its focus from an indefinite 'Nothing', which might be everything that is, to 'the nothing' which forms into a final, hard, obstructive *thing* in the end. In 'Les Plus Belles Pages' he writes that 'Nothing exists by itself' (222). This might mean that everything only exists in relation to others—the explanation given by the poet himself in his 'Note' (867). But it might also mean that nothing, that strangely self-sufficient fact, indeed 'exists by itself'. Stevens loves such constructions. 'Nothing is final' (121), he declares in 'Like Decorations in a Nigger Cemetery' (121). An airy nothing can always, of course, turn to a form in the imagination. Poetic form itself might be understood as a transaction of nothings, an empty shape holding a shaped emptiness, an urn holding ashes. On the subject of nothing, Stevens is eloquent. 'To have nothing to say and to say it in a tragic manner is not the same thing as to have something to say' (905), he jotted down in 'Adagia'. That 'something' is always a problem for poetry: 'One of the most difficult things in writing poetry is to know what one's subject is. Most people know what it is and do not write poetry' (942), he declares in a letter. Elsewhere, he writes: 'A poet's words are of things that do not exist without the words' (663). Not being there is perhaps the main subject of poetry. To find something there, the 'true subject', is to miss the poem. While 'things' were always important to Stevens, here they are almost identical to words, in the sense that they 'do not exist' outside words. He does not quite say that words are the only things that matter; but he does suggest that the 'things' signalled by words belong only to words, and have no life apart from them. This encourages the kind of interplay he loves: those ditherings, meta-meanings, tangents, evasions, changes, seemings, frettings, which fill his poems. His delight in words which move and express movement for its own sake, rather than for description's sake, is the key to his work

There is a passage in 'The Noble Rider and the Sound of Words' (1942) where he defines the imagination as an 'inherent nobility' which commands and yet constantly evades expression:

Nothing could be more evasive and inaccessible. Nothing distorts itself and seeks disguise more quickly. ... If it is defined, it will be fixed and it must not be fixed. As in the case of an external thing, nobility resolves itself into an enormous number of vibrations, movements, changes. To fix it is to put an end to it. Let me show it to you unfixed. (664)

This most abstract of poets is also, in fact, one of the least philosophical. 'It must be abstract' is a statement which, on the one hand, seems to acknowledge the huge lexicon of abstract nouns in his poetry, but on the other hand resists the intention of philosophical abstraction, namely 'the extrapolation of idea from thing'.[30] To be abstract, for Stevens, is to pull away from any fixed idea or thing. It is to set a word vibrating, moving, changing, in relation to its reference. This is almost the opposite of philosophical abstraction, which pins ideas down to a single meaning: the good, the beautiful, the true. Stevens, by contrast, aims for an unfixing of meaning, as well as a disclosure of that unfixing: 'Let me show it to you unfixed.' This is the key to his extraordinary voice as a poet. 'Nothing could be more evasive and inaccessible.' *Nothing*, indeed, could be. Being able to disclose evasion and inaccessibility, so that 'nothing' is seen or heard, is one of his great gifts.

In the late poetry in particular, the representational potential of language is reduced to a minimum. Instead, there is a kind of reverse-reference in it; an emptying of meaning from the poem which leaves form bereft. It is as if the sense of nothing seems to have spread in these late works, leaving words somehow internally evading their purpose, their representational efficiency. As he asks in 'Notes Toward a Supreme Fiction' (1947):

> There's a meditation there, in which there seems
>
> To be an evasion, a thing not apprehended or
> Not apprehended well. Does the poet
> Evade us, as in a senseless element? (343)

Increasingly his poetry comes to sound like meditations on the creative act as an evasion of sense rather than a focussing on it. This is language as gesture, as waving. 'In poetic gesture,' writes Kristine Santilli, 'the poetic words are transformed into sound that dwells somewhere between meaning and word, in the interaction between the two.'[31] That 'interaction', the representational distancing which allows the 'senseless element' to come into play, is what characterizes the literary generally. And the word which, for Stevens as for so many others, defines that dynamic of evasion, that ambiguously gestural apprehension of meaning, is 'form'.

* * *

[30] Edward Kessler, *Images of Wallace Stevens* (New Brunswick, N.J.: Rutgers University Press, 1972), 37.

[31] Kristine S. Santilli, *Poetic Gesture: Myth, Wallace Stevens, and the Motions of Poetic Language* (London: Routledge, 2002), 69.

This is a word to which he returns obsessively, particularly in the later work—there are well over a hundred instances in his poetry as a whole.[32] Like most writers, he is not concerned with form as verse-form. Even before reading Focillon, he dismisses these as uninteresting. 'You can compose poetry in whatever form you like' (789), he declares in 'The Irrational Element in Poetry' (1936). Nor does that choice involve any particular credentials of invention. 'A free form does not assure freedom. As a form, it is just one more form' (801), he explains. It is after reading Focillon, however, that Stevens starts to press the word into a slightly more complex service. In 'A Comment on Meaning in Poetry' (1948), he argues categorically that 'poetic form is not a question of literary mode.' It is not a matter of a poem's free or traditional structure, but rather 'a question of what appears within the poem itself... the things created and existing there' (824). This takes form into the region of poetry's internal workings, its oblique and difficult relation to what it is merely about. Form is an appearance and a disappearance, a gesticulation to and from reference. It is what the poem becomes, in the course of its writing, which is also not a finished item but an ongoing meaningfulness. In 'Woman Looking at a Vase of Flowers' (1942), he writes: 'The crude and jealous formlessness | Became the form and the fragrance of things' (224). Form also has to be won from its opposites: matter or formlessness. It is not a thing or a literary mode, but an activity of language, a moving quality at the heart of the poem, which also, in both senses, becomes it.

'Description Without Place' (1947), for instance, is a critique of the pastoral tradition and of romantic nature poetry. Unlike those, with their confiding, descriptive conventions, this is a poem with no observing poet, no place in which to stand (though there are some named places), and where description happens outside location. This 'most impersonal'[33] poem, as Vendler calls it, also reads like a riddle on the words 'seem' and 'seeming', which occur twenty-seven times in all. 'It is possible that to seem—it is to be, | As the sun is something seeming and it is.' A 'seeming' is one of those apparitional words, a kind of shine that also goes out, disclosing and disguising itself at the same time. It is a word which stresses the dynamic of objects, rather than their shape or fixity, correlating the seen to the effort of seeing. Here, it has something

---

to do with the 'green queen' (296) of nature, but what exactly it is that seems, or to whom, is not important. The poem is full of people: the youngest poet, the dark musician, the dying soldier, Calvin, Anne of England, Neruda, Nietzsche, Lenin, and to each of these the 'seemings' of the world pass as things, in a chance panning of history a little like Pater's slumberous gloss on the Mona Lisa. Any one event is no more than a seeming, or form, as Stevens stirs his pot of favourite words:

> Nietzsche in Basel studied the deep pool
> Of these discolorations, mastering
>
> The moving and the moving of their forms
> In the much-mottled motion of blank time.
>
> His revery was the deepness of the pool,
> The very pool, his thoughts the colored forms,
>
> The eccentric souvenirs of human shapes,
> Wrapped in their seemings, crowd on curious crowd … (299)

So thought is form, and form one of the 'eccentric souvenirs of human shapes'. Through Nietzsche, Stevens captures the forms of thought as constantly shifting, their memories crucially off-centre, 'eccentric'. As in the whole poem, repetition blocks reference and increases movement: 'The moving and the moving', 'the pool, | The very pool', 'crowd on curious crowd'. In this effect of verbal crowding, the idea of human crowds seems very distant—are they curious for something, or just curious-looking? Meanwhile, these 'eccentric souvenirs', like all Stevens' other souvenirs, thicken the sense of mere memories. The movement of 'eccentric', like its etymology, is planetary, unstoppable, while 'souvenirs' offers its usual sense of tactile, and tacky, nostalgia. Meanwhile, what is remembered is a sense of the human, those 'human shapes', but only at several removes, distanced by milling thought-forms and memory-crowds.

Then, in one fine line, Stevens takes the word 'form' and animates it. 'The forms that are attentive in thin air' (301), he writes. These forms sit up, with a listening look that also listens to nothing we can hear. 'Forms that are attentive' expresses that invisibility of form in Stevens, something which is 'attentive' without an object to attend *to*. By removing human presences, he sometimes risks imaginative sterility, an over-extended recycling of words. But at his best he achieves an attention which is all the more acute for being distantly, elegiacally haunted by something or someone somewhere—like a souvenir. Attention, here, is an end in itself. The pattern is like that in 'The Bouquet', where a squinting effect, as of flowers distorted by glass or water, leads, not to understanding or interpretation, but only to redoubled attention: 'the eccentric twistings of the rapt bouquet | Exacted attention with attentive force' (386). The movement of 'eccentric' requires a doubling or trebling of a sense of effort. Such 'attentive force' is a good description of the kind of 'attention' required by poetry: it is intransitive and tautological, an attention achieved almost for its own sake. Stevens' object, then, is not to see objects clearly or truly, but to catch 'forms that are attentive'. It does not too much matter where Nietzsche is, if this ever happened, or what his thoughts were. What matters is that they are 'forms'—a word full of the vague, animate presence of something which calls attention to itself while rebuffing the conventions of ordinary knowledge.

The last lines of 'Description Without Place' sound like a philosophical proposition about the imagination's placelessness:

> It matters, because everything we say
> Of the past is description without place, a cast
>
> Of the imagination, made in sound;
> And because what we say of the future must portend,
>
> Be alive with its own seemings, seeming to be
> Like rubies reddened by rubies reddening. (302)

The poet's need for abstractions is a need for a vocabulary withdrawn from things, not for the things represented by that vocabulary. 'Description Without Place' may risk 'a dangerous aridity',[34] from which some critics recoil, but its method of imagining nothing, and therefore finding another kind of attention, is characteristic of Stevens' work from beginning to end. Here, the 'cast | Of the imagination, made in sound' plays brilliantly between a mould, something solid if only in outline, and also an angler's line, thrown to chance. Stevens' self-reflexive poetry is constantly casting itself anew, in forms which let meaning, purpose, place, for instance, simply go through them. What remains is something 'made in sound', like the last line, with its lovely aesthetic surprise: 'rubies reddened by rubies reddening'. Stevens reduces the future to the gemlike flame of the instant, of the moment's sake, which glows by its own intrinsic nature. The poem ends with this bracelet of sound and colour, a phrase as jewelled as any in Pater or Wilde, and as tautologically emptied of everything except its own fine brilliance.

[34] Joseph N. Riddel, *The Clairvoyant Eye: The Poetry and Poetics of Wallace Stevens* (Baton Rouge: Louisiana State University Press, 1965), 198.

'Description Without Place' may mark a dead end, of abstraction and emptiness in poetry, but it is an end to which late Stevens constantly presses. The idea that poetry is a form, or memory, but without a specific object, itself having become the object, only gains in rich variations in his work. Throughout, it has carried a sense of unfinished business, of words for their own sakes: 'a voice ... speaking without form', 'edgings and inchings of final form', 'undetermined form', 'sprawling form', an 'abstraction approaching form', 'a blind thing fumbling for its form', 'a gesticulation of forms', 'forms of farewell', 'forms formless in the dark', 'form gulping after formlessness'. Form, for Stevens, is a word with a rich difficulty of reference. As a figure for the way poems work, it loses or approaches meaning, carrying always a sense of movement and effort. Above all, it suggests the workings of memory, of those 'eccentric souvenirs' which can be summoned, obliquely and idiosyncratically, from the stirred pool of the mind. Those quirky objects, formed from the surrounding formlessness, express Stevens' peculiarly indirect and elegiac understanding of poetic language itself.

It is not surprising, then, that form should figure prominently in the poet's elegy for his friend Henry Church. Church had been the dedicatee of 'Notes Toward a Supreme Fiction': 'And for what, except for you, do I feel love?' (329). His death in 1947 resulted in the nearest thing to a personal elegy that Stevens ever wrote: 'The Owl in the Sarcophagus' (1947). That he wrote so few formal elegies is, as Ramazani points out,[35] surprising, since the subject of death absorbed him as a man and as a poet. 'I gave up writing plays,' he recalled in 1951, 'because I had much less interest in dramatic poetry than in elegiac poetry.'[36] To Church's widow he explained, a little hedgingly, that his new poem 'was written in the frame of mind that followed Mr. Church's death. While it is not personal, I had thought of inscribing it somehow, below the title, as, for example, Goodbye H.C.'[37] Stevens' sense of the personal is typically uneasy. 'Goodbye H.C.', by comparison with the usual i.m., is both intimate and casual. In the event Stevens let the poem go without dedication, retaining, as Woolf does in *The Waves*, its privacy and impersonality. 'The Owl in the Sarcophagus' remains, however, for all its obscurity, a poem about how to say goodbye, and therefore to some extent about the nature of elegy itself.

---

[35] Jahan Ramazani, *Poetry of Mourning: The Modern Elegy from Hardy to Heaney* (Chicago & London: University of Chicago Press, 1994), 87.
[36] Stevens, *Letters*, 729.   [37] Ibid. 566.

It is also a poem full of forms. They move about in shadowy ways and do not quite settle into the allegorical mode they set up. The owl of the title may be, as Joseph Riddel suggests, 'a self that consciously bears within it the presence of its own nothingness',[38] or, as Hillis Miller puts it, 'Minerva, the mind', living in the 'sarcophagus' of the body.[39] The owl within, as in 'Hoot, little owl within her' (223), may be either the imagination or just a darkness at the core. But this mind–body dualism then gives way to three new figures: sleep and peace, 'two brothers', each of them 'high' and 'visible to the eye', and a third, which is different:

> And a third form, she that says
> Good-by in the darkness, speaking quietly there,
> To those that cannot say good-by themselves.
>
> These forms are visible to the eye that needs,
> Needs out of the whole necessity of sight.
> The third form speaks, because the ear repeats,
>
> Without a voice, inventions of farewell.

This is Stevens' own goodbye, sneaked into the poem, not as an address to the dead by the living, but as an idea in the ear, simply. Whose ear does not matter. Robert Frost once began a lecture with: 'I want to call your attention to the function of the imagining ear.'[40] The ear, in Stevens' poem, is cut off from desire, purpose, intention, person. Rhythmically and rhymingly, it is only an adjunct of form: 'The third form speaks, because the ear repeats.' We, the reader, duly hear that assonantal echo in the line's surprising balancing act. The third form, certainly, is female; she is 'The earthly mother and the mother of | The dead'. But she is also speech merely, a word in the ear, 'good-by' said somewhere, in another's voice. While the forms of sleep and peace belong in a medieval dream-vision, in a decodable allegory of death, the third form is Stevens' own. She is nothing that can be seen, but she can be heard. She is the form of sound, a shape in the ear, which is the shape of speech that cannot otherwise be said. She is, perhaps, just the imagination of a word: 'good-by'.

---

[38] Riddel, *The Clairvoyant Eye*, 240.

[39] J. Hillis Miller, 'Wallace Stevens' Poetry of Being', in *The Act of the Mind: Essays on the Poetry of Wallace Stevens*, ed. Roy Harvey Pearce and J. Hillis Miller (Baltimore, Md.: Johns Hopkins University Press, 1965), 143–62, 152.

[40] Robert Frost, *Collected Poems, Prose, and Plays* (New York: The Library of America, 1995), 687.

In this modernist elegy, Stevens does not yearn for the form of the beloved lost body, and he does not imagine a meeting with the dead. Instead, he imagines a shaped sound in the ear, neither his own nor the dead man's, but just anyone's ear. Moreover, that sound happens in a flash:

> And she that in the syllable between life
>
> And death cries quickly, in a flash of voice,
> Keep you, keep you, I am gone, oh keep you as
> My memory, is the mother of us all ... (371)

Once again, it is hard to know whose voice this is. She might be the form of time, of the moment, of speech, or of memory. In a sense she does not belong to anyone or anything, though she instigates a complexity of pronouns: 'she', 'I', 'you', 'us'. Her message: 'oh keep you as | My memory' does not quite mean 'remember me', but remember yourselves as me, 'gone' as soon as said. This strange souvenir might be all there is. The third form, no sooner syllabled than lost, is a going that is always gone. Like Pater's moment for the moment's sake, this is a snatching at time that is already passing into 'memory'. In this extraordinary syntactical construction, the form speaks only 'between life | And death', in the line-break's tiny, purposeful pause.

The other two forms, by comparison, seem simple. Sleep is calm and composed, 'an ever-changing, calmest unity' (372). Peace is evidently its religious equivalent, but decorative, Christmassy and kitsch: 'The prince of shither-shade and tinsel lights' (373). Then the poem returns to the third form, 'the mythology of modern death', which provides the only possible, true elegy for Stevens. Unlike sleep and peace, the third form is not visual but aural:

> She spoke with backward gestures of her hand.
> She held men closely with discovery,
>
> Almost as speed discovers, in the way
> Invisible change discovers what is changed,
> In the way what was has ceased to be what is. (374)

So discovery, speed, and change is always now, in the split-syllable moment between 'what was' and 'what is'. Stevens' third form may be mother earth, in a long tradition of female responsibility for birth and death; but she is also mother elegy, whose voice is heard 'in the way' of speed and change. Only by such impersonal syntax, scattered pronouns, and ambiguous nouns can Stevens say, simply, 'goodbye H.C.' That human impulse in the poem is diverted into forms, those things which shift, uncannily, between living and dead, elegist and addressee, past and future. The poet takes the word 'form', which has a long tradition in elegy as the remembered bodily form of the dead, and typically empties it of human presence. Still, it expresses the dynamic of elegy: its uncertainty, its loss, its casting for what has gone in a shape which mirrors the emptiness it knows. The third form is mysterious and powerful for being a form of grieving memory, set loose from subject and object, I and you.

Certainly, Stevens writes not a farewell to his friend, but 'inventions of farewell'. These 'inventions' are played, like Mozart's divertimento, at a distance from death, in an atmosphere of evasions and tangents, of weirdly displaced syntax and grammar, which seem hardly to bear upon the event in question. That event, the death of Henry Church, happens outside the poem, outside the piano room of its sounds, its speech. But just as in 'Mozart, 1935', the repetition 'Be thou, be thou' (107), *inside* the poem, also captures the awful 'cries' (108) in the streets outside, so here, the voice of the third form repeats a phrase, like a keepsake, *in* the poem, which also speaks for the dead man outside, and for his grieving elegist: 'Keep you, keep you, I am gone, oh keep you as | My memory'. The third form thus ventriloquizes the human cry to be remembered, to remember, to make in the end a 'souvenir' of a reality which might otherwise be forgotten. So Stevens, once again, lets us hear the cry of the human, the cry of ordinary despair and sorrow, caught up somewhere in the elaborate inventions of the poem and its, indeed, memorial form. If the poet stays inside the piano room, in an aesthetic space which seems shut to the world outside, wrapped in its difficult self-referentiality, this is perhaps only to hear better the cries from outside. Although Stevens seems to banish person, place, event, and feeling from his late poems, achieving an impersonality which is harshly obscure, in fact to listen carefully to his music is often to hear, somewhere, the displaced cry of the human. That cry may be diverted, slanted, evaded, but it returns in another voice or another form. So the strange third form 'says | Good-by in the darkness, speaking quietly there, | To those who cannot say good-by themselves'. Through her, Stevens, who could not write 'Goodbye H.C.' himself, does finally, formally, write it.

Such cries can be heard everywhere in this poetry, diverting its emotions but also re-playing them. While the 'unseeking cry of the very late poems',[41] as Vendler calls it, is a sound which seems to have lost its purpose and reference altogether, yet a cry always has some call on the

---

[41] Vendler, *On Extended Wings*, 4.

ear. In the poem, 'The Course of a Particular' (1951), a tiny, unspecific thing runs its Lucretian course, but starts with a cry which instantly catches the attention: 'Today the leaves cry.' This keeps the sound ringing on, intransitively, as if asking for an explanation. How do leaves cry, and what about? 'The poem is the cry of its occasion, | Part of the res itself and not about it' (404), Stevens writes elsewhere. Intransitive cries suggest a conception of poetry, not as description but as the thing itself. In 'Lyric Poetry and Society' Adorno writes something similar, when he claims that the lyric poet 'intones in language until the voice of language itself is heard'.[42] Stevens himself writes:

> they are in the final finding of the ear, in the thing
> Itself, until, at last, the cry concerns no one at all. (460)

Neither divine nor human, this is the sound of 'the thing | Itself', rounded back into saying nothing, concerning nothing. That such a cry 'concerns no one at all' is a declaration of indifference which the poem strives to achieve, and triumphantly asserts at the end. But the presence of an 'ear' complicates the fact. Someone or something somewhere must be listening to all these cries.

Indeed, that word is repeated nine times in this short poem. That leaves should cry at all is such a travesty of any sound they might make that the human meaning insinuates itself from the start. 'It is a busy cry, concerning someone else', Stevens discloses in stanza two. So the cry is indeed 'concerning', even concerned? The sense of 'someone else', out there, out of hearing or sight, presses on the words as if from another place. Leaves don't cry, unless 'someone else' says so, or hears it. The sense of that 'someone' somehow personifies the sound that the whole poem makes through the unlikely rustle of its leaves. 'And the streets are full of cries' (108), Stevens wrote in 'Mozart, 1935', acknowledging the sounds outside the piano room. 'The Course of a Particular', so many years later, is also full of them. Although the poem purports to deny the 'busy cry, concerning someone else', in fact, in its obsessive repetitions, it cries out on someone else's behalf. This is a poem full of cries, human, divine as well as leafy. In the sheer absurdity of leaves that 'cry' we hear all the other cries that the poem mentions. It is as if the word keeps up that pleading call, for which there is no help, no answer, no explanation in the poem, but which prevails, and fills 'the

---

[42] Theodor Adorno, 'Lyric Poetry and Society', trans. Bruce Mayo, *Telos*, 20(1974), 59.

final finding of the ear'. That such a cry finally 'concerns no one at all' does not mean that it was not also 'concerning someone else'. Concern, and absence of concern, play ambiguously through this poem which, for all its evasions and distances, still leaves us with a sense, somewhere, of infinite crying.

So this increasingly abstract and inhuman poetry, which seems to set itself against responsibilities of sense or conscience—the stones on the roof or something bumping downstairs—in fact very often, indirectly, attends to those clatters and bumps, to the cries of a world outside. Stevens' aestheticist self-involvement, as of 'A voluminous master folded in his fire' (329), is a verbal as well as temperamental tendency. He loves words which, either because of their 'souvenir' foreignness or their reckless abstraction, pull away from clear meaning, and assert instead the rights of 'pure poetry'—a poetry listening to itself singing. At the same time, Stevens knows that he is never completely immured from the cry outside. That cry insists, and the poem also concerns it. His long career as a poet begins and ends with an aestheticist attention to words for their own sakes, to the shapes of sound over sense, form over matter. But this is not, ultimately, to shut out sense; it is, rather, to keep it knocking urgently, appealingly, even threateningly, at the door of the piano room.

∾

Poetic form, which
makes difficult things
possible, also makes
easy ones impossible.

Frank Kuppner

It's the cage which sings
and not the bird ...

Jane Griffiths

9

W. S. Graham: In the Mind's Ear

W. S. Graham has been, until recently, nearly invisible as a poet. A Glaswegian who lived in Cornwall for most of his life, a Scot who rejected the nationalist ideals of the Scottish Renaissance, a modernist born too late, a post-modernist born too early, a Forties' poet out of tune with the plain-speaking 'Movement', an experimentalist too formal and romantic for the avant-garde, Graham has never fitted into any of the movements or canons of literary history. He is a reminder, not only of the accidents and prejudices that drive such movements, but also of the exclusions and distortions created by them. Certainly, he cannot easily be sidelined into any one camp: romantic, modernist, formal, experimental, mainstream, avant-garde. Instead, his is a voice around which literary history itself might have to reshape.

There is a sense in which Graham's first four volumes, including his first with Faber, *The White Threshold* (1949), wrong-footed his future reputation. Written under the spell of Dylan Thomas, these early works are in the main a rich and riotous experiment with words. Already one can detect that instinct for verbal rhythms and sounds, that 'primitive identification between breaking wave rhythms and the physical basis of verse rhythms',[1] which will become Graham's characteristic note. Thomas was his Keats—the poet who gave him an entry into language, into the possibilities of words as cherishable objects of attention. In these packed, baroque, sometimes far-fetched poems, one can hear what W. N. Herbert has called 'the tremendous pressure of the language's feet'.[2] This dense and sensuous verbalism is probably the reason why the poet's potential early supporters, Hugh MacDiarmid and Edwin Morgan, were less than enthusiastic. In addition, the times were against Graham. MacDiarmid's response to his first book, *Cage Without Grievance* (1942),[3] betrays the slant of the socio-political anxieties of the age. The verse, he writes, has 'no root in its native soil' and fails to answer 'to the crucial needs and possibilities of our time. It is not responsible work in this sense.' He thus raises against Graham that favourite critical word of the 1940s: responsibility. Being 'responsible' to the times is the poet's duty. Without such responsibility the work risks being, in a phrase still charged with the power of its contrary irresponsibility, 'purely aesthetic'.[4] Graham himself seems to have remembered this criticism, and many years later half-admitted his poetry's 'too aesthetic inclinations'.[5] But he never conceded the point about political responsibility, and at the time turned MacDiarmid's criticism against him by demanding 'more poetry in Scotland to be made of words instead of heather and homerule and freedom'.[6] Although he outgrew the influence of Dylan Thomas, Graham's early insistence on words alone as poetry's primary matter never altered. Answering Edwin Morgan's similarly lukewarm response to this volume, he pointed out: 'I am always so [*sic*] first to say love the words the single words that have a heart and a world in them', and begged 'Please Morgan ... they are great poems only to me but they should not be so bad for you.'[7] Anguished at dispraise from a poet he admired, Graham also hinted at a self-confidence which would

---

[1] Tony Lopez, 'Graham and the 1940s', in *W. S. Graham: Speaking Towards You*, ed. Ralph Pite and Hester Jones (Liverpool: Liverpool University Press, 2004), 26–42, 39.

[2] W. N. Herbert, 'The Breathing Words', *Edinburgh Review*, 75(1986), 101–3, 102.

[3] 'Cage Without Grievance', in *W. S. Graham: New Collected Poems*, ed. Matthew Francis (London: Faber, 2004), 17–55. All subsequent references to Graham's poems are taken from this volume and will be cited in the text.

[4] Quoted in Tony Lopez, *The Poetry of W. S. Graham* (Edinburgh: Edinburgh University Press, 1989), 11.

[5] *The Nightfisherman: Selected Letters of W. S. Graham*, ed. Michael and Margaret Snow (Manchester: Carcanet Press, 1999), 279.

[6] Ibid. 22.   [7] Ibid. 15.

not be derailed, however much his 'great poems' went unrecognized by others.

It may be that the title, *Cage Without Grievance*, is already staking out a territory inimical to his Scottish contemporaries. MacDiarmid, for instance, disliked the hint of political quiescence in it: 'The poet should be not a contented cage-bird in no matter how ornate a cage',[8] he grumbled, reading the title rather literally. Whether or not Graham is echoing Robert Frost's account of the difference between prose and poetry: 'Grievances are a form of impatience. Griefs are a form of patience',[9] his rejection of grievance in poetry sounds like a characteristic challenge to the new climate of political-poetic responsibility in the 1940s. Like Stevens, Graham clings to an aestheticist tradition against the pressure of the times. It is MacDiarmid in fact who puts an object in the cage, hearing, in his own Romantic image of the bird, the very sense of grievance Graham claims to be without. The cage, for Graham, may not be a bird cage at all. It may contain some other kind of beast. Or else it may be a cage with nothing in it.

Graham's letters suggest that his early, 'too aesthetic' concern with words underwent changes but was never abandoned. To 'love the words the single words' for the words' sake rather than for their message remains his credo, even if as a poet he learns to use words more sparingly. Certainly, his letters continue to reject the idea of something in it, of a simple content, even of a 'contented cage-bird' which might be made to sing. Poetry, he argues, must not 'hand us out a little nutshell truth which we have pleasure in agreeing with'.[10] Like Stevens, who chafed at having to paraphrase 'The Man with the Blue Guitar', Graham warns Charles Causley that to 'discuss those ideas which are, you might say, take-away-able would be to curtail what the poem says to you'.[11] This is not just the poet's usual injunction to trust the poem, not the poet; it is also a lifelong concern to disengage the poem from being too straightforward a messenger of sense. The poem does not contain ideas or birds which might be released from words. Writing to Morgan a year later, Graham offers a neat little parable about the dangers of responsible message-giving: 'People write and write so sweating that it should say something worthy and valuable to humanity that some comparative

[8] Quoted in Lopez, *The Poetry of W. S. Graham*, 1989, 11.
[9] *Robert Frost: Collected Poems, Prose, and Plays* (New York: The Library of America, 1995), 743.
[10] *The Nightfisherman*, 163.   [11] Ibid. 144.

wisdom is tortured into the world ... so that the poet is assured and a bit certain that it is good ... and the public are a bit certain they are not being hoaxed (for here is something we understand) and another bad poem is made, a nice rivetted up wagon.'[12] Such collusions between poet and reader may be briefly reassuring in the uncertain climate of what modern poetry is, or should be, in the war-torn Forties, but ultimately they are only likely to lead to (band)wagons of 'comparative wisdom'. By contrast, the good poem is unwise, uncertain, unreassuring, even perhaps a kind of hoax.

Three years later, Graham published his only prose piece about writing: *Notes on a Poetry of Release* (1946). This fine but all too short account contains a fascinating paragraph about authorial intention. Like 'comparative wisdom' or any other 'take-away-able' idea, intention is not something the reader should seek or the poem convey. However, Graham does not simply do away with it in the cause of formalist purity. Instead, he subjects it to an extraordinarily tortuous piece of argument, which concedes as much as it denies. He writes:

I must begin with first the illusion of an intention. The poem begins to form from the first intention. But the intention is already breaking into another. The first intention begins me but of course continually shatters itself and is replaced by the child of the new collision. I try to have the courage to let the last intention be now a dead step and to allow myself to be taken in hand. Yet I must not lose my responsibility, being that explorer who shoots the sun, carries samples of air back to civilisation, and looks his forward. The poem is more than the poet's intention. The poet does not write what he knows but what he does not know.[13]

Even the 'first intention', it seems, though a necessary beginning, is only an 'illusion'. It offers an ambiguous origin, half real, half imaginary, from which the poet must then break. For Graham this illusion of a beginning is the starting point for the poem 'to form'. What forms, however, is not the intention itself, or even the 'illusion of an intention', but the poem which is actually there from the beginning: 'The poem begins to form from the first intention.' Even more strangely, the poem forms as the intention de-forms, for 'the intention is already breaking into another.' That 'already' makes the first intention already a second or a third, which are somehow also there at the beginning. Thus poems forming come out of intentions breaking—a collocation of 'form' and

---

'breaking' which will be repeated throughout Graham's poetry. This repeat backdating of intentions, each breaking out of one which went before, then leads to another kind of beginning: 'The first intention begins me', Graham writes. This means 'gets me started', but it also, grammatically, hints at 'originates me' or 'begets me', so that 'me' is made emphatically the object of a force outside itself, even in some sense born from it. At this point there seems to be an endless begetting by intentions, or rather, illusions of intentions—that first illusion being the parental-grammatical source of each 'child' of collision and shattering. The poet must accede, courageously, to this violent procreation, which is not his, exactly, but rather takes him 'in hand'. He thus allows himself to be ousted by a drama which was his only by a kind of originating illusion.

Not that he is totally irrelevant and powerless, however. At this point Graham recalls the word levelled against him by MacDiarmid: 'Yet I must not lose my responsibility.' He seems suddenly to need to get a grip on this breaking-replacing narrative of intentions. His responsibility is not social or moral, however much the poet imagines himself as a mythical hero, contributing to the work of 'civilisation'; it is only a responsibility to 'allow' the poem to happen, and above all to 'not know'. All this takes 'courage'—a kind of giving up of self to a 'me', which is not an authority, an originator, an intentional actor, but only part of the process of breaking and forming which constitutes the poem, and which is always 'more than the poet's intention'. In the end this is a tussle to lose intentions, in the interests of the poem's own curious, contradictory formations.

Graham is evidently uneasy about responsibility—a word which also troubles Yeats and Stevens—but he does not throw it off altogether. Instead, he redirects it towards the unpredictable workings of poetry itself. 'I must not lose my responsibility' means letting the poetry follow its own intentions, those which break and form continually, and will not settle into a simple cause and effect. Vivienne Koch, who knew Graham well and championed his poetry in America, suggests, in a review of 1947, that this is the key to his work: 'The responsibility of a poet *to* as well as *for* his poem implies a radical shift in emphasis from the kind of responsibility elected so often in recent times by the poets themselves',[14] she writes. Evidently, the pressure of 'recent times' was felt acutely in the

---

[14] Vivienne Koch, 'The Technique of Morality', *Poetry Quarterly*, 72(1947), 216–25, 216.

war decade of the 1940s. Graham's way of shifting responsibility, but not shedding it, is to allow the poem to be an almost autonomous product of multiple illusory intentions, each of which shatters before the next. In this way it develops another surprising potential. In 1944, faced with a request from an anthologist for some poems which would not be too difficult and would 'remember the Great British Public', Graham recalls the poet's dilemma: whether to write to order and produce what will reassure, or else, as he puts it, 'to make a poem which will release the reader to a responsibility of his own'.[15] Here, once again, he takes MacDiarmid's word and redirects it to the reader and the reader's freedom. *A Poetry Of Release*, in which intentions are relinquished and responsibilities passed on, is a complex drama of evasions and freedoms all round.

Thus Graham rejects the political purposes of the age, and insists on responsibility to the words of a poem, to that shaped significance which will not translate directly into messages but releases the reader into responsible freedom. Not only does he resist intentionalism but, like Stevens, he also invokes a phrase which has a long history of opposition to political messages: 'Parts are a wee bit like "pure" poetry, serenely other-world-creating poetry',[16] he admits of his work. As late as 1949 he is still invoking a term with its roots deep in nineteenth-century aestheticism. The notion of ' "pure" poetry', offered in apologetic, baffled quotation marks, signals the old resistance to intentional purpose and political responsibility. The phrase still conveys, however hazily, a whiff of opposition to the rivetted-up wagons of meaningful poetry.

However, it was a real-life event rather than a poetic theory which gave Graham the inspiration and the word for a new kind of writing. In 1947 he was invited to go out with a local fishing crew on a working boat, and soon after he started the long poem for which he would be best known. In January 1948 he wrote from New York that he was 'trying to be more simple', adding: 'I feel the need to make some kind of (even structural) formality.'[17] Although the earlier verse is usually metrical and stanzaic, in no sense informal or free, it is clear that the notion of 'formality' here offers something new. It is an odd word to choose and the construction only complicates it. A 'formality' is different from a poetic verse-form, though evidently related. It might suggest the stiffness of something said out of politeness or impersonal routine. 'It's a formality' implies mere deference to forms, in particular those that are filled in. (Sometimes, however, these are not a 'mere formality', as

---

Graham's own menacing poem, 'Fill in this Form' (312–13), suggests). But 'the need to make some kind of … formality' also sets formality up as an end in its own right. Instead of a routine protocol, it is a thing which takes some effort, some making. Graham's sentence wavers between the two meanings of 'formality' as he seeks to draw a hard-won object out of an empty formula.

The poem which comes out of this concern is 'The Nightfishing' (1955), undoubtedly a new departure while also being very much about departures: a journey into night, the sea, the past, the self, and the dead. Compared with the tightly crammed early verse, the language is fluid, easier, more spacious and relaxed. Making a 'formality' does not mean, for Graham, writing in strict form, though his musical ear never lets up on 'the beat established silently in the centre of the words'.[18] Form is not a box or cage into which to shut meaning, with all its grievances. It is, rather, a sense of direction without directors, a lucidity of sound and structure which may not necessarily make lucid sense. 'The Nightfishing' has a driving, half-literal, half-metaphorical narrative, which nonetheless achieves a 'formality' which the tighter, packed verse-forms of the early work lacks. This has something to do with the spaced, repeated distribution of its sounds on the page.

The poem opens with two lines which will resonate like metaphorical signposts throughout the work:

> Very gently struck
> The quay night bell.

These lines, spaced on all sides and set apart from what follows, are the sound of a sound. After their slow, audible call and calling, something sets sail:

> This staring second
> Breaks my home away
> Through always every
> Night through every whisper
> From the first that once
> Named me to the bone.
> Yet this place finds me
> And forms itself again. (105)

---

[18] Quoted in Edwin Morgan, 'W. S. Graham and "Voice" ', in *The Constructed Space: A Celebration of W. S. Graham*, ed. Ronnie Duncan and Jonathan Davidson (Lincoln: Sunk Island Publishing, 1994), 76–83, 77.

Wherever we are, 'this place' is a place that has cut loose from narrative logic. There is no familiar personal pronoun at the helm of these sentences. Instead, the two subjects: 'This staring second' and 'this place' ensure that something other than the poet drives the sense. Graham, as a poet, very often finds himself more readily in 'me' than in 'I', in a word which is acted upon rather than acts. In fact, he does not find himself at all in these lines. Instead, he is found, both by the whispered name given at birth and by the place itself which 'finds me'. A strange foundling of his own lines, he is discovered by the two deictics which seem to be trying to pin something down. But what follows each of the opening subjects is a restlessness which defies 'this'. First, 'Breaks my home away' seems juggled from more familiar phrases: breaks away from home, home is away, away from home. But 'Breaks my home away' undercuts even the last, most tenuous home and sends it out and 'away'. Homeless even now this 'second', the very idea of home seems to break away from itself. Secondly, 'this place' is followed by a construction that is deeply displacing: it 'forms itself again'. Having been found, the poet has not found a place, but only somewhere still forming. Of course, all this beautifully describes the changing motion of the sea. But the sea has not yet been mentioned, except indirectly by the bell. Instead, the idea of being at home, being named and being found, runs through the estranging grammar of the passage like lost wishes.

At the very start, then, Graham connects the ideas contained in two verbs which often shadow each other in his work: 'Breaks' and 'forms'. 'The poem begins to form from the first intention. But the intention is already breaking into another', he writes in *A Poetry of Release*. The beginning of 'The Nightfishing' similarly juxtaposes breaking and forming, suggesting that something shaped and formed is founded on something lost and broken. In the process, home is forfeited, exchanged for something altogether less homely: 'this place'. From the start, this is a journey out from familiar persons or places, including the self. The key word 'forms' is already at work in Graham's strange construction, which makes the place, like those first intentions, a matter of constant self-structuring: 'And forms itself again.' A similar event is repeated later in the poem, where the idea of 'home' inspires another breaking and setting out:

> Each word is but a longing
> Set out to break from a difficult home. Yet in
> Its meaning I am. (108)

Here 'home' is the homed-into significance of a word which, in poetry at least, is 'difficult'. At the same time there is a movement away from 'home', a 'break' which is full of 'longing'. The to-and-fro movement makes the meaning, as well as the place of the poet, that Coleridgean 'I am', a matter of continual flux. Graham's line-broken syntax puts the poet, eventually, in his place, which is not at the wheel, steering the intention of these lines, but somehow bobbing up and down on them. For the poem, it seems, functions like the sea: it is vast, directionless, a place on which one has no place, a home which is a constant setting out from home. The 'forming and breaking sea' (116), as Graham later puts it, expresses the contradiction of a poetic form which shapes like something breaking. This putting together and coming apart is what makes poetic form, in this work, such a moving force.

The theme of setting out from home returns with variations throughout 'The Nightfishing', giving the voyage a sense of uncanny repeats, even while the boat strikes further and further out. So, in another desperately grasped deictic, the poet asserts:

> Here, formal and struck into a dead stillness,
> The voyage sails you no more than your own.
> And on its wrought epitaph fathers itself
> The sea as metaphor of the sea. (108)

At this point Graham plays on a word which looks both forward and back. That 'struck' recalls the necessary striking out from shore of this home-leaving 'voyage', but it also recalls the 'quay night bell' at the start which 'Very gently struck'. So one word captures what goes and what stays, what strikes out and what strikes, what 'sails you' and also keeps 'a dead stillness'. This is after all a voyage to, and of, the dead, and it has a Charon-like unearthliness about it. The memory of Stevens' dictum, 'every poem an epitaph', seems to mingle with Keats's name writ on water, to make the combined 'wrought epitaph' of the sea. This is writing which will not stay still, which shifts on the waters of syntax and grammar, and yet is 'wrought' to a high degree. Graham's relatively new word 'formal', which tolls through 'The Nightfishing', also helps to recall the sound of the bell rhythmically 'struck'. Literally, the bell is an invitation to the voyage and a warning of danger. Figuratively, however, it tolls a death: the 'formal' disappearing act of the poet into his poem, as it takes him away from homes of all kinds. As Graham describes a fishing trip into the dangers of the night sea guided only by the quay bell, he also strikes out into a new kind of poetry, indeed one that is 'formal and struck', as if all the more acutely aware of the empty space all round.

The sound of that night bell gives Graham, not only a figure for the ambiguous dangers and pleasures of this surreal journey, but also for the kind of poetry he wants to write. Being 'formal and struck into a dead stillness' is a cluster of meanings to which the poem constantly returns. This is a journey of or to the dead, which might also, for all its movements, go nowhere, except to a 'stillness'. But it is also a journey timed and marked by sounds, in particular by the first, all-important, formal striking of the bell. The clarity and the rhythm of that sound are a goad and an ideal. As Graham was finishing the poem in November 1949, he recalled a meeting with T. S. Eliot, his publisher, which greatly cheered him: 'he said that I had "a good sense of form and a wonderful sense of rhythm" ', he wrote, adding: 'He thought no young poet had produced a long poem with any formal structure, which he thought was necessary.'[19] Evidently the word 'form' is on his mind as he relishes Eliot's praise, just as it has been on his mind throughout the writing of 'The Nightfishing'. Although the sea voyage leaves the sound of the night bell far behind, in fact that sound goes on being 'struck', as if in the mind of the poem, in key passages throughout.

So Graham writes at one point:

> In those words through which I move, leaving a cry
> Formed in exact degree and set dead at
> The mingling flood, I am put forward on to
> Live water ... (109)

This repeats the bell's 'formal and struck' quality as well as its mortal warning in the pun of 'set dead'. But now the sound of the bell has become the sound of the poet's own voice: 'a cry | Formed in exact degree'. Gravitating once again to the word 'form', Graham finds in it a way of describing how a 'cry' might become 'exact', without perhaps losing its crying-ness. Through the shifting nature of words and water, something is 'Formed', the word carrying a load of responsibility for what happens, without, it seems, any directing subject. The 'I', already on the move 'through' words, hardly seems to be the intentional activator of 'Formed'. At the same time, 'I' moves through a complex syntax which somehow makes that first 'cry' a matter of exact, and therefore poetic, form. Like Stevens' repeated 'cry' in

---

[19] *The Nightfisherman*, 103.

'The Course of a Particular', Graham imagines form as the hollow thing in which cries might still resound. He does not write 'I leave a cry | Formed in exact degree', but lets 'those words' become the subject, thus setting the 'I' moving, going forward, and meanwhile 'leaving a cry' which is no one's in particular and has nothing to disclose. The syntax takes the cry away from the 'I' and lets it resonate, like the night bell, like the poem, on its own. 'Art expression', Graham explained many years later, 'is a voice between two things. Abstract formality and the very human gesture.'[20] The 'very human gesture', whatever it may be, is lost, recalled, and saved in the 'formality' a poem makes.

In 1949, some months before completing 'The Nightfishing', Graham wrote to Morgan: 'the sea with no exactness but with nonetheless intensity and positivity ... Edwin, I really love being on the sea. There I have feeling of freedom and cleanness and being part of a great energy which has nothing to do with any morality and is completely unhuman.'[21] The poet of 'The Nightfishing', like other ancient mariners, is on a godless sea, beyond morality and humanity. But his is not really a story of rebellion or alienation; in fact his is not really a personal story at all. It is a kind of sound-story, in which the sea engulfs human event or purpose in what Fiona Green has called the 'poetry's tidal push and pull'.[22] The sea, for Graham, is less a place or time than it is the formal condition of losing place, time, even self, for the sake of sea-shapes and 'sea-worked measures' (116). To turn 'The Nightfishing' into an allegory of death, rebirth, faith, even of writing itself, is to miss the extent to which it resists translation at every turn. 'I think it just might make its wee disturbance in the language. I think (in a dramatic way) it makes a place, organic and believable, within its lines. ... If it made somebody seasick (a good unliterary measurement) I would be pleased',[23] Graham explained in 1955, the year of its publication. The poem is its own place, but one full of disturbances and upheavals, to which the truest critical reaction might be to be sick. Brilliantly, Graham suggests that the very formal, self-validating abstractness of this work is a physical property, a whoozy ungrounding of the very grounds of sense.

---

[20] *The Nightfisherman*, 197.   [21] Ibid. 92–3.

[22] Fiona Green, 'Achieve Further through Elegy', in *W. S. Graham: Speaking Towards You*, 132–57, 148.

[23] *The Nightfisherman*, 141.

Towards the end of the poem, although there is a sense of arrival, the place remains obscure and shifting:

> So this is the place. This
> Is the place fastened still with movement,
> Movement as calligraphic and formal as
> A music burned on copper. (117)

'I think (in a dramatic way) it makes a place', Graham wrote in retrospect of the whole poem. 'The Nightfishing' begins and ends with the idea of 'this' place, a here and now of no fixed address, somewhere not found but made. Certainly by the end, after the long night's journey and the thrill of the herring catch, there is a narrative homecoming of a kind. The boat returns to shore, the poet returns to his house, and the poem seems to round back to its questionable beginning: 'So this is the place.' What has been found is the sea at home, or rather the sea at home in the lines that are written. The poem, of course, has never left home: it is its own 'calligraphic and formal' fact, its own place. And 'this' place at the end is only where it started from: a 'this' no better known than before, and still on the move in the strange mobility and lift of Graham's subject-eluding, seaworthy syntax. There is no author to head this calligraphy, no hand to write it. The lines continue to leave out the poet-fisherman, who might anyway have died in the story, while finding only themselves, 'fastened still with movement', which is the still movement of a poem on the page.

Somewhere in the background of this, and other passages which play on the paradox of movement and stillness, can be heard the lines Graham was fond of quoting from Eliot's 'Burnt Norton':

> Only by the form, the pattern,
> Can words or music reach
> The stillness, as a Chinese jar still
> Moves perpetually in its stillness.[24]

Behind this passage, too, the 'silent form' of Keats's Grecian urn moves still. That work continues to shape the idea of 'the form, the pattern' of art for the two modernist poets in the 1940s. Graham's own sense of form and formality is deeply indebted to Eliot's play of stillness and movement in 'Burnt Norton', but he replaces the Nineties' preciosity of the 'Chinese jar' with something more naturally contradictory: 'That forming and

---

[24] *The Complete Poems and Plays of T. S. Eliot* (London: Faber, 1969), 175.

breaking sea' (116). It is important to Graham to be able to feel the fluent edges of form, to know its breakdown as well as its hold, to let his lines imitate the irregular yet rhythmic metrics of 'sea-worked measures'. The sea, that 'simultaneously liquid and recalcitrant medium',[25] as Adam Piette puts it, gives Graham a figure for poetry which feels the reach of its line-ends as an altering, aural rhythm in the ear. This most musical of poets, who might himself have trained as a singer, has an understanding of form as the invisible shape of a sound, or the spectral apprehension of a returning rhythm, which is uniquely his own.

So the poem's eventual homecoming is described in sounds of words which have chimed throughout the poem:

> I leaned and with a kind word gently
> Struck the held air like a doorway ... (118)

The poet, at the end, speaks in the words and the timbre of the very first 'gently struck' (1) bell. That bell has tolled like a ground bass, a rhythm in the language which repeats the same sounds as if nothing had happened and nothing else mattered. The round-trip of the narrative, with all its thrill and danger, is founded on the beat of a bell. By the end, the poet has learned to speak like the bell, finding its 'formal and struck' character in his own words. Sharp, striking, inviting, as well as death-dealing, the bell catches the idea of a voice which knows form, not as external shape, the metrical or visual nature of the verse, but as the 'inner form' of rhythm. To hear the night bell is to hear form at work in the poem as if it were something in the listener's ear.

Three years after the publication of 'The Nightfishing', Graham theorized the counterpoint which seems to structure it:

I remember that always somewhere under the live and speaking idiom of the Voice in poetry there is the count, the beats you can count on your fingers. Yes always under the shout and whimper and the quick and the slow of poetry there is the formal construction of time made abstract in the mind's ear. And the strange thing is that that very abstract dimension in the poem is what creates the reader's release into the human world of another.[26]

There is the idiomatic voice which is 'live and speaking', telling its human story in the poem, and underneath there is time, rhythm, the beats on the fingers. This is the 'abstract dimension', a 'formal

---

[25] Adam Piette, ' "Roaring between the lines": W. S. Graham and the White Threshold of Line-Breaks', in *W. S. Graham: Speaking Towards You*, 54.
[26] *The Nightfisherman*, 162.

construction' which has nothing to do with 'the shout and whimper' of human feelings and human events. '*It Must Be Abstract*'[27] was the phrase Graham often repeated from Stevens' 'Notes Toward a Supreme Fiction'. However, as in Stevens, 'that very abstract dimension', the shape of rhythm in the ear, ultimately returns to the human rather than escaping from it. In this passage, the return is signalled by the poet's old favourite word 'release'. A poetry of release frees us for, not from, the human. The 'formal construction of time made abstract' thus becomes the place ('this' place perhaps), where 'the human world', with all its unformed cries, its shouts and whimpers, is rediscovered. This is a detour, not an avoidance. What happens in 'the mind's ear', that curiously intellectualized hearing aid, is that the shouts and whimpers of the human world can be heard all the more clearly. However impersonal—not anyone's ear, and distinctly not 'the mind's eye' though punning on that original—'the mind's ear' is itself a 'formal construction', a way with words which opens up the possibility of a new thing. Above all, 'the mind's ear' provides Graham with a place which brings together 'formality' and 'the human gesture'. In that ear, with its suggestion of a listening intelligence, the reader can hear 'the human world of another', and be reminded of the very ties of sympathy, feeling, need, which seemed to lie elsewhere. The fact that this is 'the mind's ear', not just the ear itself, hints at the responsibility of the reader who must also turn his or her mind to what might be heard.

For Graham, then, poetry is not just a 'formal construction' but 'the formal construction of time made abstract'. Its form is not in the eye but the ear, a matter of time and timing. The extent to which this is the case is marked by his favourite opening injunction, 'Listen', as in 'No, Listen, for This I Tell' (26) or 'Listen. Put on Morning' (59). By asking the reader to listen, Graham marks out the space, mid-air as well as mid-page, in which poetry happens. That dimension of sound, the way that poetry might be 'formal and struck', like a percussive instrument, means that it can hook 'the mind's ear' in a special way. Graham relishes these multi-dimensional effects. For instance, his often repeated line, 'We fall down darkness in a line of words' (27), throws him, and us, imaginatively towards the vertical. He doesn't write it slant, but lets the sense slant, as if down a lethal staircase of words, or else by a life-line to a sheer drop. Lines, for him, frequently confuse visual and aural senses, as if the poetic line were always more than a convention of typography. In one of his letters, for example, he describes listening to a Mozart violin concerto: 'The violinist in this is so very exact and "clean" in his playing. He makes almost a visual line in the air—I think of Klee's phrase—"taking a line for a walk", of course about drawing.'[28] This is typically multi-media, exploiting sound, sight, and meaning at once, against the visible and aural backdrop of 'the air'. Such a line is not static, but moves, half directed by the poet, half impelled by its own wandering, like an unruly dog that is taken for a walk

Graham once described to a friend how he liked to begin a poetry reading, and gave, for an example, the opening of 'The Nightfishing':

Right. Listen Listen make the idea of silence first so that the very first beginning of the very first word is going to be resonant, inevitable upon it. Now, Norman, think of the wonderful (forgive me) dramatic beginning again.

> 'Very gently struck
> The quay night bell.'[29]

Tom Leonard recalls the almost agonizing pause at the beginning of a reading by Graham, when he would repeat the command to 'Listen Listen', and then hold the 'quality of silence ... for the best part of an hour'.[30] Certainly, to 'make the idea of silence first' was, for Graham, to make a crucial part of the poem: in this case, the night, the quiet, the darkness, the sea. These become somehow audible before they are mentioned or known, so that the six muted notes of the night bell, heard in the two, three-stress lines of the start, sound all the more startling, lonely, far-reaching. Something has been broken into by the poem which thus shapes up dramatically against it.

Form, then, is never mere metricality for Graham, though he often enjoys traditional verse-forms—the sonnet with its 'wee iambic penta metra-gnome',[31] for instance. Instead, form is the shape of sound, which is also the shape of something breaking or moving. The metre may be part of that shape, but just as important is the silence which the poem breaks, not only at the beginning but throughout, at every line end and every punctuation mark. This is a listening poetry, which hears the contours of its own sounds as part of the story.

---

[28] *The Nightfisherman*, 78.   [29] Ibid. 167–8.

[30] Tom Leonard, 'Journeys', *Edinburgh Review*, 75(1986), 83–7, 87.

[31] *The Nightfisherman*, 337.

Certainly, Graham's opening gambits at readings could be unnerving: not only a repeated 'Can you hear me?'[32] but on one occasion, as Sebastian Barker recalls, a loud 'Fuck off' to organizer and audience, followed by a refusal to read at all.[33] The poem 'The Beast in the Space' (1970) starts with what sounds like this typical capricious rudeness: 'Shut up. Shut up. There's nobody here' (157). The order to 'Shut up' not only locates a murmur, a noise outside the verse which it must interrupt, but then also insists that, by contrast, 'There's nobody here.' Poet and audience are thus cleared out of the way, and we are invited into the poem's empty 'here'. This might be an overture to pure formalism, to an understanding of the poem as merely itself, by nobody for nobody. Like all negatives, however, 'nobody' ghosts a sense of somebody, while the repeated order to 'Shut up' leaves a still audible trail of talking, coughing, shuffling, whatever it is, breaking into the work. Graham's formalism knows its own limits. The 'space' in which 'the beast' lives is cleared only with an insistent and personal rudeness. This is a quiet which takes some effort. And indeed, as Graham's love of a pun might intimate, the beast itself is also 'shut up' in its strangely spacious cage.

The poet thus seems to construct the poem as an airy cage, free of human noises, and not as a trap to keep creatures in. However, there *is* something in it: a beast. This two-way creature is rather like an Escher print imagined poetically: 'The beast that lives on silence takes | Its bite out of either side' (157). Silence is a bite-size out of language, a kind of jigsawed alternative which lies on 'either side'. The beast, which represents poetry in its special space, free of intentions and consolations, also hints at the deep ambiguity of poetic form. For form is both inside and outside, a thing figured by space which also makes space visible and shaped. 'The Beast in the Space' is quite different from, say, a bird in a cage. It is not a prisoner, not a trapped object with a grievance. Space, after all, releases objects from captivity. The title, which puts something in space, also therefore lets it out. Meanwhile the beast, unnamed and invisible, is known only by its restless noises: it thumps, pads, sniffs, laps, bangs, snorts, growls. This is a beast which inhabits the space of the mind's ear. It is figured as sounds, particularly those repeated, rhythmical ones which start to sound like a poem. It ought to be a content, since it is contained 'in the space', but it is more like an emptiness, or rhthym, shaped. To look for representational meaning in

---

[32] Ibid. 305.
[33] Sebastian Barker, 'Memoir of W. S. Graham', *Edinburgh Review*, 75(1986), 88–91, 89.

this poem is to be thwarted. The beast is a weird go-between, something between air and sound, which has no simple allegorical meaning, but rather the opposite: 'It comes and laps my meaning up' (157). As Barthes proposed: 'Form is what is *between* the thing and its name, form is what delays the name.'[34] The poem's form is nothing very clear; it is without 'meaning', but it has a beastly outline and makes insistent noises.

This beast, then, goes between silence and sound, poet and reader, enclosed cage and open space. It 'means neither | Well or ill' (158), we are told, having of course eaten all meaning up. It does, however, keep two personal pronouns, 'I' and 'you', in a kind of correspondence. 'I remember | I am not here' the speaker confesses at one point, sounding, with Quince-like naivety, as if he has forgotten his lines, or at least has forgotten the line at the start: 'There's nobody here.' If the beast is form, the visible and audible layout of words on silence and the sound of a debate between them, it does not, finally, shut out the human. Across a last, line-ended phrase, which stretches the sense distortingly, the opening of the poem is repeated but with a difference:

Above

All, shut up. Give him your love.

Evidently, it seems, someone is still chattering in the stalls, some 'you' who has not been swept out of the way. Meanwhile the beast, for all its amoral qualities, its impersonal, rhythmic thumps and beats, the abstract jigsaw of its bites 'either side', leads back to the old human thing: 'love'. As Graham himself wrote: 'that very abstract dimension in the poem is what creates the reader's release into the human world of another.' By the end the reader is released into feeling. 'Give him your love' is this poem's last word, signing off, on behalf of the reader, an imaginary, bizarre love letter.

'The Beast in the Space' is typical of Graham in being a poem figured as an open cage—a cage without grievance. Something is 'in' it, an ambiguous, shifty creature, who makes noises and laps up meaning. The inside-outside puzzle of a spacious cage is what makes the lines take a walk, move on their stillness, look two ways. It is a verbal-aural example of the poem's formal limits, which are both necessary and infinitely extendable. The beast in the space is a kind of verse-room in which to move. As Don Brown has noted, Graham constantly stressed 'the need

---

[34] Roland Barthes, *The Responsibility of Forms: Critical Essays on Music, Art, and Representation*, trans. Richard Howard (Oxford: Basil Blackwell, 1986), 234.

to "make a shape" '.[35] But to make a shape in the ear is to perplex the notion of shape, and make a curious beast which rhythmically paces its limits, but is also outside any identifiable cages. As Amittai Aviram puts it: 'poetic form itself, as rhythm, is beyond meaning.'[36] For Graham, the need to make, as he puts it, 'rhythmic shapes'[37] is a need to understand that poetry *is* its form, its own 'formal construction', but one that is found by listening, in 'the mind's ear', to 'the human world of another'.

It is true, as Frank Kuppner,[38] Douglas Dunn,[39] and others have pointed out, that Graham can be too obsessed with language. He writes about writing too easily, and sometimes, when not sidetracked, can sound merely didactic. But in his best poems there are cross-themes: loneliness, poverty, claustrophobia, terror, the need to make a poem a letter, even if a letter 'Aimed at Nobody' (295). The brilliant, cold absences of 'Malcolm Mooney's Land', the personal elegies to painter friends, the riddling, abstract verse-games, all in their different ways make overtures to presence, conceived as human and loved. The power of Graham's letters comes from the same powerful mix. When there is nothing there, the poet speaks more powerfully. 'I hate having to say anything which needs saying. I would rather write to someone I like when I've nothing to say ... and just want to let them hear my sweet voice',[40] he declares. Free of compulsion, needs, import, or matter, the singer can sing. The 'sweet voice' of the musician comes through when there is no grievance, intention, or purpose. That word 'nothing' is found everywhere in his letters. He sends, for instance, 'LINES FOR NOTHING',[41] or 'A LITTLE LETTER FOR NOTHING',[42] or elsewhere begs: 'Remember this is a letter for nothing for nothing at all.'[43] To Elizabeth Smart, who was writing a new work, he asks: 'How are you getting on in nothing?'[44] That old aestheticist formula, 'for nothing', for no money, for no purpose, no need, is still running its resourceful course. If there is a small irony in the fact that Graham was also often asking, or hoping, for money from his correspondents, it does not detract from

---

[35] Don Brown, 'Establishing the Don Brown Route', in *The Constructed Space*, 31–6, 33.

[36] Amittai F. Aviram, *Telling Rhythm: Body and Meaning in Poetry* (Ann Arbor: University of Michigan Press, 1994), 19.

[37] Quoted in Morgan, 'W. S. Graham and "Voice" ', 77.

[38] Frank Kuppner, 'Marginalia to "Implements in their Places" ', *Edinburgh Review*, 75(1986), 94–100, 97.

[39] Douglas Dunn, Foreword to *W. S. Graham: New Collected Poems*, p. xviii.

[40] *The Nightfisherman*, 83.   [41] Ibid. 192.   [42] Ibid. 244.

[43] Ibid. 324.   [44] Ibid. 338.

'nothing' as a literary intention. To be 'getting on in nothing' is a nice juxtaposition of two senses: the careerism of 'getting on', and the bogged-down purposelessness of 'nothing'. Nothing, like nobody, offers a word in place of a thing, and thus mimes, to some extent, the ways of all literary language. As outlines of something or someone no longer there, nothing and nobody are (almost) empty forms.

In his emphasis on lines, spaces, constructions, Graham seems to be trying to write the poetic equivalent of the abstract art produced by his painter friends in St. Ives, Roger Hilton and Bryan Wynter. As with Woolf's similar interests in lines, oblongs and squares, cubist forms which defy the personal yet also memorialize it, such abstractness recalls, desires, and regrets what is human and alive. Objects that are merely 'calligraphic and formal' call for feeling. The beast in the space is restless, seeking a response. If the emotional drama is oblique to the language of the poem, it is also, for that reason, all the more powerfully there.

In another late poem, 'Approaches to How They Behave' (1970), Graham focusses once again the verbal constructions of poetry, and its difficulty. The point, he writes, is 'To be exact and yet not to | Exact the prime intention to death' (178). Letting go of intentions, and all such controlled meanings, is a way to let nothing happen instead. When it happens, however abstractly expressed, it might sound like falling in love:

> Running across the language lightly
> This morning in the hangingover
> Whistling light from the window, I
> Was tripped and caught into the whole
> Formal scheme which Art is. (182)

This is the contradiction which runs through Graham's work, laying it open to the charge of literary self-consciousness, but also giving it its peculiar emotional flavour. There is a story at work, which may not involve particular people or places, but which is there as the driving surprise of the writing itself. His abstractions or formal schemes are sharp as things, and as capable of tripping us up. Indeed, as he suggests in a letter, the poem must be 'an obstacle of communication ... which has to be climbed over or gone round but not walked through'.[45] In 'Approaches to How They Behave' it is 'tripped' up on, a 'Formal scheme' being a very definite, blocking obstacle in the path. 'Running

---

[45] *The Nightfisherman*, 141.

across the language lightly' is an odd construction, which catches up the idea of running across a lawn, running one's fingers over, rifling through, coming across. There is the rush of 'Running' and then the abstract lightness of 'across the language'. Having 'tripped', the poet is also then 'caught', whether into Art's nets or arms. The idea of the poem as an 'obstacle' gives to its 'Formal scheme', whatever that is, a definite, obstructive bulk—a thingness, which is not the things it is about. The poem lies in the way of the poet, like a boulder or mountain, so that communication involves skirting or climbing, not just walking (or seeing) straight through it.

Thus form—the made 'formality', 'the forming and breaking sea', 'the formal construction of time', the 'Formal scheme which Art is'—must also be a human communication, full of difficulties and annoyances perhaps, but nonetheless a way through or across the obstacle of language. In another poem, 'Clusters Travelling Out' (1970), Graham takes the word which, in his private vocabulary, stood for his automatic writings,[46] and loads these 'clusters' with the memory of the primitive painter Arthur Wallis, who died in the workhouse at Madron:

> Tap tap quickly along the nearest
> Metal. When you hear from me
> Again I will not know you. Whoever
> Speaks to you will not be me.
> I wonder what I will say. (191)

Exactly who inhabits this place of coded messages and desperate communications does not matter much. The messages go out along strange routes, tapped along the pipelines of the workhouse, sent without obvious purpose or intention. The sender seems neither to know who he is nor what he will say. Like the beast that taps, the poem thus goes out in a kind of code, but a code without any decodable system, since the addressee is absent and the sender possibly mad. There are only the taps, the rhythm of something sent out in lines, the clusters of sound around which no particular story clusters. At the same time, however abstract and impersonal, the poem struggles to be a letter, a communication that puts writer and reader in touch. While being lines for nothing, like Graham's own letters, these are also the lines of loneliness, despair, insanity, terror. Those human meanings cross the formal arrangements

---

[46] Matthew Francis, 'Syntax Gram and the Magic Typewriter: W. S. Graham's Automatic Writing', in *W. S. Graham: Speaking Towards You*, 86–105, 86.

of the verse like a surprising cross-purpose. 'You' and 'I' have something to say to each other, 'Tap tap quickly', even though 'I will not know you' and in any case I 'will not be me'. 'I wonder what I will say', without even a question mark, is Graham's most frequent, collapsed intention in writing. From that near-nothing, the poem's wondering communication flowers.

So form, for Graham, is a word in the ear. He conceives the poem as a sound-work, which makes 'some kind of (even structural) formality' in the way it breaks against silence and distracts sense into sound. At the same time these most abstract and musical of poems, which shape themselves more aurally than visually, have, at their best, an epistolary urgency which catches, in spite of everything, 'the live and speaking idiom … the shout and whimper' of human communication. Those sounds find their way into the formal plan of the poem by devious routes, which may not be easy to follow. But at their best, Graham's poems evoke this tension at the heart of the notion of form. Abstract and impersonal, like blocks of words that sing almost for the singing's sake, they sometimes let the human cries come through. And when they do, they can be counted as some of the greatest poems of the twentieth century.

The poem which more than any other expresses this cross-purpose is 'The Constructed Space' (1970). The title brings together two of the poet's favourite ideas: that of a construction and that of a shapeless space. He then goes on to describe the poem as a place where 'we two' face each other across the usual barrier of an 'abstract scene'. The pressure of the personal 'we two' against the 'abstract scene' is then made the point of the whole poem. It is:

> a public place
> Achieved against subjective odds and then
> Mainly an obstacle to what I mean. (162)

Not only 'subjective odds' but also 'what I mean' must be swept out of the way. The poem is 'a public place', out there in the open, and functions as 'an obstacle'. It is a thing in the way of personal meaning, which must therefore be sent in another direction, over or round it, or just off elsewhere. But this obstacle of communication is also precisely what lets communication happen. 'Anyhow here we are', the poet asserts, suggesting a buttonholing warmth, aggression, struggle, a facing of 'each other' of (at least) two presences. The human gesture of the pronoun is busy in the language. Graham is not suggesting that we are constructed out of language. He is suggesting that the construction, the 'public place', is made in order to displace us from subjective meanings or intentions. The only intention which might be recognized is already impersonal; it is, like Wordsworth's imagination in *The Prelude*, 'some intention risen up out of nothing'. Intention is met like a stranger by the wayside, en route, unforeseen, its source and origin that favourite literary place: 'nothing.' Yet 'out of nothing' comes something:

> I say this silence or, better, construct this space
> So that somehow something may move across
> The caught habits of language to you and me.

Intentions 'risen up out of nothing' give way to 'something' that 'may move', though of course it may not. Attentive as ever to the depths of words, Graham catches in 'caught' both the sense of an infection, of a powerless inheritance, and perhaps of a fleeting necessary stay which is to be clutched at. Those 'habits of language' are certainly not dispensable. They are the grid across which 'somehow something may move'. Like the spirit of God moving upon the waters, this motion is uncertain, surprising, a matter only of 'somehow'. What it creates, however, is a bond, an event between 'you and me', a spirit of human communication which crosses, with luck, the constructed space of the poem.

Not knowing who we are, or where, or when, the poem has therefore given us a 'space' where 'something may move | Across the caught habits of language'. That 'Across' is crucial. This is something which does not run smoothly along the rails of language, like the 'rivetted up wagon' of the poem loaded with worthy intentions, but crosses it, goes athwart it, like an idea caught by luck and chance. That is how it reaches 'you and me'. Whatever it is, that moment of human communication happens. The fact that it also has no name, no knowable presence in the world, is part of Graham's point and of his poetic achievement. This, like many of his poems, may be 'a letter for nothing for nothing' (324), but it is also, across the declared pointlessness and purposelessness of that old aestheticist phrase, an urgent and passionate love letter.

ᘒ

The forms are many in which the unchanging
seeks relief from its formlessness.

Samuel Beckett

Perhaps, the words will find their mark
And leave a brief glow on the dark,
Effect mutations of dead things
Into a form that nearly sings ...

Derek Mahon

10

Forms of Elegy: Stevenson, Muldoon, Hill, Fisher

Elegy is a form defined by content. Although this was not always the case, the Greek and Roman elegy having a strict verse-form and a 'fairly broad range of topics', the word in the modern period has been largely associated with 'mortal loss and consolation'.[1] As a result, according to Jahan Ramazani, the genre now 'permeates a wide range of poems about war, love, race, gender, meditation, the self, the family, and the poet'.[2] His definition, relying on that prolific 'about', hints at a list which might continue indefinitely. As long as the work is 'about' death or loss, however loosely defined, it can be classed as an elegy. It need not even necessarily be a poem. Virginia Woolf wondered if she might call her novels elegies, since their themes and moods as well as their poetic styles seemed essentially elegiac. Elegy, unlike almost all other literary genres, takes its name from what it is about, rather than from any conventional structure.

---

[1] Peter M. Sacks, *The English Elegy: Studies in the Genre from Spenser to Yeats* (Baltimore and London: Johns Hopkins University Press, 1985), 2–3.

[2] Jahan Ramazani, *Poetry of Mourning: The Modern Elegy from Hardy to Heaney* (Chicago & London: University of Chicago Press, 1994), p. x.

As a result, modern accounts of the genre have tended to rely on Freud's theories of mourning for guidance. That mourning might be 'normal' or 'melancholic',[3] curable or incurable, has offered a powerful dualistic template by which to map this most free of literary genres. According to the Freudian scheme, elegy becomes an act of mourning which may or may not be worked through in the interests of consolation. The sense of laborious and improving effort thus becomes its main characteristic. Essentially, elegy is not literary work, a craft or technique to be perfected, but moral and emotional work, undertaken by the elegist who is assumed to grieve. Although mourning itself always slides a little ambiguously from a felt grief to a necessary ritual, from personal emotion to public display, it does nonetheless take its definition from the sense of sorrow, larger or smaller, provoked by death. As a work of mourning, elegy relies on this attributive intentionalism. Its language is graded by feeling and checked along the grid of grief and consolation. By this account, Tennyson's 'In Memoriam', like Milton's 'Lycidas', charts the emotional route out of grief and follows the 'normal' process of mourning. By contrast, according to Ramazani, most twentieth-century elegies are melancholic and comfortless. They eschew the curative progress implied by Freud's first category, and instead remain essentially 'ironic and self-mocking, anti-sentimental, anti-scientific, and anti-therapeutic'.[4]

The question of what does or does not console, however, involves some fixing of the emotional stakes. After all, the most bleak and 'anti-sentimental' of elegies, Larkin's 'Aubade', might also be grimly, even upliftingly, consoling. Conversely, the consolatory ending, like Tennyson's, may only depress with triteness. The very category of mourning, as a grief to be gone through and come through, is itself a peculiarly Victorian notion, loaded with a sense of emotional improvement and normalizing outcomes. It is a category which hardly impinges on those elegies which are impersonally meditative, metaphysical, comic, mock-heroic, or just coolly observant. Here, the presumed emotions of either writer or reader are not intrinsic features of the genre, and Freud's categories seem themselves sentimental. By contrast, Samuel Johnson's brusque assertion that 'Where there is leisure for fiction there

---

[3] Sigmund Freud, 'Mourning and Melancholia', in *On Metapsychology: The Theory of Psychoanalysis*, trans. James Strachey, ed. Angela Richards (London: Penguin, 1984; first pub. 1917), 247–68, 251.

[4] Ramazani, *Poetry of Mourning*, 17.

is little grief'[5] might be a salutary reminder that elegy, as a genre, does not necessarily carry the negative and positive charges of sorrow and consolation. It may simply be a 'fiction', playing up, as all literature does, the disparities of form and content, writing and feeling, in a tangled losers' game made all the more acute by the fact that loss is also its subject matter. Rather than a work of mourning, then, with all its overtones of required emotions and hopeful solutions, elegy might be defined as a work of losing, in which language replicates the loss that gives rise to it.

This might be why the sense of form in elegy is peculiarly prominent. Form, in the sense of body-form as well as in the sense of formal outline or effigy, is a word which contains the complex dynamic of elegy itself. For elegy is a literary form defined by the body-form which lies somewhere within the container or reliquary of the text; but it is also a form left empty, feeling the hollow shell of its literary objectlessness. It is a word which suits the elegist's need to be writing about someone, formed in the work's verbal memory and imagination, as well as the knowledge that there is nothing there, except the work's leisured and formal movements. The something-and-nothing of elegy thus sets up a dynamic which brings together the emotional drama of loss which it replicates, and the essential drama of the literary itself. Nor is this doubleness peculiar to the twentieth century. As Robert Douglas-Fairhurst has shown, Robert Browning's elegy 'La Saisiaz' contains a vagueness about the word 'form' which, on the one hand, points to content: 'the question as to whether a dead person has any form other than a corpse', and on the other points to genre: 'the central and unresolved question which is raised by its own form: is this poem a dramatic monologue?'[6] Elegy, perhaps more than any other genre, conceives its poetic form as the relief somehow, the shaped remains, of something that has gone. It is a verse-form bound to, and defined by, being 'about', while also expressing the verbal and emotional limits of that 'about'. It thus brings to the fore the old form-and-content conundrum which lies at the heart of all literature.

Two twentieth-century elegies, Anne Stevenson's 'Willow Song' and Paul Muldoon's 'Incantata', both play on this disparity of form. Both

---

[5] Samuel Johnson, 'Milton', in *Lives of the English Poets*, 3 vols., ed. George Birkbeck Hill (Oxford: Clarendon Press, 1905), i. 163.

[6] Robert Douglas-Fairhurst, *Victorian Afterlives: The Shaping of Influence in Nineteenth-Century Literature* (Oxford: Oxford University Press, 2002), 176.

are personal elegies which name and identify their objects, thus casting the elegist as private mourner from the start. At the same time the strict stanza-forms, the repeats and refrains, the chiming internal and external rhymes, suggest a worked fiction, whose object has disappeared and whose character has therefore become 'merely' formal:

> I went down to the railway
> But the railway wasn't there.
> A long scar lay across the waste
> Bound up with vetch and maidenhair
> And birdsfoot trefoils everywhere.
> But the clover and the sweet hay,
> The cranesbill and the yarrow
> Were as nothing to the rose bay
> the rose bay, the rose bay,
> As nothing to the rose bay willow.

Stevenson's elegy for the poet Frances Horowitz also remembers, by the way, Desdemona, the singer of the first willow song, Ophelia, the gatherer of ineffective herbs, a disused railway and its lost mining industry, a ravaged pastoral landscape, as well as the wild flowers which, in the course of the poem's summer, fade and die. As the rose bay withers, stanza after stanza, in a repeated, sense-emptying refrain, the human object is displaced. While this is a perfect Elizabethan lyric, a song of 'simples', invoked as if they might still cure the poet's 'sweet love',[7] it is also a modern elegy, grieving a lost industrial heritage as well as the natural landscape which it scarred. Brilliantly, in the first two lines, the expected, human object is lost again in the poem's surprising swerve: 'the railway wasn't there.' Instead of addressing 'you', this elegy sidetracks from the start. Not only is 'you' not there, but neither is the railway, a double absence which then discloses something which is there: 'A long scar lay across the waste | Bound up with vetch and maidenhair'. Hidden in the words is the lost body, scarred and 'Bound up', perhaps in all three senses of the phrase: imprisoned in, implicated in, and salved with bandages. In this unconsoling elegy there is no 'you' to touch or be touched, even in imagination, and herbal remedies cannot hide the scars. The ordinary literal negative of 'the railway wasn't there' denies from the start any supra-literal appearances, and hints at a double negative which the rest of the poem confirms: she is not here, and neither is the railway.

---

[7] Anne Stevenson, *Poems 1955–2005* (Tarset: Bloodaxe Books, 2004), 378.

'Willow Song' addictively reproduces its ancient imagery of healing, but also rejects the medieval theory of signatures which might make the milli-foliate yarrow, for instance, good for binding wounds. This flowery tale can only decorate an absence. Indeed, drafts of the poem show Stevenson working to excise altogether any personal references to Horowitz, so that by the end the flowers have taken over, and an early line like 'the gloss of her red hair'[8] has been deleted and replaced by 'the loosestrife of her hair'. The flowers, with their wild names, catch at a presence which they also conceal, as if covering the landscape of a grave. The human form is contained in, and transformed by, the poem's own form: its litany of flowers, and the rhymes which continually echo the sound of 'willow': 'yarrow', 'hollow', 'sorrow', 'yellow', 'snow'. Originally called 'Song', then 'A Song for Frances', the final title, 'Willow Song', puns on the expected other willow which weeps, but also suggests that this 'rose bay' must have its own brilliant flowering. The 'rose bay willow' is the recalled (excised) red hair, buried in the ground of the poem, in the 'song' which can only flower hopelessly in its absence. It is, in a sense, both lost content and beautiful, empty form.

Elegy, then, brings the relation of form and content to the fore. It plays with content, metonymically, topographically, but also loses it to words alone. Muldoon's 'Incantata' might be echoing Stevenson's poem in its hauntingly similar floral imagery. This too is a song, a cantata, addressed to a named friend and fellow-artist: *'Mary Farl Powers'*. Its complex rhyme scheme, echoing elegies by Cowley and Yeats [9] as well as quoting 'the same ninety rhyme words'[10] of his other long elegy, 'Yarrow', both backwards and forwards, insists on a kind of formal magic. And, indeed, 'Incantata' is a feat of bravura, a show of language which displays its structural form in a tense dialectic with its conversational ease. Thus the penultimate nineteen stanzas, each introduced by the Miltonic 'Of', seem to burst their grammatical and rhyming bounds in a kind of epic aide-memoire. The sequence then ends with a sentence which might indeed be staking its claim to 'normative' mourning, a work of words which brings relief to the mourner in its supreme wish-come-true:

> than that the Irish Hermes,
> Lugh, might have leafed through his vast herbarium
> for the leaf that had it within it, Mary, to anoint and anneal,

[8] 'Anne Stevenson Archive', in the University Library, Cambridge, MS Add 9451.
[9] Tim Kendall, *Paul Muldoon* (Bridgend, Wales: Seren, 1996), 209–10.
[10] Clair Wills, *Reading Paul Muldoon* (Newcastle: Bloodaxe Books, 1998), 183.

than that Lugh of the Long Arm might have found in the midst of *lus
na leac* or *lus na treatha* or *Frannc-lus*,
in the midst of eyebright, or speedwell, or tansy, an antidote,
than that this *Incantata*
might have you look up from your plate of copper or zinc
on which you've etched the row upon row
of army-worms, than that you might reach out, arrah,
and take in your ink-stained hands my own hands stained with ink.[11]

So Muldoon lets the wish-list of wild flowers which has run through
the poem seem to work its cure. From the last 'Of', three stanzas back,
a single sentence unwinds its spell, the spell of 'this *Incantata*', which
might have Mary look up as if nothing had happened, and greet the
poet in a gesture which remembers Tennyson's hopeful dream that
Hallam might 'strike a sudden hand in mine'. The lovely symmetry of
the hexameter lets the palindromic echo of 'take in your ink-stained
hands my own hands stained with ink' make a love-match. So the poem
imagines itself as the flowery antidote it invokes: the one that will cure
cancer and bring Mary back into her life, unchanged. At the end, the
ink still fresh on his hands, the poet seems to enter the room of his final
stanza and find its lost object there: 'your ink-stained hands'. This is
the dream of all elegy, that form, in its virtual reality, its empty room,
will be able to house the beloved human form again, and so find its
longed-for consolation.

But of course this is not true. The last stanza depends on a kind of
grammatical amnesia. Each 'than that' gets further away from the thing,
two stanzas back, which inspires the comparison: 'the furrows from
which we can no more deviate'.[12] Back there, Muldoon has buried the
sense of the whole sentence. There is no deviating from 'the furrows',
however devious the ways of poetry. 'than that this *Incantata*', with its
touching resurrection in the last line, is a passage carrying its negative
from the start. The dead are in their 'furrow', or even, in a distant
half-rhyme to the very first line of the poem, in their 'long barrow'.[13]
There is no getting out of that place. The imaginary touch of hands is
a trick of grammar which can 'no more' happen than the furrows be
harrowed of their dead. Muldoon's poem, like Stevenson's, rings the
changes on that sound: barrow, widow, low, swallow, sorrow, sparrow,

---

[11] Paul Muldoon, *Poems 1968–1998* (London: Faber, 2001), 341.
[12] Ibid. 341.   [13] Ibid. 331.

flow, furbelow, mellow, yellow, furrow, row, as if to keep the echo of sorrow, and of that first unswerving 'barrow', always audibly in mind.

'Willow Song' and 'Incantata' both sing. Their objects are evoked by a language which can make music, but cannot help. For all their powers of memory and invocation, and in spite of the binding force of their rhymes, these elegies know that there is nothing else. Their forms are hollow, somehow lonely. The addressed object neither hears nor knows. In the end, these elegies stand as witnesses to the fact that their gestures are rhetorical and their handwaving empty-handed. More than any other genre, elegy shows the outlines of its own verbal mode as part of what it is about: the form, inside, of the dead, and the form that is the limit of what the poem can do or say about them.

Geoffrey Hill's 'Two Formal Elegies', subtitled *'For the Jews in Europe'*, are similarly concerned with what we mean by 'Formal', and how that affects the named, if impersonal, subject. The very word in the title refers not to verse-form—both poems are sonnets—but to something formal in their tone or attitude, the manner or pitch of their speech, the impersonality of their pronouns. These elegies are formal, not in any technical sense, but in the inevitable detachment, the cool helplessness of their speech before an unspeakable topic. How then, they seem to ask, might 'we' talk about 'them'? When the dead are plural and so many, the poet has no rights of personal sentiment, of mourning and consolation. Yet the first elegy begins: 'Knowing the dead, and how some are disposed'.[14] This might sound intimate, a knowing, as if of some personal 'disposition',[15] as Christopher Ricks notes, until the next phrase dispels the illusion and digs out, in a Pateresque move, the Latin etymology of 'disposed' in the phrase 'subdued under rubble'. Underneath, even dragged through 'rubble', there is an unknown thing. 'Knowing the dead' thus takes on a quite different meaning. Not known to 'us' personally, the object of this elegy is simply 'the dead' become 'rubble'. Then, having brought us so discomfitingly close, the sentence ends, four lines later, with another surprise: 'Knowing the dead ... we grasp, roughly, the song.'[16] Whether 'roughly' means approximately, crudely, or violently,[17] the notion of 'song' is a shock. After such knowledge, can there be 'song'? Hill drags the sense of his opening lines

---

[14] Geoffrey Hill, *For the Unfallen: Poems 1952–1958* (London: Andre Deutsch, 1959), 31.

[15] Christopher Ricks, 'Geoffrey Hill 1: "The Tongue's Atrocities"', in *The Force of Poetry* (Oxford: Clarendon Press, 1984), 285–318, 291.

[16] Hill, *For the Unfallen*, 31.   [17] Ricks, *'Geoffrey Hill'*, 291.

through the rubble of mass graves, but still insists on 'roughly, the song'. Song, in this context, may be an aesthetic silliness or scandal, but it is also the thing that must somehow be grasped. Just how difficult to grasp is contained in the tangible richness of the word 'roughly', which also hints at a recoil from what we'd perhaps rather not touch at all.

Yet that 'the song' must win through all sorts of knowing and un-knowing is the point of the syntax. Hill's 'we' in 'we grasp' is both himself, finding a way to write, and the reader who must try to under-stand it. His song, like Celan's music, knows the dirt of what it must sing about, but sings nonetheless. This old trope for poetry will always, especially in the case of political elegy, admit to being a purposeless sound. Nevertheless, the poet's business is 'song', nothing more, nothing less. Even beside the mass graves of the twentieth century, this poet must grasp the nearly intransitive, merely formal, condition of music.

Form, then, develops an extra resonance in elegy. On the one hand it points to the mere formalities of poetry in the face of death or atrocity. Whether as song or meditation, the poem is a useless formula, thrown back on the magic of its words. On the other hand elegy is also peopled by forms, by presences which, even without any supernatural intention, hover in the poem, ghosting its pronouns, ghosting even so dead a noun as 'the dead'. The question of where the dead are—in the mind, in the past, the landscape or the grave—leaves them rattling around in the poem's pod, never quite 'subdued'. They move there, verbally shifting between their lives and their deaths, in a space that holds them verbally, but cannot 'grasp' them. Elegy promotes this heightened sense of form's responsibility to something outside. It is a form of words about lost human forms, both ghostly with absent content. Meanwhile, the wish to see, touch, or grasp the dead, as ancient as Odysseus reaching to embrace his mother in Hades, is a conceit no less strong for being displaced else-where, onto the 'song'. The dead are by definition absent from their own forms, though forms are all that is left, in memory at least, to the living.

* * *

'Never have people seemed so absent from their own deaths',[18] writes Roy Fisher, in a line which catches, wittily, the absurd absenteeism

[18] Roy Fisher, *The Long and the Short of It: Poems 1955–2005* (Tarset: Bloodaxe Books, 2005), 34. All subsequent references to Fisher's poetry are taken from this volume and are cited in the text.

of the dead. 'The Entertainment of War' (1957) is a curious work, at once a comic elegy, a war poem, and a personal commemoration of four members of the poet's own family who were killed by a falling bomb. Knowing the dead, however, comes with no charge of grief or guilt to the poet's recalled ten-year-old self. Instead, he seems merely entertained by his morning-after knowledge. 'A mile away in the night I had heard the bombs | Sing' (33), he remembers. To make a song of it, as all these elegists do, is to find a certain necessary detachment, even to aestheticize the sound of bombs in music, or poems: 'Sing'. Fisher then recalls the things rescued or pillaged from the house: 'My cousin's pencils lasted me several years'; so does that cousin's 'notepad'. These are relics, as well as a legacy. The poem details their survival, for 'several years', with awful, literal accuracy, as it does the comparable survival of the grandfather, who 'for five years tried to share the noises in his skull' (34), then walked out and died. Being 'so absent from their own deaths' is a state replicated by the poem's extraordinary detachment. It is as if there is no one here who is not somehow absent from feeling, at least from any disclosed or curable feeling. The grandfather cracks up slowly and the boy scribbles in his notepad.

Without the family connection it might have been impossible for Fisher to adopt this tone of humorous impersonality and treat war almost as a poetic entertainment. There is no mourning in the child's-eye view of what happens or in the child's simple need for pencils. Flat detail, roped into regular three-line stanzas, sets human trauma alongside the appearance of the blasted house that is 'so tidy it seemed nobody had ever been there' (33). The poem, too, has the formal tidiness of an inventory, coolly drawn up by an outside witness. Objects survive or disappear, as luck would have it. Nor can these suddenly unhoused dead be reclaimed as heroes, victims, or cherished familiars. Fisher's refusal to mourn seems to make a mockery of war and of the 'marginal people' it wipes out. The result is one of the coldest elegies ever composed, its absences written deep into its language. Being 'so absent from their own deaths' is a double negative which leaves the dead almost out of verbal account altogether, literally flattened into masonry and muddy ground.

There is, however, a legacy from them: 'This bloody episode of four whom I could understand better dead | Gave me something I needed to keep a long story moving' (34). The cousin's pencils are at work in the poem's undermeanings. This apparently least 'moving' of poems, which seems to have missed its emotional register altogether, also admits that its griefless event is never over. Understanding the dead *as* dead will be Fisher's special and ongoing story. He is the legatee of their 'pencils' and the teller of a 'long story' which, like 'The Entertainment of War', keeps them lightly but constantly in mind. 'A good deal of what I'm on about is the lives of the dead, their lost histories', the poet once admitted. Yet his sense of the impersonality of the dead puts them beyond either personal or political emotion. As he himself added, about the very phrase 'the dead': 'Making it singular makes it, by intention, a more abstract and extensive term which has to take its chance.'[19] Making it abstract allows the language of elegy to be, not tied to feeling, poet's or reader's, but chancy, adventurous, moving beyond its instant. 'The Entertainment of War' may seem careless, aloof, banal, but this absence of feeling, like the absence even of death to the dead, is part of the point. The wartime bombings of Birmingham, which so confused personal and political events for the ten-year-old boy, originated the poet's continuing sense of the dead as beyond grief, pity, sense, but also never to be forgotten. They remain like a penumbra, or stain, everywhere in the brickwork of his poetry.

'By no means separate the dead | from anything' (189), Fisher declares in a later poem, letting the line-break take the force of the joining. In 'They Come Home' (1984), he describes bringing his parents-in-law home from the crematorium, 'owl-size in their jars', via 'the car-exhaust workshop' where they are 'lifted up high' in a tiny, unmystical ascension on the ramp, before being composted in the garden. Their last 'whisper of human dust' is then binned with the rest of the household refuse to be sent to the municipal incinerator. 'They Come Home' is a funny, updated piece of graveyard verse, the literal-mindedness of which also betrays a touching, yearning whimsy: 'owl-size' might mean they are wise, 'whisper' might be the sound of their voices. The dead come home in this poem, not to be housed, but to mix with useful, ordinary things which are also, in their turn, on the way out: the rusting car, the 'discontinued kitchen', 'the clearings-out' of household rubbish. Within this general exiting, 'By no means separate | From anything at all' (190), the dead leave the print of their peculiar, casual absence.

Fisher has called his fixation with small-scale close-ups, with 'window-frames and bricks and things', a troubling 'super-realism'.[20] There are no metaphysical views in his poetry, but paradoxically there is a kind

---

[19] Roy Fisher, *Interviews Through Time and Selected Prose* (Kentisbeare: Shearsman Books, 2000), 111.
[20] Ibid. 78.

of inverse long view in things themselves. 'Soot, sunlight, brick-dust; and the breath that tastes of them' (35), he writes in an early prose poem, 'By the Pond' (1960). Such lists as these turn 'super-realism' to ghostliness. Here, there is a 'breath' exuded from mere things, as if something lived. By the end, the poet insists: 'I can see no ghosts of men and women, only the gigantic ghost of stone.' (36). A 'ghost of stone' is a strange compound, massively itself, yet already doubling into a ghost of itself, as if so much of mere matter might be unbearable. Ghosts, in this poetry, are inseparable from things, from that reality, even super-reality, to which the dead come home. At the same time, even a 'ghost of stone' is more, or less, than just stone. It is as if the communal graves of wartime Birmingham everywhere leak into the architecture of Fisher's poems. This means that, although the brick structure of the city is his main imaginative prospect, 'where there was nothing to see | but immediacy, a long wall' (275), that 'immediacy' is also haunted. Walls, as Sean O'Brien[21] has pointed out, are one of Fisher's favourite close-ups, their dead-endedness part of the point. However, this materialist vision, a '*belief* in the priority of matter',[22] is also not quite matter-of-fact. Walls, bricks, and stones can turn unreal from too much looking, too close a stare, so that the 'ghost of stone' might turn into a stony ghost. The sense of the dead infiltrates the most ordinary and material of walls. Their absenteeism is what keeps them in, ghosting Fisher's landscapes, remaining, indeed, not 'separate | from anything at all'—although the tiny hiatus of the line-break also suggests that this inseparability is not easily achieved.

The paradox, then, of a material vision so hyper-real that it becomes surreal goes to the heart of Fisher's poetics. He is a poet who sees so visually close that his works are almost, as the title of one of his own poems puts it, 'Without Location' (1975).[23] In this unlocated place he can be 'keeping in closeup' (234) to a world 'made on a pulse' (235). This may be one of the reasons for his reputation as a difficult poet. He cannot be read 'straight', though it is, he claims, his 'practice to write as

[21] Sean O'Brien, 'Roy Fisher: A Polytheism with No Gods', in *The Deregulated Muse* (Newcastle: Bloodaxe Books, 1998), 112–22, 114.

[22] Ian Gregson, ' "Music of the Generous Eye": Roy Fisher's Poems 1955–1980', in *Bête Noire*, 6(1988), 186–96, 196.

[23] See John Kerrigan, 'Roy Fisher on Location', in *The Thing about Roy Fisher: Critical Studies*, ed. John Kerrigan and Peter Robinson (Liverpool: Liverpool University Press, 2000), 16–46, 30–1.

simply and starkly as possible'.[24] That simplicity and starkness are not the same as literal straightforwardness, however. A wall, in Fisher, is not simply a wall. This is something the poet makes clear when he repudiates those critics who analyse his work 'from the representational end or the end which appears to have a morality in it, and might be what you could call comforting'.[25] The opposite of 'comforting' representation is contained in the word 'aesthetic'. 'Duchamp', he writes, 'is a major ethical figure for me, and a major marker of the sort of inherent qualities of the aesthetic you make when you work.'[26] The word 'aesthetic' comes to hand as an explanation of some 'inherent' quality of the work, which cannot be extrapolated into narrative or paraphrase. Perhaps recalling Donald Davie's early criticism of his poetry, as of one 'who'd disappeared into aestheticism, never to return',[27] Fisher grapples with the well-worn binary of the ethical and the aesthetic, forcing the one into the service of the other. Duchamp is 'ethical' because he pursues the 'aesthetic'. This word and its variants recur throughout his writings. 'I find it very surprising that people will look at my work as if it was pure aestheticism or look at it as without moral dimension at all ... though I know that if I look at it from one angle myself, it is',[28] he points out. The word 'aestheticism', with its easy tag 'pure', is dubious, but not entirely rejected: 'though I know ... ' Davie's accusation of 'aestheticism' perhaps only drove the idea of the aesthetic, with its complex sense of inherency and its relational dance with ethics, all the more firmly into place.

One of those places is a poem which becomes both a poetic manifesto and an elegy for the dead. 'Diversions' (1976), with its *fin-de-siècle* title, its praise for the kites which are 'mindless, but all style', and its sense of the dead in the *'power of dead imaginings to return'* (305), is an elegy with a strongly resonant aesthetic. In it, the foundry patternmaker, who shapes drains, gears, doors, seems to stand for the figure of the poet himself:

> His work fulfils the conditions for myth:
> it celebrates origin,
>
> it fixes forms for endless recurrence;
> it relates energy to form;
> is useless in itself;

[24] 'People who can't float: Roy Fisher Interviewed by Ra Page', in *Prop*, 2(1996), 30.
[25] Fisher, *Interviews Through Time*, 66.   [26] Ibid. 50.
[27] 'People who can't float', 30.   [28] Fisher, *Interviews Through Time*, 81.

for all these reasons it also attracts
aesthetic responses in anybody
free to respond aesthetically ... (310)

Linking the ironworks of Birmingham to the furnace of poetry, Fisher
offers an aesthetic of Blakean energy,[29] with a Los of the imagination
at work in its foundry. Here, 'aesthetic responses' are elicited by an
industrial process which would seem as far from aestheticist preciousness
as it is possible to be. At the same time the language betrays its debts to
the past. Being 'useless in itself', the work of the patternmaker makes
something happen: 'it fixes forms for endless recurrence; | it relates
energy to form.' The word 'form', meaning precisely the mould or
pattern of the foundryman, as well as eliciting old associations with the
aesthetic, is both thick and empty, both fixed and energetic, both
the functional implement and the artistic end. It makes a link between
industrial production and the purposes of poetry which runs deep in
Fisher's imagination. At the same time, the old tropes of aestheticism
can be heard stirring. That such work is 'useless in itself' is part of its
use, while the word 'form', repeated, starts to draw attention to itself.
Form is an object of production, but also something invisibly versatile,
metamorphic, and re-creative. Associated with 'energy' and 'recurrence',
it has no meaning or purpose in itself, but appeals to our free 'aesthetic
responses'. Form is not a particular object, but a thing 'endlessly'
re-forming itself.

'Diversions' is also, like many of Fisher's poems, a furtive elegy—one
which recalls the dead, lightly, in passing, as if they were casual accidents
of the landscape. 'Dead troubles take longer than live ones' (307), he
writes, as if touching once again on the 'long story' of the dead that
started with 'The Entertainment of War'. But what do they take longer
for, or for whom? The sentence mixes the idea of having long-dead
troubles and of the dead themselves continuing to trouble. Either way,
something troubling and dead lurks in it, as it does in the word 'form',
which recurs throughout. While the patternmaker creates 'forms' for
industrial use, and the poet for poetic use, another kind also looms
for instance, in, 'the vegetable variants of body-form', which show up
like a 'negative | body-aura' (309)—as if they were something between
a photo and a saint. Elsewhere, these body-forms lurk in the strong
elegiac undertow of the work:

[29] Clair Wills, ' "A Furnace" and the Life of the Dead', in *The Thing about Roy Fisher*,
257–74, 261.

> a dissolution of my darkness
> into such forms
> as live there in the space
> beyond the clear image of an owl:
>
> forms without image;
> pointless to describe. (305)

This is indeed a poem of which it is 'pointless' to say simply what it is about. Its narrative is full of diversionary tactics, irreducible to morality, anecdote, reportage—not 'what you might call comforting'. The word 'forms', however, carries an elegiac burden of human presence, while suggesting something at the limits of presence. Reminiscent of Stevens' 'The Owl in the Sarcophagus', these 'forms' inhabit an owlish place where they cannot be seen or described. They are about as empty as a word can be, while still being a noun. In this place, wherever it is, beyond even 'my darkness', there are 'forms'—a word that seems shapeless and purposeless, but still somehow there: a presence, a potential, a variable. It is a word for nothing you can see, but it outlines a space and suggests a search, a loss, a need. Moreover, forms 'live there'. Those dead troubles, or troubles of the dead, have a way of coming back and living, 'in the space | beyond the clear image', which is the unrepresentable space into which Fisher's language pushes.

In 'A Poem Not a Picture' (1974), he again uses the word 'form' to press beyond representation. He begins: 'On a ground remarkable for lack of character, sweeps of direction form' (231). Here, the pun on 'remarkable' ensures the turn from picture to poem, from visual to tellable. This is not a remarkable picture, but an unpicturable remark. Indeed, 'making forms with remarks'[30] is Fisher's own witty summary of his own experimental poems in *City*. A remark, without being remarkable, can be a poetic form because it has an internal dynamic *to* form. The verb is at work in the noun. The phrase 'sweeps of direction form' thus gives movement a shape, without there being any particular shape to see. Moreover, the meaning does not stop at the verb, but goes on sweeping through it, as if forming were always a continuous activity. This sense of momentum, of verbal unfinished business in 'form', is characteristic of this poetry, which is no less formal for being often, as Fisher himself acknowledges, in 'a self-branching, self-proliferating form'.[31] A poem need not be a boxed shape. It may,

---

[30] Fisher, *Interviews Through Time*, 83.   [31] Ibid. 68.

instead, make 'sweeps of direction', like the impression of a gesture, mid-air. Indeed a hand, gesturing or painting, has just disappeared from view in 'sweeps of direction', leaving a movement apparently without subject or object, and also without stop.

So 'form', in this line, indeed keeps a story moving. It insists on fluidity, on a sense of design which withholds pictures, disdains closure. The word is not a casual one for Fisher. He uses it with a keen sense of its innate poetic significance, as of something carefully and deliberately constructed, however freely. 'Also a lot of what I do write is an attempt to make sense, or make art, or make form',[32] he declares. Though he is not a formal poet in the traditional sense, the shaped arrangement of a poem in the mind and on the page is what matters. The 'interest in form that I have'[33] is an interest, not in counting syllables or lines, but in finding the internal shape that makes a poem move. Form, with its multiple, dynamic meanings, is the link-word between the forming properties of words in time and the outer sound-shape the poem makes. In 'Continuity' (1969), for instance, he describes how 'the fish-trap gives the waters form, | minimal form.' The wavering net of the trap lets out as much as it lets in, while giving to 'So much free water' (375) a kind of mobile, pulsing shape. Like Graham's 'The Beast in the Space', Fisher's thing in the net is as free as it is formed. As a description of poetry it emphasizes once again that form does not contain its matter, netted or caged, but lets it flow through. This poet, certainly, is a fisher of 'free water' rather than of trapped fish.

All poems, writes Donald Davie, 'are shapes cut out of lapsing time'.[34] The conflict of shape and time, of poetry as sculpture which must be 'cut' and as music which must be timed, may be one reason why poets themselves continue to need and to redefine the word 'form'. With its hint of visual emptiness and effort, form takes time to take shape, like 'sweeps of direction' or the wavering fish-trap. A shape is a solid; a form depends on a relation with what moves through it. Something thus takes form in poetry, not instantly, once and for all, but in the 'lapsing time' of syntactical and imaginative process. In an interview, Fisher himself tries to explain this focus of attention beyond the photographic fixity of visual objects:

---

[32] Fisher, *Interviews Through Time*, 92.   [33] Ibid. 100.
[34] Donald Davie, 'Two Analogies for Poetry', in *Modernist Essays: Yeats, Pound, Eliot*, ed. Clive Wilmer (Manchester: Carcanet, 2004), 47–52, 49.

If there's a thing which I think of as my style, or even my music—albeit a subdued music—it's logopoeia. That is the part which is off hunting. How they combine is that usually the shape of the poem, if I can make it move at all, has this third category lurking somewhere. That's the beast in view. I almost have to avoid bogging down in the visual. Otherwise I'd finish up with a colour photograph which looks as though it needs paraphrasing back into a black and white, but isn't a poem.

Opting for Pound's third term 'logopoeia, 'the dance of the intellect among words'[35] rather than the pictorial 'phanopoeia' or the musical 'melopoeia', Fisher is evidently looking for a way through the visual–aural complex. To go 'among words', in the chancy way of the poet, is to make a song and dance of it perhaps, but it is also to make 'the shape of the poem ... move'. The chiselled implication of 'shape' is unshaped by that favourite and crucial word, 'move'. A poem has to move, not settle into 'the visual'. Later in the same interview, this wrestle with shape leads again to the word which always suggests movement in Fisher's work: 'making casual and conversational shapes that clearly acquired form in the course of their writing',[36] he writes of William Carlos Williams. So 'form' is not a fixer of 'conversational shapes', but a movement in them, achieved in time, 'in the course of writing'. The slip from 'shape' to 'form' shows a movement which is integral to what makes a poem. Though dogged by the photographic visual, particularly its near-view shots of bricks and stones, Fisher's verse moves through and beyond the visual to a sense of form as running in time.

The poem which most daringly pushes beyond visual shapes into moving forms is 'A Furnace'. Published in 1986, this late elegy, which accumulates all the aesthetic, industrial, and political implications of the earlier work, epitomizes the strangeness and challenge of Fisher's work. It is an elegy which follows no narrative line, carries no personal story or investment in mourning, and meets the dead, here and there, with an extraordinarily impersonal sangfroid. The challenge of the work derives less from its invisible 'spiral' structure, its claim to 'anti-time',[37] or even its free-form fragmentariness, than from the quirky, unfinished appearances of the dead in it. This is an elegy which exploits the brokenness of its verse-form in order to show the dead as forms, appearing here and there, bit by bit, as the reader learns to look and listen.

---

[35] 'People who can't float', 28.   [36] Ibid. 29.
[37] Fisher, *Interviews Through Time*, 116.

Appearing is important to Fisher. It is a word he often uses, in spite of distrusting 'the visual' on the one hand and disclaiming visionary credentials on the other. The dead in 'A Furnace' seem to need to appear, randomly, silently, not at any set time or with any sense of importance or import. They are, for instance, like the 'town gods':

> Personages who keep strange hours,
> who manifest
> but are for the most part mute,
>
> being appearances ... (66)

Although something here seems on the verge of the visible, 'manifest' withholds it. The intransitive mode suits the dead, allowing, as it does, an action of some sort, an effort or intent, but without result. What do these personages 'manifest'? Nothing, it seems. Yet the wish to show or disclose remains. These personages are 'appearances', which is a sort of apparition, but more ordinary, less ghostly, and taking longer to come about. The word is, like 'manifest', a disclosure of something with no accessible shape. In another poem, 'Wonders of Obligation' (1979), the word 'manifest' has a similarly ambiguous function. The sky is described as 'the manifest | of more forms than anyone could see' (16). Here too, 'manifest' suggests a visible show, a clarity, even a literal invoice of cargo,[38] yet containing a plethora of 'forms' which cannot be seen. Something obvious in 'manifest' is mysteriously withdrawn by 'forms'. That Fisher's poetry is full of forms does not imply that there are more things in its heaven and earth than appear at first sight. Instead, like the 'Personages', the forms of the dead come into being somehow only in the interstices of grammar itself, in the wrenched surprise of a word or phrase which comes to life. 'The manifest', like 'manifest', allows the dead to be there, working at coming into view, but never in fact giving us a picture of what they are. Like form, 'manifest' is a word which offers something and nothing, which refuses representation even while hinting at it. From that place, the dead solicit a kind of greeting.

'A Furnace' is punctuated by these appearances, these verbal haunt-ings, of the dead who are not usually named or known, but might be found suddenly anywhere, randomly and comically, in a bush, in windows and water-drops, in the space between ceiling and cupboard, in walls and bricks and wild fennel. This might add up to an almost riotous mysticism, except, as Peter Robinson suggests, it is a mysticism

---

[38] Thanks to Roy Fisher for pointing this meaning out to me.

of things and 'patternings'[39] rather than of named or active agencies. Certainly, the dead are not message-bearers or familiars, expecting recognition. They are, perhaps, just the forgotten poor of Birmingham, or, as Fisher puts it in one place, anonymous 'timeless identities | riding in the flux with no | determined form' (59). Such undetermined 'form' (and language) opens up a prospect for ghosts which is both capacious and unspecific. The word holds them, but holds them free of visible identity or presence. The city is their crematorium and graveyard, the place which recycles but also harbours them, since there is nowhere else for them to go. 'And the biggest of all the apparitions, | the great iron | thing, the ironworks' (53) is the key to it. The foundry, as elsewhere, is a striker of forms from the blaze of its furnace, which might also be the blaze of war, history, life itself. It is also, however, only another apparition in the poem, a thing that dawns on sight, slowly, with strangely invested purpose.

Forms, manifestations, apparitions, all these help to describe a world in which the dead mix with things, and come to sight (or mind) casually, chaotically, with no special emphasis or significance. Too close for comfort sometimes, Fisher's poetic brickwork is elegiac, not because of any melancholy tone or theme, or any personal story in it, but in what it tries to make appear. 'They have no choice but to appear' (83), he declares of the dead at the start of the final section. Like all his appearances, this one too takes time—a time that can be heard in the extended movement of the sentence which follows, and which runs across four lines:

> We knew they existed, but not what they'd be like;
> this visitation is the form that whatever
>
> has been expected but not imaged takes
> for the minutes it occupies now. (83)

The hint of biblical promise in 'visitation', that something might be paying a visit, is lost in time—syntactical time. In order to get to 'visitation' (in reverse), something, 'whatever', has to take a 'form', though not any form of its own choosing but one 'expected' by another, unknown subject. So 'this visitation', which leaves us none the wiser as to 'what they'd be like', remains an idea dawning. The 'form' in question ought to be a ghost, a strange visitant, a person, but as so often in Fisher it is more a process of seeing which never finishes with an

---

[39] Peter Robinson, 'Last Things', in *The Thing About Roy Fisher*, 275–311, 297.

object simply seen. Instead, 'they' lie beyond representation, in a 'form' that is 'not imaged', and which thus echoes those similar 'forms without image' in 'Diversions'. It is in the nature of 'forms' to visit without a face, to be expected but never known. The purpose of this elusive elegy is not to know, see, or touch the dead. It is to let them form, as comers and goers in things, having no other ontology, no emotional or ethical purpose, except to be, fitfully, intransitively, 'manifest'.

'A Furnace' thus asks for a strangely free and unplotted reading. It is an elegy, in the sense that it is 'about' the dead, but that 'about' tells no story, gives no names, expresses no emotion, and certainly does not track a process of mourning. Instead, it glimpses here and there the 'forms' of those no longer living, forms which might be imagined in its grammatical lacunae, intransitive verbs, passive tenses, and odd tricks of phrase.

> Something's decided
> to narrate
> in more dimensions that I can know ... (53)

the poet explains in the opening section of the poem. This seems to ask for what Franklin Rogers has called 'a "volumetric" reading', a reading of the poem 'in several dimensions at once'.[40] The poem, Fisher once wrote, 'is written in a sequence which is to me musical, but it is at the same time a heap'.[41] It works in time, but it is also an unsorted instant of ideas, so that its aural and temporal properties conflict with its tangible and visual ones. To try to peg the poem to a story misses the point, for this too, like 'Diversions', is 'pointless to describe'. 'A Furnace' is a work 'intended to be made of poetry rather than hung on narrative or hung on a lot of anecdote, but which is made chiefly for being in a language which ... is made to move in its own way'. Like all attempts to define what it is that makes a poem a poem, rather than narrative or anecdote, the passage falls back on varieties of intrinsic-ness. It is a poem 'made of poetry' or of 'language'. It is what it is, confusingly beyond knowable dimensions of thought, and marked by a redundancy of suitable paraphrase.

Nonetheless, Fisher does offer a word which is one of his favourites when describing the workings of poetry: it moves. Not only does

---

[40] Franklin R. Rogers, *Painting and Poetry: Form, Metaphor, and the Language of Literature* (London and Toronto: Associated University Presses, 1985), 194.

[41] Fisher, *Interviews Through Time*, 95.

language 'move in its own way', but the reader too is expected to 'give his life up to moving through this poem'.[42] To 'keep a long story moving' was the drive behind 'The Entertainment of War', that early experiment in elegy which first acknowledged the ubiquitous fascination of the dead. To 'move in its own way' is a feature of poetic language, shifting as it does, through and against the norms of representation, as well as a feature of the dead, whose place is uncertain and changeable. In 'A Furnace', the dead are described at one point as 'material spirits | moving in rock as in air' (71). This catches the impersonal, material emphasis of Fisher's elegy. The dead are given room, and room to move, only as 'material spirits'. The key word, once again, is 'moving', which makes something which might just be solid 'rock', shift a little. The dead are there, in that slight alteration of perspective which happens between 'material' and 'spirits', between 'rock' and 'moving'. They are thus given a sort of syntactical time in which to appear. That they are 'moving' is not a tribute to any metaphysical or mystical state, merely to what poetic language can do, as the reader reads, in time.

At one point in this poem, Fisher draws on a classical story of return and meeting, but then offers a conclusion which is purely his own:

> They come anyway
> to the trench,
> the dead in their surprise,
> taking whatever form they can
> to push across. They've no news.
> They infest the brickwork. (64)

This 'trench' goes deep in the poet's imagination, back to Odysseus conversing with the dead on the one hand, and to the trenches of the First World War on the other.[43] The trench is also the local graveyard, up 'Kentish Road' (64), and the remembered bombed garden of 'The Entertainment of War'. Trenches are where the dead are found, in a figure which mixes ancient literary precedent, earthy literalism, political catastrophe, and personal memory. It is a word to which Fisher himself returns in his work. In 'The Home Pianist's Companion' (1980), for instance, he writes of Mary Lou Williams' playing that 'she will trench and | trench into the firmness of the music' (240). This catches the muscular effort of the pianist at work, but also opens up, by an imaginary wrench of verb into noun, a pit of memory, which a little

---

[42] Ibid. 96.   [43] Wills, ' "A Furnace" and the Life of the Dead', 263.

later proves its elegiac connotation when the music 'suddenly locates the dead | the utterly forgotten' (241). Those 'utterly forgotten' dead lie everywhere in the music Fisher makes. Even the pianist digs a memory-grave to them. In the passage from 'A Furnace', the trench is where the dead might be met, 'taking whatever form they can'. This lets us hear what is crucial to Fisher's work: the effort of form, its chanciness and freedom, but also its deep necessity. The dead need form in order not to be nothing. Form, however, is not 'news'. Like the other mute visitations in this poem, the dead do not come bearing messages and the living are none the wiser for their visits. 'They've no news' beautifully recalls, as well, that 'news' is not what we read poetry for. We read it for the surprise, and the form, 'whatever form', that is, it needs to get across. The dead inhabit form with difficulty, with a sense of surprise, but like all poetic content or subject matter, form is their only imaginable place.

It is typical of Fisher, however, to bring us up short with a last line: 'They infest the brickwork.' This is his favourite dead-end vision, 'immediacy, a long wall'. The dead have crowded in, prolific and close, weeds or stains in the 'brickwork'. They come home to the place which was there at the beginning of his career: 'I can see no ghosts of men and women, only the gigantic ghost of stone.' There is regret in this comment, as well as recognition. In 'A Furnace', too, it seems, the dead are forced into things, into bricks or stones or stalks. But paradoxically the reductive literalism of 'They infest the brickwork' keeps a sense of something, foreign, swarming, pervasive, just there under our noses. Material spirits, in this poetry, invert easily into spirits of matter. The difference lies only in how they appear. Meanwhile, 'They infest the brickwork' sums up where the dead are, generally, in Fisher's poetry: in the near-view objects of the industrial landscape. The verb, however belittling, allows them to be there, not dispersed or lost, but oddly manifest in 'infest'. If not visible or recognizable, they are at least, like any other infestation, deeply ingrained.

That this is the case is proved by the last sentence of the whole passage. The poet concludes this strange meeting and non-meeting with: 'My surprise | stares into the walls' (64). This 'surprise' seems to have no object except 'walls'. Yet that surprise should go on staring, as if still in the hope of seeing something by which to be surprised, is intriguing. It may be, of course, that walls in themselves are sufficiently surprising for Fisher. But it may also be that the word meets, aurally at least, that earlier 'surprise' of the dead, who come 'in their surprise, | taking whatever form they can'. Surprises all round then, and through them, a beautifully poised, implicit question as to whether anything returned or was met, in any form that might be known. 'My surprise | stares into the walls' leaves the poet at his favourite chalk-face for poetry, with bricks and things, but also with a sense of 'surprise' at what might be seen there. It is in those material objects, banal and literal as they are, that he might find the dead still 'moving'. At the same time, the unfinished business of staring, or, more curiously, of 'surprise' staring, suggests that there are no easy or comforting recognitions to be had in that place.

So Fisher makes form work hard in his poems. As for all these writers, it is less about the outside shape of his poetry, fluid, versatile, and often minimal as that is, and more about its inside seeing. When it comes to seeing the dead, it is a matter of seeing nothing there, but seeing it so that it 'moves', which of course also throws the emphasis back on seeing itself: 'staring into the walls'. He lets the dead come to the dividing trench, not to confirm an other or afterlife, not that they might be recognized or mourned by the living, but to allow a kind of verbal surprise to take place. That greeting, as in most of his elegies, is not a mystical sign or proof of anything, but it is nonetheless a greeting. The sense of the dead as nothing but form, as figures in the carpet or the brickwork, is not a disparagement of them, but a moving, even loving poetic attention to them.

As Fisher himself puts it, in a late poem which is in part an elegy for a school friend, 'The Dow Low Drop' (2000): 'True nothing | needs hands to build its many forms.'[44] The 'many forms' of his own poetry are a reminder that, particularly in elegy, form is not an external fixture, but an internal dynamic, and one which needs and founds content as well. Form is a word which gives writers a figure for something essential to literary work: for that obliqueness of style and matter, music and meaning, which demands attention, and becomes, in its way, a new kind of knowledge. In the case of elegy, that dynamic is peculiarly tense and involved, drawing, as it does, on a sense of content, the dead, which is also an absence. Such a content, however, might thus become, not nothing simply, but more challengingly and laboriously, with a need for the working 'hands' of the poet, 'True nothing'.

---

[44] This is taken from the earlier, very slightly different version of the poem, in *The Dow Low Drop: New and Selected Poems* (Newcastle: Bloodaxe Books, 1996), 191.

The monuments meant nothing of course. ...
'This is art,' they said, 'We cannot use it.'

John Ash

when the question changed its form
it was the same point driven home

Alice Oswald

11

Elegies of Form: Bishop, Plath, Stevenson

After great pain, a formal feeling comes—
The Nerves sit ceremonious, like Tombs—[1]

Emily Dickinson's 'formal feeling' is a curious construction. These lines
ought to mean that, 'After great pain', there is an end, a numbness, a
death. And indeed, there is a kind of death in the poem. At the same
time, 'a formal feeling' goes on to become the monumental feeling form
of the second line: 'Nerves sit ceremonious, like Tombs'. Like much
Victorian women's poetry, Dickinson's posthumous moment, 'After
great pain', lets feeling get free of the personal pronoun 'I' or 'she', as
well as of its object 'pain', and freewheel into wit. Out of time and place,
even out of their own body, those 'Nerves sit', all the more alertly, all the
more on edge. Exactly who or what this sitting attends on is not quite
clear. 'Nerves ... like Tombs' is a nervy contradiction, which stiffens the
'formal feeling' of the first line, while leaving an empty space where
there should be an object *of* feeling, some body within. These tomb-like
'Nerves' are erected like monuments to their own death, which may or
may not have happened yet. In the end, this is a tomb to feeling made
from the very stuff of feeling. That 'Nerves sit ceremonious' keeps them
upright, even live, while offering a commemorative headstone to what
has gone.

[1] Emily Dickinson, *The Complete Poems*, ed. Thomas H. Johnson (London: Faber,
1970), No. 341, 162.

Dickinson's lines seem to mix two ideas which have always, at least since the early nineteenth century, been associated with the word 'form'. On the one hand, it is a material construction, a house or tomb in which something is contained; and on the other, it is a body, nervous and feeling. It has the stony, monumental rigidity of a shelter, and at the same time it is alive, with the feel and tension of a living creature. It is both a container and a content. In Dickinson's witty summary, she pulls those opposites together and confounds the difference between them. Is this a tomb, or is it nerves? Is it dead or alive, feeling or unfeeling? Those questions, and that confusion, mixing outer and inner, form and content, are then intrinsic to the nature of the poem which follows. For this thing which comes 'After great pain' is not a death, exactly, but a death-like pose, a sensed after-sense.' The poem's 'formal feeling' is like an attentive tomb to something and nothing.

Form, whether it means the formal parts or the informing spirit, the thing itself or the idea it evokes, the poem or its parts, runs the gamut, as Raymond Williams observes, from 'the external and superficial to the inherent and determining'.[2] As a word, it relishes confusion, slips cavalierly from one sense to another, puns liberally. It is a licence for inexactness and an opportunity for double-think. These, however, are also the very reasons for its appeal. Its scope for invention is large and free. Promiscuously adapted to a multitude of meanings, it moves easily between them, thus, by its very nature, signalling the 'moving' quality which makes literary language work. The richness of its aestheticist legacy only adds to this mischief. Form, in the hands of Gautier, Pater, and Wilde, for instance, is a sly provocation to the bourgeois, which wards off the pressures of content, narrative, morality, use. Aligning itself with style, technique, music, with art's non-committal, non-representational tendencies, it also sneaks into view the seductive possibility that form, like style, is the man. In art, writes Pater, '*form*, in the full signification of that word, is everything, and the mere matter is nothing.'[3] That nervous qualification, 'in the full signification', is already plumping out '*form*' into something more than just a stylistic device. The lost body of form is always waiting in the wings to slip back into the picture, as it does, literally, in *Dorian Gray*: 'the painter looked

---

[2] Raymond Williams, *Keywords: A Vocabulary of Culture and Society* (London: Fontana, 1983; first pub. 1976), 138.

[3] Walter Pater, *Plato and Platonism: A Series of Lectures* (London: Macmillan, 1910), 8.

at the gracious and comely form he had so skilfully mirrored in his art.'[4] Here, form makes one of those seductive slips between life and art, body and body-image, as the painter runs his eyes down the outlines, real and figurative, of human beauty. Like Pater, Wilde enjoys one of the more archaic dictionary definitions of 'form' as 'beauty, comeliness'. A 'comely form' is doubly an object of desire, allowing body to figure in art, flesh to figure in words, and one more resourceful double-entendre to ply its (rough) trade through Victorian aestheticism.

By the time form becomes one of the defining features of twentieth-century formalism, much of this scandal-value has been lost. Clive Bell's 'significant form',[5] like Eliot's '*significant* emotion',[6] may exploit its own contradiction in terms, its sense of wanting both significance and form, but its sense is sanitized by comparison with Pater's and Wilde's. Twentieth-century formalisms tend to denude form of its racier meanings, turning it into style pure and simple, or pure and well-wrought. 'The representative element in a work of art may or may not be harmful', writes Bell, 'always it is irrelevant.'[7] By the time the challenge comes from various literary theories from the 1960s onwards, form has become associated with a formalism which, in rejecting relevance, representation, purpose, might seem in danger of becoming itself irrelevant. Terry Eagleton's 'Ideology and Literary Form', which defines 'form' as the deceptively smooth face of 'historical contradictions',[8] announces an opposition between form and ideology, form and politics, form and history, which still resonates in our consciousness, and is, indeed, part of the continuing allure and offence of the word. Yet 'form', as a word, has never gone away. For all its slipperiness, it continues to be needed by literary criticism, perhaps sometimes for want of a better. Particularly when it comes to poetry, this four-letter word has always offered something that 'text' or 'work', for instance, cannot supply: a sense of the poem's conflicting dimensions, its shape in the mind's ear as well as the mind's eye, its nearly tangible bulk and outline on the page, its dynamic interplay of sound, sense, and

---

[4] Oscar Wilde, *The Picture of Dorian Gray* (Harmondsworth: Penguin, 1949; first pub. 1891), 7.

[5] Clive Bell, *Art* (London: Chatto & Windus, 1914), 8.

[6] T. S. Eliot, 'Tradition and the Individual Talent', in *Selected Prose of T. S. Eliot*, ed. Frank Kermode (London: Faber, 1975), 44.

[7] Bell, *Art*, 25. Bell does, however, make the point that literature 'is never pure art', always being 'concerned, to some extent, with facts and ideas', 153.

[8] Terry Eagleton, 'Ideology and Literary Form', in *Criticism and Ideology: A Study in Marxist Literary Theory* (London: NLB, 1976), 114.

appearance. In addition to these, form always carries that hint of a tactical withdrawal from meaning and intention, of a retreat into the intrinsic. Form, which has historically accreted all these connotations, gives to art a sense of being already a complex of events, a dynamics of creation and interpretation. Such a dynamics might also be what gives the reader a freer, more choice, entry into what art is also about.

Discussions of form, indeed its very definition, have almost always entailed, however, even if by default, arguments about use, purpose, and relevance. Eliot's complaint about Arnold, for instance, that 'he was so conscious of what, for him, poetry was *for*, that he could not altogether see it for what it is',[9] probes a debate which recurs throughout history. The idea of being '*for*' (by implication also politically for or against) is fended off by a tautology which leaves almost, but not quite, nothing more to say. Poetry is 'what it is'. Eliot here half-echoes the most famous tautology of all in the story of 'what for': art for art's sake. His own uneasy debt to that legacy is part of the story of his own development as a modernist. Certainly Tom Paulin's attack on him is, at least in part, an attack on form's apparently trivial pursuits. 'Poetry', he mocks, is thus 'not sacral or ethical or civic, it's just a higher form of limerick'[10]—the limerick being, evidently, at the bottom of the formal heap. Peter McDonald's riposte is that, on the contrary, 'form is the serious heart of a poem.'[11] Knowing this, he claims, 'real poets know, as they have always known, that poetry cannot work to extra-poetic agendas.'[12] So 'form' remains contentious still, setting the poetic against the 'extra-poetic', the 'limerick' against 'the civic', the workings of mere style against relevance and responsibility. This continuing debate, about what the poem is and what the poem is for, also keeps criticism, perhaps, awake to the possibilities and limits of its *own* 'use', to its own necessary dependence on being *for* something, whether elucidation, interpretation, praise, dispraise, polemic, or paraphrase. Criticism is wedded to being 'for'. Meanwhile, the art work, at least in the tradition inherited from nineteenth-century aestheticism, wants also to be for itself, for nothing. The conflict between these two perhaps keeps both

[9] T. S. Eliot, 'Matthew Arnold', in *The Use of Poetry and the Use of Criticism: Studies in the Relation of Criticism to Poetry in England* (London: Faber, 1933), 103–19, 118.

[10] Tom Paulin, 'T. S. Eliot and Anti-Semitism', in *Writing to the Moment* (London: Faber, 1996), 149–60, 156.

[11] Peter McDonald, *Serious Poetry: Form and Authority from Yeats to Hill* (Oxford: Clarendon Press, 2002), 6.

[12] Ibid. 15.

on their toes. '[W]hen we write literary criticism', Paul Fry suggests in
a richly throwaway sentence, 'we still do not know what we are talking
about.'[13]

That cautionary proposition makes an interesting accompaniment
to some lines from one of the poets themselves. Heather McHugh's
'20–200 on 747' raises the very problems of what poems are for, as she
describes a journey by air in which the logic of clear sight, 20–200,
must bend to the curve of both world and poem:

> Given an airplane, chance
>
> encounters always ask, So what
> are your poems about? They're about
> their business, and their father's business, and their
> monkey's uncle, they're about
>
> how nothing is about, they're not
> about about. This answer drives them
> back to the snack tray every time.[14]

This defence of poetry against 'about about' leaves the idiot questioner
understandably dumbfounded. Not for or about, the special intran-
sitiveness of poetry drives this poet into rigmaroles of 'not', and the
baffled fellow-traveller 'back to the snack tray'. The poem wittily enacts
an answer which is no answer at all, while also being the thing in
question: a poem. The miscommunication hinges, as so often, on a
tagging preposition. Being not 'about about' sounds like an attempt
to cancel 'about' altogether, by turning it into nearly nonsense. But in
fact the misunderstanding between poet and traveller is not total. In
response to the question, 'what | are your poems about?' the poet also
gives a rather eloquent answer. 'They're about | their business, and their
father's business and their | monkey's uncle'. So they *are*, also, 'about'.
On the one hand, these are poems formally minding their own business;
but on the other, they are Christs with a mission and jokers out for a
laugh. They mix God-the-'father's business' with the whim of a 'mon-
key's uncle'. The business of poetry thus turns out to be everything's
business, high and low, sacred and civic, significant and insignificant.
The question of being 'about' is not, then, entirely irrelevant. Poetry,

---

[13] Paul H. Fry, 'The Hum of Literature: Ostension in Language', in *A Defense of
Poetry: Reflections on the Occasion of Writing* (Stanford, Ca.: Stanford University Press,
1995), 50–69, 53–4.

[14] Heather McHugh, '20–200 on 747', in *Hinge and Sign: Poems, 1968–1993*
(Hanover and London: Wesleyan University Press, 1994), 184–5.

it seems, at least for McHugh, is 'about' *not quite* 'nothing'. If wanting it to be 'about' is criticism's short-sightedness, wanting wholly not to be 'about' may be poetry's. Meanwhile, conversations between the two, however ill-tempered and high-flown, are still those of fellow-travellers.

And so 'Elegies of Form'—the slight strain and awkwardness of this title is meant to signal a difficulty. The possessive '*of* Form' is countered by something fugitive about 'Elegies', so that the phrase pulls in two directions. Indeed, there is a trouble of prepositions throughout this book, as if the very idea of form provoked a kind of grammatical fussing. A discussion about form must also, in some ways, be 'about about'—as well as about for, and after, and of. 'Elegies of form' hints at this problem, at the idea of something taken away from form, as well as possessed by it. 'Elegy', writes Coleridge, 'presents every thing as lost and gone, or absent and future.'[15] The relationship of 'form' to 'everything' may be, similarly, essentially elegiac, commemorating a loss which also cannot be forgotten. At least in the work of the three poets in this chapter, the sense of form is present, not simply as a matter of technique, but as an object, a body, in a tradition which goes back to Victorian aestheticism's playful commodifications of its own formal pleasures. The sense of elegy may be greater or lesser depending on the work, but some elegiac quality, a regret for what has gone, both gone from and gone into a poem, affects all poetry. In the case of Bishop, Plath, and Stevenson, their formal seriousness as poets is neither an accidental extra nor an ideological flag-waving. It is, rather, part of the losing game of being *for*, which is what their poems are also about. 'The art of losing', as Bishop insists, is a loss that poetry especially knows how to express.

Thus her famous villanelle, 'One Art', turns the fate of 'losing' into a practised ambition with a joke at its heart: 'Lose something every day.' The sheer pressure of the villanelle form (almost as trying as the limerick, one would think), is part of its drama of lost objects. Each one of those, from 'door keys' to the loved 'you', is briefly inventoried before the iron rule of the refrain throws it out. The poem toys with the formal control that might make losing, not just a way of life, but also a way of art. What happens, however, is that the two things come apart. By the last stanza the form, with its hammered rhyme, loses everything except itself:

---

[15] S. T. Coleridge, 'Table Talk', in *The Collected Works*, 16 vols., ed. Kathleen Coburn and Bart Winer (London: Routledge, 1971–2001), vol. xiv, ed. Carl Woodring, 226.

> —Even losing you (the joking voice, a gesture
> I love) I shan't have lied. It's evident
> the art of losing's not too hard to master
> though it may look like (*Write* it!) like disaster.[16]

So writing it makes what it is about happen. The art of losing is the poem's 'One Art'. Anne Stevenson has pointed out that: 'The personal losses written *of* in "One Art" are simultaneously, almost cheerily, written *off*.'[17] From '*of*' to '*off*', another prepositional wheeze, neatly catches the double game of the poem: it is *about* losing, and it is also, simultaneously, a losing through its own writing. The form, which is so prominently audible, finally wedges an 'it' between the poet's voice and the beloved, addressed 'you'. That 'it' is no use, in any sense. It cannot bring back what is lost, or make loss more bearable. Meanwhile, the sheer concentration of '(*Write* it!)' substitutes the poem itself for all the lost objects that have been listed. It also lets us hear the personal disaster zone of its informal aside. Brilliantly, those brackets put '(*Write* it!)' both inside and outside the poem. The phrase is, on the one hand, the poem itself, the thing that offers words in place of what is lost; and on the other it is the anguished sound of the poet, steeling herself to write as if no one could hear. The phrase is, in miniature, both poetic and extra-poetic, both the triumph of form and the cry from life—the one being the art of losing the other.

It is just possible that Bishop was recalling a passage from Robert Hitchens' racy send-up of Victorian aestheticism, published in 1894: *The Green Carnation*. Mr. Amarinth, recognizably Oscar Wilde, declares at one point: 'My temper and my heart are the only two things I never lose! Everything else vanishes. I think the art of losing things is a very subtle art. So few people can lose anything really beautifully.'[18] Aestheticism exploits and parades just this outrageous, provocative, but also guilty distance between art and life. Form for form's sake, as well as for good form, leaves, one can hear it, a great deal to be desired. Bishop's villanelle, with its mastering form, and its sense, therefore, that form matters more than feeling, carries something of the same spirit of aestheticist self-containment as Mr. Amarinth's beautiful losing. It, too,

---

[16] Elizabeth Bishop, 'One Art', in *Complete Poems* (London: Chatto & Windus, 1983), 178.

[17] Anne Stevenson, 'The Iceberg and the Ship', in *Between the Iceberg and the Ship: Selected Essays* (Ann Arbor: University of Michigan Press, 1998), 53.

[18] Robert Hitchens, *The Green Carnation*, ed. Stanley Weintraub (Lincoln, Neb.: University of Nebraska Press, 1970; first pub. 1894), 57.

'beautifully' writes *off* the disasters of *of*, while letting us hear the cost of writing 'it'.

Lorrie Goldensohn has pointed out how often Bishop's 'pictures are the just-evacuated containers of human activity.'[19] The sense of something lost to the picture, something 'runaway',[20] as Jonathan Ellis nicely puts it, is what makes Bishop's poetry elegiac at heart. Her poetry's form misses something, to which it therefore becomes a readable memorial. The poem's object has slipped out of view, leaving a construction which both is and is not self-sufficient. 'The Monument' reproduces exactly this aesthetic double-bind, of being about, but also not about:

> It is an artifact
> of wood. ...
> The monument's an object, yet those decorations,
> carelessly nailed, looking like nothing at all,
> give it away as having life, and wishing;
> wanting to be a monument, to cherish something.
> The crudest scroll-work says 'commemorate' ...[21]

'The Monument' is Bishop's 'Grecian Urn'. It is a poem about the art object which is also the art object itself, puzzling, secretive, but also telling, wishing. Like Keats's 'silent form', it stands alone, without context or condition, and it too bears some more or less significant inscription about itself. But unlike the urn, which announces its dictum of beauty and truth, Bishop's inscription is almost unreadably worn. 'The monument's an object', we are told, and its 'crudest scroll-work says "commemorate"'. A structure, a ruin, a tomb, it ought to be a monument to or for something. The instruction 'commemorate' certainly seems to direct us to an object within, or perhaps without: something missing but remembered, and likely to be dead.

However, Bishop's monumental form seems not to know what it should commemorate or mourn. Moreover its construction, of wood not stone, has an uncanny life of its own which undermines its monumental status: 'having a life, and wishing; | wanting to be a monument'. The

[19] Lorrie Goldensohn, 'Elizabeth Bishop's Written Pictures, Painted Poems', in *In Worcester, Massachusetts: Essays on Elizabeth Bishop from the 1997 Elizabeth Bishop Conference* (New York: Peter Lang Publishing, 1999), 167–75, 172.

[20] Jonathan Ellis, 'Elizabeth Bishop: *North and South*', in *A Companion to Twentieth-Century Poetry*, ed. Neil Roberts (Oxford: Blackwell, 2001), 457–68, 459.

[21] Elizabeth Bishop, 'The Monument', in *Complete Poems*, 23–5, 24.

description starts to go into reverse, backtracking from what it is, and thus acquiring an oddly yearning, emotional purpose. Like Dickinson's sitting 'Nerves', something peculiarly live has come into this tomb-like contraption. The monument wants to be monumental, and thus to remember what, or who, it is *for*. This anthropomorphic aim perhaps also quietly exposes the conventions of monument-making which the poetic tradition often invokes. 'The existing monuments form an ideal order among themselves',[22] Eliot declares of the literary tradition. 'A Sonnet is a moment's monument',[23] writes Dante Gabriel Rossetti. Both of those are gestures towards the canonical, towards form as a kind of solid structure, destined for immortality. Bishop's monument, however, is altogether less assured, as well as less orderly and important. Partly, it looks 'like nothing at all'—that 'nothing' nicely balancing the yearning for 'something' two lines later. In itself 'nothing at all', it also longs 'to cherish something', to have a purpose or point. Such something-or-nothing leaves a restless sort of commotion at the heart of this monument's peculiarly shoddy, unfinished, moving form.

Nor do the last lines offer any resolution. This would-be art object still longs to be accountable to something, remembered or imagined, inside or outside:

> The bones of the artist-prince may be inside
> or far away on even drier soil.
> But roughly but adequately it can shelter
> what is within (which after all
> cannot have been intended to be seen).
> It is the beginning of a painting,
> a piece of sculpture, or poem, or monument,
> and all of wood. Watch it closely.[24]

The monument's indeterminate form, as irregular as its metre, yearns, even at the end, to hold something, even something that 'cannot have been intended to be seen'. Yet not seeing it may even be the point. That way we learn to see better what is without (in both senses of 'without'): that is, a 'poem, or monument'. 'Watch it closely' is this poet's last word on her oddly ramshackle structure, which shelters, 'roughly but

---

[22] Eliot, 'Tradition and the Individual Talent', 38.

[23] D. G. Rossetti, *Poems*, ed. Oswald Doughty (London: Dent, 1961), 212. For a fine discussion of some monumental nineteenth-century poems see Herbert F. Tucker, 'Of Monuments and Moments: Spacetime in Nineteenth-Century Poetry', *Modern Language Quarterly*, 58(1997), 269–97.

[24] Bishop, 'The Monument', 25.

adequately', the idea, however 'far away', of what it might be for. Being *for* may point to an 'extra-poetic' quantity, but it is a quantity this poem cannot quite give up. The idea of it haunts the work, even if it is merely conjectured, desired. A tomb needs a body; a poem needs an object. When Julia Kristeva, in *Black Sun*, defines 'poetic form' as 'the sole "container" seemingly able to secure an uncertain but adequate hold over the Thing',[25] she seems to be invoking the same figure of gesturing approximation. 'But roughly, but adequately' is Bishop's idiosyncratic contribution to the aestheticist problem of form: its being, on the one hand, a perfectly useless, self-justified arrangement, with no meaning or message, and on the other, its wanting to 'shelter' something: a presence, a body—the 'bones of the artist-prince', for instance.

> After great pain, a formal feeling comes—
> The Nerves sit ceremonious, like Tombs—

Bishop's monument, like Dickinson's, is a nervous sort of tomb. The body which it should contain has become the body which it is. At the same time, the dynamic of loss can be felt in it. Art's 'formal feeling' still recalls the ordinary, messy feelings of life, which are formalized but not forgotten. If such formality must come 'After great pain', it also commemorates 'pain', the feeling that has gone. If the tomb comes to life and almost moves, it also, by its very nature, recollects life elsewhere, in the past, 'far away'.

This transaction between tomb and body is one which, for some reason, proves itself especially congenial to women poets. Throughout the nineteenth and twentieth centuries, the figure recurs, as if it continued to offer women some kind of resourceful, poetic joke. 'I was as dead as I could be',[26] writes McHugh in 'The Looker', making it sound as if being dead involved as much hard effort as writing a poem. 'Now I am dead',[27] writes Stevenson in 'Postscriptum', with a sense of satisfied achievement. Stevie Smith's 'Voice from the Tomb' calls out, in the hope that her absurd predicament might be heard: 'You never heard of me, I dare | Say. Well, I'm here.'[28] Being 'here' is a nice nowhere,

[25] Julia Kristeva, *Black Sun: Depression and Melancholia*, trans. Leon S. Roudiez (New York: Columbia University Press, 1989; first pub. 1987), 14.

[26] Heather McHugh, *Eyeshot* (Middletown, Conn.: Wesleyan University Press, 2003), 52.

[27] Anne Stevenson, 'Postscriptum', in *Poems 1955–2005* (Tarset: Bloodaxe Books, 2004), 320.

[28] Stevie Smith, 'Voice from the Tomb' (5), in *Collected Poems* (London: Allen Lane, 1975), 463.

which at least allows her to take a place in the poem. 'When I was dead',[29] Christina Rossetti recalls, in an opening gambit which, like all these others, sends the personal pronoun into a temporizing spin. When was that 'When'? 'I died for Beauty—but was scarce | Adjusted in the Tomb',[30] Dickinson recalls. Dying for 'Beauty' rather than 'Truth', she thus audibly enters her own 'Grecian Urn' and brilliantly gets herself 'Adjusted' in it. That fit takes a moment's work, as woman and tomb become accommodated to each other. Whatever the social or ideological reasons why so many women poets speak from the dead, there is certainly an aestheticist formality about it, as the human form becomes the form of the poem, and 'I' speaks from an imaginary nowhere. Bishop's poem, 'The Weed', begins in a vein similar to all of these: 'I dreamed that dead, and meditating | I lay upon a grave, or bed.'[31] This recalls a dream recorded in the poet's notebooks, where she writes: 'Dreamed I was dead, or at least in some other form of existence, and arranged on a card, like buttons.'[32] That 'arranged' is exactly Dickinson's 'Adjusted'. It takes a moment to happen, so that the difference between being alive and being dead can be felt. The surrealism of the poem, in which a live weed grows out of the poet's cold heart, then allows 'some other form' to take the place of the speaker's own. Form, indeed, is the issue and purpose of this deadly live figure. Like all these poems about being dead, inhabiting one's own death is not a sentimental trope, intended to elicit pity, but witty and disengaged. It allows the personal pronoun to loosen its hold on the person; to be not I, but 'it'—'like buttons', 'like Tombs', or poems.

This is not an attempt to enlist Bishop in a female tradition. She herself was notoriously antipathetic to such classifications, refusing 'to act as Sex Appeal'[33] when invited to be the female representative in a volume of poems. However, it does perhaps point to some intertextual memory, as women poets listen to each others' voices, and find in the 'formal feeling' of being dead a way of tricking the personal pronoun out of its biographical authority. The risky transactions of aestheticism,

[29] Christina Rossetti, 'At Home', in *The Complete Poems*, 3 vols. ed. R. W. Crump (Baton Rouge & London: Louisiana State University Press, 1979–90), i. 28.

[30] Emily Dickinson, 'I died for Beauty', no. 449, in *Complete Poems*, 216.

[31] Elizabeth Bishop, 'The Weed', in *Complete Poems*, 20.

[32] Quoted in Barbara Page, 'Elizabeth Bishop: Stops, Starts and Dreamy Divagations', in *Elizabeth Bishop: Poet of the Periphery*, ed. Linda Anderson and Jo Shapcott (Newcastle: Bloodaxe Books, 2002), 16.

[33] Elizabeth Bishop, *One Art: Letters*, sel. and ed. Robert Giroux (London: Chatto & Windus, 1994), 86.

between body and form, life and art, can thus be adapted into a figure for speaking at all.

To turn to Plath at this point is logical, but unnerving. Hers are poems in which the 'I' has had to carry an extra, and extra-poetic, haunting from the burdensome fact of her suicide. It has therefore been tempting to read them as reverse elegies, elegies to herself in advance, and thus to colour them with the un-formal feelings of real life, and death. But this is to miss the extent to which Plath's sense of form plays on a trope of aesthetic self-sufficiency which is often mischievously comic. 'I lean very strongly toward forms that are, I suppose, quite rigid',[34] she once declared, the word 'rigid', instead of 'strict', just hinting at her characteristic mortuary imagery. The rigour of form, which might also be a rigor mortis, makes it congenial to a poet who so obsessively dramatized the difficult relation between 'I' and its dead other, not as a prefiguring of her own life's end, but as part of this surreal female tradition.

'Ted says he never read poems by a woman like mine ... they are working, sweating, heaving poems born out of the way words should be said.'[35] So Plath wrote in one of her exhilarated letters home in 1956. It is interesting how the sentence swerves from 'poems by a woman', through a birth metaphor of 'working, sweating, heaving', to a conclusion which rounds into a near-effortless tautology: poems are born, not from a poet, a woman, a body, but ultimately from 'the way words should be said'. The fine surprise of that passive construction leaves people, both poet and reader, finally out of account. The rightness comes from rightness, poems from words. At the same time, the way 'they should be said' also leaves the words open to all comers, a common heritage in which the reader participates. Plath, here, audibly rehearses the act of getting out of the way, and letting poetry work on its own birth. She also, however, lets us hear exactly how much has to be got out of the way: 'working, sweating, heaving', a body work which, in her case, is also explicitly measured against the birth-work of women.

Yet, as a poet Plath returns again and again, not to the art work's beauty or truth, or even to its surreal, uncertain adequacy, but to the perfect horror of it:

---

[34] Quoted in Anne Stevenson, 'Sylvia Plath's Word Games', in *Between the Iceberg and the Ship*, 39–51, 51.

[35] Sylvia Plath, *Letters Home: Correspondence 1950–1963*, ed. Aurelia Schober Plath (London: Faber, 1976), 244.

I shall never get out of this! There are two of me now:
This absolutely white person and the old yellow one,
And the white person is certainly the superior one.

'In Plaster' is indeed about a 'rigid' form. It is also, typically, the form
of a woman. These two awkward bedfellows, one white, one yellow,
seem bound for life in a fretful bond of love and hate, desire and
disgust. The 'absolutely white' plaster one, who encases the yellow,
is cold, unbreakable, clean, and probably 'immortal'. She might be
the soul—'I gave her a soul', Plath writes—or she might be a tomb:
'Living with her was like living with my own coffin.' But this speaker
is less 'Adjusted in the Tomb' of her plaster cast than Dickinson.
Although the two persons look alike—'she was shaped just the way
I was'[36]—they are not identical. The difference, the uncomfortable
gap between them, leaves scope for unrest, quarrelsomeness, drama.
Between the form and its content, the tomb and its body, there is a
comic mismatch. Meanwhile, plaster casts, like other monuments, recall
restless, living occupants.

Plath's lifelong interest in effigies, dummies, casts, and heads, the
'some other form' of her inhuman alter egos, is the source of her
power as well as her scandal. Her sense of the inhuman can be eerily
boastful, triumphalist, as she repeatedly resurrects 'it' out of her speakers' flamboyant deaths. 'The affinity of all beauty with death', writes
Adorno, 'has its nexus in the idea of pure form that art imposes on
the diversity of the living and that is extinguished in it.'[37] Here, the
notion of 'pure form' kills, its relation to 'the diversity of the living'
is murderous. But this is perhaps just a bit too serious. Art as murder
suggests a *Dorian Gray* story accepted literally, and without Wilde's
aestheticist fun. The point about Plath, for all the horror of her 'rigid
forms', is that their 'affinity ... with death' is figurative, verbal, playful.
Life is not 'extinguished' by them (especially not her own), but it
is, by comparison, regretted, commemorated. Her poems about dead
women, like Rossetti's, Dickinson's, and Smith's before her, are not
forms of elegy, especially not forms of self-elegy, but elegies, rather, of
perfect form.

---

[36] Sylvia Plath, 'In Plaster', in *Collected Poems*, ed. Ted Hughes (London: Faber,
1981), 158–60.
[37] Theodor W. Adorno, *Aesthetic Theory*, ed. Gretel Adorno and Rolf Tiedemann, newly trans. Robert Hullot-Kentnor (London: Athlone Press, 1997; first pub.
1970), 52.

The woman is perfected.
Her dead

Body wears the smile of accomplishment ...

James Fenton rightly warns against reading 'Edge' as Plath's 'signing off' poem. A dead daughter, a mother moon, and two children is also, he points out, the story of another 'Greek necessity':[38] Medea.[39] Certainly, this is a poem about the horror of perfection. It too is 'In Plaster'. But it is also about an art object, classical, sculptured, Keats-haunted, with its 'scrolls' of drapery holding out the promise of an inscription, somewhere. 'The crudest scroll-work says "commemorate"', Bishop writes. Plath too yearns for an inscription; yearns to read the aesthetic object, as if to find what it might be 'about'. The nearest she comes to finding a message, however, is in the feet. They 'seem to be saying: | We have come so far, it is over.'[40] This is wild wit. 'Over' is a bit too literally somewhere the feet might have gone—and 'Edge' is lurking for the connection. Even in its superb, perfected form, 'Edge' contains that slightly uncomfortable adjustment and readjustment of stone and flesh, monument and body. The 'scrolls', the 'toga', the 'Greek necessity', all suggest a statue. The 'body', the 'smile', the 'feet' suggest a woman. Like the word 'accomplishment', with its distant recall of female, subartistic activities, the very accomplished perfection of the form recalls the woman before she was 'perfected'.

The brilliance of the title is that it does something similar. 'Edge', which sounds so neutral, non-human, also discloses its silent, human variations: on edge, at the edge, over the edge. Those absent prepositions would, if present, make the poem more 'about about'. By leaving them out, Plath lets us hear their absence, but also insists that this is none of them; it is just 'Edge', clean-cut, indefinite. 'has it breasts, has it edges?'[41] she asks in 'A Birthday Present', turning another 'she' to 'it'. 'Edge' suggests the hard outline of a thing, in particular the way that a poem is a shape, a set of lines or frontier on what is not said. But it is also a 'woman', rounding into those flows in her toga. Like the word 'form', which etymologically contains both the idea of outline and the idea of a physical body, so 'Edge' signals the very edge of formality to which a poem might go.

38 Sylvia Plath, 'Edge', in *Collected Poems*, 272.
39 James Fenton, *The Strength of Poetry* (Oxford: Oxford University Press, 2001), 153.
40 Plath, 'Edge', 272.   41 Ibid. 206.

All these poems, then, reflect in different ways on a legacy of aestheticist self-containment. They are about objects which have been taken out of context, and museumed or monumentalized as art. The woman's 'smile of accomplishment' is complete and complacent, indeed like the Mona Lisa's. At the same time, these poems are restless, commemorative, elegiac. 'The woman is perfected. | Her dead | Body ...' Plath quietly rhymes 'perfected' with 'dead', as if to nerve her statue from life, or from a memory of life. If form is the woman here, then, as in Pater and Wilde, there is also no 'pure form'. Human meaning troubles the art work, edging its perfection, pressing upon its completed arrangement of words. Form does not kill life, as Adorno suggests; it borders, relationally, on it.

Thus form, which looks two ways, inwards and outwards, still seems to offer a way of understanding what poems are about, and not about. It is a limit as well as a self-sufficiency; an edge as well as an object. 'No poem worthy of the name can be formless, whether it is written according to metrical rules or in free verse', writes Anne Stevenson. 'The sounds, rhythms, pitch, and intensity of the lines ARE the poem. Every poem IS its form.'[42] As with Bishop and Plath, the aestheticist legacy haunts her own serious play with form. Form is the poem, the poem its form. The two cannot be separated. At the same time, form, as 'sounds, rhythms, pitch', is not content. It is perhaps not an accident, then, that the formal conundrum of Henry James's short story, 'The Figure in the Carpet', should give Stevenson the title of one of her own poems:

> Might be human,
> might be design:
> a diamond face, half mouth,
> half upright hair;
> two square-rimmed eyes
> that stare
> in a sad direction.
> He—or is it she?—
> wipes the clear
> left eye
> with a wrist
> more paw than hand.

[42] Anne Stevenson, 'The Trouble with a Word like Formalism', in *Between the Iceberg and the Ship*, 105–11, 107.

The other arm,
crippled, perhaps,
(it will not bend)
holds a cross
which is part
of the interlocking risk
of pattern
or of art.[43]

In James's story, the figure in the carpet is a figure for the essentially unparaphrasable secret of art. In Stevenson, it is literally a pattern in a carpet. But both texts also set that figure against some 'extra-poetic' explanation, which they also nonetheless invoke. In James's story the detective critic hunts for clues to the meaning of art. 'I see—it's some idea *about* life, some sort of philosophy',[44] he innocently hopes. But of course the more he asks '*about*', the less likely he is to find it. The figure is not 'about about'. Neither is Stevenson's—at least not out of the carpet. Within the carpet, it 'Might be human, | might be design'. This grotesque crossbreed, half-finished, half animal, half cripple, will not come humanly right. The cross is the point, as it is the point in many of her poems. The 'interlocking risk | of pattern | or of art' is irresolvably cruciform, and the resulting, crosspatched creature is fixed in it for good. However, like so many of these poems about the art object, something troubles the plan. The 'design' recalls a human form, and the cross recalls something suffered as well as drawn. Stevenson's rewriting of James's story conveys a sense of wistful regret, of maimed hurt: for instance, the paw hand that wipes the all too 'clear | left eye' of tears it cannot weep. The poem's aestheticist sense of its own design and form takes the pressure of the alternative: of something that lies outside, 'in a sad direction'.

Stevenson, like Plath and Bishop, sees form, not just as a matter of technique or pattern, though that is part of it, but also as a matter of resistance. It is the thing that cuts the poem off, from meaningful duties, civic or ethical, in order to be a thing in itself, in its own carpet of design and plan. The figure may cry out for human purpose, human feeling; but in the end it is what it is, and that is only a poem. So this figure 'wipes the clear | left eye', as if retaining a memory of tears which are no

[43] Anne Stevenson, 'The Figure in the Carpet', in *Poems 1955–2005*, 290.
[44] Henry James, 'The Figure in the Carpet', in *The Figure in the Carpet and Other Stories*, ed. Frank Kermode (Harmondsworth: Penguin, 1986), 357–400, 368.

longer there. The line beautifully evokes the real-life feeling of pain or sorrow which might be recalled by this clear-eyed creature of the carpet. In one of her essays Stevenson touches on the unpredictable autonomy of form. 'I couldn't, of course, have predicted any of the formal features of the poem before it began to sing of itself',[45] she writes. That 'of itself' means both about, and by. In a prepositional nutshell, the poem sings about what it sings about. The tautology of 'sing of itself', like Plath's 'the way words should be said', lets the poem round back into its own justification, its own meaning, beyond intention or control. 'Tautology', writes Barthes, 'is a faint at the right moment, a saving aphasia, it is a death, or perhaps a comedy, the indignant "representation" of the *rights* of reality over and above language.'[46] In other words, tautology, while rounding up against reality, also indignantly represents reality, with its superior '*rights*'. Art for art, then, or form for form's sake—those faints of meaning—are ways of saying nothing for the sake of what art cannot say, and cannot help. It is 'a death, or perhaps a comedy'.

> How habitable is perfected form? ...
>
> What's the use of a held note or held line
> That cannot be assailed for reassurance?[47]

So Seamus Heaney, in 'Squarings', reflects on aestheticist tropes of perfection and formality. Rejecting, by implication, aestheticism's 'condition of music', the 'held note', he calls for poetry's 'use' and 'reassurance'. Yet form and use pull, as they always have done, in opposite directions. His question about form's habitableness might also, however, be recalling Stevenson's question in her poem 'Making Poetry': 'And why inhabit, make, inherit poetry?' Her answer invokes the need for an imperfect shelter, roomy, if empty, a habitation which is not comfortably 'habitable', but which must, in all its contradictions, be inhabited. In addition, it is one which must be 'shared' with others. Poetry, she concludes, is:

> the shared comedy of the worst
> blessed; the sound leading the hand;
> a wordlife running from mind to mind

---

[45] Stevenson, 'A Chev'ril Glove', in *Between the Iceberg and the Ship*, 120–31, 124.

[46] Roland Barthes, 'Myth Today', in *Mythologies*, sel. and trans. Annette Lavers (London: Granada, 1973; first pub. 1957), 109–59, 152–3.

[47] Seamus Heaney, 'Squarings, xxii', in *Seeing Things* (London: Faber, 1991), 51–108, 78.

through the washed rooms of the simple senses;
one of those haunted, undefendible, unpoetic
crosses we have to find.[48]

To 'find', not bear, the cross, as if it were a suffering complexity
to be sought, is to discover the place where the poem comes across
its own 'undefendible, unpoetic' opposite. This heavenly mansion
of art is, finally, empty of the poet, and full only of the 'crosses'
which are its various figures in the carpet. In it, there is 'comedy',
'sound', 'wordlife'—active, abstract ideas which sing of themselves,
and command their own verbs. Not the hand, but 'the sound leading
the hand', is what makes the poem come to life, and offer its strange,
comfortless, windy habitation. It thus seems to represent what Stevenson
has elsewhere called 'the *independent nature of the imagined*'.[49] To
find the cross between figure and fact, design and human, form and
pain, is the insight which Stevenson draws from the old mottos and
provocations of art for art. 'Making Poetry' means making an airy,
inhabitable monument of the senses—one which encloses nothing, yet
lets the 'unpoetic | crosses' of real life be heard or found there.

Stevenson's poetry everywhere seeks out this cross-purpose. Form
is not a closed house, an impregnable fortress or shut ivory tower. It is
not a 'pure' place, untouched by the pressure of the 'unpoetic'. Instead,
it is open to all those outside forces. In 'From the Men of Letters', for
instance, the speakers in the habitable 'room in language' are forced
to notice the ones outside, 'whose | disasters encourage our art'. Other
people's sorrows press on this poem's embarrassed form. The literati,
the poets, the academicians, high and dry in their language rooms,
thus end up hopelessly asking: 'How will their experience | forgive
our tall books?'[50] The 'tall books', 'tall' as all literary towers, cannot
redress, but neither can they ignore the 'disasters' outside. This is
the reason for that other characteristic of the towers, whether tall or
open: guilt. Stevenson's lines might be condensed to something even
simpler and harsher: how can life's experience forgive the formality
of art?

To hear the formality of form, then, is to hear, not only its figurative
self-containment, but also its modesty tropes, its elegies and guilts.
Art, writes Levinas, 'essentially disengaged, constitutes, in a world of

---

[48] Stevenson, 'Making Poetry', in *Poems 1955–2005*, 17.
[49] Stevenson, 'On Elizabeth Bishop', in *Between the Iceberg and the Ship*, 52–70, 56.
[50] Stevenson, 'From the Men of Letters', in *Poems 1955–2005*, 289–90.

initiative and responsibility, a dimension of evasion'.[51] The more self-contained in its form, the more poetry might register its guilt at only being able to '(*write* it!)' — in brackets. That bracketing off which form visibly is, and which it expresses in different ways, is the subject of one last poem by Stevenson:

> The worm in the spine,
> the word on the tongue—
> not the same.
> We speak of 'pain'.
> The sufferer won't suffer it
> to be tamed.

'To witness pain is a different form of pain' does, very simply, what all poems do: it lets words tell the difference. Precisely by being formal, arranged and adjusted on the page, it announces an 'evasion'. The slight note of complacency in the title, which suggests that to witness pain is no different than to experience it, is belied by the words which follow, and which insist that it is 'not the same'. Thus between 'worm' and 'word', the difference sounds. Between 'suffer it' and 'suffer it', two meanings diverge. The 'different form' of what a poem is rounds back into itself, into a helpless, guilty, beautifully finished thing which can make, precisely, no difference.

Then, in two lines set apart from the others, the poet acknowledges the utter apartness of words, even words about pain:

> Outside, we pace in guilt
> Ah, 'guilt', another name.[52]

For a moment we are conned into hearing a mistake: that guilt is 'another name' *for* 'pain'. But that is precisely *not* what is said. The 'name' is not *for* anything. It is merely 'another name', like all the others which cannot be 'suffered' by the sufferer. Stevenson lets the foreshortened phrase bring us back to words, to names, poems, and to that ' "guilt" ' in inverted commas which is not the same as guilt unnamed. 'Ah, "guilt", another name' lets us hear how this is also just 'another name', and therefore removed, privileged, lucky. Whether in 'guilt' or ' "guilt" ', the pacers outside are those who deal in names and are not in pain. 'After great pain, a formal feeling comes.' Stevenson,

[51] Emmanuel Levinas, 'Reality and Its Shadow', in *The Levinas Reader*, ed. Sean Hand (Oxford: Blackwell, 1989), 129–43, 141.

[52] Stevenson, 'To witness pain is a different form of pain', in *Poems 1955–2005*, 170.

like Dickinson, knows how long that 'After' takes, and therefore how much art might need forgiving.

Form, then, the sense of the poem's self-contained outlines, its safety in names, its brackets and inverted commas, might be the very thing which, far from resolving contradiction, keeps it visible and audible—part of the cross 'we have to find'. Between poems and the world there is a world of difference. But that is exactly the point of contact too, the point of relief. Poems edge on what they are not, on the thing they come 'After', evasively, guiltily, elegiacally—'pain' for instance. Form is the poem's body, an object of almost tangible attention, its 'sounds, rhythms, pitch, and intensity'. But form is also a design, an outline, a habitable room, an empty shelter, which lets meaning in and out. It is something and nothing, and both of those matter. Flaubert once famously declared that he dreamed of writing a book about nothing— *'un livre sur rien'.*[53] Being 'about | how nothing is about' is also 'something'—and something that poetry can do, perhaps even better than prose, because its formal arrangements on the page constantly break on their own margins, edges. Texts for something, then, and 'Texts for Nothing',[54] in Beckett's characteristically aestheticist title, poetry's form is a constantly readjusting, unsatisfied 'what for'.

This is the point, and also the no point, of one last poem, by the poet with whom I started. Heather McHugh's 'What Poems Are For', with its angling preposition, recalling so many problems of 'for', is a final reminder that being not 'about about' might also, still, be *'for* something'—even if, as the last line tells, what 'that' is is a quite small, even wittily empty-handed gift:

> They aren't for everything.
> I better swallow this, or else
> wind up shut up by openness so utter.
> Nip and tuck, poems are for
>
> a bit, a patch, a mended
> hem, carnation's cage—and then
> the heart may bloom, the sex may roar, the moment
> widen to be the well the child

[53] Gustave Flaubert, Letter to Louise Colet, 16 January 1852, in *Oeuvres Complètes de Gustave Flaubert*, 16 vols. ed. Société des Études littéraires françaises (Paris : Club de L'Honnête Homme, 1970–1975), ii. 158.

[54] Samuel Beckett, 'Texts for Nothing', in *The Complete Short Prose: 1929–1989*, ed. S. E. Gontarski (New York: Grove Press, 1995), 100–54.

fell in forever—yes—but not until
I've checked the pinafore
and laced the meat,
puttied the stones, and pinched

the flowers back. I can't give you
a word to hold the dead. I can't give you a name
to hold a god, a big enough denomination. Find yourself

a church instead, where roofs are all allusions
to the sky, and words are all
incorrigible. Timelessness, and time,

they are not mine to give. I have
a spoon, a bed,
a pen, a hat.
The poem
is for something,
and the world is small.

I'll give you that.[55]

---

[55] Heather McHugh, 'What Poems Are For', in *Hinge and Sign*, 179.

Whatever you say, say nothing.

Seamus Heaney

12

Nothing, but: An Afterword

If 'form' is a word which has left its legacy on two centuries and more of aestheticist and post-aestheticist writing, there is another word which has often seemed to shadow it, and that is the word 'nothing'. Nothing, which has appeared here and there in the works of all the writers in this book, seems to carry a special resonance when it comes to understanding what poetry is for. Like 'form', it is a word which already toys with its own content, enjoying the hologram effect of being a thing and an absence, a sound and an emptiness, there and not there. The nineteenth-century aesthetes invoke it frequently as a (perhaps false) modesty trope, in order to advocate the insignificance of content and the importance of form and style. Thus the poet who 'has "nothing to say"', as Wilde puts it, is the true poet, the one who 'gains his inspiration from form, and from form purely'.[1] Having 'nothing to say' is a way of allowing the shape or sound of writing to be heard, rather than its substance understood.

Form, then, is what remains when all the various somethings—matter, content, message—have been got out of the way. Form, perhaps, is the sense of nothing. Wallace Stevens is writing in this same tradition when he suggests that poetry's 'Nothing much'[2] might be preferable to weighty somethings, and that those poets who 'have nothing to say'[3] are likely to be the better artists. His own poetic games with 'nothing' love to milk the ambiguity of a word which shifts between denoted

---

[1] Oscar Wilde, 'The Critic as Artist', in *Intentions* (London: Methuen, 1919; first pub. 1891), 153–217, 201.

[2] Wallace Stevens, *Collected Poetry and Prose*, sel. Frank Kermode and Joan Richardson (New York: The Library of America, 1997), 384.

[3] Ibid. 905.

absence and presence: 'Nothing that is not there and the nothing that
is',[4] is a line which maddeningly proliferates the senses of 'nothing',
while still pointing to something looming and pressing, out 'there'. W.
S. Graham, too, circles round the word, as he tries to find what it is that
gives the singer, and the singer's mere voice, breathing-space. Like Roy
Fisher, whose 'True nothing' deflects attention back to the method, to
'the hands'[5] which do the work of writing, Graham finds in it a way
of declaring that poetic language has nothing to declare, except its own
delightful presence.

The poet who waxes most lyrical on the subject of 'nothing', and
whose whole modernist aesthetic relies on the rebuff of that word, is
Laura Riding. Like others, she founds her modernism on an aestheticist
trope which, in denying relevant theme or message, asserts a variation
of art for art's sake. Thus she declares, in *Contemporaries and Snobs*,
that 'subject-matter has always exhausted rather than nourished creative
energy.'[6] Thus, in a neat reversal, she suggests that having something to
say is in fact the writer's problem. 'What is a poem?' she asks elsewhere,
and answers succinctly: 'A poem is nothing. By persistence the poem
can be made something; but then it is something, not a poem.'[7] This
comment is, as a later passage makes clear, a jibe at criticism, with all its
persistent methods for turning poems into something. 'The conversion
of nothing into something is the task of criticism',[8] she points out.
Here poet and critic are placed in an opposition which seems deep-set
and irresolvable. The critic evades the poem's true nothing, in order to
assert various, important somethings which criticism needs. This is the
point made by Vernon Lee, too, when she points to the 'chronological
and ethnological propriety' which 'we, poor critics'[9] always bring to
a text. Whether it is Henry James's critical busybody in 'The Figure
in the Carpet' or Heather McHugh's conversational everyman in the
aeroplane, the questions asked by criticism seem, these writers suggest,
to miss the point. For the point is that the work is the work, art is
art, and the critic's explanations, being so much 'about about', are

[4] Stevens, 'The Snow Man', in *Collected Poetry and Prose*, 8.

[5] Roy Fisher, 'From *The Dow Low Drop*', in *The Dow Low Drop: New and Selected
Poems* (Newcastle: Bloodaxe Books, 1996), 191.

[6] Laura Riding, *Contemporaries and Snobs* (London: Jonathan Cape, 1928), 79.

[7] Laura Riding, *Anarchism is Not Enough*, ed. Lisa Samuels (Berkeley, Ca.: University
of California Press, 2001; first pub. 1928), 16.

[8] Ibid. 18.

[9] Vernon Lee, *Belcaro: Being Essays on Sundry Aesthetical Questions* (London: W.
Satchell, 1880), 127.

always wide of the mark. Riding's conclusion, however, is interesting, in that it does not just waive off the critic, and assert art's inviolable self-justification. Instead, she argues, poetry is nothing because it is another kind of knowledge. The poem, she writes, 'is all the truth it knows, that is, it knows nothing'.[10] So Socrates' old axiom about the wisdom of knowing nothing is invoked to help account for the wise nothings of poetry—that it offers itself as a kind of knowing which needs, if not explanations of what it is about, at least attention, hard work, respect.

In all these texts, then, the aestheticist programme of deflecting matter into form, message into style, is reiterated in different ways. The work itself is 'nothing', only because it might turn up the frequency of our attention on the way that poetic words also know something. Whether that attention is drawn to sound effects, densities of language or strangenesses of syntax, it is those that hold the key to the work. 'Nothing' is a word which thus redirects our understanding towards that listening, attending, hearing, as if for their own sakes, in the intransitive mode. For instance, in a recent poem by Jane Griffiths, 'Women and Secrets', the poet describes a nothing which is heard in the night, and which the reader expects the poem to disclose. But in fact it ends with nothing explained. '*I heard nothing.* No explanation, | but the upright jolt of waking. And then?'[11] So this ominous no-sound leads to 'No explanation', just that hair-raising wakefulness. In a sense, this is where all poems lead. Once all the 'abouts' have been listed, the horrors imagined, and the plots mapped out, what remains is a listening, shocked into nervous attention, which cannot ever answer the leading question of the too rational critic: 'And then?'

Perhaps, however, this opposition of something and nothing, criticism and poetry, is not exactly the impasse that Riding suggests. 'Nothing', as I have also shown, is a word with subtly altering pressure points. In Auden and Stevens it can readily be pressed into a different service. 'For poetry makes nothing happen'[12] is, on the one hand, a negative denigration of poetry, and on the other, a positive assertion. Like so many plays on 'nothing', it enjoys the way that opposites can mix. It may be, then, that 'nothing' is also the very thing that keeps critics and

[10] Riding, *Anarchism is Not Enough*, 11.

[11] Jane Griffiths, 'Women and Secrets', in *A Grip on Thin Air* (Tarset: Bloodaxe Books, 2000), 25.

[12] W. H. Auden, 'In Memory of W. B. Yeats', in *Collected Poems*, ed. Edward Mendelson (London: Faber, 1976), 197–8, 197.

poets together, intrigued fellow passengers on poetry's '747'. Certainly, there is some other knowledge which art might have, which is not the takeaway-able message which might justify the critic's theory or creed. Such a knowledge has more to do with what aestheticism, in its long historical legacy, continues to probe and exploit: that art is somehow there for its own sake, in its own insignificantly pleasurable world, 'for nothing'; but that that is also precisely what we might need to know, in the less pleasurable world of reality outside.

'For art comes to you proposing frankly to give nothing but … '[13] Pater's last words ring memorably into the future. As all these writers testify, poetry's 'nothing' is not a programme for frivolity, carelessness, mere hedonism; it is a programme for attention, for finding out what it is that 'nothing' knows. It is easy to know something; it merely has to be understood and remembered. But to know nothing requires constant, perhaps constantly unsatisfied, effort. Pater's is a straightforward 'nothing but', which insists on the free and frank giving of art. By contrast, David Harsent's recent poem, 'Despatches', from his avowedly political collection *Legion*, takes that phrase and makes one tiny adjustment to it. This poem, which is full of nothings, the lies, evasions, jokes, and consolations of wartime, ends with the same words, but unpunctuated, unfinished: 'nothing, in fact, but'.[14]

Thus the old colloquialism is prised open, attended to, and like so many of these word games, made to mean the opposite of itself as well. This is not 'nothing but', but 'nothing, in fact, but'. It is nervous, unsure of what comes after. Perhaps this hanging, uncertain 'but', with its provisional warning and unease, offers a key to aestheticism's own playful, but guilty and elegiac awareness of the limits and edges of art's formality. Moreover, if poetry is all on the side of 'nothing', and criticism all a matter of making 'something', then 'nothing, in fact, but' might also be a reminder that, at some point, the two must come together, that the one needs the other, even if only to mark out the differences, in the end, between form and the matter it holds off.

---

[13] Walter Pater, *The Renaissance: Studies in Art and Poetry* (London: Macmillan, 1910), 239.

[14] David Harsent, 'Despatches', in *Legion* (London: Faber, 2005), 28–9, 29.

Bibliography

Adorno, Theodor W., 'The Essay as Form', in *Notes to Literature*, vol. 1, ed. Rolf Tiedemann, trans. Shierry Weber Nicholson (1958; New York: Columbia University Press, 1991), 3–23.

_____ *Aesthetic Theory*, ed. Gretel Adorno and Rolf Tiedemann, newly trans. Robert Hullot-Kentor (1970; London: Athlone Press, 1997).

_____ 'Lyric Poetry and Society', trans. Bruce Mayo, *Telos*, 20(1974), 59.

Aldington, Richard (ed.) *The Religion of Beauty: Selections from the Aesthetes* (London: Heinemann, 1950).

Anderson, Linda, and Shapcott, Jo (eds.), *Elizabeth Bishop: Poet of the Periphery* (Newcastle: Bloodaxe Books, 2002).

Anstruther-Thomson, C., *Art and Man: Essays & Fragments*, intro. Vernon Lee (London: The Bodley Head, 1924.)

Armstrong, Isobel (ed.), *New Feminist Discourses: Critical Essays on Theories and Texts* (London: Routledge, 1992).

_____ 'The Collapse of Object and Subject: *In Memoriam*', in *Critical Essays on Alfred Lord Tennyson*, ed. Herbert F. Tucker (New York: G. K. Hall, 1993).

_____ 'And Beauty? A Dialogue: Debating Adorno's Aesthetic Theory', *Textual Practice*, 12(1998), 269–89.

_____ *The Radical Aesthetic* (Oxford: Blackwell, 2000).

Attridge, Derek, *The Rhythms of English Poetry* (London: Longman, 1982).

_____ *The Singularity of Literature* (London: Routledge, 2004).

Auden, W. H., 'The Public v. the Late Mr William Butler Yeats', in *W. B. Yeats: A Critical Anthology*, ed. William H. Pritchard (Harmondsworth: Penguin, 1972).

_____ *Collected Poems*, ed. Edward Mendelson (London: Faber, 1976).

Aviram, Amittai F., *Telling Rhythm: Body and Meaning in Poetry* (Ann Arbor: University of Michigan Press, 1994).

Barker, Sebastian, 'Memoir of W. S. Graham', *Edinburgh Review*, 75(1986), 88–91.

Barthes, Roland, *Mythologies*, sel. and trans. Annette Lavers (1957; London: Granada, 1973).

_____ *The Responsibility of Forms: Critical Essays on Music, Art, and Representation*, trans. Richard Howard (1982; Oxford: Basil Blackwell, 1986).

Bates, Milton J., *Wallace Stevens; A Mythology of Self* (Berkeley, Los Angeles: University of California Press, 1985).

Beckett, Samuel, *The Complete Short Prose: 1929–1989*, ed. S. E. Gontarski (New York: Grove Press, 1995).

Beer, Gillian, *Virginia Woolf: The Common Ground* (Edinburgh: Edinburgh University Press, 1996).

_____ 'The Dissidence of Vernon Lee: *Satan the Waster* and the Will to Believe', in *Women's Fiction and the Great War*, ed. Suzanne Raitt and Trudi Tate (Oxford: Oxford Clarendon Press, 1997).

_____ 'Revenants and Migrants: Hardy, Butler, Woolf and Sebald', *Proceedings of the British Academy*, 125(2004), 163–82.

Beerbohm, Max, *The Works of Max Beerbohm* (London: Macmillan, 1922).

Bell, Clive, *Art* (London: Chatto & Windus, 1914).

Benjamin, Walter, *Illuminations*, ed. Hannah Arendt, trans. Harry Zorn (London: Pimlico, 1999).

Bernstein, Charles (ed.), *The Politics of Poetic Form: Poetry and Public Policy* (New York: Roof, 1990).

Bishop, Elizabeth, *Complete Poems* (London: Chatto & Windus, 1983).

_____ *One Art: Letters*, ed. Robert Giroux (London: Chatto & Windus, 1994).

Bloom, Harold, 'Tennyson, Hallam, and Romantic Tradition', in *The Ringers in the Tower: Studies in Romantic Tradition* (Chicago: University of Chicago Press, 1971).

Boland, Eavan, *Object Lessons: The Life of the Woman and the Poet in Our Time* (London: Vintage, 1995).

Bolla, Peter de, 'The Discomfort of Strangeness and Beauty: Art, Politics, and Aesthetics', in *Politics and Aesthetics in the Arts*, ed. Salim Kemal and Ivan Gaskell (Cambridge: Cambridge University Press, 2000).

_____ *Art Matters* (Cambridge, Mass.: Harvard University Press, 2001).

Booth, James, *Philip Larkin: Writer* (London: Harvester, 1992).

Bowlby, Rachel, 'Walking, Women and Writing: Virginia Woolf as Flâneuse', in *New Feminist Discourses: Critical Essays on Theories and Texts*, ed. Isobel Armstrong (London: Routledge, 1992).

Bradley, A. C., 'Poetry for Poetry's Sake', in *Oxford Lectures on Poetry* (London: Macmillan, 1926), 3–34.

Briggs, Julia, *Night Visitors: The Rise and Fall of the English Ghost Story* (London: Faber, 1997).

Brimley, George, 'Alfred Tennyson's Poems', in *Cambridge Essays* (Cambridge: Cambridge University Press, 1855).

Brooks, Cleanth, *The Well Wrought Urn: Studies in the Structure of Poetry* (1947; London: Methuen, 1968).

Brooks, Peter, 'Aesthetics and Ideology—What Happened to Poetics?', in *Aesthetics and Ideology*, ed. George Levine (New Brunswick, N.J.: Rutgers University Press, 1994), 153–67.

Brown, Don, 'Establishing the Don Brown Route', in *The Constructed Space: A Celebration of W. S. Graham*, ed. Ronnie Duncan and Jonathan Davidson (Lincoln: Sunk Island Publishing, 1994), 31–6.

Brown, Marshall. *Turning Points: Essays in the History of Cultural Expressions* (Stanford, Ca: Stanford University Press, 1997).

Browning, Oscar, *Memories of Sixty Years* (London: Bodley Head, 1910).

Burkhardt, Jacob, *The Civilization of the Renaissance in Italy*, trans. S. G. C. Middlemore, intro. Peter Burke, notes Peter Murray (London: Penguin, 1990).

Butler, Christopher, *Pleasure and the Arts: Enjoying Literature, Painting, and Music* (Oxford: Oxford University Press, 2004).

Caballero, Carlo, ' "A Wicked Voice": On Vernon Lee, Wagner, and the Effects of Music', *Victorian Studies*, 35(1992), 386–408, 394.

Campbell, Nancie, *Tennyson in Lincoln: A Catalogue of the Collections in the Research Centre*, 2 vols. (Lincoln: Tennyson Society, 1971–3).

Carey, John, *What Good are the Arts?* (London: Faber, 2005).

Cari, Titi Lucreti (Lucretius), *De Rerum Natura*, with a translation and notes by H. A. J. Munro, vol. 1 (Cambridge: Deighton Bell and Co., 1864).

Cavaliero, Glen, *The Supernatural and English Fiction* (Oxford: Oxford University Press, 1995).

Celan, Paul, *Selected Poems*, trans. and intro. Michael Hamburger (1986; London: Penguin, 1990).

——*Collected Prose*, trans. Rosmarie Waldrop (1986: Manchester: Carcanet, 1999).

Chai, Leon, *Aestheticism: The Religion of Art in Post-Romantic Literature* (New York: Columbia University Press, 1990).

Chapman, Alison, and Stabler, Jane (eds.), *Unfolding the South: Nineteenth-Century British Women Writers and Artists in Italy* (Manchester: Manchester University Press, 2003).

Colby, Vineta, *Vernon Lee: A Literary Biography* (Charlottesville and London: University of Virginia Press, 2003).

Coleridge, S. T., 'Table Talk', in *The Collected Works*, 16 vols., ed. Kathleen Coburn and Bart Winer (London: Routledge, 1971–2001), xiv.

——*Coleridge's Notebooks: A Selection*, ed. Seamus Perry (Oxford: Oxford University Press, 2002).

Colvin, Sidney, 'English painters and painting in 1867', *Fortnightly Review*, ns 2 (October 1867), 473–6.

Connolly, Cyril, *Enemies of Promise* (1938; London: Penguin, 1961).

Cooper, David E. (ed.), *A Companion to Aesthetics* (Oxford: Blackwell, 1992).

Croce, Benedetto, *The Aesthetic as the Science of Expression and of the Linguistic in General*, trans. Colin Lyas (Cambridge: Cambridge University Press, 1992).

Dale, Peter Allan, *The Victorian Critic and the Idea of History: Carlyle, Arnold, Pater* (Cambridge, Mass.: Harvard University Press, 1977).

Darwin, Charles, *The Origin of Species*, ed. Gillian Beer (1859; Oxford: Oxford University Press, 1996).

Davie, Donald, 'Two Analogies for Poetry', in *Modernist Essays: Yeats, Pound, Eliot*, ed. Clive Wilmer (Manchester: Carcanet, 2004).

Dickinson, Emily, *The Complete Poems*, ed. Thomas H. Johnson (London: Faber, 1970).

Diffey, T. J., 'A Note on Some Meanings of the Term "Aesthetic"', *British Journal of Aesthetics*, 35(1995), 61–6.

Donoghue, Denis, *Walter Pater: Lover of Strange Souls* (New York: Alfred A. Knopf, 1995).

—— *Speaking of Beauty* (New Haven and London: Yale University Press, 2003).

Douglas-Fairhurst, Robert, *Victorian Afterlives: The Shaping of Influence in Nineteenth-Century Literature* (Oxford: Oxford University Press, 2002).

Dowling, Linda, *Language and Decadence in the Victorian Fin de Siècle* (Princeton: Princeton University Press, 1986).

—— 'Walter Pater and Archaeology: The Reconciliation with Earth', *Victorian Studies*, 31(1988), 209–31.

Duncan, Ronnie, and Davidson, Jonathan (eds.), *The Constructed Space: A Celebration of W. S. Graham* (Lincoln: Sunk Island Publishing, 1994).

Eagleton, Terry, 'Ideology and Literary Form', in *Criticism and Ideology: A Study in Marxist Literary Theory* (London: NLB, 1976).

—— *The Ideology of the Aesthetic* (Oxford: Blackwell, 1990).

Edmundson, Mark, *Literature against Philosophy, Plato to Derrida: A Defence of Poetry* (Cambridge: Cambridge University Press, 1995).

Eliot, George, *Middlemarch,* intro. W. J. Harvey (Harmondsworth: Penguin, 1965).

Eliot, T. S., 'Arnold and Pater', in *Selected Essays: 1917–1932* (London: Faber, 1932), 379–91.

—— 'Matthew Arnold', in *The Use of Poetry and the Use of Criticism: Studies in the Relation of Criticism to Poetry in England* (London: Faber, 1933), 103–19.

—— *The Complete Poems and Plays of T. S. Eliot* (London: Faber, 1969).

—— *The Waste Land: A Facsimile and Transcript*, ed. Valerie Eliot (London: Faber, 1971).

—— 'Tradition and the Individual Talent', in *Selected Prose of T. S. Eliot*, ed. Frank Kermode (London: Faber, 1975).

Ellis, Jonathan, 'Elizabeth Bishop: *North and South*', in *A Companion to Twentieth-Century Poetry*, ed. Neil Roberts (Oxford: Blackwell, 2001), 457–68.

Empson, William, *Seven Types of Ambiguity* (1930; Harmondsworth: Penguin, 1961).

—— 'Mr Wilson on the Byzantium Poems', in *W. B. Yeats: A Critical Anthology*, ed. William H. Pritchard (Harmondsworth: Penguin, 1972), 288–94.

Etlin, Richard A., *In Defense of Humanism: Value in the Arts and Letters* (Cambridge: Cambridge University Press, 1966).

Evans, Lawrence (ed.), *Letters of Walter Pater* (Oxford: Clarendon Press, 1970).

Feagin, Susan L., and Maynard, Patrick (eds.), *Aesthetics* (Oxford: Oxford University Press, 1997).

Felstiner, John, *Paul Celan: Poet, Survivor, Jew* (New Haven and London: Yale University Press, 1995).

Fenton, James, *The Strength of Poetry* (Oxford: Oxford University Press, 2001).

Filreis, Alan, *Modernism from Right to Left: Wallace Stevens, the Thirties, & Literary Radicalism* (Cambridge: Cambridge University Press, 1994).

Finch, Annie (ed.), *After New Formalism: Poets on Form, Narrative, and Tradition* (Ashland, Or.: Story Line Press, 1999).

Findlay, L. M., 'The Introduction of the Phrase "Art for Art's Sake" into English', *Notes and Queries*, 218 (July 1973), 246–8.

Finneran, Richard J. (ed.), *Yeats: An Annual of Critical and Textual Studies*, vol. ii (Ithaca and London: Cornell University Press, 1984), 209–26.

Fisher, Roy, 'People who can't float: Roy Fisher Interviewed by Ra Page', in *Prop*, 2(1996), 30.

—— *The Dow Low Drop: New and Selected Poems* (Newcastle: Bloodaxe Books, 1996).

—— *Interviews Through Time and Selected Prose* (Kentisbeare: Shearsman Books, 2000).

—— *The Long and the Short of It: Poems 1955–2005* (Tarset: Bloodaxe Books, 2005).

Fishman, Solomon, *The Interpretation of Art: Essays on the Art Criticism of John Ruskin, Walter Pater, Clive Bell, Roger Fry and Herbert Read* (Berkeley and Los Angeles: University of California Press, 1963).

Flaubert, Gustave, *Oeuvres Complètes de Gustave Flaubert*, 16 vols., ed. Societé des Études littéraires françaises (Paris: Club de L'Honnnête Homme, 1970–5).

Focillon, Henri, *The Life of Forms in Art*, rev. and trans. Charles Beecher Hogan and George Kubler (1934; New York: George Wittenborn, Inc., 1948).

Ford, Mark, 'The Insurance Man', *Times Literary Supplement* (29 November 2002), 8–9.

Forster, E. M., *Two Cheers for Democracy* (London: Edward Arnold & Co., 1951).

Foster, R. F., *W. B. Yeats: A Life*, 2 vols. (Oxford: Oxford University Press, 1997 and 2003).

Francis, Matthew, 'Syntax Gram and the Magic Typewriter: W. S. Graham's Automatic Writing', in *W. S. Graham: Speaking Towards You*, ed. Ralph Pite and Hester Jones (Liverpool: Liverpool University Press, 2004), 86–105.

Freedman, Jonathan, *Professions of Taste: Henry James, British Aestheticism, and Commodity Culture* (Stanford, Ca.: Stanford University Press, 1990).

Freud, Sigmund, 'Mourning and Melancholia', in *On Metapsychology: The Theory of Psychoanalysis*, trans. James Strachey, ed. Angela Richards (1917; London: Penguin, 1984).

Frost, Robert, *Collected Poems, Prose, and Plays* (New York: The Library of America, 1995).

Fry, Paul H., *A Defense of Poetry: Reflections on the Occasion of Writing* (Stanford, Ca.: Stanford University Press, 1995).

Fry, Roger, *Vision and Design* (1920; London: Chatto & Windus, 1925).

Gadamer, Hans-Georg, *The Relevance of the Beautiful and Other Essays* (Cambridge: Cambridge University Press, 1986).

Gallagher, Catherine, 'Formalism and Time', in *Modern Language Quarterly*, 61(2000), 229–51.

Gautier, Théophile, *Mademoiselle de Maupin*, intro. Geneviève van den Bogaert (1835; Paris: Garnier-Flammarion, 1966).

Gibson, Robert, *Modern French Poets on Poetry* (Cambridge: Cambridge University Press, 1961).

Goldensohn, Lorrie, 'Elizabeth Bishop's Written Pictures, Painted Poems', in *In Worcester Massachusetts: Essays on Elizabeth Bishop from the 1997 Elizabeth Bishop Conference* (New York: Peter Lang Publishing, 1999), 167–75.

Graham, W. S., *The Nightfisherman: Selected Letters of W. S. Graham*, ed. Michael and Margaret Snow (Manchester: Carcanet Press, 1999).

—— *W. S. Graham: New Collected Poems*, ed. Matthew Francis (London: Faber, 2004).

Gray, Thomas, *Gray and Collins Poetical Works*, ed. Austin Lane Poole (London: Oxford University Press, 1937).

Green, Fiona, 'Achieve Further through Elegy', in *W. S. Graham: Speaking Towards You*, ed. Ralph Pite and Hester Jones (Liverpool: Liverpool University Press, 2004), 132–57.

Gregson, Ian, ' "Music of the Generous Eye": Roy Fisher's Poems 1955–1980', in *Bête Noire*, 6(1988), 186–96.

Griffiths, Eric, 'Tennyson's Breath', in *Critical Essays on Alfred Lord Tennyson*, ed. Herbert F. Tucker (New York: G. K. Hall, 1993), 28–47.

Griffiths, Jane, *A Grip on Thin Air* (Tarset: Bloodaxe Books, 2000).

Gunn, Peter, *Vernon Lee: Violet Paget, 1856–1935* (London: Oxford University Press, 1964).

Guyer, Paul, *Values of Beauty: Historical Essays in Aesthetics* (Cambridge: Cambridge University Press, 2005).

Hair, Donald S., *Tennyson's Language* (London: University of Toronto Press, 1991).

Hallam, Arthur Henry, *Remains in Verse and Prose* (London: John Murray, 1863).

—— *The Poems of Arthur Henry Hallam, Together with his Essay on the Lyrical Poems of Alfred Tennyson*, ed. Richard le Gallienne (London: Elkin Matthews, 1893).

—— *The Writings of Arthur Hallam*, ed. T. H. Vail Motter (London: Oxford University Press, 1943).

—— *The Letters of Arthur Henry Hallam*, ed. Jack Kolb (Columbus, Oh.: Ohio State University Press, 1981).

Hamilton, Walter, *The Aesthetic Movement in England* (London: 1882).

Harsent, David, *Legion* (London: Faber, 2005).

Haskell, Dennis, ' "Long-Legged Fly" and Yeats's Concept of Mind', *Yeats Annual*, 10(1993), 250–6.

Heaney, Seamus, *Seeing Things* (London: Faber, 1991).

Herbert, W. N., 'The Breathing Words', *Edinburgh Review*, 75(1986), 101–3.

Higgins, Lesley, 'Jowett and Pater: Trafficking in Platonic Wares', *Victorian Studies*, 37(1993), 43–72.

Hill, Geoffrey, *For the Unfallen: Poems 1952–1958* (London: Andre Deutsch, 1959).

Hitchens, Robert, *The Green Carnation*, ed. Stanley Weintraub (1894; Lincoln, Neb.: University of Nebraska Press, 1970).

Hopkins, Gerard Manley, *The Poems of Gerard Manley Hopkins* (London: Oxford University Press, 1967).

Hughes, Ted, *Birthday Letters* (London: Faber, 1998).

Hunt, Leigh, review (1842), quoted in *Tennyson: The Critical Heritage*, ed. John D. Jump (London: Routledge & Kegan Paul, 1967), 126–36.

Huxley, Leonard (ed.), *Life and Letters of Thomas Henry Huxley*, 2 vols. (London: Macmillan, 1900).

Inman, Billie Andrew, *Walter Pater's Reading: A Bibliography of His Library Borrowings and Literary References, 1858–1873* (New York and London: Garland Publishing, 1981).

Iser, Wolfgang, *Walter Pater: The Aesthetic Moment*, trans. David Henry Wilson (Cambridge: Cambridge University Press, 1987).

James, Henry, *The Golden Bowl*, vols. 23 and 24 (New York: Scribners, 1909).

―――― *Letters*, 4 vols., ed. Leon Edel (London: Macmillan, 1974–84).

―――― *The Figure in the Carpet and Other Stories*, ed. Frank Kermode (Harmondsworth: Penguin, 1986).

Jay, Martin, *Force Fields: Between Intellectual History and Cultural Critique* (London: Routledge, 1993).

Johnson, R. V., *Aestheticism* (London: Methuen, 1969).

Johnson, Samuel, 'Milton', in *Lives of the English Poets*, 3 vols., ed. George Birkbeck Hill (Oxford: Clarendon Press, 1905).

Joseph, Gerhard, *Tennyson and the Text: The Weaver's Shuttle* (Cambridge: Cambridge University Press, 1992).

Joughin, John H. and Malpas, Simon (eds.), *The New Aestheticism* (Manchester: Manchester University Press, 2003).

Joyce, James, *Portrait of the Artist as a Young Man* (1916; Harmondsworth: Penguin, 1960).

―――― *Ulysses*, ed. Jeri Johnson (1922; Oxford: Oxford University Press, 1993).

Jump, John D. (ed.), *Tennyson: The Critical Heritage* (London: Routledge & Kegan Paul, 1967).

Kant, Immanuel, *The Critique of Judgement*, trans. James Creed Meredith (1790; Oxford: Clarendon Press, 1952).

Kaufman, Robert, 'Everybody Hates Kant: Blakean Formalism and the Symmetries of Laura Moriarty', *Modern Language Quarterly*, 61(2000), 131–55.

Keats, John, *Poetical Works*, ed. H. W. Garrod (Oxford: Oxford University Press, 1970).

Kemal, Salim, and Gaskell, Ivan (eds.), *Politics and Aesthetics in the Arts* (Cambridge: Cambridge University Press, 2000).

Kendall, Tim, *Paul Muldoon* (Bridgend, Wales: Seren, 1996).

—— (ed.), *Twentieth-Century War Poetry from Britain and Ireland* (Oxford: Oxford University Press, forthcoming).

Kermode, Frank. *Wallace Stevens* (1960; London; Faber, 1989).

—— *An Appetite for Poetry: Essays in Literary Interpretation.* (London: Collins, 1989).

Kessler, Edward, *Images of Wallace Stevens* (New Brunswick, N.J.: Rutgers University Press, 1972).

Killham, John (ed.), *Critical Essays on the Poetry of Tennyson* (London: Routledge & Kegan Paul, 1960).

Kimball, Roger, 'A Metaphysical Loss Adjustor', *Times Literary Supplement* (16 January 1998), 25.

Kirwan, James, *Beauty* (Manchester: Manchester University Press, 1999).

Koch, Vivienne, 'The Technique of Morality', *Poetry Quarterly*, 72(1947), 216–25.

Kolb, Jack (ed.), *The Letters of Arthur Henry Hallam* (Columbus, Oh.: Ohio State University Press, 1981).

Kristeva, Julia, *Black Sun: Depression and Melancholia*, trans. Leon S. Roudiez (1987; New York: Columbia University Press, 1989).

Kuppner, Frank, 'Marginalia to "Implements in their Places"', *Edinburgh Review*, 75(1986), 94–100.

Kuch, Peter, '"Laying the Ghosts?"—W. B. Yeats's Lecture on Ghosts and Dreams', *Yeats Annual*, ed. Warwick Gould, 5(1987), 114–35.

Langer, Susanne K., *Feeling and Form: A Theory of Art Developed from Philosophy in a New Key* (London: Routledge & Kegan Paul, 1953).

Larkin, Philip, *Selected Letters: 1940–1985*, ed. Anthony Thwaite (London: Faber, 1992).

Lee, Hermione, *Virginia Woolf* (London: Chatto & Windus, 1996).

Lee, Vernon, *Belcaro: Being Essays on Sundry Aesthetical Questions* (London: W. Satchell, 1880).

—— 'The Responsibilities of Unbelief: A Conversation between Three Rationalists', *The Contemporary Review*, 43(1883), 685–710.

—— 'An Eighteenth-Century Singer: An Imaginary Portrait', *Fortnightly Review*, 56(1891), 842–80.

—— *Renaissance Fancies and Studies: Being a Sequel to Euphorion* (London: Smith Elder, 1895).

_____ and Anstruther-Thomson, C., 'Beauty and Ugliness', *Contemporary Review*, 72(1897), 544–69 and 669–88.

_____ *Hauntings: Fantastic Stories* (1890; London: John Lane, 1906).

_____ 'The Riddle of Music', *Quarterly Review*, 204(1906), 207–27.

_____ *Studies of the Eighteenth Century in Italy* (1880; London: Fisher Unwin, 1907).

_____ *Laurus Nobilis: Chapters on Art and Life* (London: John Lane, 1909).

_____ *Vital Lies: Studies of Some Varieties of Recent Obscurantism*, 2 vols. (London: John Lane, 1912).

_____ *The Beautiful: An Introduction to Psychological Aesthetics* (Cambridge: Cambridge University Press, 1913).

_____ *The Poet's Eye* (London: Hogarth Press, 1926).

_____ *The Handling of Words, and Other Studies in Literary Psychology* (1923; London: John Lane, 1927).

_____ *For Maurice: Five Unlikely Stories* (London: John Lane, 1927).

_____ *Music and Its Lovers: An Empirical Study of Emotional and Imaginative Responses to Music* (London: George Allen & Unwin, 1932).

_____ *Vernon Lee's Letters*, with a Preface by her Executor (Privately printed: 1937).

Le Gallienne, Richard (ed.), *The Poems of Arthur Henry Hallam, Together with his Essay on the Lyrical Poems of Alfred Tennyson* (London: Elkin Matthews, 1893).

Leighton, Angela, *Victorian Women Poets: Writing Against the Heart* (Hemel Hempstead: Harvester, 1992).

_____ 'Resurrections of the Body: Women Writers and the Idea of the Renaissance', in *Unfolding the South: Nineteenth-Century British Women Writers and Artists in Italy*, ed. Alison Chapman and Jane Stabler (Manchester: Manchester University Press, 2003), 222–38.

_____ 'Pater's Music', *Journal of Pre-Raphaelite Studies*, 14(2005), 67–79.

Leonard, Tom, 'Journeys', *Edinburgh Review*, 75(1986), 83–7.

Levi, Primo, *The Voice of Memory: Interviews 1961–1987*, ed. Marco Belpoliti and Robert Gordon, trans. Robert Gordon (1997; Oxford: Blackwell, 2001).

Levinas, Emmanuel, *The Levinas Reader*, ed. Sean Hand (Oxford: Blackwell, 1989).

Levine, George (ed.), *Aesthetics and Ideology* (New Brunswick, N.J.: Rutgers University Press, 1994).

Levinson, Jerrold (ed.), *Aesthetics and Ethics: Essays at the Intersection* (Cambridge: Cambridge University Press, 1998).

_____ (ed.), *The Oxford Handbook of Aesthetics* (Oxford: Oxford University Press, 2003).

Longenbach, James, *Wallace Stevens: The Plain Sense of Things* (Oxford: Oxford University Press, 1991).

Longley, Edna, 'The Singing Line: Form in Derek Mahon's Poetry', in *Poetry in the Wars* (1986; Newcastle: Bloodaxe Books, 1996).

Longley, Edna, *Poetry and Posterity* (Newcastle: Bloodaxe Books, 2000).

Longley, Michael, *The Ghost Orchid* (London: Cape Poetry, 1995).

Lopez, Tony, *The Poetry of W. S. Graham* (Edinburgh: Edinburgh University Press, 1989).

_____ 'Graham and the 1940s', in *W. S. Graham: Speaking Towards You*, ed. Ralph Pite and Hester Jones (Liverpool: Liverpool University Press, 2004), 26–42.

Lyon, John, 'War, Politics and Disappearing Poetry: Auden, Yeats, Empson', in *Twentieth-Century War Poetry from Britain and Ireland*, ed. Tim Kendall (Oxford: Oxford University Press, 2007 forthcoming).

McDonald, Peter, *Mistaken Identities: Poetry and Northern Ireland* (Oxford: Clarendon Press, 1997).

_____ *Serious Poetry: Form and Authority from Yeats to Hill* (Oxford: Clarendon Press, 2002).

_____ 'Beside Himself', review of Robert Lowell's *Collected Poems*, in *Poetry Review*, 93(2003–4), 62–70.

_____ 'Yeats and the Life of the Dead', Typescript of a Lecture given at the Yeats International Summer School, 2005.

McHugh, Heather, *Hinge and Sign: Poems, 1968–1993* (Hanover and London: Wesleyan University Press, 1994).

_____ *Eyeshot* (Middletown, Conn: Wesleyan University Press, 2003).

McLuhan, H. M., 'Tennyson and Picturesque Poetry', in *Critical Essays on the Poetry of Tennyson*, ed. John Killham (London: Routledge & Kegan Paul, 1960).

MacNeice, Louis, *Modern Poetry: A Personal Essay*, intro. Walter Allen (1938; Oxford: Clarendon Press, 1968).

_____ *The Poetry of W. B. Yeats* (London: Oxford University Press, 1941).

McNeillie, Andrew, 'Bloomsbury', in *The Cambridge Companion to Virginia Woolf*, ed. Sue Roe and Susan Sellers (Cambridge: Cambridge University Press, 2000).

_____ *Now, Then* (Manchester: Carcanet, 2002).

Mahon, Derek, *Collected Poems* (Loughcrew: Gallery Press, 1999).

Mann, Thomas, *Death in Venice*, trans. H. T. Lowe-Porter (1912; Harmondsworth: Penguin, 1955).

Martin, Robert Bernard, *Tennyson: The Unquiet Heart* (Oxford: Clarendon Press, 1983).

Maxwell, Catherine, 'From Dionysus to "Dionea": Vernon Lee's Portraits', *Word and Image*, 13(1997), 253–69.

_____ 'Vernon Lee and the Ghosts of Italy', in *Unfolding the South: Nineteenth-Century British Women Writers and Artists in Italy*, ed. Alison Chapman and Jane Stabler (Manchester: Manchester University Press, 2003), 201–21.

Mays, J. C. C., '*In Memoriam*: An Aspect of Form', *University of Toronto Quarterly*, 35(1965), 22–46.

Meisel, Perry, *The Absent Father: Virginia Woolf and Walter Pater* (New Haven and London: Yale University Press, 1980).

Miller, J. Hillis, 'Wallace Stevens' Poetry of Being', in *The Act of the Mind: Essays on the Poetry of Wallace Stevens*, ed. Roy Harvey Pearce and J. Hillis Miller (Baltimore, Md.: Johns Hopkins University Press, 1965), 143–62.

Millier, Brett C., *Elizabeth Bishop: Life and the Memory of It* (Berkeley, Los Angeles: University of California Press, 1993).

Mix, Katherine Lyon, *A Study in Yellow: The Yellow Book and Its Contributors* (London: Constable, 1960).

Moore, George, *Avowals* (1919; London: Heinemann, 1924).

Moore, Marianne, *Predilections* (London: Faber, 1956),

Morgan, Edwin, 'W. S. Graham and "Voice"', in *The Constructed Space: A Celebration of W. S. Graham*, ed. Ronnie Duncan and Jonathan Davidson (Lincoln: Sunk Island Publishing, 1994).

Muldoon, Paul, *Poems 1968–1998* (London: Faber, 2001).

O'Brien, Sean, 'Roy Fisher: A Polytheism with No Gods', in *The Deregulated Muse* (Newcastle: Bloodaxe Books, 1998), 112–22.

Oliver, Douglas, *Three Variations on the Theme of Harm: Selected Poetry and Prose* (London: Paladin, 1990).

——— 'Poetry's Subject', in *PN Review*, 105(1995), 52–8.

——— *Arrondissements,* ed. Alice Notley (Cambridge: Salt, 2003).

Orwell, George, 'W. B. Yeats', in *W. B. Yeats: A Critical Anthology*, ed. William H. Pritchard (Harmondsworth : Penguin, 1972).

Page, Barbara, 'Elizabeth Bishop: Stops, Starts and Dreamy Divagations', in *Elizabeth Bishop: Poet of the Periphery*, ed. Linda Anderson and Jo Shapcott (Newcastle: Bloodaxe Books, 2002), 12–30.

Parrish, Stephen Maxfield (ed.), *A Concordance to the Poems of W. B. Yeats*, programmed James Allan Painter (Ithaca, N.Y.: Cornell University Press, 1963).

Pater, Walter, 'Poems by William Morris', *Westminster Review*, 34(1868), 300–12.

——— *The Renaissance: Studies in Art and Poetry* (1873; London: Macmillan, 1910).

——— *Marius the Epicurean,* 2 vols. (1885; London: Macmillan, 1910).

——— *Imaginary Portraits* (1887; London: Macmillan, 1910).

——— *Appreciations, with an Essay on Style* (1889; London: Macmillan, 1910).

——— *Plato and Platonism: A Series of Lectures* (1893; London: Macmillan, 1910).

——— *Miscellaneous Studies* (1895; London: Macmillan, 1910).

Paulin, Tom, 'T. S. Eliot and Anti-Semitism', in *Writing to the Moment* (London: Faber, 1996), 149–60.

Peacock, Molly, 'From Gilded Cage to Rib Cage', in *After New Formalism: Poets on Form, Narrative, and Tradition*, ed. Annie Finch (Ashland, Or.: Story Line Press, 1999), 70–8.

Pearce, Roy Harvey, and Miller, J. Hillis (eds.), *The Act of the Mind: Essays on the Poetry of Wallace Stevens* (Baltimore, Md.: John Hopkins University Press, 1965).

Pessoa, Fernando, *The Book of Disquiet*, ed. and trans. Richard Zenith (1998; London: Penguin, 2001).

Piette, Adam, ' "Roaring between the Lines": W. S. Graham and the White Threshold of Line-Breaks', in *W. S. Graham: Speaking Towards You*, ed. Ralph Pite and Hester Jones (Liverpool: Liverpool University Press, 2004), 44–62.

Pite, Ralph, and Jones, Hester (eds.), *W. S. Graham: Speaking Towards You* (Liverpool: Liverpool University Press, 2004).

Plath, Sylvia, *Letters Home: Correspondence 1950–1963*, ed. Aurelia Schober Plath (London: Faber, 1976).

—— *Collected Poems*, ed. Ted Hughes (London: Faber, 1981).

Plato, *The Republic*, trans. Francis Macdonald Cornford (London: Oxford University Press, 1941).

Poe, Edgar Allan, 'The Poetic Principle', in *Poems and Essays on Poetry*, ed. C. H. Sisson (1850; Manchester: Carcanet, 1995).

Pole, David, *Aesthetics, Form and Emotion*, ed. George Roberts (London: Duckworth, 1983).

Pound, Ezra, *Gaudier-Brzeska: A Memoir* (1916; Hessle, E. Yorkshire: Marvell Press, 1960).

—— 'Brancusi', in *Literary Essays of Ezra Pound*, ed. T. S. Eliot (1954; London: Faber, 1960).

—— *Ezra Pound and Music: The Complete Criticism*, edited with commentary by R. Murray Schafer (London: Faber, 1978).

—— *The Cantos of Ezra Pound* (London: Faber, 1987).

Prettejohn, Elizabeth (ed.), *After the Pre-Raphaelites: Art and Aestheticism in Victorian England* (Manchester: Manchester University Press, 1999).

Pritchard, William H. (ed.), *W. B. Yeats: A Critical Anthology* (Harmondsworth: Penguin, 1972).

Psomiades, Kathy Alexis, *Beauty's Body: Femininity and Representation in British Aestheticism* (Stanford, Ca.: Stanford University Press, 1997).

Quinn, Justin, 'How to Live. What to do', *PN Review*, 121(1998), 26–31.

Raitt, Suzanne, and Tate, Trudi (eds.), *Women's Fiction and the Great War* (Oxford: Oxford Clarendon Press, 1997).

Ramazani, Jahan, *Poetry of Mourning: The Modern Elegy from Hardy to Heaney* (Chicago & London: University of Chicago Press, 1994).

Read, Herbert, *Form in Modern Poetry* (1932; Plymouth: Vision Press Limited, 1989).

Reagan, Stephen (ed.), *The Politics of Pleasure: Aesthetics and Cultural Theory* (Buckingham: Open University Press, 1992).

Rich, Adrienne, 'Format and Form', in *After New Formalism: Poets on Form,*

Narrative, and Tradition, ed. Annie Finch (Ashland, Or: Story Line Press, 1999), 1–7.

Richards, I. A., *Principles of Literary Criticism* (1924; London: Routledge & Kegan Paul, 1960).

Ricks, Christopher, *The Force of Poetry* (Oxford: Clarendon Press, 1984).

—— 'Literature and the Matter of Fact', in *Essays in Appreciation* (Oxford: Oxford University Press, 1998).

Riddel, Joseph N., *The Clairvoyant Eye: The Poetry and Poetics of Wallace Stevens* (Baton Rouge: Louisiana State University Press, 1965).

Riding, Laura, *Contemporaries and Snobs* (London: Jonathan Cape, 1928).

—— *The Poems of Laura Riding* (1938; Manchester: Carcanet, 1980).

—— *Anarchism is Not Enough*, ed. Lisa Samuels (1928; Berkeley, Ca.: University of California Press, 2001).

—— *A Survey of Modernist Poetry and a Pamphlet against Anthologies* (1927; 1928; Manchester: Carcanet, 2002).

Riley, Denise, 'Doug's Prose', in *A Meeting for Douglas Oliver* (Cambridge: Street Editions and Poetical Histories, 2002), 18–21.

Robbins, Ruth, 'Vernon Lee: Decadent Woman?', in *Fin de Siècle/Fin du Globe: Fears and Fantasies of the Nineteenth Century*, ed. John Stokes (Basingstoke: Macmillan, 1992).

Robinson, Peter, 'Last Things', in *The Thing about Roy Fisher: Critical Studies*, ed. John Kerrigan and Peter Robinson (Liverpool: Liverpool University Press, 2000), 275–311.

—— *Poetry, Poets, Readers: Making Things Happen* (Oxford: Clarendon Press, 2002).

Roe, Sue, 'The Impact of Post-Impressionism', in *The Cambridge Companion to Virginia Woolf*, ed. Sue Roe and Susan Sellars (Cambridge: Cambridge University Press, 2000), 164–90.

—— and Sellars, Susan (eds.), *The Cambridge Companion to Virginia Woolf* (Cambridge: Cambridge University Press, 2000).

Rogers, Franklin R., *Painting and Poetry: Form, Metaphor, and the Language of Literature* (London and Toronto: Associated University Presses, 1985).

Rooney, Ellen, 'Form and Contentment', *Modern Language Quarterly*, 61(2000), 17–40.

Rossetti, Christina, *The Complete Poems*, 3 vols., ed. R. W. Crump (Baton Rouge & London: Louisiana State University Press, 1979–90).

Rossetti, D. G., *Poems*, ed. Oswald Doughty (London: Dent, 1961).

Sacks, Peter M., *The English Elegy: Studies in the Genre from Spenser to Yeats* (Baltimore and London: Johns Hopkins University Press, 1985).

Santilli, Kristine S., *Poetic Gesture: Myth, Wallace Stevens, and the Motions of Poetic Language* (London: Routledge, 2002).

Scarry, Elaine, *On Beauty and Being Just* (Princeton, NJ: Princeton University Press, 1999).

Schaffer, Talia, and Psomiades, Kathy Alexis (eds.), *Women and British Aestheticism* (Charlottesville and London: University Press of Virginia, 1999).

Schiller, Friedrich, *On the Aesthetic Education of Man, in a Series of Letters*, trans. Reginald Snell (London: Routledge & Kegan Paul, 1954).

——— *On the Aesthetic Education of Man: In a Series of Letters*, ed. and trans. Elizabeth M. Wilkinson and L. A. Willoughby (Oxford: Clarendon Press, 1967).

Schuchard, Ronald, ' "As Regarding Rhythm": Yeats and the Imagists', in *Yeats: An Annual of Critical and Textual Studies*, vol. II, ed. Richard J. Finneran (Ithaca and London: Cornell University Press, 1984), 209–26.

——— ' "The Countess Cathleen" and the Chanting of Verse, 1892–1912', *Yeats Annual*, ed. Wayne K. Chapman and Warwick Gould, 15(2002), 36–68, 40–1.

Scruton, Roger, *The Aesthetics of Music* (Oxford: Clarendon Press, 1997).

Shrimpton, Nicholas, 'Pater and the "Aesthetical Sect" ', in *Walter Pater and the Culture of the Fin-de-Siècle*, ed. E. S. Shaffer, *Comparative Criticism*, 17(1995), 61–84.

Singer, Alan, and Dunn, Allen (eds.), *Literary Aesthetics: A Reader* (Oxford: Blackwell, 2000).

Small, Helen, 'Tennyson and Late Style', *The Tennyson Research Bulletin*, 8(2005), 226–50.

Smith, Stevie, *Novel on Yellow Paper* (Harmondsworth: Penguin, 1951).

——— *Collected Poems* (London: Allen Lane, 1975).

Smyth, Ethel, *Maurice Baring* (London: Heinemann, 1938).

Steiner, George, *Language and Silence: Essays 1958–1966* (1967; London: Faber, 1985).

——— *Real Presences: Is There Anything in What We Say?* (London: Faber, 1989).

Stevens, Wallace, *Letters of Wallace Stevens*, ed. Holly Stevens (London: Faber, 1967).

——— *Wallace Stevens: Collected Poetry and Prose*, sel. Frank Kermode and Joan Richardson (New York: The Library of America, 1997).

Stevenson, Anne, *Between the Iceberg and the Ship: Selected Essays* (Ann Arbor: University of Michigan Press, 1998).

——— 'The Trouble with a Word like Formalism', in *After New Formalism: Poets on Form, Narrative, and Tradition*, ed. Annie Finch (Ashland, Or.: Story Line Press, 1999), 217–23, 219.

——— *Poems 1955–2005* (Tarset: Bloodaxe Books, 2004).

——— 'Anne Stevenson Archive', University Library, Cambridge, MS Add 9451.

Stokes, John, ed. *Fin de Siècle/Fin du Globe: Fears and Fantasies of the Nineteenth Century* (Basingstoke: Macmillan, 1992).

Symonds, John Addington, *Renaissance in Italy: The Revival of Learning* (1877; London: Smith Elder, 1897).

Tennyson, Alfred, *The Poems of Tennyson*, 3 vols., ed. Christopher Ricks (London: Longmans, 1987).

Tucker, Herbert F. (ed.), *Critical Essays on Alfred Lord Tennyson* (New York: G. K. Hall, 1993).

_____ 'Of Monuments and Moments: Spacetime in Nineteenth-Century Poetry', *Modern Language Quarterly*, 58(1997), 269–97.

Turner, Frank M., 'Lucretius among the Victorians', *Victorian Studies*, 16(1973), 329–48.

Turner, Frederick, *Beauty: The Value of Values* (Charlottesville & London: University Press of Virginia, 1991).

Turner, Paul, *Tennyson* (London: Routledge, 1976).

Tyndall, John, *Six Lectures on Light* (London: Longmans, Green & Co., 1873).

Uehling, Theodore E., Jr., *The Notion of Form in Kant's Critique of Aesthetic Judgment* (The Hague, Paris: Mouton, 1971).

Vail Motter, T. H. (ed.), *The Writings of Arthur Hallam* (London: Oxford University Press, 1943).

Vendler, Helen, *On Extended Wings: Wallace Stevens' Longer Poems* (Cambridge, Mass.: Harvard University Press, 1969).

_____ *Wallace Stevens: Words Chosen Out of Desire* (Cambridge, Mass.: Harvard University Press, 1986).

_____ *The Music of What Happens: Poems, Poets, Critics* (Cambridge, Mass.: Harvard University Press, 1988).

_____ *The Given and the Made: Recent American Poets* (London & Boston: Faber, 1995).

Walker, Alice, 'Advancing Luna and Ida B. Wells', in *Any Woman's Blues*, ed. Mary Helen Washington (London: Virago, 1980).

Walsh, Thomas F., *Concordance to the Poetry of Wallace Stevens* (University Park, Penn.: Pennsylvania State University Press, 1963)

Wharton, Edith, *A Backward Glance* (1933; New York: Scribners, 1964).

Wilde, Oscar, 'The Critic as Artist', in *Intentions* (1891; London: Methuen, 1919), 93–217.

_____ 'The Decay of Lying', *Intentions* (1891; London: Methuen, 1919), 1–54.

_____ *The Picture of Dorian Gray* (1891; Harmondsworth: Penguin, 1949).

Williams, Carolyn, *Transfigured World: Walter Pater's Aesthetic Historicism* (Ithaca and London: Cornell University Press, 1989).

Williams, Raymond, *Keywords: A Vocabulary of Culture and Society* (1976; London: Fontana, 1983).

Wills, Clair, *Reading Paul Muldoon* (Newcastle: Bloodaxe Books, 1998).

_____ ' "A Furnace" and the Life of the Dead', in *The Thing about Roy Fisher*, ed. John Kerrigan and Peter Robinson (Liverpool: Liverpool University Press, 2000), 257–74.

Wilmer, Clive (ed.), *Modernist Essays: Yeats, Pound, Eliot* (Manchester: Carcanet, 2004).

Winterson, Jeanette, *Art Objects: Essays on Ecstasy and Effrontery* (London: Jonathan Cape, 1995).

Wolfson, Susan, *Formal Charges: The Shaping of Poetry in British Romanticism* (Stanford, Ca.: Stanford University Press, 1997).

_____ 'Reading for Form', in *Modern Language Quarterly*, 61(2000), 1–16.

Wood, Michael, *Literature and the Taste of Knowledge* (Cambridge: Cambridge University Press, 2005).

Woolf, Virginia, *A Letter to a Young Poet* (London: Hogarth Press, 1932).

_____ *Three Guineas* (London: Hogarth Press, 1938).

_____ *Roger Fry: A Biography* (London: Hogarth Press, 1940).

_____ *Collected Essays*, 4 vols., ed. Leonard Woolf (London: Chatto & Windus, 1966).

_____ *The Letters of Virginia Woolf*, 6 vols., ed. Nigel Nicolson and Joanne Trautmann (London: Hogarth Press, 1978).

_____ *The Diary of Virginia Woolf*, 5 vols., ed. Anne Olivier Bell, ass. Andrew McNeillie (London: Penguin, 1982).

_____ 'Solid Objects', in *The Complete Shorter Fiction of Virginia Woolf*, ed. Susan Dick (London: Hogarth Press, 1985), 96–101.

_____ *The Complete Shorter Fiction of Virginia Woolf*, ed. Susan Dick (London: Hogarth Press, 1985).

_____ *The Essays of Virginia Woolf: 1904–12*, ed. Andrew McNeillie (London: Hogarth Press, 1986).

_____ *A Passionate Apprentice: The Early Journals 1897–1909*, ed. Mitchell A. Leaska (London: Hogarth Press, 1990).

_____ *Mrs Dalloway*, intro. Elaine Showalter, ed. Stella McNichol (1925; London: Penguin, 1992).

_____ *Jacob's Room*, ed. Sue Roe (1922; London: Penguin, 1992).

_____ *The Waves*, ed. Kate Flint (1931; London: Penguin, 1992).

_____ *The Years*, ed. Hermione Lee, notes by Sue Asbee (1937; Oxford: Oxford University Press, 1992).

_____ *To the Lighthouse*, intro. Hermione Lee, ed. Stella McNichol (1927; London: Penguin, 1992).

Wordsworth, William, *Poetical Works*, ed. Thomas Hutchinson, rev. Ernest de Selincourt (London: Oxford University Press, 1936).

Yeats, W. B. (ed.), *The Oxford Book of Modern Verse: 1892–1935* (Oxford: Clarendon Press, 1936).

_____ *The Variorum Edition of the Poems of W. B. Yeats*, ed. Peter Allt and Russell K. Alspach (New York: Macmillan, 1957).

_____ *Mythologies* (London: Macmillan, 1959).

_____ *Essays and Introductions* (London: Macmillan, 1961).

_____ *Vision Papers*, 3 vols., *Sleep and Dream Notebooks, 'Vision' Notebooks 1 and 2, Card File*, ed. Robert Anthony Martinich and Margaret Mills Harper (London: Macmillan, 1992).

_____ *Explorations*, selected by Mrs W. B. Yeats (London: Macmillan, 1962).

_____ *The Secret Rose, Stories by W. B. Yeats: A Variorum Edition*, 2nd edn revised and enlarged, ed. Warwick Gould, Phillip L. Marcus, and Michael J. Sidnell (Basingstoke: Macmillan, 1992).

_____ *W. B. Yeats: Later Essays*, ed. William H. O'Donnell, with assistance from Elizabeth Bergmann Loizeaux (New York: Charles Scribner's Sons, 1994).

_____ *The Collected Letters of W. B. Yeats*, ed. John Kelly, vol. II, 1896–1900, ed. Warwick Gould, John Kelly, Deirdre Toomey (Oxford: Clarendon Press, 1997).

_____ *Autobiographies*, ed. William H. O'Donnell and Douglas N. Archibald (New York: Scribner, 1999).

Index